Volume 4 in the Collected Works of M. A. K. Halliday

The Language of Early Childhood

M. A. K. Halliday

Edited by Jonathan J. Webster

著作权合同登记号　图字:01-2006-7146

图书在版编目(CIP)数据

婴幼儿的语言＝The Language of Early Childhood:英文/(英)韩礼德
(Halliday, M. A. K.)著. —北京:北京大学出版社,2007.11
(韩礼德文集)
ISBN 978-7-301-13012-4

Ⅰ.婴… Ⅱ.韩… Ⅲ.儿童语言－研究－英文 Ⅳ.H003

中国版本图书馆 CIP 数据核字(2007)第 172998 号

First published 2004 by Continuum

This collection © M. A. K. Halliday 2003

All rights reserved. No part of this publication may be reproduced or transmitted in any form or by any means, electronic or mechanical, including photocopying, recording or any information storage or retrieval system, without permission in writing from the publishers.

The Work is published by arrangement with the Continuum International Publishing Group.

该作品由 Continuum 国际出版有限公司授权出版。

书　　　名:婴幼儿的语言
著作责任者:〔英〕韩礼德　著
责 任 编 辑:孙凤兰
标 准 书 号:ISBN 978-7-301-13012-4/H·1895
出 版 发 行:北京大学出版社
地　　　址:北京市海淀区成府路 205 号　100871
网　　　址:http://www.pup.cn
电　　　话:邮购部 62752015　发行部 62750672　编辑部 62767315
　　　　　　出版部 62754962
电 子 邮 箱:zpup@pup.pku.edu.cn
印 刷 者:北京汇林印务有限公司
经 销 者:新华书店
　　　　　650 毫米×980 毫米　16 开本　27.5 印张　580 千字
　　　　　2007 年 11 月第 1 版　2007 年 11 月第 1 次印刷
定　　　价:55.00 元(配有光盘)

未经许可,不得以任何方式复制或抄袭本书之部分或全部内容。
版权所有,侵权必究　举报电话:010－62752024
　　　　　　　　　　电子邮箱:fd@pup.pku.edu.cn

Collected Works of M. A. K. Halliday

Volume 1: *On Grammar*
Volume 2: *Linguistic Studies of Text and Discourse*
Volume 3: *On Language and Linguistics*
Volume 4: *The Language of Early Childhood*
Volume 5: *The Language of Science*
Volume 6: *Computational and Quantitative Studies*
Volume 7: *Studies in English Language*
Volume 8: *Studies in Chinese Language*
Volume 8: *汉语语言研究(汉译版)*
Volume 9: *Language and Education*
Volume 10: *Language and Society*

总 序

胡壮麟

由香港城市大学汉语、翻译和语言学系系主任 Jonathan J. Webster 教授主编的,并由英国 Continuum 公司自 2002 年陆续出版的《韩礼德文集》,总共 10 卷,已全部出齐。北京大学出版社获得 Continuum 公司的授权后,负责文集在中国境内的出版,并组织国内专家为读者撰写导读。这无疑是我国出版界和语言学界的一件大事。

就当代语言学研究来说,20 世纪下半叶一直表现为生成语言学和功能语言学的对峙,说得具体些,当乔姆斯基在 50 年代末一度以他的转换生成语法掀起一场革命,并成为国际上,特别是美国的语言学研究的主流时,能揭竿而起并与之抗衡的便是韩礼德的系统功能语法。[①] 如果说乔姆斯基的理论得益于后来成为他"革命"对象的美国结构主义,韩礼德则公开宣称他继承和发展了欧洲的弗斯学派、布拉格学派和哥本哈根学派。正是这两种力量的冲突、挑战和互补推动了这半个世纪精彩纷呈的语言学研究。

《韩礼德文集》在中国的出版还具有重要的意义,那就是韩礼德的成就除了受到欧洲语言学传统的影响外,也从中国语言学传统获得滋养。他早年师从罗常培先生和王力先生,在韩礼德的论著中不时绽放出这些大师的思想火花。[②]《文集》的第 8 卷是最好的历史见证,在这个意义上,《文集》的出版是一次学术上的回归,为我国语言学研究如何实现全球化和本土化的结合提供了宝贵的经验。为此,北京大学出

[①] 胡壮麟、朱永生、张德禄、李战子,《系统功能语言学概论》,北京大学出版社,2005 年 9 月。
[②] 胡壮麟,《王力与韩礼德》,《北京大学学报·英美语言文学专刊》1991 年第 1 期,第 49—57 页。收入张谷、王辑国编,《龙虫并雕,一代宗师——中外学者论王力》,广西教育出版社,第 200—216 页。

版社采纳了我们的建议,在出版10卷《文集》的同时,将第8卷全部译成中文,另行出版中文版,以供汉语界参考。

《文集》充分反映了韩礼德所走过的治学道路,其轨迹分见于各卷的主要内容。韩礼德首先研究现代汉语(第8卷),打好了音系学和方言调查的扎实基础。回英国后,进入对普通语言学的研究(第1卷和第3卷),继承、发展和建立科学的语言学研究的理论,把握前进的方向。为了在欧美学术界获得一席之地,韩礼德在此时期把英语作为研究分析对象(第7卷)。在研究方法上,他注意第一手材料的收集(第4卷),将语言学研究从句子层面提高到在具体语境中出现的语篇和话语(第2卷),因此他的研究是经得起实际的检验的。韩礼德特别注意语言学理论的价值在于它的应用,能否说明社会生活中的问题,并为社会服务,前者见之于第10卷的"语言与社会",后者反映于第9卷的"语言与教育"。曾经有位学者向韩礼德提问,为什么转换生成语法在中国国内打不开局面,而系统功能语法却响应者众多?这两卷的内容有助于人们找到答案。20世纪下半叶是现代科学技术,特别是电子技术,获得飞速发展的时代。韩礼德时年七八十岁,他能在自己的晚年,关注语言与科学技术的关系(第5卷和第6卷),这种活到老、学到老的精神令人钦佩不已。

最后,《文集》只概括了韩礼德2002年以前的主要论著和节选,因此有关韩礼德的学术思想和成就有待我们进一步挖掘和学习。其次,这几年韩本人一直是老骥伏枥,笔耕不辍,勤于思索。如2006年3月26日韩礼德教授在香港城市大学的"韩礼德语言研究智能应用中心"成立大会上,做了题目为"研究意义:建立一个适用语言学"的主旨报告。韩提出适用语言学(appliable linguistics)的长期目标是为了建立语言的意义发生系统,其工作机制是以社会理据来解释和描写语义发生,可见韩礼德已经认识到语言学研究最终要解决对"意义"的描写。对这个问题,结构主义和生成主义学派是不研究的,系统功能语言学在功能语义学方面只是刚刚起步,这将是语言学界在新世纪为之共同奋斗的目标。

参加《韩礼德文集》导读编写者均为我国著名学府的学者,在系统功能语言学研究方面享有盛誉,仅在此表示感谢。

总　序

卷别/导读作者

第1卷　论语法/黄国文（中山大学教授/博导）

第2卷　语篇和话语的语言学研究/朱永生（复旦大学教授/博导）

第3卷　论语言和语言学/方　琰（清华大学教授）

第4卷　婴幼儿的语言/李战子（南京国际关系学院教授/博导）

第5卷　科学语言/杨信彰（厦门大学教授/博导）

第6卷　计算机与定量语言/林允清（北京师范大学教授/博导）
　　　　　　　　　　　　/于　晖（解放军外国语学院副教授/博士）

第7卷　英语语言研究/何　伟（北京科技大学副教授/博士）

第8卷　汉语语言研究/彭宣维（北京师范大学教授/博导）

第8卷　汉语语言研究（汉译版）/彭宣维（北京师范大学教授/博导）

第9卷　语言与教育/张德禄（中国海洋大学教授/博导）

第10卷　语言与社会/任绍曾（浙江大学教授）

导　　读

李战子

　　对婴幼儿语言的研究能帮助人们认识语言的本质,以及语言在人的发育过程中的作用。在本书中,韩礼德详尽研究了自己的儿子在九个月到两岁半之间语言能力发展的情况。他使用的方法就是用纸和笔记下他儿子奈吉尔的话语,积累成丰富的语料,从功能和语义的角度对语料进行分析。他将儿童学习母语过程分为三个阶段:第一阶段是原始母语阶段;第二阶段是原始母语到成人语言的过渡阶段;第三阶段是学习成人语言阶段。通过分析他试图验证这样一个假设:儿童是逐渐地拓展他的语言功能的。

　　该书的第一部分讨论婴儿和原始母语的发展。在这个阶段,奈吉尔的语言由语用性功能发展到交际和反思的功能。第二部分考察儿童语言到母语的过渡阶段。在该阶段,原始母语末期出现的实用功能与理性功能的对比被重新解读为成人语言的人际和概念元功能。在原始母语的语义和语音层面之间又增加了词汇语法层,而且随着奈吉尔语篇的语言资源开始成熟和发展,他的话语显示了更强的组篇结构。第三部分探讨了语言发展和学习中的持续过程,及其对老师和学生的意义。儿童与身边其他人(父母、老师、同龄人)的交流互动在帮助儿童构建社会现实的过程中发挥着重要作用,并且为儿童达到社会所要求的语言能力作准备。韩礼德将语言与学习的关系总结为三个层面:即学习语言,通过语言学习其他知识,学习语言本身。

　　第一部分包括六篇论文。在第一篇"将儿童描述成意义的存在"(1998)中,针对传统观点,即认为儿童语言发育是逐步达到一个外在的、固定的目标,韩礼德根据20年来对儿童语言发展的研究提出了创新的观点:婴幼儿是在学习如何表达意义,是在建立一种潜势,并且从本质上看,这正好和人类语言最初发展的过程相吻合。

该部分随后的五篇是韩礼德20世纪70年代中后期的论文。在第二篇"学习如何表达意义"(1975)中,韩礼德基于伯恩斯坦的研究提出了七个语言功能:工具功能、规约功能、互动功能、个人功能、启发功能、想象功能和信息功能。韩礼德通过研究奈吉尔的语言发展试图证明他的假设:即儿童的语言功能差不多以上述的顺序出现,而且信息功能肯定最后出现;在原始母语阶段这些功能是独立的,每句话只有一个功能,而掌握全部功能(可能最后一个功能除外)是向成人语言系统转变的充要条件。到第二阶段的末期,儿童语言已经进入了成人期语言,已经建立了多层多功能的系统。他已经学会了如何表达意义,接下来的语言发展在于将其意义潜势拓展到更广阔的文化中。基于伯恩斯坦的研究,韩礼德认为由于语言的功能性基础,在典型的日常情景中表达的具体意义成为儿童构建文化语境的主要来源。儿童早期对语言的使用对语言系统的本质提出了某些要求,决定了语言系统赖以组织的功能性基础,其结果是当这些早期的使用习惯变为普遍的社会语境时,语言系统能够通过它们作为文化传播的主要手段。这样,语言在社会学习的过程中开始发挥中心作用。

在第三篇"早期语言学习:一种社会语言学方法"(1976)中,韩礼德描述了奈吉尔的语言由原始母语发展到成人语言的过程。作为系统的原始母语和成人语言的区别是原始母语包含语义和语音层但不包括词汇语法层。该篇还着重论述了奈吉尔在九到十二个月之间原始母语的发展过程,他的语言功能由实用功能(得到想要的东西,提出要求)发展到使用语言互动,表达自己的思想感情。

将奈吉尔的语言发育解读为一个社会符号过程是第四篇"语言发育的社会符号观"(1974)的主题。奈吉尔在第一阶段习得的意义潜势使其完成独立于语言的功能,但同时在同样的过程中,他也是在为自己构建社会符号——一个文化模型,而自己是其中的一员。这样,他在学习语言的同时也是在通过语言学习文化,他所构建的语义系统成为文化传播的主要形式。

第五篇"童年早期的意义和现实构建"(1978)从主体间创造性来讨论语言发育。学习表达意义是一个创造的过程,由此儿童通过与周围人的互动构建一种符号潜势,该潜势使儿童接触到构成社会现实的意义。这一观点在第六篇"对话的个体发生"(1979)中得到了进一步的阐释。该篇主要讨论奈吉尔的语言发展到交换意义行为,即对话。奈吉尔使用原始母语表达非语言的行为或状态,例如"我想要那个","我们一起吧"等。而信息交换直到两岁前的一两个月才发生。

第二部分包括第七至十一篇论文,主要关注儿童语言发育的第二阶段和第三阶段。进入第二阶段后,实用功能与理性功能的区别渐渐消失,因为话语已经既是概念性又是人际性的了。此外,语言系统中加进了词汇语法层和语篇性。在第七篇"进入成人期语言"(1975)中,韩礼德指出:儿童在两岁末掌握成人语言系统意味着儿童已经成功地为自己构建了一个三层的符号系统,该系统的组织方式与成人语言一样。当然,这并不是说儿童已经掌握了成人语言,但是基础已经有了。第七篇还考察了奈吉尔的语言中形成语篇的资源的发展情况。他已经能通过重音表达信息焦点,这反映了他控制信息结构的能力。他大概在一岁半到两岁时发展了一些语义模式,使得语篇具有连贯性。他的语言也显示了他对于与叙述和对话相关的特定体裁结构比较敏感。

第八篇"发育语言学对将语言看做系统的贡献"(1980)中,韩礼德指出,儿童语言研究强烈显示了语言系统的功能性解读,这些研究可以为语言理论提供更广的背景。如果我们沿着实用功能/理性功能对比发展成成人语义结构的元功能框架这个思路,我们就能准确理解对语言的功能性要求是如何形成语言系统的。

第九篇"从儿童语言到母语的过渡"(1983)中,韩礼德认为如果从互动、功能和朝向意义或符号的观点来研究的话,从语言学观点和发育观点进行的研究会互相补充。

第十篇是"对话的本质和对话的个体发生学的系统功能性解读"(1984),韩礼德将对话看做一种社会意义的交换,看做一个符号过程,因此认为对话原则上可以由语言以外的系统实现,并举了一些奈吉尔和父母交谈的例子,还讨论了奈吉尔如何发展他的对话系统。

第十一篇"对话在儿童构建意义中的地位"(1991)进一步探讨了对话的个体发生学,阐明了语篇是如何与环境互动,以致意义在两种冲突的交叉点被创造出来;一种是概念冲突,即经验的物质模式和意识模式之间的冲突,另一种是人际冲突,即参与者不同的个人历史之间的冲突。

第三部分由五篇论文组成。第十二篇"语言的相关模型"(1969)主要提供了一种与教育相关的语言观。韩礼德描述了与教育相关的研究语言的方法,可分为两部分:一部分描述儿童自己的语言经验,从其最丰富的潜势角度定义这种经验,并注意在哪里会有差距,可能对教育和发育有害;另一部分与儿童后来的经历相关——社会对他最终的语言要求,和中间阶段学校将对语言做出的要求以及他要在班级里取得好成绩所必须达到的要求。这里所说的与教育相关的模型不是语言习得模型,而是使用者实现意图所用的语言的"形象",如前文提到的工具性、规约性等。随着儿童发展起使用语言的意识,他便逐渐成为社会人或社会符号人,周围的人则是儿童构建语言与社会符号过程中的积极参与者。

第十三篇"语言发育的社会语境"(1975)中,韩礼德描述了儿童在学习社会符号即文化的同时如何学习作为学习文化的手段——语言。学习的一个基本条件是意义的组成部分(即表达者表达意义能力的不同方面)与情景的社会符号性质之间的系统联系。奈吉尔与母亲的互动被用来展示语篇的语言特点是如何由语境特点决定的。语言的发展是一个持续学习表达意义的过程,包括两个方面的持续性:不仅是从出生到成人的发展持续,还是一种贯穿学习所有部分和过程的结构性持续。儿童出生后就开始不断无意识地认识到可以用语言做事。教育如果要强化扩展儿童的语言发展,就需要建立在这种认识上。

第十四篇"儿童语言发展的三个层面:学习语言,通过语言学习其他知识,学习语言本身"(1980)建议将课堂上的语言学习与儿童从自己经验中已经了解的语言知识相联系。

第十五篇"以语言为基础的学习理论"(1993)建议将学习理论建立在对学习时使用的语言所了解的基础上。韩礼德在直接观察儿童在家和在校使用语言的情况的基础上,确认了21个儿童语言发育的特点,这些特点对于以语言为基础的学习理论是非常重要的,例如,其中包括构建信息、表达或然性、理解抽象意义、使用语法隐喻等等。

最后一篇"语法和教育知识的构建"(1999)论述了某些儿童是如何学习语言的,或者更确切地说,是如何通过语言学习其他知识的;也就是他们如何在学习语言的同时使用语言学习其它与他们世界相关的知识。

从全书看,韩礼德对婴幼儿期的语言的研究并不是他的业余兴趣,而是他构建的系统功能语法理论的有机组成部分。他曾与英语是母语的教师一起工作,他们常常问他儿童是如何发展自己的语言能力的,韩礼德就此展开了一段深入研究,即作为参与者和观察者,用纸和笔记录了他儿子奈吉尔从九个月到两岁半的语言能力发育情况。全书各篇紧紧围绕两个目的,一是开创性地、极为细致地研究了儿童是如何逐渐通过表达意义掌握语言,一是同时试图阐释人类语言逐渐发展的过程,——既作为建构经验意义的资源,也作为激活人际意义的资源。韩礼德对奈吉尔的早期语言发展做了详尽的记录，收录在该书所附的光盘中。韩礼德关于语言发展的研究还具有教育学上的重要意义，有助于我们理解语言意义创造在教育的各个阶段中——从学龄前的聊天到学术写作——所具有的中心地位。对于社会学家、教育学家、系统功能语言学研究者以及研究语言发展的学者，这本书都具有非常重要的理论价值。

CONTENTS

    Preface   xvii

    Acknowledgements   xxi

PART ONE: INFANCY AND PROTOLANGUAGE

    Editor's Introduction   3

1. Representing the Child as a Semiotic Being (One Who Means) (1998)   6

2. Learning How to Mean (1975)   28

3. Early Language Learning: A Sociolinguistic Approach (1976)   60

4. A Sociosemiotic Perspective on Language Development (1974)   90

5. Meaning and the Construction of Reality in Early Childhood (1978)   113

6. The Ontogenesis of Dialogue (1979)   144

PART TWO: TRANSITION FROM CHILD TONGUE TO MOTHER TONGUE

    Editor's Introduction   155

7. Into the Adult Language (1975)   157

8	The Contribution of Developmental Linguistics to the Interpretation of Language as a System (1980)	196
9	On the Transition from Child Tongue to Mother Tongue (1983)	209
10	A Systemic-Functional Interpretation of the Nature and Ontogenesis of Dialogue (1984)	226
11	The Place of Dialogue in Children's Construction of Meaning (1991)	250

PART THREE: EARLY LANGUAGE AND LEARNING

	Editor's Introduction	267
12	Relevant Models of Language (1969)	269
13	The Social Context of Language Development (1975)	281
14	Three Aspects of Children's Language Development: Learning Language, Learning through Language, Learning about Language (1980)	308
15	Towards a Language-Based Theory of Learning (1993)	327
16	Grammar and the Construction of Educational Knowledge (1999)	353
	Bibliography	373
	Appendices	382
	Index	405

PREFACE

Nigel 0–1
It was a November evening, in London. Nigel was twelve days old.
He had come from the hospital four days earlier, and seemed pleased at the move. But today he had been crying miserably, and his mother, who had suddenly become a worrier at the thought of this other life for which she was responsible, was in distress.
The time came to bath him. As she undressed him, she noticed an unpleasant boil in the crook of his elbow.
"Come here," she said to me. "Look at this."
That same instant, Nigel stopped crying.
It was his first act of communication. He knew his mother had found out what was wrong, and that was what mattered.
The boil must have gone on hurting, at least until the doctor came and treated it.
But Nigel didn't cry again.

(Personal notes)

The language of children has much to tell us about what language is and the role it plays in our development as human beings. Prompted by his experience of working with teachers of English as a mother tongue and their questions about how children develop their ability to use language, Professor Halliday conducted an intensive study as a participant–observer of his own son's developing linguistic ability from 9 months to $2\frac{1}{2}$ years of age. The methodology was simple – using notebook and pencil to record Nigel's utterances. The data proved rich, providing a wealth of insight into how a child learns how to mean.

Language is as language does. Approaching the data from a functional and meaning-oriented perspective, Professor Halliday tests the hypothesis that a child gradually expands the functional load of his utterances using language initially only to get what he wants, then for purposes which may also be described as regulatory, interactional, personal, heuristic, imaginative, and finally informative. Part One focuses on infancy and the development of protolanguage. We observe Nigel as his language develops from being primarily pragmatic and active to becoming also communal and reflective. Part Two looks at the transitional phase from child tongue to mother tongue. During this phase, the functional contrast between pragmatic and mathetic that has appeared at the end of the protolanguage is reinterpreted in terms of the interpersonal and ideational metafunctions of adult language. Between the semantics and phonology of protolanguage is added lexicogrammar, and the child's discourse exhibits greater texture as his text-forming resources begin to mature and develop.

Language development is a continuous process of learning how to mean through language. Part Three explores this continuity in language development and learning, and discusses its implications for teachers and students. Interaction between the child and others who are part of his world – parents, teachers, peers – plays a crucial role in helping the child construe a sense of social reality, and prepares him to meet the linguistic demands of society. The findings from Professor Halliday's own study of Nigel's language development, which continue to be corroborated by others' studies of child language development, reveal the close relationship between language and learning. This relationship between language and learning is summed up well by Professor Halliday's threefold perspective: learning language, learning through language, learning about language. Building on what the child already knows about language, which in turn has been learned through language, is essential to improving the educational attainment of our children. In fact, learning theory itself has much to learn from how children learn language.

Listening to Nigel learning how to mean is a revelation of how language dynamically develops through interaction and self-expression. These conversations of a very small child provide answers to questions raised by educators and linguists about the nature of learning and language. The data validate a theoretical perspective that gives priority to function over form. The proof of the theory is in the learning.

Nigel 2–2½
The first week after Nigel's second birthday we went away, to stay with friends in southern California.
I had finished making notes on his language. I had followed the development of his meaning potential up to the end of his second year, and that was to be all; now I was going to process what I had.

It was so restful after the exertion of keeping up with him that I kept to this resolution for a whole week — apart from a few scattered observations that I made out of sheer habit.

Back home in Providence, I wavered. There were so many new meanings all coming in all the time; why stop because of a date line? Perhaps I should carry on taking notes a little longer, say till the end of the year? I found myself once more reaching out for pad and pencil.

(Personal notes)

ACKNOWLEDGEMENTS

'Representing the Child as a Semiotic Being', paper presented at the conference "Representing the Child", Monash University, 2–3 October 1998.

'Learning How to Mean', from *Foundations of Language Development: A Multidisciplinary Perspective*, edited by Eric Lenneberg and Elizabeth Lenneberg, published by Academic Press, 1975, pages 239–65. Reprinted by permission of Academic Press. © 1975 Elsevier Science (USA).

'Early Language Learning: A Sociolinguistic Approach', from *Language and Man, Anthropological Issues*, edited by William C. McCormack and Stephen A. Wurm, published by Mouton de Gruyter, 1976, pages 97–124. Reprinted by permission of Mouton de Gruyter.

'One child's protolanguage', from *Before Speech: The Beginnings of Interpersonal Communication*, edited by Margaret Bullowa, published by Cambridge University Press, 1979, pages 171–90. Reprinted by permission of Cambridge University Press.

'A Sociosemiotic Perspective on Language Development', from the *Bulletin of the School of Oriental and African Studies* 37.1 (W. H. Whiteley Memorial Volume), published by the School of Oriental and African Studies, 1974, pages 98–118. Reprinted by permission of Cambridge University Press. © School of Oriental and African Studies.

'Meaning and the Construction of Reality in Early Childhood', from *Modes of Perceiving and Processing of Information*, edited by Herbert L. Pick, Jr and Elliot Saltzman, published by Lawrence Erlbaum Associates, 1978, pages 67–96. Reprinted by permission of Lawrence Erlbaum Associates.

ACKNOWLEDGEMENTS

'The Ontogenesis of Dialogue', from *Proceedings of the Twelfth International Congress of Linguists*, Innsbruck, 1978, edited by Wolfgang U. Dressler, published by Innsbrucker Beiträge zur Sprachwissenschaft, 1979, pages 539–44. Reprinted by permission of Innsbrucker Beiträge zur Sprachwissenschaft.

'Into the Adult Language', from *Learning How to Mean: Explorations in the Development of Language* (in the series *Explorations in the Study of Language*), published by Edward Arnold, 1975, pages 82–119. Reprinted by permission of Edward Arnold.

'On the development of texture in child language', from *The Development of Conversation and Discourse*, edited by Terry Myers, published by Edinburgh University Press, 1979, pages 72–87. Reprinted by permission of Edinburgh University Press.

'The Contribution of Developmental Linguistics to the Interpretation of Language as a System', from *The Nordic Languages and Modern Linguistics: Proceedings of the Fourth International Conference of Nordic and General Linguistics*, Oslo, 1980, pages 1–18. Reprinted by permission of Universitesforlaget AS, Oslo.

'On the Transition from Child Tongue to Mother Tongue', from *Australian Journal of Linguistics* 3.2, published by the Australian Linguistic Society, 1983, pages 201–16. Reprinted by permission of the Australian Linguistic Society (http://www.tandf.co.uk).

'Language as code and language as behaviour: a systemic-functional interpretation of the nature and ontogenesis of dialogue', from *The Semiotics of Culture and Language*, Vol. 1, *Language as Social Semiotic*, edited by R. P. Fawcett, M. A. K. Halliday, S. M. Lamb and A. Makkai, published by Frances Pinter Publishers Ltd, 1984, pages 3–35. Reprinted by permission of Continuum.

'The Place of Dialogue in Children's Construction of Meaning', from *Dialoganalyse III: Referate der 3, Arbeitstgung*, edited by Sorin Stati, Edda Weigand and Franz Hundsnurscher, published by Max Niemeyer Verlag GmbH, 1991, pages 417–30. Reprinted by permission of Max Niemeyer Verlag GmbH, Tübingen.

'Relevant Models of Language', from *The State of Language, Educational Review* 22.1, published by Carfax Publishing, 1969, pages 26–37. Reprinted by permission of Taylor & Francis.

ACKNOWLEDGMENTS

'The Social Context of Language Development', from *Learning How to Mean: Explorations in the Development of Language* (in the series *Explorations in the Study of Language*), published by Edward Arnold, 1975, pages 120–45. Reprinted by permission of Edward Arnold.

'Three Aspects of Children's Language Development: Learning Language, Learning through Language, Learning about Language', from *Oral and Written Language Development: Impact on Schools* (Proceedings from the 1979 and 1980 IMPACT Conferences), edited by Yetta M. Goodman, Myna M. Haussler and Dorothy Strickland, published by International Reading Association, Newark, Delaware, 1980, pages 7–19. Reprinted by permission of International Reading Association, Newark, Delaware.

'Towards a Language-Based Theory of Learning', from *Linguistics and Education* 5.2, published by Elsevier Science, 1993, pages 93–116.

'Grammar and the Construction of Educational Knowledge', from *Language Analysis Description and Pedagogy*, edited by Barry Asker, Ken Hyland and Martha Lam, published by Language Centre, Hong Kong University of Science and Technology, 1999, pages 70–87. Reprinted by permission of the Editor, *Language Analysis, Description and Pedagogy*.

PART ONE

INFANCY AND PROTOLANGUAGE

Editor's Introduction

Children are "meaning-full human beings". It is on this note that Chapter 1 in this part, 'Representing the Child as a Semiotic Being', begins. Presented to the conference "Representing the Child" held at Monash University in October 1998, this chapter offers a perspective born out of two decades of research into children's language development. Rather than seeing children's language development "as a kind of progressive approximation to a goal, a goal that was extrinsically fixed and defined, so that each new step was seen as an imperfect attempt to attain it", Professor Halliday maintains that "What small children are doing is learning how to mean; [...] The child is building up a potential; and in doing so is essentially tracking the processes whereby language first evolved."

The next five chapters in this first part date back to the mid-to-late 1970s, when Professor Halliday began working on children's language development. Included are 'Learning How to Mean' (1975); 'Early Language Learning: A Sociolinguistic Approach' (1976); 'A Socio-semiotic Perspective on Language Development' (1974); 'Meaning and the Construction of Reality in Early Childhood' (1978); and 'The Ontogenesis of Dialogue' (1979). These works detail the findings from his study of a child called Nigel, from 9 months to $2\frac{1}{2}$ years. In Chapter 2, 'Learning How to Mean', Professor Halliday notes how the impetus behind this intensive study of Nigel's developing language system "came from working over a number of years with teachers of English as a mother tongue, who were attempting to grapple with the fundamental problem of language in education [...] Their experience showed that we are still far from understanding the essential patterns of language development in the preschool child, in the deeper sense of being able to answer the question, 'How does the child learn how to mean?'"

Building on the work of Basil Bernstein, Professor Halliday proposes a set of seven functions, the first six serving as the basis of interpreting the language of very young children: (1) instrumental, (2) regulatory, (3) interactional, (4) personal, (5) heuristic, (6) imaginative, and (7) informative. Through studying Nigel's language development, Professor Halliday aimed to test his hypothesis "that these functions would appear, approximately in the order listed, and in any case with the 'informative' (originally called 'representational') significantly last; that in Phase I, they would appear as discrete, with each expression (and therefore each utterance) having just one function; and that the mastery of all of them – with the possible exception of the last – would be both a necessary and a sufficient condition for the transition to the adult system."

The learning of one's mother tongue is described as comprising three phases: "Phase I, the child's initial functional-linguistic system; Phase II, the transition from this system to that of the adult language; Phase III, the learning of the adult language." The first two phases are the subject of Chapter 3, 'Early Language Learning: A Sociolinguistic Approach', in which Professor Halliday maps out the steps in Nigel's language development from protolanguage to adult language. The difference between protolanguage as a system and adult language being that "[protolanguage] consists of a semantics and phonology (or other expressive means) with no lexicogrammar in between". This chapter also focuses on Nigel's development of protolanguage during the period from 9 to 12 months. We see how Nigel's use of language progresses from the pragmatic and active end of the scale – using language to get what he wants (instrumental), and making requests (regulatory) – to the communal and reflective – using language as a way of being together (interactional) and expressing his own thoughts and feelings (personal). Interpreting Nigel's language development as a sociosemiotic process is the subject of Chapter 4, 'A Sociosemiotic Perspective on Language Development'. Incorporated into these two chapters are portions of another paper, 'One Child's Protolanguage' (1979).

Chapter 5, 'Meaning and the Construction of Reality in Early Childhood', approaches language development in terms of intersubjective creativity, in which "Learning to mean is a process of creation, whereby a child constructs, in interaction with those around, a semiotic potential that gives access to the edifice of meanings that constitute social reality." A child creates meaning through interacting with others. The child constructs reality "through intersubjective acts of meaning". This view of language development "as a process of intersubjective creation, whereby a child, in interaction with significant others –

mother, family, peer group, teachers – creates in himself the systems of meanings, wordings and expressions that we call language" is further elaborated in the final chapter of this part, 'The Ontogenesis of Dialogue', which focuses on Nigel's progress towards exchanging acts of meaning, or dialogue. Nigel uses protolanguage to encode non-linguistic acts or states, such as 'I want that', 'do that', 'let's be together', 'I like that' or 'I'm curious about that'. Information as a commodity for exchange, whether giving or demanding – "where the exchange of symbols is not a means towards the exchange of something else (goods-and-services) but actually constitutes, or manifests, the exchange itself" – does not occur until one or two months before two years of age.

Chapter One

REPRESENTING THE CHILD AS A SEMIOTIC BEING (ONE WHO MEANS) (1998)

I am taking the words "representing the child" in two distinct but, I think, not unrelated senses – probably as intended by the organizers of the present conference. One is notational and interpretative: how we can record and theorize children's behaviour; in this case, their semiotic behaviour – how they mean. The other is obligational: how we can act on children's behalf and look after their interests. I used to stress this latter point when I first worked on children's language development, back in the early 1970s: that we should pay children the courtesy of treating them as meaning-full human beings. It was rather necessary to say this at that time; now, I hope, this much can be taken for granted.

Putting these two motifs together means first taking children's *acts of meaning* seriously, as having value in themselves, and second interpreting them, where appropriate, as *instances* of underlying *systems* – systems of meaning potential. (I shall come in a moment to the question of when it becomes appropriate to do that.) This is one kind of dual focus that I shall try to adopt: focus on the instance and, at the same time, focus on the system. There is also another kind: a dual focus whereby we represent each stage in a child's development in its own terms, while at the same time seeing it as part of an ongoing temporal progression: focus on the *moment*, and focus on what we might call the *momentum*. And I might add a third point here, also in a way a kind of dual focus: that in "representing" we are always both recording and interpreting. Representing is, by its nature, a theoretical kind of activity.

Paper presented to conference "Representing the Child", Monash University, 2–3 October, 1998.

One only has to observe about the first half-hour of a newborn infant's life to recognize that here is a social creature, whose personality is formed out of the conjunction of material and semiotic modes of being. Like any other small mammal, of course, the human child is bonded to its mother **materially**, for food, warmth and loving care; but beyond that, the human infant is also bonded **semiotically**, from the start, through the exchange of attention. Already in the early 1970s Colwyn Trevarthen had recorded, on film, how within a few weeks of birth the newborn baby would address its mother, and respond to being addressed: when its mother's face came into view, the baby's whole being became animated, with movement of arms, legs and head, and facial gestures of all kinds, to which the mother responded in her turn. When the mother's attention was withdrawn, the baby's movements subsided and its body became listless and inactive. As yet there is no clear distinction in the baby's behaviour between material and semiotic acts; all such bodily activity is, of course, displacement of matter, subject to the laws of physics; but it is also, as Catherine Bateson had observed, a kind of "protoconversation" – the sharing of attention between infant and mother is actually an exchange of **meaning**. If we were using the terms favoured by natural scientists we would talk about "matter" and "information", as the two phenomenal domains which we inhabit (cf. Williams 1992); these are incommensurable, matter being measured in mass, length, etc., information in bytes. But "information" is a misleadingly loaded term, and even the assumption that it can be measured (like matter) needs to be questioned. I prefer to talk about "matter" and "meaning" – the material and the semiotic. Matter is displaced, meaning is exchanged; I suppose we could use the general term "movement" for both. My point is that in trying to understand early infancy we are faced with a unity of the material and the semiotic. The human infant cannot yet talk, just as it cannot yet walk; neither its body nor its brain has developed to that degree. But both body and brain are being stretched in anticipation of both these tasks.

Representing the newborn child's protoconversation (or "protosemiosis") is easy: it just needs a VCR, a video-audio recording of the event. This because the baby's behaviour is not yet **systemic**: apart from the rather clear distinction between the two states, addressing and not addressing, which is a choice of on or off, within the "addressing" behaviour itself there is no systematic variation in meaning. To demonstrate this point, suppose we now leap forward – say three years. At three years old the child is a fluent speaker of a least one human language, maybe two or three; and also controls various other semiotic modalities besides: producing and recognizing facial expressions and other patterns of non-verbal bodily behaviour, recognizing two- and three-dimensional representations (pictures and models), and operating with a range of symbolic value systems, some realized through language and others not. Representing the semiotic potential of a three-year-old is a very different matter.

Let me stick with the three-year-old for just a moment, to outline just what such representation entails. First and foremost, of course, it means representing the child's language. This is now, by age three, fully systemic; that is to say, each instance has meaning by virtue of *selection* – as a choice from a vast network of possibilities, all the things that might have been meant but were not. We would need to represent this network of options. But it is not just a single network, because the child's language is now stratified: it has a grammar and a phonology as its core, each of these with its own systemic potential, and each in turn interfacing with the material world – the grammar impinging on the world of the child's experience and interpersonal relationships, via the interface level of semantics; the phonology impinging on the world of the child's own body (the "signifying body"; see Thibault, forthcoming), via the interface levels of phonetics and kinetics; and each of these interfaces has, in turn, its own systemic potential. In other words, recognizing what children can do with language – what they can mean – by the age of three years means using some form of representation, such as system networks, to display their powers in semantics, in lexicogrammar, in phonology and in phonetics, as well as, of course, the relations they have established among all these different strata of language. Without this kind of theoretical interpretation, a simple record of children's utterances can give only an impoverished account of their striking ability to mean.

Now we have the theoretical resources for representing this ability to mean, because the language of the three-year-old, although still fragmentary by comparison with that of adults, already has the formal organization of the adult language system. So we can represent it the way we represent adult languages: using phonetic and phonological notations for the expression strata, structural and/or feature representations for the strata of the "content". But what about the stages that are rather earlier in time, intermediate between birth and the advanced age of three? How do we track children's progression after those first semiotic encounters within a few days of being born?

Let us set up a schematic framework for the first half of this period, from birth to 18 months, showing the child's development on both fronts, the material and the semiotic. When we take these together, we find notable parallels between phases of moving and phases of meaning.

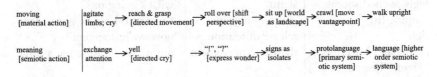

Figure 1 Moving and meaning

And this is where we may notice an interesting phenomenon. At each phase of their semiotic development, children have to create forms of expression — "signifiers", if you like, although the "sign" in its strict sense is a feature only of a particular phase. Where do these signifying expressions come from? They are not imitations of symbolic forms, because the infant brain is not yet able to interpret adult symbols — nor is the infant body yet able to produce them. What happens is that bodily actions (including both movements of the limbs and the sound-producing movements of the vocal organs) get borrowed, as it were — coopted into use as symbolic expressions. There is a regular and constant passage from the material to the semiotic, the semiotic powers raiding the material domain for meaning-making resources (rather in the way that, in human societies, cultural practices that start off by being socially functional get coopted for use in ritual, symbolic contexts).

The first instance of this transference takes place relatively early in infancy, when the cry gets transformed into a yell. A yell is a **directed** cry, a cry that is turned into a message; this semiotic development is analogous to the material development whereby the action of stretching the arms and clasping the fists is gradually transformed into reaching out and grasping — in other words, to action that is **directed** towards some object in the field of vision. (In the semiotic sphere, of course, "directed" means directed at a person, or addressed.) But this same process of material-to-semiotic transformation continues right through into the protolanguage, although, of course, with increasing variation among individual children. The following are some examples from the data:

Form of expression	Material context [original source]	Transformed semiotic significance [meaning as message]
cry	pain	"do something!"
high-pitched squeak	alarm	"what's going on?"
clasping fist	grasping object	"I want (to hold/be given) that"
sigh	release of tension	"now we're together"
raising and lowering arm ("beating time")	rhythmic movement	"put music on, sing me a song"
alternation of w/y posture	sucking + vocalization	"I want to be cuddled"

Possibly the use of intonation (rising and falling pitch) as a primary semiotic resource falls into the same category, although the material origins are not so clear. Traces of this process remain in "adult" language, such as *yuk!* derived from the sound of vomiting, and *yum!* from smacking the lips to get the last morsels of a taste.

From very early in its development, the brain of the infant is simultaneously directing the body to move — to **control** itself and its environment — and directing it to mean — to **construe** itself and its environment. Of course, the construal takes place within the brain itself, as the infant's primary consciousness develops epigenetically into the higher-order consciousness that is (apparently) uniquely human; but all such construal is a social process, dependent on social symbols — and that takes us back to the body, since such symbols have to take on material (perceptible) form.

When infants learn to roll the body over, to move from prone to supine and then from supine to prone, they now for the first time control their own perspective, and can observe the world systematically from these two complementary angles. By this time they have become highly curious, wanting to observe whatever is going on around them; and this curiosity may also be transformed into meaning, with some vocal sign such as a squeak, meaning 'what's going on?' again derived, like the yell, from a self-monitored material event, a noise of alarm; and just as they respond to the yell, caregivers typically interpret these squeaks semiotically, and respond to them by giving some explanation. But it is at the next stage, when infants learn to sit up, that their view of the world becomes integrated into a coherent landscape; and it is at this stage that they decide (so to speak!)

to mean in earnest – to give full value to the semiotic act, as a distinct and self-sufficient form of activity. At first this takes the form of a few isolated simple signs, with meanings such as 'I'm curious; what's happening?', 'I want that', 'I don't want that', 'play with me' and suchlike – although even here we begin to notice different functional orientations; and the isolates are now clearly emerging as ***signs***: that is, as content/expression pairs, such that both the content (the signified) and the expression (the signifier) remain stable over a period of time (even though it may be, in our adult terms, a very short period, sometimes as little as around three to five days).

This relative stability of the sign is a necessary condition for enabling such isolates to develop into a ***semiotic system***; and this is the next phase – that of the protolanguage. The protolanguage is the child's first semiotic system. In terms of "meaning and moving", the interlocking development of material and semiotic resources, protolanguage is associated with crawling. When infants learn to crawl (that is, to move themselves unaided from place to place), they are able to see the world in three dimensions, shifting the angle of observation at their will; and this gives an added dimension to their perceptions. It is at this phase that they become able to construe their meaning potential into systems, in this way developing their first real language, in which meaning is created paradigmatically: each utterance has meaning because it is an instance of a systemic choice. And this is where we need to pause and take stock.

The protolanguage is child tongue, not mother tongue. It is created by the child, in interaction with its caregivers and any other members of its small meaning group (who normally respond to it in their own adult tongue), as a primary semiotic which will eventually lead, via a transitional phase, into the "mother tongue" of childhood, adolescence and beyond. But it is still itself a primary semiotic (that is, a semiotic of primary consciousness), not a higher-order semiotic as adult languages are; that is to say, it has no lexicogrammar (no structures and no words) in it. Its elements are still simple signs, content/expression pairs. What is new is that these are no longer isolated elements; they enter into systemic contrasts, within a small number of definable functional domains. I was able to identify four such domains to start with: the instrumental, the regulatory, the interactional and the personal. I referred to these as ***microfunctions***, to contrast with the more abstract functional components of the later, transitional and mother tongue, phases of children's speech.

As far as the expression is concerned, children will create their protolinguistic signifiers out of anything that is to hand, or to mouth – provided that they can perform it and that those who exchange meanings with them respond. One source I have already referred to is by borrowing from the material domain. Another source is imitation – which can also be a source of confusion for those involved, if it is an imitation of adult speech sounds, because the meaning is not (and cannot be, because the protolanguage is not yet referential) that which the others are disposed to assign to it. Other expressions seem to be just plucked out of the air, so to speak – out of the child's repertory (of sound or gesture) as it happens to be at the time.

It is when we consider the task of "representing the child", however, that with the protolanguage an entirely new issue arises. Up to this point, the child's behaviour has been pre-systemic: signs have been created instantially, and existed only at the level of performance – they could be recorded, as sounds or gestures, but not theorized in general terms. There was no general principle behind them, no systemic potential – and hence no predictability. The phase of one or two isolated signs is transitional; by the time of the protolanguage – and this is what justifies us in referring to it as a form of "language" – the meanings have become systemic. That is to say, each individual act of meaning is the instantiation of some meaning potential; the challenge now is to represent that meaning potential in such a way that the meaning of each instance can be explained by reference to it. Instances, individual acts of meaning, have to be observed within their contexts of situation; the observer's stance then has to be shifted, to allow observation from a distance, so that the child's meaningful activity can be viewed as a whole and that a comprehensive, explanatory picture can be built up.

At least some, and typically perhaps the great majority of, protolinguistic expressions are – like those of the adult language – vocal. How are these vocal expressions to be represented? Most linguists have used standard phonetic representations (like those in Tables 1–6 in Appendix 2), on the grounds that the child is in fact producing articulatory and prosodic (intonational) patterns using the same bodily resources as the adult. But such notations are not really appropriate. At this stage children's vocalizations are postural rather than phonemic: they begin as patterns of movement, among the three basic postures of the human articulatory organs, known in prosodic theory as "y-prosody" (lips spread + front of tongue raised), "w-prosody" (lips rounded + back of tongue raised) and "a-prosody" (lips open + tongue lowered), and also between higher and lower levels of pitch. What this means is that articulation begins as a kind of prosody rather than the other way round. Prosody in adult languages has typically been represented (if at all) as if it was a funny kind of articulation, with "suprasegmental phonemes", and pitch shown as points instead of contours. This is problematic even with adult speech; with children it is clear that the prototype is prosodic, and that articulatory segments are then specialized out. By the time of the protolanguage, the child's phonological resources have typically expanded to include intermediate vowel postures and some consonantal articulations (associated plosives and nasals); but they are still not sequences of segments entering into separate oppositions, as the phonemes of the adult language do. As far as I know we have as yet no adequate form of phonetic representation for this phase.

How long does the protolanguage last? Typically, I think, round about six to nine months, although this should not be taken at all exactly, since it has no clear limits in time: it develops gradually from simple signs, and in its turn is gradually abandoned in the transition to the mother tongue. During its time of ascendancy (a typical age range might be 10 to 18 months), it is constantly changing, as new meanings are added to the system and some old ones modified or dropped. This poses a further problem for representation: when to take cross-sections in time. When I did my own first round of work on the protolanguage, I tried various time intervals for resetting the system network, and eventually settled on an optimum interval of once every six weeks: less than that, one could be picking up too many isolated instances (that is, that did not, in fact, become systemic); more than that, one could be losing track of the way the system was developing. I was able to track the protolanguage of one child through six six-week stages (over about eight months, from 0;10 to 1;6 – by the next time round, at $1;7\frac{1}{2}$, the child had clearly embarked on the transition to the mother tongue) (Halliday 1975; cf. also Painter 1984, Oldenburg-Torr 1997).

What do we learn from such a step-by-step representation of individual children's protolanguage? I think there are mainly two kinds of insight that can be gained. On the one hand, we get a clear picture of the functionality of the protolanguage, of how the child is already using language to live by and has a rather clear sense of the domains of life within which language figures prominently and with effect – what in the first paper I ever wrote on child language I referred to as the child's "relevant models of language". These are the contexts which have value for small children as the domains of semiotic activity. On the other hand, we can come to see how children expand their meaning potential – and what are the limits imposed on this expansion by the nature of the protolanguage itself: since it has no lexicogrammatical system, it cannot function to construct a model of experience or to develop a dynamic of dialogue. These possibilities are opened up by a higher-order semiotic, one with a grammar in it; there is strong pressure for the child to move into the mother tongue! Putting these two perspectives together we can gain a coherent picture of the child's early semiotic development: how children are steadily increasing the number of "semogenic vectors", the various parameters that open up the total potential for meaning. First they tease apart the content from the expression; then they separate the system from the instance; then they open up further strata, further levels of organization within the content and within the expression; then they prise apart the distinct functional components inside each stratum. With each step they are opening up a new domain in which to move, so construing a multidimensional semiotic space analogous to the increasing dimensionality of the bodily space in which their material existence is located.

Throughout this developmental history, the body is involved twice over. In the first place, it is involved as itself, so to speak: as the "doer", or mover, in the child's material existence. In the second place, it is involved as the "meaner", the signifying agent in the child's semiotic existence. By the time of the protolanguage, these two functions have specialized out and become separated: observe any parent and you will find they are very seldom in doubt about which domain any instance of the child's bodily activity belongs to, the material or the semiotic (they know it unconsciously, of course; they are not aware of making any such distinction, and it is certainly no use trying to find out by asking them!). Both kinds of activity, of course, are controlled by the infant's brain; but it would be wrong to think of this as a ready-made brain guiding the body through its various phases of development. On the contrary: the brain itself is developing, being shaped, moulded, wired up – whatever the metaphor we like to deploy – precisely by the ongoing, cumulative instances of material and semiotic behaviour.

What we are trying to do, it seems to me, is to represent the child's semiotic behaviour as a **meaning potential**, something that is functional because it is constantly changing as the child's interaction with the environment expands and develops. Once it becomes **systemic**, such that each performance of an act of meaning is an **instance** of an underlying system that is instated in the infant's brain – in other words, once it becomes a *language*, even if still "proto-", child tongue not yet mother tongue – we can represent it in the form of a network; and, while each network taken by itself is a representation of just one "moment" in the developmental progression, the sequence of several such networks presents a moving picture of the expanding consciousness of the child. A good way of showing this is to use the retrospective technique that was devised by Joy Phillips (1985): she drew up the network for a particular phase of development, then used it to foreshadow the development that led up towards it, filling it in step by step as the child progressed. This also reveals where features are brought in to the system and then drop out again, which is an interesting aspect of the earlier phases in learning the mother tongue. Figures 2 and 3 exemplify Phillips' approach.

Let me come back now to the transition from protolanguage to mother tongue – the move into "language" in its typical sense of post-infancy human speech. This is, in fact, the transition from primary to higher-order consciousness, using Edelman's model of the evolution of the brain (Edelman 1992); and it involves what is in evolutionary terms a considerable leap forwards, so that there appears to be a massive discontinuity – in the popular view, the child is beginning to talk. (Protolanguage is not recognized in the culture as a form of talk, even though parents carry on long conversations with their infants at the protolinguistic stage.) The discontinuity is real enough; but it also tends to mask what is an equally real continuity in the child's development of meaning, including the functions that meaning takes on in everyday life. To return to the analogy I was drawing between meaning potential and moving potential, whereas protolanguage is associated with crawling, language is associated with walking; and the transition to an upright posture is so sudden, and so striking, that it tends to obscure the essential continuity in the framing of the human body, and in the significance of freedom of movement for human existence.

To represent the transition from child tongue to mother tongue we need to take account of two interdependent factors, the stratal and the functional. In stratal terms, what happens is that the child deconstructs, or rather deconstrues (using "construe", as throughout, for constructing in the semiotic mode), the protolinguistic sign, and insinuates a grammar "in between" the meaning and the expression. By this move the primary semiotic system (that is, the semiotic system as construed by the infant's primary consciousness – a level of consciousness shared

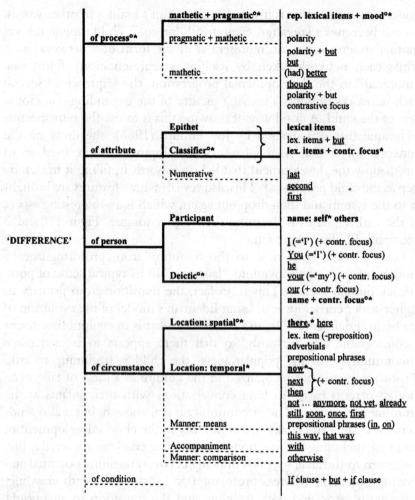

Figure 2 Nigel's construal of 'difference' at 1;7½ –1;9 (from Phillips 1985)
★ occurring for the first time, ° one occurrence only, up to this point.

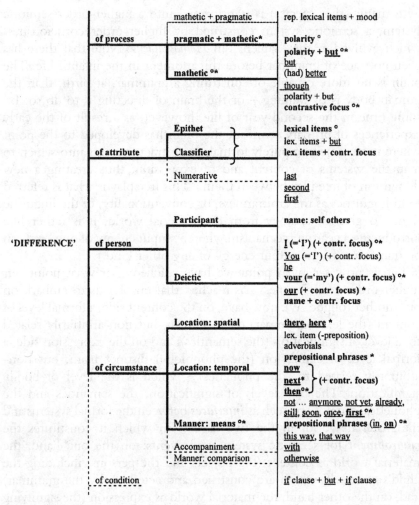

Figure 3 Nigel's construal of 'difference' at 1;9–1;10½ (from Phillips 1985)

with many other species) is transformed into a higher-order semiotic system, a semiotic system construed by higher-order consciousness which evolved as the "sapiens" in *Homo sapiens*. Note that there has been no trace of grammar before this moment in the infant's life. The brain is no more capable of construing a grammar, at birth, than the human body is of walking – or the brain of directing it to do so. By some time in the second year of life, however, as a result of the early experiences of primary semiosis, the brain has developed to the point where it can construe purely formal, or abstract, systems into which to map the systems of content and of expression, thus creating a new dimension of free play between them. (This free play is what is referred to in linguistics as the arbitrariness, or conventionality, of the linguistic sign. To give an analogy from the material world, it is rather like introducing a gearing mechanism whereby input energy of one kind can be transformed into output energy of any other kind.)

Let us now see what point we have reached – or what point our higher-order consciousness has reached that enables us to embark on our mother tongue. We now have, on the content side, a formal level of content (the lexicogrammar) distinct from, but non-arbitrarily related to, a level of signification (the semantics); and on the expression side, a formal level of expression (the phonology) distinct from, but non-arbitrarily related to, the phonetics – which is the level of bodily signification. The two levels of signification, the semantics and the phonetics, can now be seen as **interfaces** between the formal systems and the material world, in the two aspects in which it constitutes the **environment** for semiotic systems and events: on the one hand, the material world as content (the objects and the persons, including the child's own self, which are construed and acted on by the grammar) and, on the other hand, the material world as expression (the signifying body, analogously "construed" by the phonology).

This has been presented in somewhat abstruse theoretical terms; but before I illustrate it let me refer to one other factor that I mentioned in connection with the transition into the mother tongue, namely the functional one. We have seen how, in the protolanguage, children first **systemized** their acts of meaning, by reference to a small number of functional contexts: obtaining goods-and-services ("instrumental"), manipulating others ("regulatory"), exchanging attention ("interactional"), manifesting their own affective states ("personal"), playing and imagining ("imaginative"). These contexts arise in the course of daily life and the meanings the child produces arise out of them; that is how the caregivers are able to interpret them, just as pet-owners identify the meanings produced by their household pets, which are evolutionarily parallel to the human protolanguage – they also are the manifestations of forms of primary consciousness. The functional orientations of the mother tongue are very different from those of the protolanguage; in fact the entire concept of linguistic "function" has to be reconstrued. In language (here as opposed to protolanguage), while it is still possible to talk informally about the "functions" of individual utterances in their contexts of situation, functionality has become **intrinsic to the system**: every instance is in fact multifunctional, because this feature is built in to the grammar – you cannot switch it off. It is impossible to activate just one "function" at a time. In our higher-order semiotic every act of meaning is at once a construing of experience and an enacting of interpersonal relationships (grammatically speaking, every clause selects both in transitivity and in mood). This is the extraordinary semiotic leap that children take in the second year of their lives, from the point where their range of meaning is an inventory of simple signs to the point where they have constructed for themselves an effectively infinite resource for making sense of the world and interacting with the people in it. Our next step in representing the child has to be that of representing **how** they make this catastrophic transition.

I remarked at the beginning that the infant brain is simultaneously directing the body both to move and to mean – to act materially and to act semiotically. The semiotic act, or "act of meaning", involves the two planes of *content* and *expression*; and each of these two planes interfaces with the material world. The interface on the expression plane is what I have called, following Thibault, the signifying body – at first the whole body, then gradually specializing out to certain parts of it (face, hands, vocal organs) and then, when the child attains the higher-order semiotic, that of language, the vocal organs take over as the dominant player (this interface is what we call "phonetics"), except in "sign", which uses mainly hands, arms and face. On the content plane, the interface is what we call "semantics"; here children are making sense of their experience of the world they find round about them (and also that they find inside themselves, the world of their own consciousness); and in the same breath, so to speak, interacting with those around them, and so enacting their own social being. As they move into this transitional phase of semiosis, leading from the primary semiotic of the protolanguage to the higher-order semiotic of the mother tongue, there is a remarkable collaboration set up by the brain between these two interfaces, something that is made possible by the brain's development to the level of higher-order consciousness. The critical factors in this development, as far as the semantic interface is concerned, are two: memory, and consciousness of self.

With memory, the child is able to construe *classes* of phenomena out of repeated instances, using a re-entrant mapping to impose categories on its experience of the world. Linguistically, this means that the child is now able to construe "common" terms – generalized common nouns as opposed to individuated proper nouns; and this is the beginning of *reference*, referential meaning. (The early individuated signs of the protolanguage are not yet referential; a protolinguistic *mama* means something like 'I want (you) mummy'.) With self-consciousness, the child is able to make a systemic distinction between two modes of meaning, the declarative ('this is how things are') and the imperative ('this is how I want things to be'); this distinction is something that was noticed a long time ago by observers of children's first incursions into language (e.g. Lewis 1936), and more recent evidence confirms that it is a typical strategy for the transition into the mother tongue (Halliday 1975, see also Chapter 9; Painter 1984, 1989; Oldenburg-Torr 1997). In grammatical terms, these two steps constitute, respectively, proto-transitivity and proto-mood; taken together, they make it possible for the child to transform experience into meaning – to reflect on and to act on the world and the people in it in one semiotic swoop.

But for them to be able to do this the other interface must also be involved – the body as domain of expression: now becoming specialized, as we have seen, to expression in the form of vocally originated sound. We noted that in the content there were these two motifs: construing experience, by setting up categories and their interrelations to model the child's experience of the world, and enacting social processes, by getting along with others and in so doing shaping the child's own self. Let us call these two motifs the "ideational" and the "interpersonal", as used in systemic functional grammar. Now, somehow these two motifs have to be carried along simultaneously yet independently, so that all possible meanings of the one kind can be combined with all possible meanings of the other kind. How can this freedom of movement – or rather, freedom of meaning – be achieved?

Adult languages do it in highly elaborated ways. They have an array of resources in their grammars: choice of words, the words' phonetic shape, the ordering of elements, repetitions, morphological variation, particles, patterns of intonation, and the like; and all this allows for a great deal of play – every language has its own characteristic way of deploying these different resources. But underlying this variation is a basic principle which runs something along these lines: that interpersonal meanings tend to have a slightly longer, or even significantly longer, time frame than ideational ones. Thus, if one thinks of an instance of a clause: ideationally it will consist of various elements (an event, participants in that event, circumstantial elements of various kinds – like *I saw the great man on television the other night*, which is made up of five distinct constituent parts); but interpersonally it is likely to take on colouring as a whole. If it is a statement, or if it is a question, then the whole thing is a statement, or the whole thing is a question; if it is said with disapproval, or sarcastically, then the whole thing is disapproving, or sarcastic; and so on. So in some respect or other, interpersonal meanings tend to be enacted prosodically, by repeating things, choosing a particular voice quality or pitch contour, beginning or signing off with a distinctive type of particle, and so on: some form of expression whose domain is more extended than that of elements of referential meaning.

How do children work their way in to the immense complexity that this interplay of meanings involves? This is where the body again plays a critical part – the part of the body that has become specialized for signifying through language; namely, the voice. The organs of **articulation** – primarily tongue and lips, also soft palate and larynx – move around very quickly; their posture can change many times a second, producing rapidly varying acoustic impacts. By contrast, features of timbre and voice quality, patterns of melody and rhythm, take longer both to unfold and to produce contrasting sound effects. These latter are what are referred to collectively as **prosodic** features (using the term in a less abstract and more strictly phonetic sense than I was doing earlier). The one-year-old has already developed some mastery of both prosodic and articulatory features in the protolanguage, but has not yet learnt to separate them: a protolinguistic sign is a fixed combination of the two, such as dà spoken glottalically and on a falling tone. As a critical step – **the** critical step, as far as the expression plane is concerned – the child now separates out these two types of phonation, and learns to combine one pattern of articulation with two distinct prosodies – different tones, or different voice qualities. This might have happened randomly before; but now it becomes systemic: the articulation pattern carries one consistent meaning, and the prosody carries another. To give an actual example from my own data: at 13 months Nigel created an articulatory/

prosodic system as follows: three articulatory patterns, *ama/dada/anna*, meaning respectively 'Mummy', 'Daddy', 'Anna', combined with two prosodic patterns, rising tone/falling tone, meaning respectively 'where are you?' and 'there you are!' (Figure 4).

Figure 4 Nigel's first stratification of the content plane. Here for the first time a system of experiential meaning (three personal names) becomes separated from, and freely combinable with, a system of interpersonal meaning (two moods). This is the child's first step towards a lexicogrammatical stratum.

This system yielded a set of six terms, each combining proto-reference with proto-speech-function: the articulations have taken the first step on the way to becoming **names**, the prosodies have taken the first step on the way to becoming **moods**.

A favourite transition strategy, by which the child breaks through into the transitivity and mood systems of the adult grammar, is to develop this pattern into a general principle. Figure 5 gives some examples showing the way that Nigel did it. The two tones, rising and falling, were functionally quite distinct. With the rising tone, the meaning was 'somebody do something!', 'I want (some particular good or service)'; some answer, in deeds or (increasingly, over time) in words, was being demanded and had to be forthcoming for the speech act to have been, in Nigel's view, successful (that is, he would go on saying it until it was responded to). I referred to this type as **pragmatic**. With the falling tone, the meaning was 'that's the way things are'; no response was expected, although the listener often provided one: "yes that's a green bus", "no, that's blue/that's a van" and so on. I called this type **mathetic** because they had a learning function; where the pragmatic foregrounded the **instance** ('do that now!'), the mathetic assigned the instance to a **system** ('that's a case of . . .'), locating it within a semantic space made up of categories and relationships. Over a period of six months or so (1½ to 2), the mathetic developed into the adult declarative mood; the pragmatic developed into interrogative and imperative, both of which for a time kept their rising tones before Nigel eventually shifted the imperatives and the Wh-interrogatives over into the falling tone to conform to adult English.

So the prosodic contrasts turned into a system of mood. They became the foundation for the interpersonal component in the grammar, with its speech functions, modalities, systems of appraisal and so on. The articulatory contrasts became the foundation for the ideational component; they developed into the process, participants and circumstantial elements that make up the transitivity system, construing the categories and relations with which we model our experience of the world. At first, the experiential domains of the pragmatic ('what I want') and the mathetic ('what's going on') remain distinct; but it is not long before they start to overlap, and pairs appear such as *mummy bòok* (falling tone) 'that's Mummy's book', and *mummy bóok* (rising tone) 'I want Mummy's book', and by the time the child is ready to ask questions (that is, when the meaning 'I want' extends to information as well as goods-and-services), the experiential domain of the two become in principle identical: whatever you can tell, you can also ask, and whatever you can ask, you can also tell. And this again is made possible by the signifying body: our vocal resources have evolved in such a way that any articulation can be combined with any prosody. This in turn is what has enabled human language to evolve the way it has done, such that every act of meaning, in our higher-order consciousness, is a complex activity involving both construing (referring to some features of experience) and enacting (setting up some form of interpersonal relationship). Resources for the former evolved out of vowel and consonant articulations like *wiyuwiyu*, *nananana*, *abu* and so on; resources for the latter evolved out of rising and falling pitch, breathy and creaky voice quality and the like. Thus the twofold nature of the

chuffa stúck	N. calling for help in freeing toy train
find fóryou	'I've lost something; find it for me!'
throw úp	'throw the rabbit up in the air again'
low wáll	N. about to jump off suitcase, asking to be
high wáll	caught; first used when jumping off walls, low and high, in park
squéeze	'squeeze the orange for me'
gláss	'I want my milk in a glass'
orange lèmon	'sing "Oranges and lemons"'; accompanied by music gesture, which is alternative realization of pragmatic; hence falling tone
turn róund	N. repeating instruction given when fitting shapes into puzzles: 'is that what I have to do?'
play chúffa	'let's play with the train'
open fóryou	(usual form of request for box, etc., to be opened)
back tóothpaste	'put the toothpaste back in the cupboard'
more grávy	also: more ómelette, -léttuce, -tomáto, -bréad, -bún, etc.
bounce táble	'I want to bounce my orange on the table'
cárry	'carry me!'
háve it	(usual form of 'I want that thing')
tóast	'I want some toast'; also <u>breakfast</u>, <u>tomato</u> etc.
hit flóor	'I'm going to hit the floor with the hammer'
that sóng	'sing that song you've just sung'
háve that	(same as <u>have it</u> above)
hedgehog bóok	'I want the book with the hedgehog picture in it'
play ráo	'I want to play at lions'
train under túnnel ... getit fóryou	both halves rising tone
dówn ... table ... sugar ... spóon	'put the sugar down on the table for me to put my spoon in it'; rising tone on <u>down</u> and <u>spoon</u>

Figure 5 Examples of pragmatic and mathetic: Nigel 1;6–1;9

REPRESENTING THE CHILD AS A SEMIOTIC BEING

molasses nòse	'I've got molasses on my nose' (with accompanying expression of delight)
big bàll	frequent when playing with ball; also: little bàll
mummy bòok	frequent on picking up book and finding no pictures inside ('it's Mummy's book')
red swèater	on seeing it; also: red jùmper (same object)
black brùsh	also <u>green</u>, <u>red</u>, <u>blue</u>, <u>yellow</u> with <u>stick</u>, <u>light</u>, <u>peg</u>, <u>car</u>, <u>train</u> etc.
bìg one	applied to goods train, bubble; tonic on <u>big</u>, as in adult form
baby dùck	in picture; also: mummy dùck
too bìg	frequent; sometimes appropriate, as when trying to push object through wire mesh; sometimes inappropriate, as when trying to reach ball with stick (='too far')
that bròke	'that's broken'
loud mùsic	frequent comment as loud passage starts
chuffa stòp	in game (Father bouncing N., N. being 'fast train'; Father stops)
two green pèg	
green stick fìnd	'the green stick's been found'
old green tràin ... green old tràin	both halves falling tone; the second, though less probable, would have been the appropriate one in the context
dada black brùsh	'Daddy's black brush'
no more wàter	
toothpaste ... òn ... tòothbrush	falling tone on <u>on</u> and again on <u>toothbrush</u>; not fully formed as a single structure
tree fall dòwn	later: big tree fall dòwn
dada got bàll ... nila got bàll	
ball go under càr	cf. water gone plùghole

Figure 5 continued.

body's interfacing with the content, as repository of experience and as participant in the social process, is matched by the twofold nature of its interfacing with the expression, producing (and also of course responding to) articulatory and prosodic patterns. All this activity is stage-managed by the child's rapidly developing brain.

For a long time children's language development, or "language acquisition" as it came to be rather misleadingly called, was thought of as a kind of progressive approximation to a goal, a goal that was extrinsically fixed and defined, so that each new step was seen as an imperfect attempt to attain it. Although the child's efforts are no longer dismissed as irrelevant "mistakes", but rather are seen as strategies and tactics for learning, there is still the view that the mother tongue is what the child is striving to "acquire" right from the start. In my view this conception is wide of the mark. What small children are doing is learning how to mean; and the guiding principle is neither approximative (imitating what is around) nor performative (guided by an innate grammar) but epigenetic. The child is building up a potential; and in doing so is essentially tracking the processes whereby language first evolved. Up until the beginning of the transit into the mother tongue, typically well into the second year of life, the child's language development owes nothing to the language spoken around, except in the indirect sense that the meanings of the child's protolanguage are negotiated with adults who speak that language; you cannot tell, from observing a child's protolanguage, what its mother tongue is going to be. It is only when the transition begins, and the child starts to leap over thousands of generations of human evolution, that we start to see the influence of the mother tongue; and even then the child persists along its own developmental trajectory – even to the point where the patterns being generated conflict with those that the mother tongue displays (compare Nigel's use of rising tones on his early imperatives and *Wh*-interrogatives – but many such examples could be cited).

So what are the outstanding problems in representing the child, as one who is learning how to mean? Critically, I think, we have to find ways of representing this process as the building up of a semiotic potential, analogous to the building up of the physical potential that is taking place in the child's own body. Ultimately, both are aspects of the development of brain power; and no doubt every part of the brain is talking to all the other parts as these immense resources are being built up. The language development of a small number of individual children has been studied intensively in recent years; but it will be a task for the next millennium to expand this effort and integrate it with studies of individual brain development on the one hand and large-scale corpus studies of natural data from very small children on the other. And we hope that linguistic theory may mature to the point where it can be involved in, and might even contribute to, what E. O. Wilson calls "consilience", the coming together of scientific understanding not just in physics and biology but also in the social (and I would add the semiotic) sciences. One gain we can surely expect from this will be a deeper understanding of human infancy and childhood.

Chapter Two

LEARNING HOW TO MEAN
(1975)

Adult language comprises three interrelated systems: phonological, lexicogrammatical (vocabulary, morphology, syntax) and semantic. Language development studies in the 1960s focused mainly on the lexicogrammatical level; they were also predominantly psycholinguistic in their orientation. More recently, interest has extended into semantics; the present paper is concerned with the learning of meaning, and proposes a complementary approach in sociolinguistic terms.

The paper suggests a sociosemantic interpretation of language development, based on the intensive study of one child, Nigel, from 9 months to $2\frac{1}{2}$ years. Nigel first developed (Phase I) a two-level system, having sounds and meanings but no words or structures, in which the meanings derived from the elementary social functions of interaction with others, satisfaction of needs and the like. This continued to expand for six to nine months, at which time the child entered the stage of transition to the adult language (Phase II, corresponding to what is generally taken as the starting-point). This was characterized by the interpolation of a lexicogrammatical level between meaning and sound, and by the mastery of the principle of dialogue, the adoption and assignment of speech roles. It was also marked by a generalization of the initial set of social functions to form a basic opposition between "language as learning" and "language as doing".

The transition was considered complete when the child had effectively replaced his original two-level system by a three-level one and moved from monologue into dialogue; he then entered the adult system (Phase III). He could now build up the meaning potential of the adult language, and would continue to do so all his life. From a sociolinguistic point of

---

First published in *Foundations of Language Development. A Multidisciplinary Perspective*, edited by Eric Lenneberg and Elizabeth Lenneberg. London: Academic Press, 1975, pp. 239–65.

view the major step consisted in once again reinterpreting the concept of "function" so that it became the organizing principle of the adult semantic system, being built into the heart of language in the form of the ideational (representational, referential, cognitive) and the interpersonal (expressive–conative, stylistic, social) components of meaning. All utterances in adult speech contain both these components, which are mapped on to each other by the structure-forming agency of the grammar. The original social functions survive in their concrete sense as types of situation and setting, the social contexts in which language serves in the transmission of culture to the child.

1 Introduction

Considered in the perspective of language development as a whole, the latest period of intensive study in this field – the last decade and more – has been characterized by what may, in time, come to seem a rather one-sided concentration on grammatical structure. The question that has most frequently been asked is, "How does the child acquire structure?".[1] The implication has been that this is really the heart of the language learning process; and also perhaps, in the use of the term "acquisition", that structure, and therefore language itself, is a commodity of some kind that the child has to gain possession of in the course of maturation.

The dominant standpoint has been a psycholinguistic one, and the dominant issue, at least in the United States where much of the most important work has been carried out, has been between "nativist" and "environmentalist" interpretations (Osser 1970). There seems, however, to be no necessary connection between these as general philosophical positions and the particular models of the processes involved in the learning of linguistic structure that have been most typically associated with them (cf. Braine 1971). The nativist view lays more stress on a specific innate language learning capacity; it does not follow from this that the child necessarily learns by setting up hypothetical rules of grammar and matching them against what he hears, but there has been a widely held interpretation along these lines. Environmentalist views, by contrast, emphasize the aspect of language learning that relates it to other learning tasks, and stress its dependence on environmental conditions; again, this is often assumed to imply an associationist, stimulus-response model of the learning process, although there is no essential connection between the two.

In the investigation of how the child learns grammatical structure, attention has naturally been focused on the nature of the earliest structures which the child produces for himself, where he combines certain elements – typically, but not necessarily, words – that he also uses in isolation, or in other combinations. There are in principle two ways of looking at these: one adult-oriented and other child-oriented. The child's structures may be represented either as approximations to the forms of the adult language or as independent structures *sui generis*. The first approach, which is in a sense presupposed by a nativist view, involves treating many of the child's utterances, perhaps all of them at a certain stage, as ill formed; they are analysed as the product of distortions of various kinds, particularly the deletion of elements. This brings out their relationship to the adult forms, but it blocks the way to the recognition and interpretation of the child's own system. In the second approach, the child's earliest structures are analyzed as combinations of elements forming a system in their own right, typically based on the contrast between closed and open-ended classes; the best-known example is Braine's (1963) "pivotal" model, with its categories of "pivot" and "open". Such an analysis has been criticized on the grounds that it fails to account for ambiguous forms (for example, Bloom 1970: *mommy sock* = (i) 'Mummy's sock', (ii) 'Mummy is putting my socks on'); but this is an aspect of a more general limitation, namely that it does not account for the meaning of what the child says. Nor does it easily suggest how, or why, the child moves from his own into the adult system; if language development is primarily the acquisition of structure, why does the child learn one set of structures in order to discard them in favour of another? For an excellent discussion of these and related issues, see Brown (1973).

None of the above objections is very serious, provided it is recognized, first, that structural analysis is a highly abstract exercise in which both types of representation are valid and each affords its own insight; and second – a related point – that language development is much more than the acquisition of structure. But by the same token, the form of representation of the grammatical structures of the child's language is then no longer the central issue. The fundamental question is, "How does the child learn language?". In other words, how does he master the adult linguistic system, in which grammar is just one part, and structure is just one part of grammar? How does he build up a multiple coding system consisting of content, form, and expression – of meaning relations, the representation of these as lexico-structural configurations, and the realization of these, in turn, as phonological patterns?

A consideration of this question in its broader context is embodied in what Roger Brown calls a "rich interpretation" of children's language: the approach to language development through the investigation of meaning. This is not, of course, a new idea. But when the psychologists' traditional two-level model of language (as sound and meaning) came to be overtaken by that of structuralist linguistics – which was still in terms of two levels, but this time of sound and form – it rather receded into the background.[2] With the now general recognition of the basically tri-stratal nature of the linguistic system (and Prague theory, glossematics, system-structure theory, tagmemics, stratification theory, and the later versions of transformation theory are all variants on this theme), the semantic perspective has been restored. The "rich interpretation" may still rest on a structural analysis of the utterances of children's speech; but, if so, this is an analysis at the semological level in which the elements of structure are functional in character. Most typically, perhaps, they are the transitivity functions of the clause, such as Agent and Process (Schlesinger 1971); but it is worth commenting here that all functional categories, whether those of transitivity, like Fillmore's (1968) "cases", or those of thematic structure (Gruber 1967), and including traditional notions like subject and modifier (Kelley 1967), are semantic in origin (Halliday 1970), and could therefore figure appropriately in such a description.

The approach to structure through meaning may also be either child-oriented or adult-oriented. For example, the utterance *now room* (see below), which could be glossed as 'Now let's go to (play in) (daddy's) room', could be analysed on the adult model as something like Imperative + Process + Agent + Locative + Temporal, with Imperative, Process and Agent deleted; or, in its own terms, as something like Request for joint action + Arena, with nothing omitted or "understood".

Once again, these are abstract representations, and neither can be said to be wrong. But a child-oriented semantic analysis of the latter kind, which is very suggestive, carries certain further implications. Since the elements of the structure are not being explained as (approximations to) those of the adult language, there is presumably some other source from which they are derived and in terms of which they have any meaning. Why, for example, would we postulate an element such as "Request for joint action"? This is explicable only if one of the functions of language is to call for action on the part of others, to regulate their behaviour in some way. No doubt this is true; but to make it explicit implies some specification of the total set of functions of language, some kind of a functional hypothesis that is not just a list of uses of language but a system of developmental functions from each of which a range of meanings, or **meaning potential** is derived.

At this point the attempt to understand the structure of the child's utterances leads directly to questions about the linguistic system as a whole, and specifically about the functions for which that system first develops. There is an important link between the two senses of "function", first as in "function in structure" and second as in "functions of language"; the former, when interpreted semantically, imply the latter. But whether or not the line of approach is through considerations of structure, once the interest is focused on how the child learns a system of meanings this points to some investigation in functional terms. It becomes necessary to look beyond the language itself, but to do so without presupposing a particular conceptual framework, because this is precisely what the child is using language to construct; and herein lies the value of a functional approach. Early language development may be interpreted as the child's progressive mastery of a functional potential.

There is yet a further implication here, one which takes us into the social foundations of language. If, for example, language is used, from an early stage, to regulate the behaviour of others, and it is suggested that the mastery of this function is one of the essential steps in the developmental process, this assumes some general framework of social structure and social processes in terms of which a function such as "regulatory" would make sense. More particularly – since we are concerned with the language of the child – it presupposes a concept of cultural transmission within which the role of language in the transmission process may be highlighted and defined. Here the concept of meaning, and of learning to mean, is in the last analysis interpreted in sociological terms, in the context of some chain of dependence, such as social order (transmission of the social order to the child), role of language in the transmission process (functions of language in relation to this role) and meanings derived from these functions.

In this way the functional interpretation of the child's meanings implies what might be termed a sociolinguistic approach (cf. Osser 1970), in which the learning of language is seen as a process of interaction between the child and other human beings. From this perspective, which is complementary to the psycholinguistic one (and not in any sense contradictory), the focus of attention is on the linguistic system as a whole, considered as having a (functionally organized) meaning potential, or semantic system, at one end, and a vocal potential, or phonological system, at the other. In this context, structure no longer occupies the centre of the stage; it enters in because it is one form of the realization of meanings. This has certain important consequences for the investigation of language development. The analysis does not depend on utterances of more than one element, that is, on combinations of words as structural units. This is significant because, although the word in the sense of a lexical item or lexeme (that is, vocabulary) soon comes to play an essential part in the development of the linguistic system, the word as a structural unit, which is a different concept, does not do so, or not nearly so prominently; it is merely one type of constituent among others, and the young child has no special awareness of words as constituents (this point is brought out by Braine (1971: 87), who, for some reason, finds it surprising). From the functional point of view, as soon as there are meaningful expressions there is language, and investigation can begin at a time before words and structures have evolved to take over the burden of realization.

It then emerges that the child has a linguistic system before he has any words or structures at all.[3] He is capable of expressing a range of meanings that at first seem difficult to pin down, because they do not translate easily into adult language, but that become quite transparent when interpreted functionally, in the light of the question, "What has the child learnt to do by means of language?". The transition from this first phase into the adult system can also be explained in functional terms, although it is necessary to modify the concept of function very considerably in passing from the developmental origins of the system, where "function" equals "use", to the highly abstract sense in which we can talk of the functional organization of the adult language. However, this modification in the concept "function of language" is itself one of the major sources of insight into the process whereby the adult system evolves from that of the child.

In what follows we shall suggest a tentative framework for a functional, or sociolinguistic, account of early language development. This will recognize three phases: Phase I, the child's initial functional-linguistic system; Phase II, the transition from this system to that of the adult language; Phase III, the learning of the adult language. The account does not presuppose any one particular psychological model of language acquisition or theory of learning. Linguistically, it assumes some form of a realization model of language; the descriptive techniques used are those of system-structure theory, with the *system* (a set of options with a condition of entry) as the basic concept (Firth 1957; Halliday 1973), but such a representation can be readily interpreted in stratificational terms (Lamb 1970; Reich 1970). The sociological standpoint is derived from the findings and the theoretical work of Bernstein. But the particular impetus for the detailed study of a developing language system, which provides the observational basis for this sketch, came from working over a number of years with teachers of English as a mother tongue, who were attempting to grapple with the fundamental problem of language in education (for the results of their work, see Doughty *et al.* 1971; Mackay *et al.* 1970). Their experience showed that we are still far from understanding the essential patterns of language development in the preschool child, in the deeper sense of being able to answer the question, "How does the child learn how to mean?"

2 Phase I: functional origins

2.1 Developmental functions: a hypothesis

Seen from a sociolinguistic viewpoint, the learning of the mother tongue appears to comprise three phases of development. The first of these consists of mastering certain basic functions of language, each one having a small range of alternatives, or "meaning potential", associated with it.

A tentative system of developmental (Phase I) functions was suggested (see Chapter 12) as follows:

Instrumental	*I want*
Regulatory	*Do as I tell you*
Interactional	*Me and you*
Personal	*Here I come*
Heuristic	*Tell me why*
Imaginative	*Let's pretend*
Informative	*I've got something to tell you*

The hypothesis was that these functions would appear, approximately in the order listed, and in any case with the "informative" (originally called "representational") significantly last; that, in Phase I, they would appear as discrete, with each expression (and therefore each utterance) having just one function; and that the mastery of all of them – with the possible exception of the last – would be both a necessary and a sufficient condition for the transition to the adult system. The implication of this is that these functions of language represent universals of human culture, which may in turn have further implications for an understanding of the evolution of language.

The hypothesis was tested, and the pattern of development from Phase I to Phase III followed through in detail, in an intensive study of the language development of one subject, Nigel, from 9 to 24 months of age. This will be the main source of information for the present account.

2.2 The functional interpretation of child language

The criterion adopted for regarding a vocalization by the child as an utterance (that is, as language) was an observable and constant relation between content and expression, such that, for each content–expression pair, the expression was observed in at least three unambiguous instances and the content was interpretable in functional terms. (In practice the distinction between random vocalizations and systematic forms proved to be obvious, and the latter were observed with far more than minimal frequency.) This means that the content was, in each case, derivable as a possible option in meaning from some point of origin that could reasonably be interpreted as a context for effective verbal action (Firth 1950), whether or not in the above list. We may compare here Leopold's observation (1939–49) that his daughter at eight months showed "the intention of communication, which must be considered the chief criterion of language" (vol. I: 21). Judged by the criterion adopted, Nigel's vocalizations at nine months were still prelinguistic, or just on the threshold of language. At $10\frac{1}{2}$ months, however, he had a language consisting of a meaning potential in each of four functions. We shall refer to this as NL 1, meaning "Nigel's Language 1" (Figure 1).

At this stage, there is no grammar. That is to say, there is no level of linguistic "form" (syntax, morphology, vocabulary) intermediate between the content and the expression. In stratificational terms, the child has a semology and phonology but not yet a lexology. Furthermore, the system owes nothing to the English language (a possible exception being [bø] *I want my toy bird*); the sounds are spontaneous and, in general, unexplained, although two or three are

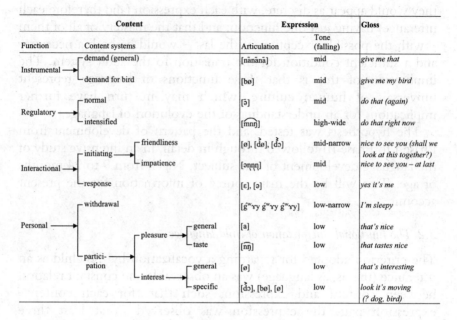

Figure 1 NL1: Nigel's language at 0;9–0;10½

attested as imitations of natural sounds the child has heard himself make and then put to systematic use. (Parenthetically, it should be noted that a phonetic alphabet such as the IPA notation is quite inappropriate as a means of representing the child's speech sounds at this stage; it is far too specific. What is wanted is a system of notation showing generalized postures and prosodic values.)

Rather, it might be said that the ***expression*** owes nothing to the English language. As far as the content is concerned, the English language probably has played a part, by virtue of the fact that it embodies meanings such as 'I want that' somewhere in its semantic system, and the adult hearer therefore recognizes and responds to such meanings. It is of course immaterial, in this regard, whether such meanings are or are not cultural and linguistic universals.

Nigel's language was studied continuously and the description recast every 1½ months, this being the interval that appeared to be optimal: with a longer interval one might fail to note significant steps in the progression; with a shorter one, one would be too much at the mercy of random non-occurrences in the data. Table 1 (p. 39) shows the number of options within each function at each stage from NL 1 (9 to 10½ months) to NL 5, the end of Phase I (15 to 16½ months). Those for NL 6, which is considered to be the beginning of Phase II, are added for comparison, although it should be stressed that they are not only less reliable but also, as will emerge from what follows, less significant as an index of the system.

2.3 Characteristics of Phase I systems

The set of options comprising NL 1 represents what a very small child can do with language – which is quite a lot in relation to his total behaviour potential. He can use language: to satisfy his own material needs, in terms of goods or services (instrumental); to exert control over the behaviour of others (regulatory); to establish and maintain contact with those that matter to him (interactional); and to express his own individuality and self-awareness (personal). Moreover, any one option may have a very considerable range, not only in the sense that it can be used very frequently (that is, on numerous occasions, not counting repetitions within one occasion; it is necessary to distinguish "instances" from "tokens" at this stage), but also, and more significantly, in the sense that many of the options are very general in their applicability. There is a tendency, in fact, for each function to include an unmarked option whose meaning is equivalent to the general meaning of the function in question; for example, in the instrumental function there is one option meaning simply 'I want that', where the object of desire is clear from the context – contrasting with one or more specific options such as 'I want my bird'. There are various modifications of this pattern; for instance, there may be one unmarked term for an initiating context and another for a response ('Yes, I do want that'). But the principle is clearly operative, and perhaps anticipates the "good reason" principle, that of "select this option unless there is a good reason for selecting some other one", that is such a fundamental feature of adult language.

The functions observed in Nigel's Phase I turned out to be those of the initial hypothesis. This will cease to be true in Phase II, but in one important respect the hypothesis fails already: there is no sign of a developmental progression within the first four functions. As a matter of fact, the only two expressions recorded before nine months that fulfil the criterion for language were in the interactional and personal areas. Furthermore, the imaginative function seems to appear before the heuristic, although a reinterpretation of certain elements (the "problem area" referred to in the next paragraph) in the light of Phase II observations suggests that this may be wrong and that the heuristic function begins to appear at NL 4 (13½ to 15 months) at the same time as the imaginative. The two are closely related: the heuristic function is language in the exploration of the objective environment – of the "non-self" that has been separated off from the self through the personal function – while the imaginative is language used to create an environment of one's own, which may be one of sound or of meaning and which leads eventually into story, song, and poetry. Finally, the informative function has not appeared at all. What does emerge as some sort of developmental sequence, in Nigel's case, is (1) that the first four functions listed clearly precede the rest, and (2) that all others precede the informative. The informative function does not appear until nearly the end of Phase II, round about NL 9 (21 to 22½ months), but this was not entirely unexpected, since the use of language to convey information is clearly a derivative function: one which presupposes various special conditions including, for one thing, the concept of dialogue.

The functions themselves, however, emerge with remarkable clarity. Not only did it prove surprisingly easy to apply the general criterion for identifying a vocal act as language (since the learning of a system cannot be regarded as a function of that system, anything interpreted as linguistic practising was automatically excluded – Nigel in fact did very little of this), but it was also possible, throughout NL 1 to 5, to assign utterances to expressions, expressions to meanings, and meanings to functions with relatively little doubt or ambiguity. There was one significant exception to this, a problem area lying at the border of the interactional and the personal functions, which proved extremely difficult to systematize; subsequent interpretation suggests that it was, in fact, the origin of heuristic language, or rather of a more general learning function that is discussed more fully below. Otherwise, although the functions clearly overlap in principle, or at least shade into one another, the value of an element at all levels in the system was usually not difficult to establish.

More important, the fact that the meaning could be derived from functions that were set up on extralinguistic grounds justifies our regarding these early utterances as expressions of language – a step that is necessary if we are to understand the genesis of language as a whole. Phase II, which corresponds to what has usually, in recent years, been taken as the (unexplained) point of origin of the system, is here regarded as being already transitional, and explained as a reinterpretation of the elementary functions in a more generalized form. Ultimately, these evolve into the abstract functional components of the adult grammatical system, and these components then serve as the medium for the encoding, in grammar, of the original functions in their concrete extensions as what we would call simply "uses of language".

Table 1 Number of options within each function at different language stages

	Instru-mental	Regul-atory	Inter-actional	Personal	Heur-istic	Imagin-ative	Inform-ative	Total
Phase I								
NL 1 (9–10½ months)	2	2	3	5	–	–	–	12
NL 2 (10½–12 months)	3	2	7	9	–	–	–	21
NL 3 (12–13½ months)	5	6	7	9	–	2	–	29
NL 4 (13½–15 months)	5	6	7	11	(?)	3	–	32
NL 5 (15–16½ months)	10	7	15	16	(?)	4	–	52
Phase II								
NL 6 (16½–18 months)	31	29	16	61[a]	3	5	–	145

[a] This figure includes all expressions used in observation and recall, reinterpreted in Phase II as "mathetic" (deriving from personal-heuristic).

3 Phase II: the transition

3.1 Vocabulary and structure

The transition to the adult system begins, with Nigel, at NL 6 (16½ to 18 months). This phase is characterized by two main features: (1) a shift in the functional orientation, which is described below, and (2) major and very rapid advances in vocabulary, structure and dialogue.

Vocabulary and structure are in principle the same thing. What emerges at this point is a grammar, in the traditional sense of this term as a level of linguistic "form" (the lexological stratum). This is a system intermediate between the content and the expression, and it is the distinguishing characteristic of human, adult language. The options in the grammatical system are realized as structure and vocabulary, with vocabulary, as a rule, expressing the more specific choices.

3.1.1 Vocabulary

NL 6 has some 80 to 100 new meanings, and, for the first time, the majority of the meanings are expressed by means of lexical items – the expressions are English words. In the first instance these are used holophrastically, which in the present context is defined in functional terms: the lexical item forms, by itself, an utterance that is functionally independent and complete. With Nigel, this did not continue very long; he happened to be one of those children who hardly go through a "holophrastic stage", for whom the holophrase is merely the limiting case of a linguistic structure. In any case the holophrase is, in itself, of little importance, but it serves to signal the very crucial step whereby the child introduces words – that is, a vocabulary – into his linguistic system.

Why does the child learn words? Do they fit into and enrich the existing functional pattern, or are they demanded by the opening up of new functional possibilities? The answer seems to be, not unexpectedly, both. Many of the words that are learnt first are called for by existing functions. Of these the majority, in Nigel's case, are at first restricted to one function only; for example, *cat* means only 'hello, cat!' (interactional), *syrup* means only 'I want my syrup' (instrumental). A few begin to appear in more than one function, at different times; for example, *hole* means now 'make a hole' (instrumental), now 'I want to (go out for a walk and) put things in holes' (regulatory), and now 'Look, there's a hole' (personal–heuristic; see below). Just once or twice we find a combination of functions in a single instance; for example, *cake* meaning 'Look, there's a cake – and I want some!' This last is very striking when it first occurs. With the adult, all utterances are plurifunctional; but for a child the ability to mean two things at once marks a great advance. Thus, as far as the existing functions are concerned, the learning of vocabulary (1) engenders new meanings within these functions and (2) allows for functions to be combined. The latter will then impose definite requirements on the nature of linguistic structure, since the principal role of structure, in the grammar, is that of mapping one functional meaning on to another.

However, many of the new words – the majority, in Nigel's case – do not fit into the earlier functional pattern. In the first place, they have clearly not been learnt for pragmatic contexts. Indeed many of them are not particularly appropriate to the instrumental or regulatory functions for example, *bubble, toe, star, hot, weathercock*. Even those that are do not appear in these functions until later on – the words *dog* and *bus*, for example, although perfectly well understood as also referring to certain toys, are not used to ask for those toys, or in any other pragmatic sense.

It might be surmised, then, that the impetus to the learning of new words would come from the emergence of the informative function, from the child's desire to use language for conveying information. But this is not so. At 18 months Nigel has no conception of language as a means of communicating an experience to someone who has not shared that experience with him; it is only much later that he internalizes the fact that language can be used in this way. A further possibility might be that the child is simply practising, using new words just in order to learn them. This also must be rejected, if it implies that the child is learning language in order to learn language; he cannot seriously be thought to be storing up verbal wealth for future uses he as yet knows nothing about. But the notion of learning is the relevant one, provided it is interpreted as learning in general, not simply the learning of language. For Nigel, the main functional impetus behind the move into the lexical mode is, very distinctly, that of learning about his environment. Most of the new vocabulary is used, at first, solely in the context of observation and recall: 'I see/hear . . .', including 'I saw/heard . . .'.

In terms of the developmental functions, this appears to be a blend of the personal and the heuristic, resulting from some such process as the following. First, the self is separated from the "nonself" (the environment). Second, a meaning potential arises in respect of each: personal reactions, for example pleasure, and attention to external phenomena, for example 'Look!' Third, new meanings arise through the combination of the two: involvement with, and reaction to, features of the environment; for example, 'Look, that's interesting!' Fourth, the child develops a linguistic semiotic for the interpretation and structuring of the environment in terms of his own experience.

Hence the new words function mainly as a means of categorizing observed phenomena. Many of them represent items having properties that are difficult to assimilate to experience, typically movement (for example, *dog, bee, train, bubble*) and visual or auditory prominence (for example, *tower, light, bus, drill*); while others are simply phenomena that are central to the child's personal explorations – in Nigel's case, particularly things in pictures. The child is constructing a heuristic hypothesis about the environment, in the form of an experiential semantic system whose meanings are realized through words and structures, and which is used in contexts of observation and recall – and before long also of prediction.[4]

This "learning" function of language – perhaps we might refer to it as the **mathetic** function – appears to arise as a synthesis of the two principal non-pragmatic Phase I functions: the personal, which is the self-oriented one, and the heuristic, which is other-oriented. Nigel's earliest instances, at the beginning of Phase II, are markedly other-oriented; but this function soon becomes a means of exploring the self as well, and so takes up, on a higher level, the meaning of the original Phase I "personal" function. We can trace the history of this mathetic function of language in Nigel's case from the very beginning; it is of interest because it reveals what was, for one child, the primary mode of entry into grammar.

Prominent in NL 1 is an interactional option in which some pleasurable experience, usually a picture, is used as the channel for contact with another person: [dɔ̌], etc., glossed as 'nice to see you, and shall we look at this together?' In NL 2, this apparently splits into two meanings, though still with considerable overlap: one has an interactional emphasis, [dɔ̌], [ɛ̀ya] , etc., 'Nice to see you (and look at this!)'; the other is personal, [dɔ̌], [dɛ̀ə], etc., 'That's nice', reacting to a picture or bright object and not requiring the presence of a second participant. By NL 3, the former has become simply a greeting, and the expression for it is replaced, in NL 4, by *hello* [alou̯wa], alongside which appear individualized expressions of greeting *mummy, daddy, Anna*. The latter remains as an expression of personal interest; but meanwhile a third form arises at the intersection of the two, [ādà], [adādàdà], etc. which represents the earliest type of **linguistic** interaction, glossed as 'Look at this! – now you say its name' – used only where the object is familiar and the name already (receptively) known. In NL 5, this naming request specializes out and becomes the form of demand for a new name, [adỹdà] 'What's that?'; and this is used constantly as a heuristic device. Meanwhile, alongside the general expression of personal interest there have appeared a few specific variants, 'Look that's a . . .', which are expressed by English words. At first these occur only in familiar contexts, again typically pictures; but in NL 6 they come to be used in the categorization of new experience, in the form of observation and recall: 'I see a . . .', 'I saw a . . .'. Then, within a very short time (less than one month), and still largely in this same mathetic function, the vocabulary begins to be backed up by structures. We can thus follow through, with Nigel, the process whereby the use of names to record and comment on what is observed, which is a universal feature of child language at a certain stage, arises out of meanings and functions that already existed for the child before any vocabulary had been learnt at all.[5] (see also Chapter 10)

3.1.2 Structure

With Nigel, the structural explosion followed very closely on the lexical one. That it is part of the same general process, the development of a stratum of *grammar* intermediate between the content and the expression, is shown, however, not so much by the shortness of this interval, which with some children is much longer, but by the fact that both vocabulary and structure first appear in the same functional contexts. All that was said, in functional terms, about the learning of vocabulary could apply to structure also.

At the outset of Phase II, Nigel displayed two types of proto-structure, or rather two variants of the same type: a specific expression, within a certain function, combined either (1) with a gesture or (2) with a general expression from the same function. Examples: [dà:bɨ] *Dvořak* + beating time (music gesture), 'I want the Dvořak record on' (instrumental function); [ndà] *star* + shaking head (negation gesture), 'I can't see the star' (personal); [ɛ`lɔu] (command + *hole*), 'Make a hole' (regulatory); [ù æyì:] (excitement + *egg*), 'Ooh, an egg!' (personal). Shortly after this came word strings. These were of two words only (for example, [bʌ`bu nɔumɔ̀]) (*bubble, no-more*) 'The bubbles have gone away'), except when in lists, when there might be as many as six (for example, *stick, hole, stone, train, ball, bus* 'I saw sticks', etc.) and each word still has its own independent (falling) tone contour. The first "true" structure, in the sense of a string of words on a single tone contour, appeared at 19 months, just four weeks after the first major excursion into vocabulary; and within two more weeks various types of structure were being produced, as in the following sets of examples:

1. *mummy come, more meat, butter on, squeeze orange, mend train, help juice* ('help me with the juice'), *come over-there, now room* ('now let's go to the room'), *star for-you* ('make a star for me'), *more meat please.*
2. *green car, two book* ('two books'), *mummy book* ('Mummy's book'), *bee flower* ('there's a bee on the flower'), *bubble round-round* ('The bubbles are going round and round'), *tiny red light, two fast train.*

These structures fall into two distinct groups, on functional criteria. Those under (1) are **pragmatic**, corresponding to the instrumental and regulatory functions of Phase I; those of (2) are what we have called **mathetic**, deriving from the personal–heuristic functions.[6]

Quite unexpectedly, this binary grouping was made fully explicit by Nigel himself, when within the same two-week period (the end of NL 7, 19 to 19½ months) he introduced an entirely new distinction into his speech, that between falling and rising tone. From this point on, all pragmatic utterances were spoken on a rising tone and all non-pragmatic (mathetic) ones on a falling tone. The distinction was fully systemic, and was maintained intact for some months; it provided a striking corroboration of the significance of pragmatic/mathetic as a major functional opposition. If Nigel is at all typical, this opposition (though not, of course, Nigel's particular form of realization of it) seems to be fundamental to the transition to Phase III, the adult system; we shall return to it below. Here it is relevant because it enables us to see the development of structure in Phase II as an integral part of the total language learning process.

What is the relation of linguistic structure to the functions of language? Let us take the examples, from Nigel at the beginning of Phase II (NL 7, 18 to 19½ months), of *more meat, two book,* and *green car.* All three seem at first sight to display an identical structure, whether this is stated in child-oriented terms, for example Pivot + Open, or in adult-oriented terms, for example Modifier + Head. But *more meat* occurs only in a pragmatic function, whereas the other two occur only in a mathetic function. Moreover, this is a general pattern; we find *more omelette, more bread,* and so on, all likewise pragmatic only, and *two train, mummy book* ('Mummy's book'), *green peg, red car,* and so on, all mathetic only. It is this functional specialization that relates these structures to the earlier stage of language learning. By a subsequent step, they become functionally derestricted, so that the structure represented by *more meat* becomes compatible with the mathetic sense 'Look there's some ...', and that of *green car* with the pragmatic sense of 'I want the ...'. At first, however, each structure is tied exclusively to just one function or the other.

The structural analysis of *more meat* might be "Request + Object of desire", relating it to the instrumental function from which it derives. The elements of the structure are pragmatic not experiential ones. By contrast, *green car* may be analysed in experiential terms, as perhaps "Visual property + Object observed". In terms of the introductory discussion, this interpretation of structure is child-oriented semantic: semantic in order to relate it to function, child-oriented to show the part it plays developmentally, which is obscured if we assume from the start a final outcome in the shape of a structure of the adult language. Exactly how a structure such as that represented by *more meat*, initially pragmatic, comes later to take on a non-pragmatic function, first in alternation and then in combination with the pragmatic, is an interesting and difficult question; presumably in this instance the request element *more* comes to be reinterpreted experientially as a comparative quantifier (in Nigel's case, via the aspectual sense of 'I want (you) to go on ...ing'; for example, *more play rao* 'I want us to go on playing lions'); while the request function is generalized and taken over by the modal system in the grammar (in Nigel's case, via the systematic use of the rising tone). We have chosen here what is probably a rather simple example; but the point is a general one. In the beginning, all Nigel's structures, like his vocabulary, are functionally specific; they are either pragmatic (Set 1 on p. 44), or mathetic (Set 2). Only after an interval are they transferred to the other function; and this takes place, not by a shift out of one box into another, but rather by a recasting of the concept of "function" on to a more abstract plane so that all expressions become, in effect, plurifunctional.

Herein lies the essential unity of structure and vocabulary. Words and structures, or rather "words-and-structures", that is, lexicogrammatical units, are the expression of options at a new level appearing in the child's linguistic system intermediate between meaning and sound. This is the stratum of linguistic form, or grammar; and it appears that grammar develops, with the child, as the means of incorporating the functional potential into the heart of the linguistic system. It allows for meanings that derive from different functions to be encoded together, as integrated structures, so that every expression becomes, in principle, functionally complex. Grammar makes it possible to mean more than one thing at a time.

3.2 Dialogue

The early development of the grammatical system has been fairly thoroughly explored. What has been much less explored, although it is of fundamental importance, is how the child learns dialogue.

Nigel learnt to engage in dialogue at the same time as he started to learn vocabulary, towards the end of NL 6 (just before 18 months), and dialogue could serve as well as vocabulary to mark the beginning of his Phase II. There was some "protodialogue" in Phase I: at NL 2, Nigel had three specific responses, to calls, greetings, and gifts, and by NL 5 he could answer questions of the type 'Do you want ...?', 'Shall I ...?', that is, those where the answers required were instrumental, regulatory, or interactional in function. But he could not initiate dialogue; nor could he give responses of a purely linguistic kind.[7]

Dialogue can be viewed as, essentially, the adoption and assignment of roles. The roles in question are social roles, but of a special kind: they exist only in and through language, as communication roles – speaker, addressee, respondent, questioner, persuader, and the like. But they are of general significance developmentally, since they serve both as a channel and as a model for social interaction. Whenever someone speaks, he normally takes on the role of addresser ('I'm talking to you'), and assigns the role of listener ('attend!'); but in dialogue these roles have to be made more specific, not merely 'I'm talking to you' but, for example, 'I am demanding information, and you are to respond by supplying it'. Dialogue involves purely linguistic forms of personal interaction; at the same time, it exemplifies the general principle whereby people adopt roles, assign them, and accept or reject those that are assigned to them.

The mysteries of dialogue were unravelled by Nigel in the two-week period at the opening of NL 7 (18 to 18½ months). At the end of this time he could:

1. Respond to a Wh-question (provided the answer was already known to the questioner); for example:
    "What are you eating?"
    NIGEL: *Banana.*

2. Respond to a command; for example:
    "Take the toothpaste to Daddy and go and get your bib."
    NIGEL (does so, saying): *Daddy ... noddy ... train*, that is 'Daddy, (give) noddy (toothpaste to him, and go and get your bib with the) train (on it).'
3. Respond to a statement; for example:
    "You went on a train yesterday."
    NIGEL (signals attention, by repeating, and continues the conversation): *Train ... byebye*, that is, 'Yes, I went on a train, and then (when I got off) the train went away.'
4. Respond to a response; for example:
    NIGEL: *Gravel*.
    RESPONSE: "Yes, you had some gravel in your hand."
    NIGEL: *Ooh* (that is, 'It hurt me').
5. Initiate dialogue; for example:
    NIGEL: *What's that?*
    RESPONSE: "That's butter".
    NIGEL (repeats): *Butter.*

The question 'What's that?' is, however, his only option for initiating dialogue at this stage. Apart from this, it is outside his functional potential to demand a linguistic response; he cannot yet assign specific communication roles. But he has gone some way in being able to accept those that are assigned to him.[8] As long as the child's responses are limited to exchanges such as:

("Nigel!")
NIGEL: [ø̀] 'Yes, I'm here.'
("Do you want some cheese?")
NIGEL: [nò] 'No, I don't want it.'
("Shall I put the truck in the box for you?")
NIGEL: [à] 'Yes, do.'

he is simply using language in its original extralinguistic functions; this is not yet true dialogue. The ability to respond to a Wh-question, however, is a significant innovation; the child has mastered the principle of the purely communicative functions of language, and is beginning to take on roles that are defined by language itself. This is the first step towards the "informative" use of language, which is late in appearing precisely because it is language in a function that is solely defined by language – a complex and difficult notion.

Once the child can engage in dialogue, new possibilities arise in relation to the functions he has already mastered: the elaboration of existing options, persistence and change in functional "tactics" and so on. Dialogue also plays an essential part in the development of the generalized mathetic function, not only making it possible for the child to ask for new names but also allowing for systematic exploration of the environment and extended patterns of verbal recall. But no less important than this is the role of dialogue in anticipating and leading into Phase III, the mastery of the adult system. Through its embodiment of linguistic role-playing, dialogue opens the way to the options of mood (declarative, interrogative, etc.), and thus to the entire interpersonal component in the language system. This is the component whereby the speaker intrudes or, as it were, builds himself into the linguistic structure, expressing his relations with other participants, his attitudes and judgements, his commitments, desires, and the like (Halliday 1973). Thus in the course of Phase II, with the help of an increasing amount of imitative, role-playing speech – and also of sheer argument, which plays an essential part – the child learns to participate linguistically, and to intrude his own angle, his individuality, and his personal involvement into the linguistic structure. In this way language becomes for him an effective channel of social learning, a means of participating in and receiving the culture. Meanings are expressed as verbal interaction in social contexts; this is the essential condition for the transmission of culture, and makes it possible for certain types of context to play a critical part in the socialization process (Bernstein 1971).

Phase II is thus characterized by two major advances towards the adult linguistic system. On the one hand, the child adds a grammar, a level of linguistic form (syntax and vocabulary) intermediate between content and expression, so developing the basic tri-stratal organization of the adult language. The grammar is a system of potential, a network of options that is capable of "receiving" from the content level and "transmitting" to the expression;[9] in so doing it forms structure, accepting options from various functionally distinct content systems and interpreting these into integrated structural patterns. It is a nexus of systems and structures, as defined by Firth (1957). On the other hand, the child learns dialogue; he learns to adopt, accept, and assign linguistic roles, and thus to measure linguistic success in linguistic terms. From now on, success consists no longer simply in obtaining the desired material object or piece of behaviour, but rather in playing one's part, in freely accepting the roles that one is assigned, and getting others to accept those that one has assigned to them.

Phase II can be said to end when the child has mastered the principles of grammar and of dialogue, and thus effectively completed the transition to the adult language **system**. (He is still, of course, only just beginning his mastery of the adult **language**.) But Phase II is transitional also in the functional sense, in that the child is moving from the original set of discrete developmental functions, where "function" equals "use", through an intermediate stage leading to the more abstract concept of "function" that lies at the heart of the adult language. Naturally the two aspects of the transition, the functional and the systemic, are closely interconnected; they are the two sides of the developmental process. The development of the functions, however, is significant for interpreting the development of the system – in the sense that language evolves in the way it does because of what it has to do. In the final section, we shall sketch out in tentative fashion the nature of the child's functional progression into the adult language.

4 Phase III: into language

4.1 Functions of the adult system

Can we relate the "function" of Phase I, where it refers to a set of simple, unintegrated **uses** of language – instrumental, regulatory, and so on – to "function" in the sense of the highly abstract, integrated networks of relations that make up the adult language system?

The answer will depend on our interpretation of "function" in the adult language. Functional theories of language have attempted, as a rule, not so much to explain the nature of language in functional terms, as to explain types of language use; their points of departure have been, for example, ethnographic (Malinowski 1923), psychological (Bühler 1934), ethological (Morris 1967), or educational (Britton 1970). But although the categories and terminologies differ, all of these incorporate in some form or other a basic distinction between an ideational (representational, referential, cognitive, denotative) and an interpersonal (expressive–conative, orectic, evocative, connotative) function of language.

If we now adapt this functional perspective to a consideration of the nature of language itself, we find that the adult linguistic system is in fact founded on a functional plurality. In particular, it is structured around the two-way distinction of *ideational* and *interpersonal*. The grammar of an adult language is a tripartite network of options, deriving from these two basic functions together with a third, that of creating text – the ***textual*** or, we could equally well say, "textural" function of language. This last is not treated in most functional theories because it is intrinsic to language; it is an enabling function, providing the conditions whereby the other functions can effectively be served. The textual function arises out of the very nature of language, and we need not therefore look for its independent origin in the developmental process. How, then, does the child progress from the functional pattern of his Phase I linguistic system to the ideational–interpersonal system which is at the foundation of the adult language?

This is the point at which Nigel provided an interesting and unexpected clue. Like all children (cf. Leopold 1939–49, vol. III: 1–30) he had made systematic use of intonation from the start, all his expressions being characterized by particular pitch contours: typically, varieties of falling tone, though with some exceptions; all personal names, for example, were high level. Early in Phase II, Nigel introduced, within one week (NL 7: $19\frac{1}{4}$ to $19\frac{1}{2}$ months), a systematic opposition between rising and falling tone; this he maintained throughout the remainder of Phase II with complete consistency. Expressed in Phase I terms, the rising tone was used for all utterances that were instrumental or regulatory in function, the falling tone for all those that were personal or heuristic, while in the interactional function he used both tones but with a contrast between them. We can generalize this distinction by saying that Nigel used the rising tone for utterances demanding a response, and the falling tone for the others. The few exceptions were themselves systematic; for example, demands for music had, as expected, a rising tone unless they were accompanied by the music gesture, in which case the tone was falling, showing that the gesture was an alternative realization of the option "request for music" – and that the falling tone is to be regarded as the unmarked term in the system. The important point to note here is that Nigel is **not** using intonation as it is used in adult English, since the contrasts in meaning that are expressed by intonation in English (Halliday 1967) are still outside his functional potential. He is adapting the elementary opposition between rising and falling, which he knows to be significant, to a functional system that is within his own limitations and which, as it happens, is perfectly transitional between Phase I and Phase III. This is the distinction that was referred to earlier between the pragmatic function, or language as doing (Nigel's rising tone), and the mathetic function, or language as learning (Nigel's falling tone). The one aspect that lies outside this system is the imaginative or play function of language, which at this stage takes the form of chants and jingles with special intonation patterns of their own.

This distinction between two broad generalized types of language use, the mathetic and the pragmatic, that Nigel expressed by means of the contrast between falling and rising tone, turns out to be the one that leads directly to the abstract functional distinction of ideational and interpersonal that lies at the heart of the adult linguistic system. In order to reach Phase III, the child has to develop two major zones of meaning potential: one ideational, concerned with the representation of experience, the other interpersonal, concerned with the communication process as a form and as a channel of social action. These are clearly marked out in the grammar of the adult language. It seems likely that the ideational component of meaning arises, in general, from the use of language to learn, whereas the interpersonal arises from the use of language to act. The fact that Nigel made the distinction between the mathetic and the pragmatic fully explicit by means of intonation was, of course, merely his own route through Phase II; it is not to be excepted that this distinction will be expressed in the same way by all children, or even that it will necessarily be made explicit at all. But for Nigel this was a major step in his development of a grammatical system, as he progressed from the simple duality of content and expression that is characteristic of Phase I.

It is not to be thought that Phase II "mathetic" is **synonymous** with ideational, or "pragmatic" with interpersonal. Pragmatic and mathetic are generalized functional categories of the content, in the developmental system of the child, in which every utterance is, in principle, **either** one **or** the other. Ideational and interpersonal are abstract functional components of the grammar, in the developed, tri-stratal system of the adult; here every utterance is, in principle, **both** one **and** the other at the same time. What changes is the concept of "function"; and from this point of view, Phase II is the developmental process whereby "function" becomes distinct from "use". In other words, the notion "function of language" splits into two distinct notions: that of "use of language" and that of "component of the linguistic system". We shall try to summarize this process, together with other aspects, of the entry into Phase III, in the final section that follows (Figure 2).

5 Summary of functional development

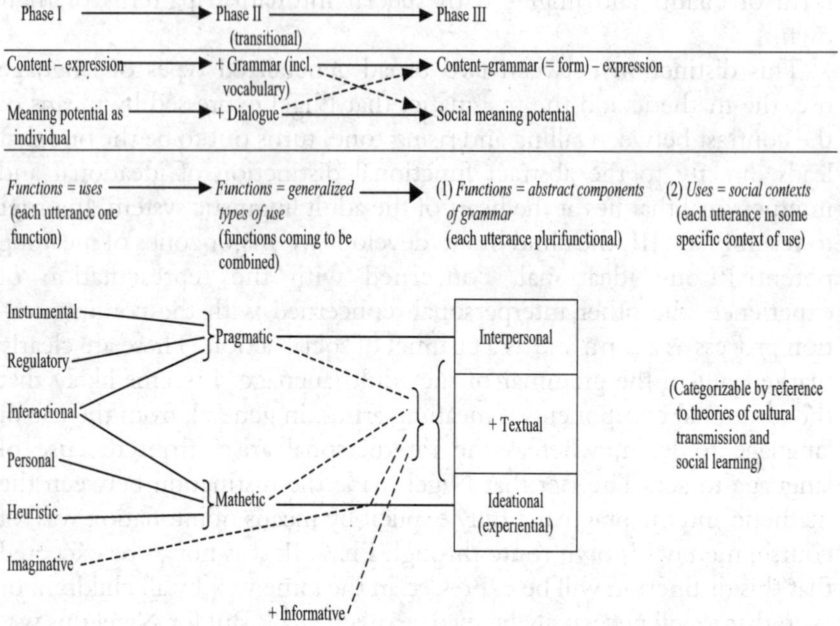

```
Phase I ─────────────► Phase II ─────────────► Phase III
                       (transitional)
```

Phase I	Phase II	Phase III
Content – expression	+ Grammar (incl. vocabulary)	Content–grammar (= form) – expression
Meaning potential as individual	+ Dialogue	Social meaning potential

Functions = uses (each utterance one function)	Functions = generalized types of use (functions coming to be combined)	(1) Functions = abstract components of grammar (each utterance plurifunctional)	(2) Uses = social contexts (each utterance in some specific context of use)

Instrumental ─┐
Regulatory ───┤─ Pragmatic ─────────── Interpersonal
Interactional ┘   (Categorizable by reference
Personal ─────┐   + Textual   to theories of cultural
Heuristic ────┤─ Mathetic ───────────   transmission and
Imaginative ──┘   Ideational   social learning)
                                        (experiential)
              + Informative

Figure 2

1. The origins of language development can be interpreted as the learning of a set of functions, each with its associated "meaning potential". The system is a functional one, in which function is identical with use; each utterance has one function only, and the meanings are such as 'give me that, I'm interested, let's be together'. The initial functions are instrumental, regulatory, interactional, and personal; these are then followed by the heuristic and the imaginative. Each item in the language is a simple content–expression pair; there is no level of linguistic "form" (no grammar).

2. At a certain stage, the child begins to use language in a "mathetic" function, for the purpose of learning. This arises as a generalization from the personal and the heuristic; language in the identification of the self and, as a corollary, in the exploration of the non-self. This function is realized through verbal observation and recall (and, later, prediction). It generates a range of new meanings for which the child needs resources of vocabulary (for example, names of objects and processes) and of structure (for example, class and property, process and participant).

3. Simultaneously there appears to take place a generalization of the remaining functions under a "pragmatic" rubric, which includes the use of language both to satisfy one's own needs and to control and interact with others (subsuming what is sometimes called "manipulative" language). This also generates new meanings, for which other structures are required (for example, request plus object of desire), and also other lexical items. With Nigel, however, only a minority of words were first learnt in this function, perhaps because often the specific meaning is recoverable from the situation (for example, 'I want that thing there').

4. The grouping into mathetic and pragmatic functions appeared, with Nigel, as the dominant characteristic of Phase II, the transitional phase. The distinction is that between language as learning and language as doing; between **separating** the self from the environment, thus identifying the one and interpreting the other, and **interacting** with the environment so as to intrude on the things and people in it, manipulating them and expressing attitudes towards them. With Nigel, nearly all words and structures were first used to express meanings in either one or the other of these two functions, not in both; after an interval, the resources that had been mastered in the one function were then transferred to the other. But, at the same time, all utterances were becoming plurifunctional (see 10 below).

5. In its inception, the mathetic–pragmatic distinction corresponds to one of "response required" (pragmatic) versus "response not required" (mathetic). This probably accounts for the remarkably explicit form given to this distinction by Nigel, who used a rising tone to express the pragmatic meaning and a falling tone for the mathetic. The question whether the mathetic–pragmatic distinction represents a general Phase II strategy must be left open at this stage; the use of intonation to express the distinction is, of course, Nigel's own idea.

6. As far as the linguistic system is concerned, Phase II consists of learning grammar; that is, of introducing into the system a level of linguistic form interposed between content and expression and made up of sets of options realized as structure and vocabulary. The need for a grammar arises out of the pragmatic and the mathetic functions; the latter, which is probably of greater significance for cognitive development, seems to provide the main impetus, at least for the learning of vocabulary. The introduction of grammatical structure makes it possible, however, to combine both functions in one utterance.

7. At the same time as he is learning grammar, the child also learns dialogue. This is the other major step characterizing Phase II. Here the

main impetus probably comes from the pragmatic functions, with their emphasis on involvement. With dialogue, the child acquires a potential for adopting and assigning linguistic roles, which in turn calls for further resources in the grammar (for example, a set of options in mood – declarative, interrogative, and so on – and the structures used to realize them).[10]

8. Functionally speaking, the grammar of the adult language comprises two major components: (1) ideational, embodying the speaker's experience and interpretation of the world that is around him and inside him, and (2) interpersonal, embodying his own involvement in the speech situation – his roles, attitudes, wishes, judgements, and the like. To express this another way, the linguistic system has evolved so as to serve, for the speaker, the "observer" function on the one hand, and the "intruder" function on the other. These two **metafunctions**, together with a third, the "textual" function, are incorporated into the system of the adult language as distinct sets of options, each having strong internal but weak external constraints (that is, a choice within one function affects other choices within the same function but not, in general, those outside it). Each set of options is realized through distinct structures that are mapped on to one another in the production of utterances.

9. It follows that, in Phase III (the adult system), "function" is no longer synonymous with "use". The adult has indefinitely many uses of language; but the typical utterance of the adult language, whatever its use, has both an ideational and an interpersonal component of meaning. For example, every main clause embodies selections – and therefore is structured – simultaneously in transitivity (ideational) and in mood (interpersonal).

10. It appears, then, that the "metafunctions" of the Phase III grammatical system arise, indirectly but unmistakably, out of the primary uses of language that the child develops in Phase I. On the evidence of Nigel, the transition takes place by a process of generalization from these primary functions, which yields the two broad function types of pragmatic and mathetic. The pragmatic is oriented towards meanings such as 'I want', 'will you?', 'may I?', 'let's', so it provides the context for the interpersonal systems of the grammar, typically those of mood, modality, person, attitude, and the like. The mathetic is oriented towards experiential meanings, and so provides the context for ideational systems such as those of transitivity (the grammar of processes), time and place, qualifying and quantifying, and so on.

11. Hence the child's Phase I functional system, which is a system of the **content** in a "content, expression" language, evolves along the familiar lines of generalization followed by abstraction into the Phase III (adult) functional system, which is a system of the **form** in a "content, form, expression" language. The concept of function has itself evolved in the process (cf. Figure 2). In Hjelmslevian terms, the functional basis of language has shifted from the "content substance" (in a system having no level of form) to the "content form". The child, at Phase II, makes the crucial discovery that, with language, he can both observe and interact with the environment at the same time; this is the significance of Nigel's *cake*, meaning 'that's cake – and I want some!' By the time he enters Phase III, the child has a great many "uses" of language; but all of them are actualized through the medium of the ideational and the interpersonal "functions"; in other words, through his twofold meaning potential as observer and as intruder.

12. Meanwhile, therefore, the original Phase I functions have not just disappeared. It is these that have become the uses of language – or rather, perhaps, they have become the generalized contexts of language use. In addition to those that seem to have been the key to the transition process, two others had been postulated, the imaginative and the informative. The imaginative, or play, function of language is present already in Phase I; by the end of Phase II, the child is playing not only with sounds but with forms and meanings as well, reciting, distorting, and inventing rhymes, routines, and stories. Eventually – but not until well into Phase II – he adds the informative function, the use of language to communicate an experience to someone who did not share it with him; this is a highly complex function, since it is one that is solely defined by language itself.[11] At the same time, language still serves, for the child, the uncomplicated functions from which he first learned it. Their scope, however, is now immeasurably enlarged, in breadth and in depth; in other words, in the meaning potential that is associated with each.

6 Conclusion

By the end of Phase II, the child has entered the adult language. He has built up a system that is multi-stratal (content, form, expression) and multifunctional (ideational, interpersonal, textual). From this point on, he is adding to what he already has. He has learnt **how** to mean; his language development now consists in extending the range of his meaning potential to broader cultural horizons.

In order to follow this process further, we should have to go outside the linguistic system and into the culture. The child's uses of language are interpretable as generalized situation types; the meanings that he can express are referable to specific social contexts, and at least in some instances may be approached through a context-specific semantic analysis such as is exemplified in Turner (1973).

Bernstein (1971) has shown that certain types of social context are critical to the process of cultural transmission; the language of these contexts plays a crucial part in the child's socialization. Now, as we have seen, all language behaviour, including that which characterizes these critical contexts, is mediated through the basic functions of language, the observer function and the intruder function; and the meanings that are expressed are linked, in this way, to what Malinowski (1923) called the "context of situation". But because these functions are not simply aspects of the use of language, but are part of – indeed, are the heart of – the linguistic system, the specific meanings expressed are at the same time instances of general semantic categories, and hence are interpreted in the "context of culture" (to use another of Malinowski's concepts).

What is the significance of this for the child? The significance is that, because of the functional basis of language, the particular, concrete meanings that are expressed in typical everyday situations become, for him, the primary source for **building up** the context of culture. By the time he reaches Phase III, each instance of 'I want' or 'may I?' or 'let me take part' or 'what's going on?' is encoded in words and structures that serve in some measure to categorize the social order and the child's own part in it. So it happens that the child's own early uses of language impose certain requirements on the nature of the linguistic system, determining the functional basis on which it is organized; with the result that, as these early uses evolve into generalized social contexts of language use, the linguistic system is able to act through them as the primary means for the transmission of the culture to the child. In this way language comes to occupy the central role in the processes of social learning.

Notes

1. For example, Braine (1971) introduces his comprehensive survey of work on "the acquisition of language" with the words "This review is concerned only with the acquisition of linguistic structure. Thus, work on child language where the concern is with social or intellectual development will not be reviewed. Even within the area defined, the

subject of lexical development will be reviewed only very sketchily [p. 3]." No mention is made of the development of the semantic system.
2. Just how far the latter view prevailed can be seen in the following quotation from Ervin and Miller (1963): "The most important contribution that modern linguistics has brought to child language studies is the conception of what a language is. A language is a system that can be described internally in terms of two primary parts or levels – the phonological (sound system) and the grammatical. A complete description of a language would include an account of all possible phonological sequences and also a set of rules by which we can predict all the possible sentences in that language [p. 108]."
3. Cf. Leopold (1939–49) "Meanings were always developed before sound forms [vol. I: 22]." As it stands this is difficult to interpret; but I take it to mean "before the appearance of sound forms recognizably derived from the adult language".
4. In a recent article, Ingram (1971) proposes adapting Fillmore's "case" theory of structural function to one-element utterances, with a category of "semantic transitivity", corresponding in general to the concept of "Process" as a structural role (Halliday 1970); he then suggests that the child identifies objects in terms of their potential "semantic function" (that is, their role in transitivity), such as their ability to move or to operate on other objects, and that this defines for the child concepts such as "Agent" and "animate". This agrees in principle with what is being suggested here, although Ingram's account of transitivity seems to be too simple; but Ingram fails to relate his notions to the language-function perspective of the child – on the one hand, his assumption seems to be that "semantic" can be equated with "ideational", whereas on the other hand, many of his own examples are of utterances having a predominantly pragmatic function.
5. Despite a commonly held belief to the contrary, the speech the child hears around him is, in the typical instance, coherent, well formed, and contextually relevant. In interaction with adults he is not, in general, surrounded by intellectual discourse, with its backtracking, anacolutha, high lexical density and hesitant planning; but by the fluent, smoothly grammatical and richly structured utterances of informal everyday conversation. (Of the first hundred clauses spoken in Nigel's presence on one particular day, only three were in some way "deviant".) He has abundant evidence with which to construct the grammatical system of his language. What he hears from other children, naturally, is different – but in ways that serve as a guide for his own efforts. This is not, of course, an argument **against** the nativist hypothesis; it merely removes one of the arguments that have been used to claim the **necessity** of a nativist interpretation.
6. Cf. the distinction drawn between the "manipulative" and "declarative" functions in Lewis (1936), an important work with which I was unfamiliar

at the time of writing. The concept of pragmatic function is very similar to Lewis' manipulative; the mathetic is somewhat different from Lewis' declarative, since Lewis interprets this in terms of self-expression, and the demand for an expressive response, rather than as a mode of learning.

7. He could not, in other words, respond to utterances where the response would have lain outside his functional potential. He could express the meanings 'yes' and 'no' in the senses of 'yes I want that' or 'no I don't want that' (instrumental), or 'yes do that' or 'no don't do that' (regulatory). But he had no general polarity (positive–negative) system; nor could he respond to any question seeking information, such as "Did you see a car?" or "What did you see?"

8. Nigel cannot at this stage respond explicitly to a yes–no question. But he sometimes does so by implication; for example:

    "Are you going shopping?"
    NIGEL: *Bread . . . egg*, that is 'I'm going to buy bread and eggs.'

9. Or the other way round, in the reception of speech. Our concern here is with productive language, and relatively little is yet known about the processes whereby the child develops his understanding of what is said to and around him. But it is likely that the crucial step here, too, is the development of this third, intermediate level in his own linguistic coding system.

10. It is the system of mood that is eventually going to determine the patterns of rising and falling tone. How does Nigel adapt this to his own interpretation of rise and fall? At this stage, he has no system of mood other than that expressed by his own use of the distinction of rise and fall, that is, the pragmatic/mathetic system; the demand for a new name, [adȳdà] 'What's that?', cannot really be regarded as an interrogative – it is true that it always has a falling tone, but this is not because it is a Wh-question (he has no Wh-questions at this stage), but rather because it has a mathetic function. When he does learn the Wh-question form, *where* + personal name, this at first has either tone, with (it seems) a difference in meaning between the two; but subsequently this and all other Wh-questions take on the rising tone, presumably on the grounds that an answer is a form of response (even though a purely linguistic one), and that demanding an answer is therefore a type of pragmatic function. Later still he learns the yes–no interrogative form, but this is not used for asking questions at all; it is used solely as the realization of the informative function, to communicate experience not shared by the hearer; for example, *Did you fall down* 'I want you to know that I fell down – you didn't see the event', contrasting with *You fell down* 'I fell down – as you saw'.

11. The imaginative and informative functions call for the narrative mode (within the ideational component) as distinct from simple observation and

recall. This, in turn, requires discourse, that is, text that is structured so as to be relevant not only to the situation but also to the verbal context, to what is said before and after. What we referred to as the "textual" component in the linguistic system can be seen developing, with Nigel, in response to the needs of dialogue and of narrative.

Chapter Three

EARLY LANGUAGE LEARNING: A SOCIOLINGUISTIC APPROACH
(1976)

This chapter[1] is about the learning of the mother tongue in the period extending roughly from 6 to 18 months. It might equally have been called a **sociosemantic** approach, because I am considering the learning of the mother tongue as the learning of a system of meanings. The child who is learning language is learning how to "mean"; in this perspective the linguistic system is seen as a **semantic potential**, or range of possible meanings, together with the means of their **realization**, or expression.[2]

The viewpoint that I am taking is a functional one, in the sense that meaning is in turn related to linguistic function – to the functions that language is made to serve in the life of the growing child. There are two reasons for looking at it in this way. The first is that the functional approach is of value in its own right in that it gives us some insight into the reasons why the child takes the steps he does. If we have a functional viewpoint, we can suggest why it is that the child builds up the system in this particular way – for example, why there comes a point where he has, as it were, to move into the adult language, to build certain of its features, such as structure and vocabulary, into his total potential.

The second reason for looking at the process from a functional point of view is that it also gives us some insight into why the adult language has evolved in the way it has. The human brain would have been capable of constructing a dozen-and-one different types of semiotic system; why is it, then, that language evolved in this particular way as a semiotic

---

Two works are combined in this chapter: 'Early language learning: a sociolinguistic approach', first published in *Language and Man, Anthropological Issues*, edited by William C. McCormack and Stephen A. Wurm. The Hague: Mouton, 1976, pp. 97–124. 'One child's protolanguage', first published in *Before Speech: The Beginnings of Interpersonal Communication*, edited by Margaret Bullowa. Cambridge University Press, 1978, pp. 171–90.

system with the particular properties that it has? If we examine this question developmentally, we can see that the adult linguistic system is structured in a way which very closely reflects its functional origins.[3]

There is still relatively little literature on the early period, before 18 months or so; probably because it is quite difficult during this period to recognize that the process of language learning is taking place at all. This is the period before the child has really started to use the adult language as his model. It might be said, in fact, that the language that is learnt at this stage owes nothing at all to the adult language that the child hears around him.

This would be an oversimplification, since in fact the child **may** use imitations of the adult phonology as part of the resources for expressing his meaning. But, equally, he **may not**; and the point is that it does not matter at this stage whether he does or not. Children vary enormously at this age in the extent to which they attempt to construct some kind of imitative phonological system. It is not entirely clear why they vary in this way; presumably, partly because of differences in their innate ability to imitate adult speech sounds and partly because of differences in the environment – how much speech they hear, but also, and perhaps more important, from how many different people, how much from adults and how much from other children, how much is addressed to them, how much their own efforts are reinforced, and so on. And also, no doubt, because of differences in personality: children differ very much in how they respond to other people's reaction to their own efforts, how far they are perfectionists – there are some children who appear simply not to attempt things, at least in public, until they are satisfied with their own performance.

So there may be all sorts of factors contributing to the very noticeable difference among children at this age – some of them attempt a great deal of phonetic imitation, others practically none. In both cases there is a source of difficulty for the investigator. If the child does imitate the phonology of the adult language, then one is inclined to use this as the criterion for deciding whether his sounds are linguistic or not, whereas it is really not the relevant point. His own system is a system of meanings, and some or all of these meanings may be expressed through sounds borrowed from the adult language. On the other hand, none of them may be, and in that case the investigator tends not to recognize that there is any language learning taking place at all. In fact there is: there is a great deal of language learning at this stage. The child is already both responding to and producing signals of a linguistic kind.

In the very first instance, he is learning that there is such a thing as language at all, that vocal sounds are functional in character. He is learning that the articulatory resources with which he is endowed can be put to the service of certain functions in his own life. For the child using his voice is doing something; it is a form of action, and one which soon develops its own patterns and its own significant contexts. With what criteria, then, do we decide that the sounds which the child is making do in some sense constitute a linguistic system, if they are not themselves identifiable as sounds drawn from the adult language – or if they **may not** be, since it does not matter at this stage whether they are or are not? Here we have a further reason for adopting a functional standpoint. As any parent knows, we can observe at a very early stage, typically perhaps beginning in the period from six to nine months, that the child begins using vocal sounds consistently and systematically, developing some kind of constant relation between sounds and meanings. But these meanings are not something which can be glossed in terms of the adult language, something which we can enter into a dictionary and which corresponds to the meanings of words and phrases and structures in the adult language. They are meanings which we can interpret if we begin with some kind of functional hypothesis, a hypothesis about what it is that the child is doing with his voice, what it is that he is making the speech sounds do for him; in other words, if we recognize that there are certain fundamental goals or purposes that the child achieves through the use of vocal sound. He uses his voice to order people about, to get them to do things for him; he uses it to demand certain objects or services; he uses it to make contact with people, to feel close to them; and so on. All these things are meaningful actions.

I have attempted a fairly intensive study of the language of one particular child beginning at this early stage; and I have compiled a number of descriptions of his language covering the period from 9 to 18 months. It seems odd to refer to these as "grammars" when the one level that is totally absent from the child's linguistic system at this period is that which we know as grammar (it has neither structure nor vocabulary in it), so let me revert to an earlier terminological practice and call them descriptions. I have written a number of descriptions of this child's language which I think are complete. (If they are, then they are the only complete descriptions of any language that I have ever written or am ever likely to write.) It might be of interest to say briefly what form these descriptions take and how they were arrived at.

1 Observing infant speech

The intensive study of the language development of a single child, in the form of a journal kept by a parent or other intimate adult, was rather unfashionable during the middle period of the twentieth century, when language development studies were largely the province of psychologists; psychologists tended to prefer an experimental approach involving large samples of children with the focus on a single clearly defined problem, such as "What is the probability that a child of three years six months will be able to understand a sentence with a passive in it?" This sort of enquiry can be carefully controlled and monitored and the sample chosen to reflect any given population; it is, however, subject to the limitation that children (like everyone else) do tend to behave in untypical ways under experimental conditions. Recently many cognitive psychologists, and psychologically inclined linguists, have favoured a semi-structured approach in which medium-sized populations of children are recorded, say, for half an hour in a playroom once a fortnight for six months; their language and other behaviour is open-ended but some structure is introduced, for example, by the kinds of toys that are provided. The aim may be to establish the range of linguistic functions typically engaged in by children of the particular age range. The journal method, by comparison, is unstructured; the child is not asked any questions, or put into any situations; nothing is elicited from him; he is simply observed, under natural conditions. The disadvantages are clear: the "sample" is just one child, or at most two or three within the one family, and this hardly justifies making general statements about how children learn their language.

At the same time there are certain advantages. The natural setting ensures that the developmental picture is a real one; not only in the general sense that what is being recorded is natural behaviour and not artificially structured or elicited, but also in that the leading edge of language development, in the history both of the individual and of the community, always lies in casual spontaneous speech. The family context, with parent or other intimate as observer, ensures that the greater part of what the child says is understood; and perhaps more important, that the child understands what is being said to him.

Finally, the uninterrupted ongoing interaction with the child, which makes it possible to observe selectively and take note of whatever is relevant, ensures that the record has no gaps in it, and that the investigator knows what the child's total system is at any one time. This last is fundamental: every new development can be seen and interpreted against the background of the child's overall resources, in terms of just what he is able to mean at the time. This is possibly only with a continuous diary-type record.

In my own work I attempted to build up a picture of this kind, tracking the semantic development of my own child from early infancy. Having had the good fortune to be trained in linguistics as a dialect field-worker, I was accustomed to being both participant and observer at the same time, and to keeping an ongoing record of verbal interaction in varieties of phonetic script. Appendix 1 is a condensed account of the development of the protolanguage in the first three stages: (1) to nine months; (2) nine to ten and a half months; (3) ten and a half to twelve months.

I made notes of the child's utterances, using the traditional equipment of the fieldworker, well suited to this stage, a notebook and pencil. I listened in, sometimes taking part in the situation and sometimes staying outside it, hiding behind doors and furniture; and I noted down any meaningful expression that I thought I was observing for the first time. Then I also noted down expressions which I considered to be the same as those I had observed before; not every time I heard them, of course, which would be impossible, but at fairly frequent intervals, the point being that at this stage it is not enough to assume that because some item has been observed to occur it is now part of the child's linguistic system.

Language learning at this stage is not a steady advance; like other forms of learning, it has its ups and downs. Elements of the system come and go; they get learnt and they get forgotten, or else modified or altered. For example, for a period of something around four months, the child I was working with, Nigel, had a particular sound which he used for commenting on the presence of an airplane flying overhead, and it was a sound which, it is fair to guess, was his imitation of the noise of the airplane. After a while, it simply dropped out of the system; and then later on, after an interval, a gap of about three months, came another word for an airplane which was an imitation of the adult word. I would not, incidentally, regard these two terms as synonymous. The functional meaning of the item which we interpret as "airplane" in the first instance was rather different from the functional meaning of the second one; the semantic system had changed in the interval. Other elements which entered into the system and subsequently disappeared included a number of forms of demand and of response to offers; these are shown in Tables 1–6 in Appendix 2.

Then, at intervals of six weeks, I interpreted these notes into a description of the system, so that the system was reinterpreted and described afresh each six weeks. This seemed to be the optimum interval. If I had chosen a longer period, then certain significant steps in the development would have been left out, whereas if I had chosen a shorter period I would have been at the mercy of random non-occurrences, items which simply had not been observed over the period but which should have been recognized as present in the system. So a month and a half seemed to work out the best for the purpose. This practice I began at nine months, because before the age of nine months Nigel had no system at all; and indeed the very first description represents a stage that I would also regard as pre-linguistic, because it does not meet the criteria which I set up for recognizing the presence of a linguistic system. That one I have coded as NL 0, NL standing for "Nigel's language"; so we have NL 0 at nine months, NL 1 at $10\frac{1}{2}$ months, NL 2 at 12 months, NL 3 at $13\frac{1}{2}$ months, NL 4 at 15 months, NL 5 at $16\frac{1}{2}$ months, and NL 6 at 18 months.

2 The child's first language: content and expression

Now there are certain theoretical considerations which I think have to be built into any study of language development at this early stage. These centre around the concepts of what we may call the ***content*** and the ***expression***, or the meaning and the sound. The first point is that these are all you have. That is to say, the child's language system at this stage is a two-level system. It consists of a content and an expression, and each element in the system is a simple sign having just these two aspects: it is a content–expression pair. In other words, the system differs from the adult language system in that it has no intermediate level; it has no stratum of grammar (we should say ***lexicogrammar***, since this stratum includes vocabulary) intermediate between the meanings and the sounds. So we shall consider the system as made up of a content and an expression, and each element in the system as itself made up of a meaning and a sound.

Second, there are certain features that we need to specify about the content and the expression. As far as the expression is concerned, one point has already been made: the particular expressions are not, or may not be, imitations of the adult language. In principle, at this stage the expression owes nothing to the adult language at all. It is a system of vocal postures including both articulation and intonation. I say ***postures*** because I want to stress that, for the notation of the expression system, the International Phonetic Alphabet is not really appropriate; it is too specific. What one requires is something more in the nature of a prosodic notation, which is postural in this sense: it represents postures which are taken up by the articulatory organs, general configurations rather than the specific bundles of contrastive phonetic features which make up the elements of the adult sound system.

By analogy, we can make the same point about the content. In general, we cannot represent the content of the child's system at this stage in terms of the words and structures of the adult language. We cannot match the child's meanings with the elements of the adult semantic system, which are again much too specific. We need in similar fashion a kind of postural notation for the content. What does this mean in fact? It means we need a form of functional representation. The content, in other words, has to be specified in relation to the functions of language.

This point needs to be elaborated in order to explain why we consider that these early vocalizations constitute language. Let us return, first, to the nature of the system itself. It is very clear that we cannot define language at this early stage in terms of either structures or of words. In the first place, there are no structures; each utterance consists of one element only. This is not to imply that an utterance which consists of one element only can never have a structure; there are many items (clause types, phrase types, etc.) of the adult language which do consist of one element, and these are undoubtedly structures, so that the utterances which stand as tokens of these types are themselves structured. But one cannot recognize a one-element structure except by reference to the existence of at least some structures of two or more elements, and these are not present in the child's system. There are no two-element utterances; hence there is no structure, and hence we cannot describe language acquisition at this stage in terms of structure, or in terms of any measure, mean length of utterance for example, which implies the presence of structure.

In the second place, there are no words. The point has already been made that the child's utterances are not imitations of adult words – they are not words in the sense of items deriving their phonological shape from the English lexicon. Neither, however, are they words in the more important sense of vocabulary items with matching definitions. Putting these two facts together, that there is no structure and that there are no words, we can summarize by saying that the language we are describing has no level of *form*; as we said earlier, it does not possess a lexicogrammar, a level of organization consisting of a grammar and a vocabulary.

This would suffice to exclude it from the domain of language, since language is normally defined as a tri-stratal system, having a semantics, a grammar, and a phonology. In the last resort, of course, it does not matter whether we call the system the child develops at this stage language or not, provided we relate it to the total picture of language development. But in order to bring out the underlying continuity between the child's system and that of the adult, we identify those features of the former which show it to be language in the making.

What it has is a set of content–expression pairs, and this enables us to define one criterion for characterizing and for accepting anything as an element in that system, namely, that there should be a constant relation between the content and the expression. Let me give an illustration of this. Whenever, for example, Nigel says *nananana* it always means something like 'I want that thing now'; and when he expresses the meaning 'I want that thing now' by means of a vocal symbol, he always does so by saying *nananana*. This meaning–sound relation can therefore be part of a language. Let us refer to this requirement of a constant relation between content and expression as the requirement of ***systematicity***.

The other requirement that we can set up on the basis of the child's system is that of ***functionality***. In order to qualify as part of his language, the child's vocalizations were required to be not only systematic but also functional. This means that the content should be such that it can be interpreted by reference to a prior established set of functions. To continue with the same example, the meaning 'I want that thing now' is derivable from one of the functions that we are postulating as the set of original developmental functions from which the child starts, namely the instrumental function, the use of language to satisfy the child's material needs. In other words there is no system of content as such, in abstraction from the context of situation. There is only content **with respect**; that is, with respect to the functions that language serves in the life of the developing child.

We are not here setting up some arbitrary meanings that are, as it were, floating in the air. We are setting up meanings in terms of certain generalized contexts of language use. The child is learning to be and to do, to act and to interact in meaningful ways. He is learning a system of meaningful behaviour; in other words, he is learning a semiotic system.

Part of his meaningful action is linguistic. But none of it takes place in isolation; it is always within some social context. So the content of an utterance is the meaning that it has with respect to a given function, to one or other of the things that the child is making language do for him. It is a semiotic act which is interpretable by reference to the total range of semiotic options, the total meaning potential that the child has accessible to him at that moment.

The question then is: what are the functions that we recognize as determining the child's semiotic system at this stage, and how do we arrive at them? Here we have, as always, to keep a sense of proportion, and to try and face both ways, shunting between sensible observation on the one hand and imaginative but at the same time goal-directed theory on the other. On the one hand, we can see ourselves, as any parent can see, what the child is doing when he is uttering speech sounds, and what contributions these speech sounds are making to his total activity. We have some reasonably clear impression of function in a context; and we can characterize this very adequately in quite general terms in relation to the context of a situation. In other words, proceeding solely from observation, and using just the amount of common sense the researcher ought to possess if he did not suspend it while on duty, we could reach generalizations such as "this child says *nananana* whenever he wants to get something handed to him". And we could reach this on a purely inductive basis, or as nearly inductive as one ever gets: the educated adult cannot really proceed without imposing some kind of theory as he goes along.

On the other hand, while we could draw some interesting conclusions in this way, there would be a very severe limitation on how far we could go. If we want to understand the nature of the developmental process, and in particular to make the bridge between the language that the child creates for himself at the very first stage and the adult language that he comes out with at the end, then we have to relate the generalizations that we make about these uses of language to some hypothesis about the overall functions of language in the life of social man.

Clearly we will not be able to do this from a purely empirical standpoint, since by the time a child is, say, two and a half, we will no longer be able to give any kind of significant general account of his uses of language. By this time, like the adult, he already uses language for so many different purposes that if we try to list them, we shall simply get an endless catalogue; or rather, we shall get a whole series of catalogues with no reason for preferring one over another. We have to find some other more theoretical basis for matching the observations about language use with some theoretical construct of a functional nature. And there are two possible sources for this type of a theory of language functions, one from within language itself and one from outside it.

3 Sources of functional concepts

Let us look at each of these briefly in turn. If we consider first the linguistic system itself, we find that the adult language displays certain features which can only be interpreted in functional terms. These are found, naturally, in the area of meaning: the semantic system of the adult language is very clearly functional in its composition. It reflects the fact that language has evolved in the service of certain particular human needs. But what is really significant is that this functional principle is carried over and built into the grammar, so that the internal organization of the grammatical system is also functional in character. If we consider language as a meaning potential, an open-ended and theoretically infinite range of options in meaning, then we find that these options are grouped into a very small number of sets such that each set of options is subject to strong internal constraints but very weak external constraints. In other words, when the speaker makes selections in the system (which are essentially selections in meaning), a choice that he makes in one set of options has a great deal of effect on the other choices that he makes within the same set, but practically no effect on the choices he makes among the options in the other sets. These sets of options constitute the functional components of the semantic system.

Broadly speaking we can characterize these functional components as follows. First, there are the *ideational* options, those relating to the content of what is said. With this component, the speaker expresses his experience of the phenomena of the external world, and of the internal world of his own consciousness. This is what we might call the *observer* function of language, language as a means of talking about the real world. It also includes a subcomponent concerned with the expression of logical relations which are first perceived and interpreted by the child as relations between things.

Second, there is the *interpersonal* component of the semantic system, reflecting the function of language as a means whereby the speaker participates in the speech situation. This we may call the *intruder* function of language. Through the options in this component, the speaker adopts a role, or a set of roles, *vis-à-vis* the participants in the speech situation, and also assigns roles to the other participants, while accepting (or rejecting) those that are assigned to him; he expresses his own judgements, his own attitudes, his own personality, and in so doing exerts certain effects on the hearers. These have been known as the "expressive–conative" functions of language. The options that the speaker takes up in this area of meaning, while they are strongly interrelated among one another, are in large measure independent of the options which he takes up of an ideational kind, those under the first heading.

And then, finally, there is a third semantic function which is in a sense an enabling function, one without which the other two could not be put into effect; this we shall refer to as the **textual** function, the function that language has of creating text. It is through the options in this component that the speaker is enabled to make what he says operational in the context, as distinct from being merely citational, like lists of words in a dictionary, or sentences in a grammar book. The textual function we can regard as being that which breathes life into language; in another metaphor, it provides texture, and without texture there is no text.

We can take account of this functional organization of the semantic system of the adult language in helping us to determine what are likely to be the developmental functions from which the child starts. Somehow, the child moves from the one to the other, from his own system to that of the adult; and our hypothesis must be such as at least to show that it would have been possible for him to make the transition. Ideally, of course, we would like it to be rather stronger, in the sense that it should show some clear motivation why the child should move into the adult language as the means of extending the functional potential that he already has. All this is looking at the question from inside language.

Outside language, we turn to some kind of social theory that accommodates language as an essential element, and in particular one that embodies some notion of functional contexts of language use that are likely to be critical for the child. Here we turn, obviously, to the work of Basil Bernstein (1971), whose theory of social structure and social change embodies a concept of cultural transmission in which he has been able to identify a number of what he calls "critical socializing contexts", types of situation involving the use of language which play a key part in the transmission of culture to the child. Bernstein has identified a certain number of such contexts in what amounts to a sociological theory of linguistic functions. At one point he enumerates four such contexts, which he refers to as the regulative, the instructional, the imaginative or innovative, and the interpersonal. The fact that in Bernstein's work language is the central factor in cultural transmission makes it likely that contexts which Bernstein recognizes as critical for cultural transmission will also be critical in the language learning process.

4 Phase I functions

We can now put together the various strands that make up a pattern in thinking about language in functional terms: in the first place, observations relating to the use of language by a very small child and, in the second place, theoretical considerations about linguistic function, which break down in turn into those which are essentially linguistic in nature, functional theories of language and of the semantic system, and those which are essentially extralinguistic in nature, sociological theories embodying a concept of cultural transmission and processes of socialization.

Taking these factors into account, I suggest a set of functions which would serve for the interpretation of the language of a very young child; that is, as an initial hypothesis for some kind of functional or sociolinguistic approach to early language development. The particular set of functions which I suggest is as follows: (1) instrumental, (2) regulatory, (3) interactional, (4) personal, (5) heuristic, and (6) imaginative. Let me comment briefly on each of these in turn.

1. The *instrumental* function is the function that language serves of satisfying the child's material needs, of enabling him to obtain the goods and services that he wants. It is the 'I want' function of language; and it is likely to include a general expression of desire, some element meaning simply 'I want that object there' (present in the context), as well as perhaps other expressions relating to specific desires, responses to questions 'do you want ...?' and so on.

2. The *regulatory* function is related to this, but it is also distinct. It is the function of language as controlling the behaviour of others, something which the child recognizes very easily because language is used on him in this way: language is used to control his own behaviour and he soon learns that he can turn the tables and use it to control others. The regulatory is the 'do as I tell you' function of language. The

difference between this and the instrumental is that in the instrumental the focus is on the goods or services required and it does not matter who provides them, whereas regulatory utterances are directed towards a particular individual, and it is the behaviour of that individual that is to be influenced. Typically therefore this function includes meanings such as, again, a generalized request 'do that', meaning 'do what you have just been doing' (in the context), 'do that again'; as well as various specific demands, particularly in the form of suggestions 'let's do ...' such as 'let's go for a walk', 'let's play this game', 'let's sing a song' and so forth.

3. The *interactional* function is what we might gloss as the 'me and you' function of language. This is language used by the child to interact with those around him, particularly his mother and others that are important to him, and it includes meanings such as the generalized greetings 'hello', 'pleased to see you', and also responses to calls 'yes?' as well as more specific forms. For example, the first names of particular individuals that the child learns are typically used with a purely interactional function; and there may be other specific meanings of an interactional kind involving the focusing of attention on particular objects in the environment, some favourite objects of the child which are used as channels for interacting with those around him.[4]

4. Fourth, there is the *personal* function. This is language used to express the child's own uniqueness; to express his awareness of himself, in contradistinction to his environment, and then to mould that self – ultimately, language used in the development of the personality. This includes, thus, expressions of personal feelings, of participation and withdrawal, of interest, pleasure, disgust, and so forth, and extends later on to more specific intrusion of the child as a personality into the speech situation. We might call this the 'here I come' function of language.

5. Fifth, once the boundary between the child himself and his environment is beginning to be recognized, then the child can turn towards the exploration of the environment; this is the *heuristic* function of language, the 'tell me why' function, that which later on develops into the whole range of questioning forms that the young child uses. At this very early stage, in its most elementary form, the heuristic use of language is the demand for a name, which is the child's way of categorizing the objects of the physical world; but it soon expands into a variety of more specific meanings.

6. Finally we have the *imaginative* function, which is the function of language whereby the child creates an environment of his own. As well as moving into, taking over, and exploring the universe which he finds around him, the child also uses language for creating a universe of his own, a world initially of pure sound, but which gradually turns into one of story and make-believe and 'let's pretend', and ultimately into the realm of poetry and imaginative writing. This we may call the 'let's pretend' function of language.

Later on there is in fact a seventh to be added to the list; but the initial hypothesis was that this seventh function, although it is the one which is undoubtedly dominant in the adult's use of language, and even more so in the adult's image of what language is, is one which does not emerge in the child until considerably after the others. This is the one that we can call the *informative* function of language, the 'I've got something to tell you' function. Now, the idea that language can be used as a means of communicating information to someone who does not already possess that information is a very sophisticated one which depends on the internalization of a whole complex set of linguistic concepts that the young child does not possess. It is the only purely intrinsic function of language, the only use of language in a function that is definable solely by reference to language. And it is one which is not at all present in the phase of language development which we are considering here. In Nigel's case, for example, it did not begin to appear until a much later stage, at about 22 months. It is useful, however, to note it at this point particularly because it tends to predominate in adult thinking about language. This, in fact, is one of the reasons why the adult finds it so difficult to interpret the image of language that the very young child has internalized. The young child has a very clear notion of the functions of his own linguistic system. He knows very well what he can do with it. But what he can do with it is not at all the same thing as what the adult does (still less what the adult thinks he does) with his linguistic system.

These, then, are the initial functions with respect to which we identify the content of what the child is learning to say, the meanings that are present in this very early linguistic system. All those utterances which we identify as language can be interpreted in the light of some such set of functions as these. Within each one of these functions, we shall recognize a range of alternatives, a range of options in meaning, that the child has mastered at this particular stage; this is the set of possibilities that is open and accessible to him in this particular function of language.

It is this notion of a range of alternatives, a set of options, that I think provides the real foundation of a functional approach to early language development. Somewhat surprisingly, perhaps, the distinction between what is and what is not part of the system seems very easy to draw at this stage; at least I found it so. It was very rare that there was any doubt as to whether a particular sound was or was not functional in the defined terms, and so was or was not an expression in the language.

This is part of the value of the functional approach: it provides a criterion for identifying what is language and what is not. It should be noted that this criterion excludes all instances which are interpreted as linguistic practice. When the child is practising speech sounds, or later on words, phrases, structures, or whatever they are, this is not regarded as language in use; it is not an instance of meaning. This is merely tantamount to saying that the learning of a particular system cannot be categorized in terms of the use of that system, and therefore in the present study those utterances which were purely directed towards the learning of the system were omitted from consideration. It happened that Nigel was a child who did very little practice of this kind; some children apparently do a great deal more.

5 Sounds and meaning of Phase I

Tables 1–6 in Appendix 2 show the system of options that Nigel had in his language at each of the six-week intervals which I referred to earlier, from $10\frac{1}{2}$ months to 18 months. At nine months it was possible to identify just two expressions which apparently fulfilled the criteria for being language; they had constant meanings which could be interpreted in terms of these functions, one being interactional, the other personal. These need hardly be regarded as constituting a linguistic system, because in each case there were no alternatives; there was one possible meaning only in this function, and no choice.

The set of options that Nigel has at $10\frac{1}{2}$ months, represented in Table 1 (see Appendix 2), is I think the earliest that we can significantly characterize as a linguistic system. At $10\frac{1}{2}$ months, the child can already use his vocal resources in four out of the six functions that we have identified. In the instrumental function he has one utterance which is a general demand meaning something like 'give me that' and referring always to some object which is clearly specified in the environment.

This contrasts with the specific demand for a favourite object, in this case a toy bird; and it is possible that this represents the one element in the system whose expression is in fact borrowed from the adult language: it may be an imitation of the word *bird*. In the regulatory function he has a generalized request, which is always directed to a specific individual, requiring him or her to do something that is again clearly specified in the context, usually by the fact of its having been done immediately before, so that it is equivalent to 'do that again'; this contrasts with an intensified form of the same meaning which carries with it the additional feature of urgency, which I have attempted to convey by the gloss 'do that right now'.

In the interactional function he has a couple of initiating expressions and one response. Of the former, one is a form of greeting, used typically when another person comes newly to his attention, for example someone coming into the room as he wakes up; the utterance directs attention to a particular object, typically a picture, which is then used as the channel for the interaction. The nearest one can get to this in a gloss is something like "How nice to see you, and shall we look at this picture together?" suggesting that the picture becomes the focus of what is in fact a form of interaction taking place through language.

The other is again an intensified form, an impatient greeting unmediated by any joint action, something like "Nice to see you, and why weren't you here before?". In addition there is a response form, used in response to a call or greeting when someone else begins to interact verbally with him. And finally there is a little set of meanings within the personal function, five in all, one of which expresses a state of withdrawal and the others the opposite, a state of participation, involving the expression of some form of pleasure or of interest.

The whole system comprises a set of 12 distinct meanings, and this represents the total semantic potential that the child has at this stage. It is not, of course, his total semiotic potential, if we define "semiotic" as the information system that is embodied in the whole of the child's behaviour. But it is his total semantic system – that part of the semiotic that he encodes by means of vocal symbols. It represents what the child can do linguistically, or in other words what he can mean.[5] We have said that the child's expressions at this stage owe nothing to the adult language. The sounds he makes are not, in general, imitations of the sounds of English words. What then is the origin of these sounds? This is something to which I would certainly not attempt to give any kind of general answer. But in one or two instances it is possible to derive a hint which throws an interesting sidelight on classical theories of the origins of language.

At least one of the expressions in Nigel's earliest linguistic system originates as an imitation by the child of a sound that he heard himself make naturally. In NL 1 the form ğʷɤɪğʷɤɪğʷɤɪ appears, interpreted as having the meaning of withdrawal, and more specifically 'I'm sleepy; I want to go to sleep', within the personal function. Now this sound was originally a sound which the child made as an automatic accompaniment of the process of going to sleep. It corresponds to a vocalization of the noise of sucking, perhaps with thumb or bottle in mouth. There came a point when the child transferred the sound into his linguistic system as the expression of one of the meanings in that system. It is interesting to note that shortly afterwards he once again reinterpreted the same sound, this time in the imaginative function as a form of play: at about $13\frac{1}{2}$ months, Nigel would curl up on the floor and produce this sound in a pretence of going to sleep. There are one or two other sounds in Nigel's early systems that could possibly be traced to similar origins.

But there is no obvious source for the great majority of the child's expressions, which appear simply as spontaneous creations of the glossogenic process. As far as the content of the child's early systems is concerned, the same observation might be made: it is not, in general, derived from the meanings of the adult language. No doubt, however, the adult language does exert an influence on the child's semantic system from a very early stage, since the child's utterances are interpreted by those around him in terms of their own semantic systems.

In other words, whatever the child means, the message which gets across is one which makes sense and is translatable into the terms of the adult language. It is in this interpretation that the child's linguistic efforts are reinforced, and in this way the meanings that the child starts out with gradually come to be adapted to the meaning of the adult language. We have no way at this stage of following through this process in any detail; but it is possible to see in the progression from one stage to the next in Nigel's developing linguistic system how the functional meanings that he expresses gradually become more and more recognizable, as they come to look more and more like the meanings that are encoded in the adult language.

Let us give an example of the way in which the meanings that the child expresses do not correspond exactly to the meanings of the adult language, and the distinctions that the child makes do not correspond to the adult's linguistic distinctions. In NL 3 there is a form *yi yi yi yi* (high level tone) which Nigel used to respond when he was asked whether he wanted a particular object to be given to him, meaning something like 'yes, I want that'. There was also a form *a*: (high rise-fall) meaning something like 'yes, I want you to do what you have just offered to do', used in response to questions beginning 'shall I ...?' – for example, 'shall I draw the curtains?' or 'do you want me to put some music on?' These two meanings represent options within the instrumental function. The first is a response to the offer of some object, which is either named or referred to, for example, by *that* (or both); while the second is a response to the offer of a service, one which may also involve the naming of objects but which itself refers to the performance of an action. The two have quite different intonation patterns; the first is high level, which does not occur systematically in adult English, whereas the second one has something very like the rise-fall tone (tone 5) of the adult language, which gives a sense of 'yes, you've got it: **that's** what I'm after'. The distinction is expressed in the description as a system of options within the instrumental function, subsystem of the general meaning of ***response***; the meaning ***response*** is in turn contrasted with the meaning of ***initiation***, the initiating of a demand by the child himself.

Now any translation of these response items such as *yes*, *please*, or an explanation such as "positive response to a question", would be quite inadequate as an interpretation of these expressions. At this stage, Nigel cannot respond to questions at all, except those in which the answer serves one of the functions that is in his linguistic system, either an instrumental function or a regulatory function. In other words, he can respond to questions of the type 'do you want?' or 'shall I?' but not to questions seeking information such as 'is there?' or 'have you got?'

It is not until after 18 months that he begins to be able to respond to questions of this kind, and when he does, he does it in a very different way. There is nothing in the child's system that corresponds to the general notion of question and answer. These notions depend on a concept of dialogue, of social roles that are defined by the communication process; this concept the child has not yet mastered, and will not master until he is in the process of transition from his own ***protolanguage*** to the adult language.

Let me take another example. In NL 5 Nigel has two requests for joint action of the type expressed in adult language by *let's*; these are 'let's go for a walk' and 'let's draw a picture'. The first is expressed by a sound of his own invention, a very slow vibration of the vocal cords;

the other first by a sound which is probably an imitation of the word *draw* and later more often as *bow-wow*, meaning etymologically 'let's draw a dog', but now generalized to a sense of 'let's draw a picture'. Now these are regulatory in function – they refer to the behaviour of a particular individual; and within the regulatory function they are specific, as contrasted with the general expression meaning 'do that'. Further, they are requests for joint action of the 'let's' type, as distinct from requests for action on the part of the other person, such as 'come for lunch'. So at this stage Nigel has a little system of just two options within the meaning of 'let's'; and we can see here the earliest manifestations of what gradually develops into an important area of the adult grammatical system, namely the system of ***mood***.

6 Beginnings of the transition

This is not the place for a detailed commentary on each stage in the child's development. It is hoped that the representations given in NL 1 to NL 5 are reasonably self-explanatory. They show at each stage the child's meaning potential represented as a network of options deriving from the small set of initial functions that were postulated at the start. They show the child's meaning potential developing from an initial point at which he is able to express about 12 distinct meanings to one in which the number of meanings has increased to somewhere around 50. We have represented these meanings in ***systemic*** terms; that is to say, as options in the environment of other options. In other words, language is being represented essentially not as structure, but as system. The underlying concept is one of choice: **either** this **meaning or** that. Structure, the combination of elements one with another (**both** this **constituent and** that), is regarded as a mechanism by which meanings are expressed; moreover it is only one of the possible mechanisms, and one which is not yet present in the child's linguistic system at this stage. But this does not prevent us from recognizing that the child has a language.

NL 5 represents the final stage in what we may refer to as Phase I of the child's language development, the phase in which the child is developing a protolanguage of his own. From this point on, he begins the transition into the adult linguistic system. NL 5 is already characterized by the presence of a considerable number of expressions that are taken from the adult language, recognizable words of English; but, more important, it is characterized by the opening up of new functional meanings. The new developments that are taking place can be seen in the sort of exchange that begins to appear in the period around 16½ months. Here is a typical sequence of events.

The child asks [ád^ydà] 'what's that?' The answer is given *That's an egg*. The child imitates *egg* [ayì:], repeating the sound a considerable number of times. Shortly afterwards, the child sees the object in question, or a picture of it, and produces the same sound; and after a further interval he begins to use the same sound without the stimulus of the object, but in terms of one of the functions for which he uses language, for example, in the instrumental meaning of 'I want an egg'. Then, when he starts to engage in dialogue proper, the word turns up in contexts such as the following (near the end of NL 6, at 17½ months), where the function is no longer obviously interpretable in the earlier terms:

MOTHER: Did you tell Daddy what you had for tea?
NIGEL (to mother, excitedly):   a^yì ... ȫ ... a^yì ... a^yì 'egg, ooh! egg, egg!' gɔgˈgɔg^wa 'cockadoodledoo' (= cornflakes, because of picture on packet; also = weathercock on church so, having just returned from walk, continues with inventory of things seen) tìk^u 'and sticks!'
MOTHER: You didn't have cornflakes for tea!
NIGEL: lə̀u 'and holes!'
MOTHER: You didn't have sticks and holes for tea!
NIGEL (returning to the subject in hand):   dɔ̀uba 'and toast.'

It might be thought, as I myself thought at first, that the principal incentive for the child to learn the vocabulary of the adult language would be of a pragmatic nature, that he would learn the new words primarily in order to be able to ask for the objects they represented. But NL 6, which shows a very sudden increase in the total number of meanings to something of the order of 200, includes a considerable number of items that it would be very unlikely to find in a pragmatic context: words such as *bubble*, *star*, *blood*, *eyelid*, and *weathercock*. If one comes to examine carefully the utterances that the child makes at this stage and the particular context in which they occur, it turns out that the majority of those in which the newly acquired vocabulary items figure are not pragmatic in function at all. They occur, rather, in contexts of observation, recall, and prediction.

First, the child uses the new word to comment on the object as it comes to his attention; for example, *stick*, translated as 'I see a stick'. Second, two or three weeks later, these words come to be used in contexts of recall: not 'I see a stick' but 'I saw a stick when I was out for a walk'. In such instances Nigel often produced long lists of words, for example ('I saw') [kàkàbàbàbàuwàugɔ̀ʔgɔ̀ʔˡtìkᵘlɔ̀ulɔ̀u] 'I saw *cars, buses, dogs, weathercocks, sticks, and holes,*' likewise *sticks, holes, stones, trains, balls and buses.* Third, after another short interval again of a week or two, the same items appear in contexts of prediction: 'I shall see sticks when I go out for a walk', typically said as he was being dressed to go out.

What is the function of utterances of this kind? Clearly they are not pragmatic in the sense that utterances of an instrumental or regulatory nature can be said to be pragmatic; but equally clearly they are not meaningless. In terms of the child's semiotic potential at this stage, it seems that their function is a learning function; not in the sense that they contribute to the child's learning of language – they are quite distinct from instances where the child is practising the items in question, instances which we have already rejected from our functional analysis of the system – but in the sense that they contribute to the child's learning about his environment.

The language is being used in a function that we might code as **mathetic**. The origin of this function can be found in the initial set of functions from which we started out. Just as we can regard the **pragmatic** use of the new words as arising directly from the instrumental and regulatory functions, so we can interpret this **mathetic** function as arising primarily from a combination of two others, the personal and the heuristic. It is possible in fact to trace a direct development from some of the earlier meanings which the child had evolved under these headings: expressions of pleasure and interest on the one hand, and on the other hand the demand for the naming of an object, typically a picture, with which the child was already familiar.

Contexts of this kind, in which from about NL 4 onwards Nigel would begin to combine the personal and the heuristic in a little series of interchanges, a sort of protodialogue, lead gradually and naturally into contexts in which the child is using newly acquired vocabulary for the purpose of categorizing the phenomena of the environment and relating them to his own experience. At this stage, therefore, we can see a process of functional generalization taking place whereby the newly acquired words and structures are put to use either in a context which we are labelling pragmatic, arising from the instrumental and regulatory functions of Phase I, or in a context of the kind that we are calling mathetic, which arises out of the personal and heuristic functions, the interactional function making some contribution to both.[6]

This interpretation is one which we are led to quite naturally from an inspection of the utterances which Nigel was making at this time, utterances such as on the one hand *more meat, mend train, come over there, draw for me*, which are clearly pragmatic in the context, and on the other hand *green car, black cat, tiny red light*, and *bubbles round-and-round*, which are equally clearly not in any sense pragmatic but are representations of what the child observes around him. But it happened that Nigel made the distinction between the pragmatic and mathetic function totally explicit in his own expressions, because from this point on for six months or more, he spoke all pragmatic utterances on a rising tone and all others on a falling tone.
   The rising tone meant in effect that some form of response was required, a response either in the form of action or, after a time and increasingly throughout this period, a verbal response. The falling tone meant that no response was required, and the utterance was, as it were, self-sufficient. This particular way of encoding the pragmatic/mathetic distinction is of course Nigel's own individual strategy; but it is likely that the opposition itself is the basis of the child's functional system at this stage, since not only is it observable in the child's own use of language but, more significantly, it also serves as a transition to the functional organization of the adult language. It is the child's way of incorporating the functions into the linguistic system. In this way he arrives ontogenetically at a linguistic system whose major semantic components are in fact based on a functional opposition, that between the ideational and the interpersonal functional which we referred to earlier.

7 Grammar and dialogue

Essentially the pragmatic function of the child's transitional phase, Phase II, is that which leads into the interpersonal component of the adult system, while the mathetic leads into the ideational component. The child learns at this stage that in any use of language he is essentially being either an **observer** or an **intruder**. He is an observer to the extent that the language is serving as the means whereby he encodes his own experience of the phenomena around him, while himself remaining apart. He is an intruder to the extent that he is using language to participate, as a means of action in the context of situation.
   But whereas at the beginning of Phase II, the child can use language in only one function at a time, being either observer or intruder but not both, by the end of Phase II he has learned to be both things at once;

and this is the essential property of the adult language. In Phase II, which in the case of Nigel begins rather suddenly at stage NL 6 (16½ to 18 months) and continues until roughly the end of his second year, the child is making the transition from his own protolanguage to the adult linguistic system, and this transition involves two fundamental steps.

In the first place, the child has to interpolate a third level in between the content and the expression of his developmental system. The adult language is not a two-level system but a three-level system; it is composed not merely of meanings and sounds, but has another level of coding in between, one which, using folk linguistic terminology, we may refer to as a level of **wording**. In technical terms, in addition to a semantics and a phonology, he has a level of linguistic form, a lexicogrammar.

And the need for the lexicogrammatical level of coding intermediate between meaning and sound arises not merely because of the increased semantic load that the system has to bear, but also because there has to be a means of mapping on to one another meanings deriving from different functional origins. This is achieved by grammatical structure. Grammatical structure is a device which enables the speaker to be both observer and intruder at the same time; it is a form of polyphony in which a number of melodies unfold simultaneously, one semantic "line" from each of the functional components. With a grammar one is free to mean two things at once.[7]

The second of the two fundamental steps that the child takes in embarking on Phase II, the transition to the adult language, is that of learning to engage in dialogue. Dialogue is, for him, a very new concept. Dialogue involves the adoption of roles which are social roles of a new and special kind, namely those which are defined by language itself. We may refer to these as **communication roles**.

A speaker of the adult language, every time he says anything, is adopting a communication role himself, and at the same time is assigning another role, or a role choice, to the addressee, who, in his turn, has the option of accepting or rejecting the role that is assigned to him. In Phase I, the child has no concept of dialogue or of communication roles; but towards the end of this phase he begins to get the idea that language is itself a form of interaction, and he starts to engage in dialogue. Nigel, at the same time as he was beginning to build a grammar and vocabulary, also took the first steps in dialogue, learning to interact linguistically in a limited number of ways. He learnt to respond to an information or "Wh-" type question, one in which the respondent is required to fill in a missing item, such as "What are you eating?" He learnt to respond to a command, not only obeying the instruction it contained, but also verbalizing the process as he did so. He learnt to respond to a statement, not only repeating it but also continuing the conversation by adding his own contribution. And, finally, he learnt to initiate dialogue himself, having first of all only one option under this heading, namely the question 'what is that?' He could not at this stage ask any other questions, nor could he respond to questions of the confirmation or "Yes/no" type. But he had clearly internalized the notion that language defines a set of social roles which are to be taken on by the participants in the speech situation; and this is the essential step towards the mastering of the final one in the list of functions that we enumerated at the beginning, namely the informative function.

The use of language to inform is a very late stage in the linguistic development of the child, because it is a function which depends on the recognition that there are functions of language which are solely defined by language itself. All the other functions in the list are extrinsic to language. They are served by and realized through language, but they are not defined by language. They represent the use of language in contexts which exist independently of the linguistic system. But the informative function has no existence independent of language itself. It is an intrinsic function which the child cannot begin to master until he has grasped the principle of dialogue, which means until he has grasped the fundamental nature of the communication process.

Some way on into what we are calling Phase II, Nigel did begin to use language in the informative function; but when he did so he introduced into the system a semantic distinction of his own, another example of a semantic distinction that does not exist in the adult language, between giving information that is already known to the hearer and giving information that is not known. By this stage, Nigel had learned the grammatical distinction of declarative and interrogative; but he used this distinction not to express the difference between statement and question, since as we have already noted he had at this stage no concept of asking "Yes/no" questions, but to make a distinction between the two types of information giving. He used the declarative form to give information that he knew was already possessed by the hearer, to represent experience that had been shared by both; and he used the interrogative form to convey information that he knew the hearer did not possess, to refer to an experience which had not been shared between the two. So, for example, if he was building a tower and the tower fell down, he would say to someone who was present and who was taking part with him *The tower fell down*. But to someone who had not been in the room at the time, and for whom the information was new, he would say *Did the tower fall down?* This is a rather useful semantic distinction, and it seems a pity it should be lost in the adult language.

The important point concerning the two major new developments that define the beginning of Phase II, the learning of grammar and the learning of dialogue, is that they take place at the same time. These are the two essential characteristics of the adult linguistic system that are absent from the protolanguage that the child creates for himself. It is as if up to a certain point the child was working his own way through the history of the human race, creating a language for himself to serve those needs which exist independently of language and which are an essential feature of human life at all times and in all cultures.

Then comes a point when he abandons the phylogenetic trail and, as it were, settles for the language that he hears around him, taking over in one immense stride its two fundamental properties as a system: one, its organization on three levels, with a lexicogrammatical level of wording intermediate between the meaning and the sounding, a level which generates structures which enable him to mean more than one thing at a time; and two, its ability to function as an independent means of human interaction, as a form of social intercourse which generates its own set of roles and role relationships, whose meaning is defined solely by the communication process that language brings about.

These two developments take place more or less simultaneously. They are the crucial features of Phase II, which we have defined as the phase that is transitional between the child's protolanguage and his mastery of the adult linguistic system. By the end of Phase II, the child has effectively mastered the linguistic **system** of the adult language. He will spend the rest of his life learning the language itself.

8 Summary

Let us attempt now to summarize the main points that have arisen. We started with the hypothesis that learning the mother tongue consists in mastering certain basic functions of language and in developing a meaning potential in respect to each. The hypothesis was that these functions, namely, the instrumental, the regulatory, the interactional, the personal, the heuristic, and the imaginative, represented the developmental functions of language, those in respect to which the child first created a system of meanings; and that some ability to mean in these functions, or in a majority of them, was a necessary and sufficient condition for the learning of the adult language. It is presumed that these functions are universals of human culture, and it is not unreasonable to think of them as the starting-point not only for linguistic ontogeny but also for the evolution of the linguistic system.

Within each function the child develops a set of options, a range of alternatives whose meanings are derived from the function in question. The language which the child develops in this way is a simple content–expression system. It contains no grammar and no vocabulary; that is to say, no level of coding intermediate between the semantics and the phonology. It represents a meaning potential, what the very small child can do with his language, together with the resources for expressing the meanings in question. What the child can do at this stage is not a great deal, but it is significant in terms of his own needs.

In the case of Nigel we find the system expanding from an initial stage, NL 1 at $10\frac{1}{2}$ months, in which he has 12 choices in meaning at his command, to a stage, NL 5 at $16\frac{1}{2}$ months, when the total number of semantic options has reached 50. This is still, of course, a very slender resource by comparison with what we know as language; but it is worth noting not only that each element in the system is used very frequently – on numerous occasions, not counting repetitions – but also, and more significantly, that some elements are very general in their application.

In each function there tends to be one semantically unmarked term, whose meaning is equivalent to that function in its most general scope; for example, 'I want that' represents the generalized meaning of language in the instrumental function, where 'that' is clearly indicated by context. This appears to be the origin of what I have called elsewhere the "*good reason*" *principle* in the adult language, a very general and all-pervasive principle whereby, at very many points in the system, the speaker has an option which is unmarked in the sense that it is the option that he selects unless there is good reason for selecting something else. In many of these functions, the child will have one option which he selects as the expression of a general meaning in the absence of any reason for selecting a more specific option within the same function.

In Phase I the child uses the vocal resources of intonation and articulation. He knows from observing linguistic interaction around him that these resources are used by others in meaningful ways. He cannot, of course, copy the particular sound–meaning correspondences, but he invents a set of his own, using, for example, rise and fall in pitch to express meaning distinctions that exist within his own system. For some time, often perhaps for about six or nine months, the child continues to expand the system that he is creating along these lines by adding new semantic contrasts within the existing range of functions; he goes on inventing his own sounds, but comes increasingly to borrow the expressions from the words of the adult language.

There comes a point, however, at which he moves into a new stage of development, characterized on the one hand by the introduction of a level of vocabulary and structure and on the other hand by the beginning of dialogue. In Nigel's case this stage began at NL 6, at which the number of distinct meanings rose sharply from 50 to something approaching 200. But, by the same token, it ceases at this point to be possible to interpret the system as a simple inventory of meanings, so that there is no longer any significance to the figure that is obtained in this way. This is because the child is now entering a new phase of semantic development.

The fact that he begins to engage in dialogue, taking on different social roles and assigning these roles to others, means that we can no longer make a simple list of the meanings that the child can express. Furthermore, he is developing a semantics that is not only a lexical semantics but also a grammatical semantics, a meaning potential that is organized in sets of options which combine; each choice is by itself very simple, but the combinations form highly complex patterns. The system network that represents the semantics at this stage is no longer a simple taxonomy, as it was before.

The new meanings are incorporated into the child's existing set of functions. There is no discontinuity here in the meanings as there is in the expressions, but rather a continuing development of the potential that is already there. At the same time, however, the very expansion of this potential leads to a development of the child's functional system into a new form: from having been equivalent simply to "uses of language", the functions come to be reinterpreted at a more abstract level, through a gradual process whereby they are eventually built into the heart of the linguistic system.

This happens in two stages: first, by the generalization out of the initial set of developmental functions of a fundamental distinction between language as doing and language as learning – the pragmatic and the mathetic functions, as we called them; and second, by the process of abstraction through which this basic functional opposition is extended from the semantic system into the lexicogrammatical system, being the source of the systematic distinction in the adult language between the ideational component (that which expresses the phenomena of the real world) and the interpersonal component (that which expresses the structure of the communication situation). Thus there is a total continuity between the set of functions formulated as part of our initial hypothesis and the functional organization of the linguistic system that has always been recognized in one form or another in functional theories of language.

There is continuity at the same time on another level, in that the initial functions which language serves for the child evolve at the same time into the types of situation, or contexts of language use. The situation type determines for the adult the particular variety or register he uses and the set of semantic configurations (and the forms of their expression) that can be recognized as typically associated with the abstract properties of the context of situation.

We could express this dual continuity another way by saying that, whereas for the very small child in Phase I, the concept of *function of language* is synonymous with that of *use of language*, for the adult, however, the two are distinct, the former referring to what are now incorporated as components of the linguistic system while the latter refers to the extralinguistic factors determining how the resources of the linguistic system are brought into play. But both *function* and *use* develop in a direct line from their origins in the child's first system of meaning potential.

We have interpreted the linguistic system as essentially a system of meanings, with associated forms and expressions as the realization of these meanings. We have interpreted the learning of language as learning how to mean. At the end of Phase II, which in the case of Nigel was at about $22\frac{1}{2}$ to 24 months, the child has learnt how to mean, in the sense that he has mastered the adult linguistic system. He has mastered a system that is multifunctional and multi-stratal.

This system has a massive potential; in fact it is open-ended, in that it can create indefinitely many meanings and indefinitely many sentences and clauses and phrases and words for the expression of the these meanings. The child will spend the rest of his life exploring the potential of this system; having learnt how to walk, he can now start going places. Language can now serve him as an effective means of cultural transmission, as a means whereby in the ordinary everyday interaction in which he himself takes part the essential meanings of the culture can be transmitted to him.

The culture is itself a semiotic system, a system of meanings or information that is encoded in the behaviour potential of the members, including their verbal potential – that is, their linguistic system. The linguistic system is only one form of the realization of the more general semiotic system which constitutes the culture. But perhaps it is the most important form of realization of it, because it is a prerequisite of most if not all the others. Although there are many aspects of the social semiotic that are not encoded in linguistic forms and expressions, it is likely that most of these draw in some way or other on the system of meanings that constitutes the essence of language.

The child who has learnt how to mean has taken the essential step towards the sharing of meanings, which is the distinctive characteristic of social man in his mature state. But in following through any one child's progress we are bound to proceed with caution. Certain of his forward moves no doubt represent universal patterns of human development; others, equally certainly, are his own individual strategy, representing patterns which are not a necessary part of the semogenic process. In between these two extremes lies a vast area in which we do not know how much of what we interpret as taking place is to be projected as universal.

The steps in Nigel's progression from protolanguage to adult language have been mapped out and formulated here in terms which would allow them to be considered as part of a more general hypothesis. But a general hypothesis does not consist solely of statements of universals. It is as much a hypothesis about human variation as about human invariance, and is as much concerned with what is more or less likely as with what is certain. In the last resort it is only the end product that we can be sure is in some sense universal; and we still do not know any too much about that.

Notes

1. This paper was prepared during my tenure of a fellowship at the Center for Advanced Study in the Behavioral Sciences, Stanford, California. I should like to record my gratitude for the opportunity thus afforded.
2. The term *semantic* is not to be understood in the restricted sense of 'lexicosemantic', that is concerned with the meanings of words. It refers to the totality of meaning in language – the "semological stratum" of Lamb's

stratification theory (1970) – whether encoded in vocabulary or not. A child cannot learn word meanings unless he also has words, that is an organized vocabulary, not necessarily in the phonological shapes of the adult lexicon. But the contention of this paper is that the learning of language is essentially the learning of a semantic system, and that this process is already well underway before the child moves into the lexical mode of its realization.
3. Similarly the term **functional** is not to be understood in the sense of the specific hypothesis that the child interprets the names of objects by reference to the functions of these objects (see Lewis 1957), or that he learns word classes by reference to structural functions, for example agent of a transitive verb, which reflect the potentialities of objects in the real world (see Ingram 1971). It refers to the general notion that the child learns language as a system of meanings in functional contexts, these contexts becoming, in turn, the principle of organization of the adult semantic system (as this is recognized in "functional" theories of language; see Halliday 1973).
4. In view of the great variety in young children's use of the *mummy* and *daddy* forms and the continuing discussion around the question whether they are or are not proper names, it should be made clear that in Nigel's system these items functioned unequivocally as proper names: they were used only interactionally (and never, for example, as expression of a demand), and were attached from the start uniquely to specific individuals. The forms themselves had the distinctive phonological shape that Nigel reserved for proper names and no instance was noted of their use in any other context. See Tables 2–5 in Appendix 2.
5. We use this formulation in preference to "what he knows", considering language development not as the acquisition of knowledge but as the development of a behaviour potential. In a sociolinguistic perspective there is no need to postulate a level of cognitive organization between "can do" and "can mean".
6. Cf. Lewis' opposition (1951) of "manipulative" and "declarative" functions.
7. As this stage it becomes possible to interpret the child's semantic development in terms of a lexicosemantic theory such as that of "semantic feature acquisition" proposed by Eve V. Clark.

Chapter Four

A Sociosemiotic Perspective on Language Development (1974)

1 Semiotic beginnings

This paper is an attempt to interpret the child's early language learning as a sociosemiotic process. What is intended here by 'sociosemiotic' will be largely left to emerge from the discussion; but in the most general terms it is meant to imply a synthesis of three modes of interpretation: that of language in the context of the social system, that of language as an aspect of a more general semiotic, and that of the social system itself as a semiotic system – modes of interpretation that are associated with Malinowski and Firth, with Jakobson, and with Lévi-Strauss, among others. The social system, viewed in these terms, is a system of meaning relations; and these meaning relations are realized in many ways, of which one, perhaps the principal one as far as the maintenance and transmission of the system is concerned, is through their encoding in language. The meaning potential of a language, its semantic system, is therefore seen as realizing a higher-level system of relations, that of the social semiotic, in just the same way as it is itself realized in the lexicogrammatical and phonological systems.

A child who is learning his mother tongue is learning how to mean. As he builds up his own meaning potential in language, he is constructing for himself a social semiotic. Since language develops as the expression of the social semiotic, it serves at the same time as the means of transmitting it, and also of constantly modifying and reshaping it, as the child takes over the culture, the received system of meanings in which he is learning to share.

First published in *Bulletin of the School of Oriental and African Studies*, 37.1, 1974, pp. 98–118. This chapter also incorporates material from 'One child's protolanguage' (see p. 60).

How early does this process begin? Many studies of language development have begun at a point when the child's 'mean length of utterance' exceeds one word; but this is already too late – the child may have a well-developed semantic system long before he begins to combine words, in fact long before he has any words at all, if by 'words' we mean lexical elements taken over from the adult language. At the other end are references to a child having a communication system at the age of a few weeks or even days; no doubt he does communicate more or less from birth, but there are significant senses in which this communication differs from language, and it is specifically language that we are concerned with here because it is language that enables him to construct a social semiotic. This does not mean that a child has no language until he has a linguistic system in the adult sense, but that there are certain features in respect of which we can say that, before a given stage, the child has not got language, and after this stage he has.

The early stages of Nigel's language development have been described to a certain degree of detail in the previous chapters. Here we shall recapitulate the description just insofar as this is necessary to clarify the present interpretation; the relevant facts will be incorporated into the discussion.

With Nigel, the breakthrough into language occurred at the age of about nine months. At nine months old, he had a meaning system of five elements, of which two were vocalized and three realized as gestures. The two that were vocalized were:

[ø] mid-low falling to low	'let's be together'
[ø] mid falling to low	'look (it's moving)'

The three realized gesturally were:

grasping object firmly	'I want that'
touching object lightly [sic]	'I don't want that'
touching person or relevant object firmly	'do that (with it) again (for example, make it jump up in the air)'

Here the child was on the threshold of language. Between nine and ten and a half months, he developed a linguistic system. This system is set out in Table 1 of Appendix 2. The gestures, incidentally, disappeared by the age of 12 months.

On what grounds are we calling this a 'language'? It has no words and no structures. It is very clearly not a linguistic system in the adult sense, since it lacks the defining characteristic of such a system: it is not tri-stratal. An adult linguistic system has three strata, or levels: a semantics, a lexicogrammar (or 'syntax') and a phonology. This is what distinguishes it from all animal communication systems, which as far as we know are bi-stratal only. In similar fashion Nigel's system at this stage is bi-stratal; it has a semantics and a phonology, but nothing in between. Whether for this reason we should or should not use the terms 'semantics' and 'phonology' is not a major issue; let us say that the child has a bi-stratal protolanguage consisting of meaning and sound, or a content and an expression. The elements of the system are signs in the sense of content–expression pairs.

The reasons for regarding this as a form of language are twofold. In the first place, it has two positive features which can be used as criterial: systematicity, and functionality. There is a systematic relation between the content and the expression, and the content is interpretable in functional terms. In the second place, it shows continuity of development into the adult system. Of these it is the second point that is the more important, since it determines the relevance of the first; we know that these properties are important because they provide the essential links, the means whereby a child can grasp the nature of the adult language and interpret it as an extension of what he already has. The continuity of development, with many children (of whom Nigel was one), is not immediately apparent, if one is looking mainly at the outward manifestation of the system; but it is brought out by a consideration of the meanings, once we place these in what we are referring to as a 'sociosemiotic' context.

2 A functional semantics

In the language represented by Table 1 in Appendix 2, the expressions are clearly not, for the most part, imitations of words or any other elements of the adult language. They are the child's own invention. In general we cannot say where they come from; ding-dong, bow-wow, yo-heave-ho and other such classical sources are probably all represented somewhere. The point is simply that they are distinct from each other; although the IPA alphabet is not, at this stage, a relevant form of notation – what is needed is a prosodic or postural notation specially designed for developmental studies – it serves to suggest what was in fact the case, that there was surprisingly little neutralization of semantic contrasts by overlap in the expression. It is likely that some children make more use of imitation in the expressions of their protolanguage, using forms of words from the adult language; this is a source of difficulty for the investigator, since such forms are not at this stage being used as words (which would imply a lexicogrammatical stratum) but merely as expressions. A possible example of this is Nigel's [bø] 'I want my toy bird'; the expression may be an imitation of the **sound** of the adult pronunciation of bird but it is not the **word** bird – there are no words at this stage. It does not matter, in fact, **where** the expressions come from; their function is to signal the meanings of the child's own system.

Where then do the meanings come from? These likewise are not imitations of meanings in the adult language. They are interpretable in functional terms. The content of the system is derived from what it is the child is making the system do for him. Hence in interpreting the content we need to start with some functional-semantic hypothesis, some notion of the developmentally significant functions that, on general sociocultural grounds (as well as from our knowledge of the nature of the adult language), we should expect to determine the content structure of the child's protolanguage. For this purpose the simple framework was adopted of six basic functions: instrumental ('I want'), regulatory ('do as I tell you'), interactional ('me and you'), personal ('here I come'), heuristic ('tell me why') and imaginative ('let's pretend') (see also Chapters 3 and 12). The instrumental is language as a demand for goods-and-services, in the satisfaction of material needs; the regulatory is language used to control the behaviour of those around, and adapt it to one's wishes. These are the more pragmatic functions. There is also a pragmatic element in the interactional, since it embodies the child's need for human contact; but there the meanings are the expression of the interaction itself, rather than of a demand for it. In its personal function, language is the expression of the child's own identity, his separateness from, and uniqueness with respect to, the environment of people and things; and this creates the context for the heuristic function, which is language in the exploration of the environment that is defined as the non-self. Finally language may function in the **creation** of an environment, an environment of the imagination that begins as pure sound and works its way up the linguistic system to become a 'let's pretend' world of songs and rhymes and stories.

Meaning is meaning **with respect to** one or other of these functions. The meanings which a small child expresses in his protolanguage may be glossed by locutions in the adult language such as 'do that again' or 'nice to see you, and shall we look at this together?'; but these – like the phonetic notations referred to above – are overly specific. We cannot adequately represent what the child means by wordings such as these, or even by semantic features drawn from the adult language. What is needed is, again, some sort of semantic representation that is analogously prosodic or postural. The content systems in Table 1 of Appendix 2 are an attempt to express the meanings in systemic terms, as sets of options deriving from the functions of the initial hypothesis. The assertion is that within each of these functions the child develops a small but open-ended, indefinitely expandable, range of alternatives, and that the total set of these sets of options constitutes his semantic system at the stage in question. The functions themselves are the prototypic social contexts of the child's existence, simple semiotic structures through which he relates to and becomes a part of the social system.

If they are viewed in this light, it is easy to see that there is no place for anything like an "informative" function. The use of language in the sense of 'I've got something to tell you', which tends to obsess adults, perhaps because they have learnt it with such difficulty, is irrelevant to a small child; it has no direct social meaning. It is also inaccessible to him, since it is wholly intrinsic to language; it is a function that derives from the nature of language itself. The other six are all extralinguistic; they arise, and can be realized, independently of language, though language immeasurably extends the meaning potential that is associated with them. Nigel began with four of them simultaneously, the instrumental, regulatory, interactional and personal; after about four or five months he added the imaginative and, incipiently at least, the heuristic. Thus the functions that had been predicted were all clearly recognizable; but, unlike what might have been expected, there was no clear developmental ordering among them such that the more pragmatically oriented functions developed before the others. Non-pragmatic elements were as prominent from the start; and this became very significant when the child moved on into the next phase.

Every element showing systematic sound–meaning correspondence, and interpretable in these functional terms (these two criteria in fact defined the same set), was entered in the system, provided it was observed operationally (in a context in which it was doing a job of meaning) with a certain minimum frequency. In practice throughout the six months or so of the ***protolanguage*** phase, which we designate Phase I, all but two or three of the sounds provisionally interpreted as meaningful were observed with far more than minimal frequency, and, surprisingly perhaps, there was hardly any difficulty in identifying what was language and what was not. Practising was excluded, on the grounds that the learning of a system is not a function of that system; Nigel did very little practising as such, but made very extensive operational use of the resources he had. (It may be that practising never is associated with the protolanguage; Nigel provides no evidence either way, since he did not practise in Phase II either.) The system was reinterpreted and written up at intervals of six weeks, this being the interval which appeared to be optimal – neither so short that the account would be distorted by random non-occurrences nor so long that the system could not be seen in course of change (see Tables 1–6 in the Appendix 2).

There is a marked break between NL 5 and NL 6; NL 6 may be regarded as the beginning of what we are calling 'Phase II'. Much of the remaining discussion will centre around the interpretation of what it is that is happening in Phase II; before coming on to this, however, we shall insert a brief note about the concept of situation or social context. This concept will be discussed more fully in Chapter 7.

3 Meaning and environment

A child is learning how to mean; but meaning takes place in an environment, not in solitude. What is the nature of the environment? On the one hand, it may be thought of as 'what is going on at the time': the situation in which the language is actualized and comes to life. On the other hand, it may be conceived of as the social system, with the child himself in the middle of it.

Malinowski took account of both: he called the former the 'context of situation' and the latter the 'context of culture'. Because of his interest in pragmatic speech, his characterization of the situation tended to be rather too concrete, a kind of scenario with props and stage directions; Firth replaced this with a more abstract account which allows us to interpret the situation as a generalized **situation type**, or social context. The situation is the environment of the **text**, of the meanings that are selected or 'actualized' in a given instance. The culture is the environment of the **system**, of the total meaning potential. (Hence Firth did not develop Malinowski's context of culture; his focus of attention was not on the potential but on the typical actual.) So we can start from the concept of "situation" and define the context of culture as the set of possible situation types. This is equivalent to interpreting the social system as the total set of possible social contexts.

There is, however, another possible perspective, one that is complementary to this one. We can choose to define the situation by reference to the culture, instead of the other way round. We have defined the culture as a system of meanings, a semiotic system. A situation (always in the generalized sense of situation type) is then a semiotic structure deriving from that system.

The various "ethnographies of speaking" that attempt to describe the relevant patterns of speech settings can be interpreted and evaluated in this light, as analyses of the semiotic structure of the situation, in its capacity as a determinant of the text. The meaning potential that a child learns to express in the first phase serves him in functions which exist independently of language, as features of human life at all times and in all cultures. But, at the same time, and in the same process, he is constructing for himself a social semiotic, a model of the culture of which he is himself a member; and he is doing so out of the semiotic properties of situations, situations in which he is a participant or an observer. The understanding of this process constitutes what Berger and Kellner (1970; cf. Berger and Luckmann 1967) refer to as the "microsociology of knowledge" – the social construction of reality from the countless microsemiotic encounters of daily life. Nigel at nine months has already embarked on this venture. His meaning potential develops as the representation of the social system and of his own place in it.

In this way a child, in the act of learning language, is also learning the culture through language. The semantic system which he is constructing becomes the primary mode of transmission of the culture. But we can also turn this point back on itself and ask the question, how has the place of language in the social system determined the nature and evolution of language? However remote this question may seem from current preoccupations – and it would not have been thought fanciful a hundred years ago – it is one that we may well bear in mind while considering how, and more especially **why**, the child makes a transition from his own protolanguage into the adult linguistic system.

4 Taking over the mother tongue

Nigel continued to expand his Phase I language, extending the meaning potential within the four functions: instrumental, regulatory, interactional and personal, and later adding to these a small range of meanings in the other functions. The number of distinct meanings increased as follows:

NL 1	NL 2	NL 3	NL 4	NL 5
12	21	29	32	52

Table 5 in Appendix 2 represents the system at NL 5 (15 to 16½ months); the number of options under each heading is now:

instrumental: 10   regulatory: 7   interactional: 15   personal: 16

the remaining four being "imaginative". Looking at the system with hindsight from the standpoint of its later development, we come to see that at least one of the options should really have been interpreted as heuristic in function. By this time, however, the functional basis of the system is itself beginning to evolve into a new phase.

By NL 5, therefore, the system has expanded to something like four or five times its original measure of potential. Essentially, though, it is still a system of the same kind. The meanings continue to form a simple semantic taxonomy – with one small but extremely significant exception, which foreshadows things to come:

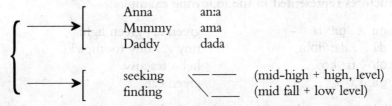

Here we have for the first time the intersection of two semantic systems, two simultaneous sets of options in free combination. Apart from this, Nigel can still only mean one thing at once.

Then, with quite dramatic suddenness, Nigel abandoned the glossogenic process. He stopped creating language for himself, and began to use the one he heard around him. This is the transitional stage we are referring to as Phase II. It corresponds to what is more usually regarded as the beginnings of language, because it is the point at which vocabulary (in the true sense, as distinct from imitations of word sounds) and structure start to appear; but from the present standpoint it is already transitional.

The changes that characterize Phase II are summarized in Chapter 2. Nigel learnt grammar, and he learnt dialogue. That is to say: 1) he replaced his own bi-stratal (content–expression) system, by the adult tri-stratal system (content, form, expression, that is, semantics, lexicogrammar, phonology); 2) he replaced his own one-way (monologue) system by the adult two-way system (dialogue). These processes began in NL 6 and were well established in NL 7 (18 to 19½ months). They are the two critical steps into the adult linguistic system; we will explain and illustrate them in turn.

5 Lexicogrammatical and semantic structures

Lexicogrammar is, in folk-linguistic terminology, the level of "wording" in language that comes between meaning and sounding; it is grammar and vocabulary. Meanings are no longer output directly as sounds; they are first coded in lexicogrammatical forms and then recoded in sounds. The outward sign of a grammar is structures; that of a vocabulary is words, or lexical items. There is no very clear line between the meanings that are coded as grammatical structures and those that are coded as lexical items; the latter represent, as a rule, the more specific or more **delicate** options. By the end of NL 7 Nigel had a vocabulary probably amounting to some 200 words, together with the structures represented in the following examples:

gɹì ... gɹī: la	green ... green light
dâ ... dā: dɒ̀bɪ	tiny ... tiny toothpick
əlōʷ tɪ: ko:	hello teacosy
gɹī: kà	green car

All these appeared on the same day, which was the first day on which he had used any structures at all (on the criterion of intonation, that is, composite forms on a single tone contour). These were followed next day by:

gɹī: kà ... bl:ɐ̄: kà ... āɲ̀ʰ	green car ... blue car ... another
mɔ̄:mìˀ	more meat
mɔ̄:mìˀ plɪ	more meat please
t'ɐ̄ bɒ̀k	two books

and within a week by *green peg*, *more omelette*, and *two* plus various items including lorries, trains and helicopters. In addition there were the following narratives, which form structures at the semantic level but not yet at the lexicogrammatical level:

ⁿdàⁿda ... pàɪ ... [blowing] Φʷ ... ƭ'ɔ̂və   uncle ... pipe ... smoke ... (like) train
ʔɔʔ ... tɪ̀ ... ı̃kwè: ... ōgɔ̀ ... bābā   broken ... tree ... take-away ... all-
                                                gone ... bye-bye
bɪ̄kè ... ōd ə̀ ... mḭ̀ ... dàda   breakfast ... oh-dear (I'm hungry)
                                                ... milk ... (and some for) Daddy
ƭ'ɔ̂və ... là ... gɹì   train ... light ... green

At this stage, the lexical items combine freely in semantic structures. They combine only with partial freedom into grammatical structures; *more*, for example, combines freely with items of food, including countables such as *more cherries*, but it does not yet combine with cars or trains. The explanation of this will appear below.

6 Interactional patterns

Dialogue is the taking on oneself, and assigning to others, of social roles of a special kind, namely those that are defined by language – the speech roles of ordering, questioning, responding and the like. Nigel had launched into dialogue just four weeks before his first structures appeared; here are some more early examples (cf. Chapter 3, section 6):

1 NIGEL: ádʸdà 'What's that?'
   MOTHER: That's a plug.
   NIGEL [imitating]: lɪkoba ... ádʸdà
2 MOTHER: That's a chain.
   NIGEL: ƭ'ʉƭ'ʉ
   MOTHER: No – not a train, a chain.
3 NIGEL [pointing to line drawn on side of bottle]: ádʸdà
   MOTHER: That's a line.
   NIGEL: ɹa: ɹa: [roaring, that is, 'a lion']
4 MOTHER: Take the toothpaste to Daddy and go and get your bib.
   NIGEL [doing so]: dàda ... n̄n̄ɔ̀ n̄n̄ɔ̀ ... ƭ'ʉƭ'ʉ 'Daddy ... (give) noddy (toothpaste to him) ... (get the bib with the) train (picture on it)'.
5 ANNA: We're going out for a walk, and we'll go and get some fish.
   NIGEL [hopefully]: tɪkɔ '(and we'll get some) sticks'
   ANNA: No, we're not getting any sticks today.
   NIGEL [plaintively]: lɔ̌ᵘ '(aren't we going to look for) holes?', or '(what can I put in the) holes?'
6 NIGEL [coming into study]: ʒē̆ɛ̆ʒʒ̆ bɔ̀uwɔ̀u 'I want to (come and) draw (originally = 'draw dogs') (with you)'
   FATHER: No, I'm working.

NIGEL: dādıkədà '(you're) playing the tabla'
FATHER: No I'm not playing dadikada; I'm writing.
NIGEL: bòuwòu '(you're) drawing'
7 MOTHER [pointing]: Who's that?
NIGEL: n:ā 'Anna'
MOTHER [pointing to self]: And who's that?
NIGEL: mā 'Mummy'
MOTHER [pointing to Nigel]: And who's that?
NIGEL: ni 'Nigel'
8 FATHER: Where's my pudding? [Five minutes later it is brought in]
NIGEL: dʒə 'there'

If we analyse these specimens of dialogue in terms of Nigel's speech role potential, we find that he can:

1. respond to a *Wh*-question (provided he knows that the answer is already known to the questioner);
2. respond to a command, acting it out and verbalizing as he does so;
3. respond to a statement, signalling attention and continuing the conversation;
4. respond to a response to something he himself has said; and
5. ask a Wh-question (but only one, namely 'what's that?')

This last is the only option he has for demanding a specifically linguistic response, and thus for **initiating** dialogue. It is important to stress that dialogue is interpreted as the exchange of **speech** roles; that is, it is language in functions that are created and defined by language itself, such as asking and answering questions. A response such as 'yes do' to "Shall I ...?" or 'yes I do' to "Do you want ...?", is not an instance of dialogue, since the responses are still extralinguistic in function; they express simple instrumental or regulatory meanings. Early in Phase I Nigel could already mean 'yes' and 'no' in such contexts, where they were fully interpretable in terms of his elementary functions; but he **could not answer a yes/no question** – because he could not use language to give information, to communicate experience to someone who had not shared that experience with him. It is for exactly the same reason that he cannot answer a Wh-question unless he sees that the answer is available to the questioner also.

Communicating new information, as we have stressed, is a complex notion, since it is a function of language that is wholly brought about and defined by language itself. Hence it is conceptualizable only at a very late stage. Nigel did not grasp it until towards the end of Phase II, when he was completing the transition to the adult language system. When he did grasp it, he superimposed a further semantic distinction of his own, between imparting information that was new and verbalizing information that was already known and shared. Since at this time he controlled the grammatical system of declarative/interrogative, but not yet the semantic system of statement/(yes/no) question, he adapted the grammatical distinction to his own use: the verbalizing of shared information was realized by the declarative and the communicating of new information by the interrogative. So, for example, on being given a present by his uncle, he turned to his mother who was present and said *Uncle gave you some marbles* (that is, 'you saw that Uncle gave me some marbles'; *you* = 'me' regularly throughout this stage). He then ran out to show his father, who had not been present, and said *Daddy, did Uncle give you some marbles?* (that is, 'you didn't see, but Uncle gave me some marbles').

If utterances such as those we have illustrated are not communicating information, what are they doing? In the context of **culture**, of course, they are communicating information. As Mary Douglas puts it, "If we ask of any form of communication the simple question what is being communicated? The answer is: information from the social system. The exchanges which are being communicated constitute the social system." This is exactly the social semiotic perspective which we are adopting here. But in the context of **situation** their function is not the communication of information to a hearer for whom it is new. Some of the utterances the child produces are clearly pragmatic in function: *more meat* means 'I want some more meat'. But others cannot be accounted for in this way, and we must look for some other interpretation. First, however, let us attempt a reconsideration of the significance of the second phase in Nigel's language development. Why does the child abandon his own language-creating efforts in favour of the mother tongue? And, in particular, why does he take the specific steps of building in a grammar and learning dialogue?

7 Limitations of Phase I system

The essential motivation behind both these moves can be seen in the inherent functional limitations of the child's Phase I system. It can no longer meet the requirements of his own social semiotic. Does this mean that it cannot express enough differentiation in meaning? In the long run, this is certainly true; but when Nigel moved into Phase II he was still very far from having exhausted the potential of his Phase I system – he could have added many more elements without undue strain on his own articulatory or his hearer's auditory resources. There is, however, a much more fundamental limitation on the protolanguage, which is that **it is impossible to mean more than one thing at once**. This can be done only by the interpolation of a lexicogrammatical stratum. The reason for this is that, in order for different meanings to be mapped on to one another and output in the form of single, integrated structures, there has to be an intermediate level of coding in between the meanings and the sounds. This function is served by the lexicogrammar.

So for example when Nigel says [lɔ˥], the meaning is already complex: something like 'there are holes – and something must be done about them'. His experience as an observer of holes is expressed in the articulation [lɔ˥], and his personal stake in the matter, his own intrusion into the situation, is expressed by the rising tone and plaintive voice quality. This is possible only because he now has a coding level of grammar and lexis, a relational system lying not at the semantic or phonological interfaces but at the heart of language, a level of purely linguistic abstractions serving as an intermediary in what Lamb used to call the "transduction" of meanings into sounds. This system can accept meanings derived from different functional origins and encode them into unified lexicogrammatical constructs, which are then output as *wordings* – patterns of ordering, word selections, intonation patterns and the like.

The example we have just given shows this functional semantic mapping in its simplest form. The expression [lɔ˥] represents a combination of the two most general functional components of meaning, the *ideational* (Bühler's "representational", Lyons' "cognitive", Hymes' "referential") and the *interpersonal* (Bühler's "conative" and "expressive", Lyons' "social", Hymes' "socio-expressive" or "stylistic"). The former is the observer function of language; it is the speaker reflecting on his environment. The latter is the intruder function of language; it is the speaker acting on his environment. It is a property of the adult language that it enables the speaker to do both these things at once – in fact it makes it impossible for him not to, though in infinitely varied and indirect ways towards which Nigel's utterance is no more than the first crude striving. But essentially this is what he is striving after: a plurifunctional system that enables him to mean more than one thing at once. It is for this that he needs a grammar.

By the same token, he needs a grammar in order to be able to engage in dialogue. Dialogue involves just this kind of functional mapping, of content elements on to situational elements; the same structure expresses both an ideational meaning, in terms of the speaker's experience, and an interpersonal meaning in terms of the speaker's adoption and assignment of speech roles. In the adult linguistic system, this requirement is embodied in the systems of transitivity and of mood. Transitivity expresses the speaker's experience of processes in the external world, and mood expresses his structuring of the speech situation; as sets of options, the two are quite independent, but they combine to form integrated lexicogrammatical structures. Nigel is still far from having either a transitivity system or a mood system. But he is beginning to interact linguistically, and to build up a potential for dialogue.

Thus it is not the fact that his Phase I 'protolanguage' cannot be understood by other people that provides the impetus for the move into Phase II. There is no sign yet that he wants to interact verbally with people other than those in his immediate environment, who understand him perfectly well; but he does want to **interact** with them, and his protolanguage does not allow for this. A simple exchange of verbal signals can, of course, be prolonged indefinitely in the protolanguage, and often is; but it is impossible to engage in dynamic role-play. The system cannot provide for the adoption, assignment, acceptance and rejection of speech roles.

Here is one brief example showing the sort of multiple meaning and multiple role-playing that Nigel has mastered by the time he is well on into Phase II; it is taken from NL 9 (21 to 22½ months):

NIGEL [having fallen and hurt himself earlier in the day; feeling his forehead]:   ádỹdà 'what's that?'
FATHER: That's plaster, sticking plaster.
NIGEL: tell Mummy take it òff '(I'm going to) …' … [running to Mother] take it óff 'take it off!'

8 Pragmatic and mathetic

We can now interpret the strategy that Nigel adopted as the basis of Phase II. In section 4 above we cited the first instance of the breakdown of the simple semantic taxonomy that characterizes the Phase I language: the combination of naming a person (one person or another) and interacting with that person (in one way or another), for example, [ān:ā] 'Anna, where are you?'. This is exactly the same phenomenon as was illustrated in the last section, where the meaning of [ló^u] was 'there are holes – and something must be done about them'; another early example was [k^{y}ē:k^y], said on seeing a cake in the middle of the table and meaning 'that's cake – and I want some!'

All these provide a preview of what is to come. If we look at the meanings of Nigel's Phase II utterances in functional terms, we find him apparently generalizing, out of the initial set of developmental functions which were recognizable in Phase I, two broad functional categories, or **macrofunctions** as we might call them: one of them demanding a response, the other not. The response that is demanded is, at first, in terms of goods-and-services: 'I want that', 'do that again' and so on; increasingly, however, it becomes a demand for a verbal response, for example, 'what's that?'. The other type of utterance, which demands no response, involves at first the observation, recall or prediction of phenomena seen or heard: 'I can see/hear', 'I saw/heard', 'I shall see/hear'; it then extends to narrative and descriptive contexts.

The first category clearly derives from the instrumental and regulatory systems of Phase I, and also in part the interactional; functionally we are calling it **pragmatic**. The developmental history of the second category was much more difficult to follow; but it can be shown to derive, by an interesting and indirect route, from the interactional, in its non-pragmatic aspect, the personal, and the heuristic functions – the last of which we can see emerging in the later stages of Phase I when we look back at these from a Phase II vantage point. This appears to happen somewhat as follows. Nigel begins (NL 1–2) by using some external object, typically a picture, as a channel for interaction with others; hence the gloss 'nice to see you – and shall we look at this together?'. He then (NL 3) separates the interactional from the personal element, the former developing into forms of greeting and the latter into 'self' expressions of interest, pleasure and the like. Then, as the split between the self and the environment becomes clearer, the interactional element reappears on a higher level, the attention being focused on an external object which the other person is required to name (NL 4–5): 'look at this – now you say its name'. At first this is used only when the object is familiar – again, typically a picture – and the name already (receptively) known; it then splits into two meanings one of which is a demand for a new name, one that is not known, the 'what's that?' form illustrated earlier. The words that name objects are at the same time being learnt productively, and are then used in the encoding of expressions of personal interest and involvement: 'look, that's a ...!'. Thus out of a combination of the personal (self-oriented) and the heuristic (environment-oriented) functions of Phase I there arises a generalized non-pragmatic mode of meaning which is in contrast to the pragmatic mode identified above.

What is the function of such 'non-pragmatic' utterances? Can we characterize their meaning in positive terms? Lewis already observed this distinction in the 1930s; he uses the term 'manipulative' for the pragmatic function, and labels the other 'declarative'. This is adequate as a description, but does not really explain what these utterances mean. Lewis appears to interpret 'declarative' in terms of self-expression, and the demand for an expressive response. It seems, however, that the function of utterances which are not pragmatic is essentially a learning one. It arises, like the pragmatic function, by a process of generalization from the initial set of extrinsic functions of Phase I; and it is complementary to it, as reflection is to action. We have suggested referring to it as the *mathetic* function; it is language enabling the child to learn about his social and material environment, serving him in the construction of reality. This function is realized, in the first instance, through the child's observing, recalling and predicting the objects and events which impinge on his perceptions.

At the beginning of Phase II, all utterances are **either** one thing **or** the other: either pragmatic or mathetic. And when we look at the new lexical items coming in to Nigel's system in NL 6–7, we find that the majority, probably more than three-quarters of them, come in in the context of the mathetic function, not the pragmatic. (Moreover, each word, and each structure, is at first specialized to one function only; they are not used in both.) This is partly explainable by reference to the greater situational dependence of the pragmatic mode; where the meaning is 'I want ...', the speaker can often point to what it is he wants, so that Nigel continued to use the unmarked instrumental and regulatory options of Phase I well on into Phase II. But the observation also recalls Lévi-Strauss' remark that in all cultures 'the universe is an object of thought at least as much as it is a means of satisfying needs'. We find this to be already a determining factor in the child's language development; language evolves in the context of his thinking about the universe no less than in the context of his exploiting it.

9 Phase II functional strategy

It is largely thanks to Nigel himself that this aspect of his Phase II strategy, the contrast between a mathetic and a pragmatic mode, can be asserted with relative confidence. At a particular moment – the last week of NL 7, one week after the structural explosion discussed in section 5 – he adopted the intonational distinction of rising/falling, which he then kept up for some months. It was noticeable that, from that date on, every utterance had one tone contour, and that the tone was either clearly rising or clearly falling in every instance. The interpretation soon became apparent. All falling tone utterances were mathetic in function, and all rising tone utterances were pragmatic in function. Some examples from NL 7–8:

PRAGMATIC
chuffa stúck	'the train's stuck; help me to get it out'
high wáll	'let me jump off and you catch me'
háve it	'I want that'
play ráo	'let's play at lions'
squeeze órange	'squeeze the orange'
bounce táble	'I want to bounce the orange on the table, can I?'
water ón	'I want the water turned on'
Anna help gréenpea	'Anna help me to eat the greenpeas'
Dada come overthere nów	'Daddy come over there now'
make cross tíckmatick ... in Dada róom	'I want to make a cross on the typewriter in Daddy's room'
chuffa under túnnel ... getit fóryou	'the train's in the tunnel; get it for me'
play rao bártok	'I want to play at lions with me holding the sleeve of the Bartok record'

MATHETIC
molasses nòse	'I've got molasses on my nose'
red swèater	'that's a red sweater'
chuffa stòp	'the train's stopped'
loud Dvǒrak	'that a loud bit of the Dvořak record'
green stick find	'the green stick's been found'
Dada black brùsh	'that's Daddy's black brush'
man clean càr	'the man was cleaning his car'
Anna make noise gràss	'Anna made a noise with a piece of grass'

clever boy fix roof on lòrry	'this clever boy fixed the roof on the lorry'
Dada come bàck ... Dada come on fast chùffa	'Daddy's come back; Daddy came on a fast train'
too dàrk ... open cùrtain ... lìght now	'it was too dark; you've opened the curtains, and it's light now'

It may be pointed out that some of these utterances could be translated into either pragmatic or mathetic forms. But Nigel himself made the distinction clear. If the tone was rising, he was not satisfied until some response was forthcoming; whereas if the tone was falling, no response was expected. The following is a typical example showing both types of utterance, the one followed by the other:

Dada got scrambled ègg ... Mummy get fóryou scrambled egg

'Daddy's got some scrambled egg; Mummy get some scrambled egg for me!'

Thus Nigel developed a clear functional strategy for Phase II, the phase that is transitional between his own protolanguage and the language of the adult system. In what sense is it transitional? Here we come back once more to the sociosemiotic perspective. Phase II is defined as the period of mastering the adult language ***system***; the end of Phase II is defined as the point when he has effectively mastered the system and can continue unhindered in his mastery of the language. It is unlikely that this point can be tied to any particular moment in time, but in Nigel's case it coincides roughly with the end of his second year, around NL 10 in the present study. The notion of transition, however, is perhaps more readily interpretable in functional terms. At the beginning of Phase II, it is 'each utterance one function'. This is what makes it possible for Nigel to put the intonation contrast to systematic use in the way he does (he cannot of course use it in the way English does, because the systems that are realized by intonation in English are as yet beyond his functional potential). Gradually in the course of Phase II he moves on, through a stage of 'each utterance typically one principal function, the other subsidiary', to a final stage of 'every utterance all functions'. This is the pattern that is characteristic of the adult language.

How does this functional development take place? Not in the obvious way, which would be by some sort of transcategorization process in which sentence types were transferred out of one box into another. It happens through a reinterpretation of the concept of function on to a more abstract level, such that it becomes the organizing principle of the linguistic system itself. We could express this by saying that the *functions* of Phase I become *macrofunctions* in Phase II and *metafunctions* in Phase III.

This, it seems, is the developmental source of the functional components of the adult linguistic system, the ideational and interpersonal referred to above. Whatever the specific **use** to which language is being put – and by the end of Phase II the child has indefinitely many uses of language (because they are indefinitely subclassifiable) – in all contexts the speaker has to be both observer and intruder at the same time. It is the pragmatic function that has provided the main context for the 'intruder' systems of mood, modality, intensity, person and the like, and the mathetic function that has provided the main context for the 'observer' systems of transitivity, extent and location, quantifying and qualifying, and so on. But it is characteristic of the adult that, whatever the social context, the expression of his meanings in language involves both reflection on and interaction with the social system.

Hence in the course of Phase II the notion of 'function' becomes totally distinct from that of 'use'. The adult has unlimited uses for language; but the typical adult utterance, whatever its use, has an ideational and an interpersonal component of meaning. At the same time, these "metafunctional" components of the adult language arise, however indirectly, out of the primary developmental functions of Phase I, where function was synonymous with use. It is in Phase II that the child makes the fundamental discovery that he can mean two things at once – he can both observe and interact with his environment at the same time; when he enters Phase III, all uses of language are mediated through this twofold meaning potential. The elementary functional contexts in which he first constructed his own protolanguage are still there; they have evolved into the semiotic structures that we recognize as situations and settings of language use. What has changed is the meaning potential that he can deploy as an actor.

A schematic representation of the process of systemic-functional development as we have postulated it is given as Figure 2 in Chapter 2.

10 Continuity of the developmental process

It is not easy to say how much of Nigel's language learning strategies represents a general pattern of transition into the adult language system, and how much is merely his own way through. Clearly the use of intonation to realize the pragmatic/mathetic distinction is an individual device; but the distinction itself may be a general feature – at least there seems nothing to suggest that it could not be. It is quite possible, on the other hand, that many children do not bother to create a Phase I language at all; almost certainly they do not all display Nigel's dramatic shift from Phase I to Phase II. But one has to be careful here. It is clear that there is no single origin for the expressions of the protolanguage, and it could well be that some children already use imitations of adult sounds in this context; these would then appear to be words, although they would not in fact be functioning as items of vocabulary – there would still be no lexicogrammatical level in the system. Moreover many children use the holophrase as a transitional strategy, which makes the introduction of the lexicogrammar a much less sudden affair.

However that may be, the point to be emphasized here is that of continuity, not discontinuity. There is, with Nigel, a discontinuity in the expression, as well as, of course, the discontinuity that arises from the introduction of a third level of coding into the system. But there is no discontinuity in the content. The social functions that have determined the protolanguage – satisfying immediate needs, controlling people's behaviour, being 'together', expressing the uniqueness of the self, exploring the world of the non-self and creating a world in the imagination – all these evolve gradually and naturally into the social contexts and situation types that we characterize as semiotic structures; and the semantic systems, the meaning potential that derives from these functions, evolve likewise. The progressive approximation of the child's meanings to those of the adult, through interaction with and reinforcement by older speakers, begins before these meanings are (necessarily) realized through the words and structures of the adult language, and continues without interruption. Without this continuity, the semantic system could not function effectively in the transmission of the social system from the adult to the child.

It is the essential continuity of the process of "learning how to mean", however early this process is considered to start, that we hope to bring out by adopting a sociosemiotic perspective. Our object of study here is still language; but it seems that additional light can be shed on language, especially where language development is concerned, if it is placed in the wider context of the social system considered as a system of meanings – hence the concept of **language as social semiotic**. From another point of view, this is a means of bringing together the sociolinguistic and the semantic interpretations of language development, which at present remain rather unconnected. From the sociolinguistic standpoint, learning the mother tongue has been interpreted as the progressive mastery of a "communicative competence", the use of language in different social contexts. But the notion of communicative competence, though valuable as a temporary structure, a heuristic device for comparative developmental and educational studies, does not relate to the nature of the linguistic system, or explain how and why the child learns it. Work in developmental semantics has focused mainly on the child's learning of the word meanings and other specific aspects of the ideational component of the adult linguistic system. But these studies do not in general relate the system to its social contexts or to the functions that language serves in the young child's life. Each of these fields of investigation constitutes, needless to say, an essential element in the total picture. But they need to be brought together, through some framework that does not separate the system from its use, or meaning from social context.

We have been perhaps too readily persuaded to accept dichotomies of this kind, with their implication that an interactional or "socio-" perspective is one in which the focus is on behaviour, performance, the use of the system 'as opposed to' the system itself. It is useful to be reminded that there are also sociological explanations, and that an interpretation of language as interaction is complementary to, and no less explanatory than, a view of language as knowledge.

A child learns a symbolic behaviour potential; this is what he 'can mean', in terms of a few elementary social functions. In the process he creates a language, a system of meanings deriving from these functions, together with their realizations in sound. The meanings are, in turn, the encoding of the higher-level meanings that constitute the developing child's social system; first his own relationships with people and objects, then the relationships among the people and objects themselves, then relationships among the symbols, and so on. In the process there comes a moment when the child abandons the glossogenic trail – which we may speculate on as a model of the evolutionary path of human language – and settles for the "mother tongue", the language he hears from others. With this, given its potential for dialogue and for multiple meaning, he can engage in an ongoing polyphonic interaction with those around him.

Since the fact that language encodes the social system has in the long run determined the form of its internal organization, the child faces no sharp discontinuity at this point; he is taking over a system that is a natural extension of that which he has constructed for himself. His own functional semiotic now reappears at a more abstract level at the core of the adult language, in the ideational and interpersonal components of the semantic system. All linguistic interaction comes to be mediated through these two functions; and since they are not just aspects of the use of language, but are at the basis of the system itself, every actual instance of linguistic interaction has meaning not only in particular but also in general, as an expression of the social system and of the child's place in it – in other words, it is related to the context of culture as well as to the context of the situation. This explains how in the course of learning language a child is also learning all the time **through** language; how the microsemiotic exchanges of family and peer group life contain within themselves indices of the most pervasive semiotic patterns of the culture.

By the middle of his second year, Nigel is firmly embarked on the learning of his mother tongue. Appendix 3 gives a specimen of conversation from the day on which he reached 18 months.

Nigel had reached this point through constant interaction with others; he had not got there by himself. The three adults in his meaning group (there were no other children in the family; he interacted with other children when the occasion arose, thrusting his toys at them and grabbing theirs, but as yet made no serious attempt to exchange meanings with them) were unconsciously tracking his language, understanding what he meant and responding with meanings of their own. Neither Nigel nor the others were imitating; but all were participating in the creation of his meaning potential. By their acts of understanding, the others shared in Nigel's language at every stage; the language-creating process was a social one, a product of the interaction between Nigel and those with whom his experiences were shared in common.

This tracking of a child's language by his mother, and perhaps others, is a remarkable phenomenon that has been paid very little notice. It is something that takes place below the level of conscious awareness; those involved cannot, as a rule, describe what they are doing, and if the mother, for example, is asked what the child has been saying she is quite likely to contend that he wasn't saying anything at all – he can't talk yet. Of course he can't talk yet, in the mother tongue. But he is talking in the child tongue; and the mother is responding all the time in a way which can be explained in no other way than as a response to language.

There is a direct continuity here from the early pre-linguistic exchanges described by Trevarthen; without noticing it, the mother has moved on with the child, and is responding to his vocal or gestural symbols as readily and as naturally as she did to the smiles and gurgles and other signs of animation that he gave in earliest infancy. At any given moment, she knows what he knows; not only does she understand him, but she knows the limits of his understanding, and talks to him so that he gets the message – not of course the literal message that the adult gets from it, but a message that he can interpret in the light of his own functional resources for meaning. Under favourable conditions this kind of tracking by others, who (again without being aware of what they are doing) talk to a child in ways that stretch his understanding without going way beyond it, can persist throughout early childhood, and it probably has a great value for him in developing his linguistic resources, both in learning language and in learning through language.

At no stage is language development an individual matter. Meaning, and learning to mean, are social processes. From the moment of birth a child is one among others, a person among people. The dominant theories among linguists and psychologists, the so-called "nativist" and "environmentalist" approaches, which were often presented as opposite viewpoints, appear now rather as variants on a single theme, that of the child as an island, an individual existent who has to 'acquire' some ready-made object 'out there' that we call language. There is no need to labour the point that such theories are the product of Western individualist ideology. The important issue at the moment is not so much the particular intellectual model we choose to impose on the language learning process, as the search for a greater understanding of the nature of early infancy, as we try to interpret the ontogenesis of language: how children begin to exchange meanings, how they construe in the course of their daily interaction a semantic system that gradually approximates to that shared by the others around them, and how while construing it they use it to construe reality – to make sense of their experience and organize it into a picture of the world that is likewise shared with the others. In understanding this we also begin to see more deeply into the nature of language itself, since ultimately language has been shaped by the functions it has to serve in the actions and reflections on reality by a child.

Chapter Five

MEANING AND THE CONSTRUCTION OF REALITY IN EARLY CHILDHOOD
(1978)

1 Functional semantics of language development

1.1 The concept of the protolanguage

Long before a child begins to speak in his mother tongue, he is engaging in acts of meaning.

The meanings may be expressed in various ways. The child may use either of the two modes, vocal or gestural; and, in the vocal mode, in which the expression is a complex pattern of intonation and articulation, he may either create new patterns of his own, or attempt to imitate sounds he hears in the speech of others. Most children probably use some combination of all three kinds of expression, though many show a preference for one particular kind. I made an intensive study of one child, Nigel, from birth to $3\frac{1}{2}$ years (Halliday 1975); Nigel showed a clear preference for the vocal mode, and for inventing sounds rather than imitating them, though he did use some gestures and vocal imitations as well. All three are variants of a single, more general mode of expression, that of bodily postures and movements, with which a child constructs his ***protolanguage***. The essential ingredient of the protolanguage is not the form of the output but the nature of the act of meaning itself.

An ***act of meaning*** is a communicative act that is intentional and symbolic. A cry of hunger is a communicative act; and so, for that matter, is clamping on to the mother's breast. Both convey a message – that the child is hungry. But neither of these acts embodies the

---

First published in *Modes of Perceiving and Processing of Information*, edited by Herbert L. Pick, Jr, and Elliot Saltzman. Hillsdale, NJ: Lawrence Erlbaum Associates, 1978, pp. 67–96.

intention to communicate; they are not symbolic acts. A symbolic act is one of which the meaning and success criteria do not reside in its own performance.

The outward form of a symbolic act is sometimes iconic. If I hit you because I'm angry with you, that is not an act of meaning. If I hit you to show that I'm angry with you, that is an act of meaning, but it is one in which the expression is related to the meaning in a non-arbitrary fashion: the symbol is an iconic one. The distinction between iconic and non-iconic symbols is, needless to say, a matter of degree; the expression may be more or less iconic, and it may be both iconic and non-iconic at the same time. At nine months Nigel had a small repertory of gestures, one of which was that of grasping an object firmly, without pulling it towards him, and then letting go. The meaning was 'I want that' (see page 131). This was a partially iconic gesture, but the act was clearly a symbolic one – it did not itself constitute an attempt at realizing the desire. Nigel was not acting directly on the object. The gesture was an act of meaning, addressed to the other person taking part in the situation.

Acts of meaning, in this specific sense, take place early in a child's life; much earlier than the time at which language development studies have usually been begun, and long before the child has anything that is recognizable as a "language" – if language is defined by the presence of adult-like linguistic structures or words. As far as I was aware, Nigel's earliest act that was unambiguously an act of meaning took place just before six months, when for the first time he produced a sound – a very short and rather quiet nasal squeak, on a high rising note – the meaning of which 'what's going on?'. On the other hand I was not prepared for acts of meaning at this early age, and I may have failed to notice earlier instances. Perhaps the sad tale that he told at the age of two months, after having his first injections, should be thought of as an act of meaning, given the very clear contrast between this and his usual cheerful narrative (see page 132).

By the age of nine months, Nigel had a **system** of acts of meaning – a **meaning potential** – which marked the beginning of his protolanguage. At this stage the protolanguage consisted of five meanings. Three, which were expressed gesturally, were in the more active mode: 'I want that', 'I don't want that', and 'do that (again)'. The other two, which were expressed vocally, were in the more reflective mode: 'let's be together' and 'look – that's interesting'. At that time, therefore, Nigel showed a correlation between the two modes of expression, vocal and gestural, and the two modes of meaning, reflective and active: reflective meanings were expressed vocally and active ones gesturally. Within four to six weeks, however, he abandoned the gestural mode almost entirely (the exception being the demand for music, expressed by "beating time"), and settled for vocal symbols in the expression of meanings of all kinds.

1.2 Systematic and social character of acts of meaning

An act of meaning is systematic in a dual sense. First, the act itself is an act of choice, of selection within a meaning potential; and the selection is non-random, in that it is coherently related to the context of situation – the semiotic structure of whatever portion of the child's reality construct constitutes the relevant environment in the given instance.

Second, the meaning potential is also systematic. It is a resource, a network of options each one of which can be interpreted by reference to the child's total model of reality and of his own place in it. The reality, and hence the meaning potential, is constantly under construction, being added to, differentiated within, and modified.

Between the ages of 9 and 16 months, Nigel's protolanguage grew from a system of five to a system of about fifty different meanings. For example, whereas at the start he had had just one meaning of an **interactional** kind, a generalized signal of participation, exchanging attention with another person through the conversational process, he now had a resource of about fifteen. These included: (1) **greetings**, where he distinguished among the different persons that he exchanged meanings with, and between initiating and responding; (2) **sharings**, with which he distinguished between shared attention and shared regret; and (3) **responses**, to specific invitations to mean. All these were coded in the system as recognizably distinct symbolic acts.

The term "act" is, however, semantically loaded; it suggests something purely subjective. But an act of meaning is a social act, again in the same dual sense as previously discussed. First, the act itself is shared, between the actor and the attender. It is shared not merely in the sense that the one is acting and the other is attending at the same time (the one "giving" meanings and the other "receiving" them), but that both are taking part in an exchange of meanings and that there is no act of meaning in isolation from such exchange. The process is one of conversation; the act becomes meaningful only when the other (who is a "significant other" by virtue of taking part in the conversational process) joins in and so gives value to the child's symbolic intent.

Second, the act of meaning is social also in the general sense, that the meaning potential from which it derives is a social construct. The semantic system, in which the child encodes his subjective reality, must be shared between the child and the significant others if his acts of meaning are to be successful. Experience may be private, but the symbolic coding of experience is social; there can be no private symbols, in this sense. But the child is not yet approximating the others' semantic system; he is creating one of his own. To say that the creation of a semantic system is a social process means, therefore, at this stage, that the others must be approximating the child's semantic system, and this is precisely what they do. It is clear from the observations of Nigel's conversation that the others not only understood him but also actively understood him; they played the conversational game according to his rules. Here is an example at 18 months:

> Nigel set himself to eating his lunch. Some fish fell off the fork.
> "Ooh!" It was another very high-pitched squeak.
> "Ooh, you lost a bit then," said Anna. "Where did it go?"
> "Byebye." Nigel looked up at Anna, inviting her to share a memory.
> "'yebye, byebye," he said.
> "Yes, all the trains went away, and you said 'byebye', didn't you?"
> "Byebye," said Nigel sadly, waving his hand. He finished his lunch.
> "No-more. No-more."
> "Where has it all gone?" Anna asked him.

It is obvious that Anna is, quite spontaneously, interpreting what Nigel says as relevant participation in the dialogue. At the same time, the semantic approximation is not a one-way process; it has its own natural dialectic. Anna responds with meanings of her own; and she interprets Nigel's meanings in terms of what is coded in her own semantic system – or (since she is an imaginative person) in terms of what is not necessarily coded but is at least codable. This, in fact, is the role of the others in the conversational process: to interpret and to respond with their own meanings. So the means exist whereby the child, even at the protolinguistic phase, has access to adult meanings in a context in which they can modify and feed into his own meaning potential.

1.3 Semantic continuity

A child's earliest protolanguage can perhaps best be interpreted by reference to a small set of extralinguistically defined semantic functions. At ten months Nigel's acts of meaning fell into four functionally defined categories: the ***instrumental*** and the ***regulatory***, which are more in the active mode of meaning; and the ***interactional*** and the ***personal***, which are more in the reflective mode. These are "extralinguistic" in the sense that they exist as modes of intent independently of being encoded into, or realized through, symbolic acts of meaning.

It seems clear that, with Nigel at least, this functional orientation of the protolanguage is the ontogenetic base of the major functional components (what I have called ***metafunctions***) of the adult semantic system, the ***interpersonal*** or active component and the ***ideational*** or reflective component (Halliday 1973).

The functional organization and functional continuity are thus properties of the system. In order to represent them we express the system as a potential – as a resource, not as a set of rules. Hence in representing Nigel's protolanguage I have used an "or"-based, not an "and"-based, model of language – one in which the underlying relation is the ***paradigmatic*** one (system) rather than the ***syntagmatic*** one (structure). A system, in this technical sense, is any set of options, or range of alternatives, together with its condition of entry.

If we follow closely Nigel's development from a protolanguage (Phase I) through a transitional stage (Phase II) to the adult linguistic system (Phase III), a striking pattern of semantic continuity emerges. The "self"-oriented systems, the interactional and the personal, at first define meanings such as 'let's be together', 'here I am', 'that's pleasing', 'that's interesting'. These then evolve, through the intermediary senses of 'let's attend to this together' and 'now you say its name', to the naming of things, beginning with persons, objects and processes; and thence through observation, recall, and prediction into the narrative mode and the ideational component of the adult semantics. This seemed to be Nigel's way in to the reflective mode of meaning.

The "other"-oriented systems, the instrumental and the regulatory, at first define meanings such as 'give me that', 'do that', and 'do that again'. These then evolve, through intermediary senses such as 'you do that', 'let's do that', and 'let me do that' (command, suggestion, and request for permission), into the exchanging of things, giving, demanding, and giving on demand; and hence through the exchange of information into the dialogue mode and the interpersonal component of the adult semantics. This was Nigel's way in to the active mode of meaning.

Central to this process of the evolution of the functional modes or components of meaning is the evolution in the concept of ***function*** itself. Nigel's earliest system of meaning potential, the Phase 1 protolanguage, is "functional" in the sense that each element in the system, and therefore each act of meaning, realizes an intent in respect of just one of a small set of extralinguistic functions (those that we identified as instrumental, regulatory, interactional, and personal, and the one or two that are added later). Nigel's conversation is meaningful in relation to his domains of social action, those of: (1) achieving material ends; (2) controlling the behaviour of the "others"; (3) establishing and maintaining contact with them; or (4) expressing his own selfhood in the form of cognitive and affective states. These are the social contexts of his acts of meaning – parts that he can play in the symbolic interaction. If we call these the "functions" of his protolanguage, then in this context "function" is equivalent to "use."

For some months (9 months to 16 to 17 months) this system continues to expand. The meaning potential is considerably enlarged; but it remains a system of the same kind. Then, towards the middle of the second year, the system undergoes a qualitative change. Hitherto, it has been a coding system with just two levels, a level of content (the meaning) and a level of expression (the sound or gesture); the elements of the system have been individual signs, content–expression pairs. Elements like "e-e-eh": 'here I am!'; or "ùh": 'do that some more'; or "dòh": 'nice to see you, and shall we look at this picture together?', are meanings coded directly into sounds, without any intervening organization. (Needless to say, the glosses need not be taken literally as statements of meaning; they are intended as an aid to understanding. But they also serve to bring out the fact that the meanings of Nigel's protolanguage are typically not meanings that are fully coded in the adult semantic.)

Just before the middle of his second year, however (though there have been previews of what was to come), Nigel introduces a third level of coding intermediate between the content and the expression, a level of formal organization consisting of words and structures. In other words, he adds a grammar – or more accurately, a lexicogrammar. The elements of the system are no longer individual signs, but configurations at three different levels: semantic, lexicogrammatical and phonological, which are related to each other by realization. The meanings are "first" realized as (encoded into) wordings and "then" realized as (recoded into) sounds. This is the way the adult language is organized.

By taking this step, Nigel made it possible for himself to combine meanings into a single complex act; and he exploited this possibility by means of a functional strategy of his own devising, by which he distinguished all acts of meaning into two broad types, the *pragmatic* and the *mathetic*. The former have a 'doing' function, and require a response from the person addressed: at first a non-verbal response, such as giving something or doing something, but later these acts increasingly call for a verbal response, such as an answer to his question. The latter require no response and serve what we may interpret as a 'learning' function. This distinction has arisen directly by generalization out of the functions of the protolanguage; but it means that Nigel can now converse in new ways, adopting and assigning roles in the conversational process (dialogue) and ranging freely over time and space beyond the confines of the here and now (narrative).

Because he has a grammar, which allows meanings to be split up and their components combined and recombined in indefinitely many ways, Nigel is able to make this distinction explicit; and he does so in an interesting way. The meaning "pragmatic" is expressed by the use of a rising tone, and the meaning "mathetic" is expressed by the use of a falling tone. In other words the functional distinction has itself now been coded, as an opposition between two **macrofunctions**;* Nigel creates this pattern more or less overnight, at 19 months, and it remains his dominant semiotic strategy throughout the rest of Phase II, the transition to an adult-like language, and into Phase III. "Function" is now no longer synonymous with "use"; it has to be reinterpreted in the sense of 'mode of meaning'.

The significant others with whom Nigel exchanges meanings respond to this new language as understandingly, and as unconsciously, as they did to his protolanguage. When the tone rises, they respond with goods-and-services, or, gradually, with new meanings – that is, they offer something in exchange. When the tone falls they listen, if they are there, but they feel no need to respond; and if they do respond, it is typically not with any new meaning but with an echo of what Nigel has said, though coded in adult words and structures, or with a prompt, inviting him to continue. Nigel, in turn, makes it clear that such responses are appropriate. This is not to imply, of course, that he always gets the response he wants; but he does get it in enough instances for the system to work. It should be noted that this semantic opposition is not at all the same as the meaning of the contrast between rising and falling tone in adult English. The two are, ultimately, related, but many of Nigel's wordings come out with what is, for the adult, the "wrong" tone. For example, all his commands and "Wh"-questions rise in tone, since they require a response; while his dependent clauses (when he begins to develop them) fall, since they do not.

In this transitional phase, however, the two modes of meaning, pragmatic and mathetic, are still alternatives: an act of meaning is always either one or the other. For example, *more méat* means 'more meat' + 'do something' (pragmatic), that is, 'give me some more meat'; *chuffa stúck* means 'train stuck' + 'do something', that is, 'get it out for me'; *high wáll* means 'high place' + 'do something', that is, 'I'm going to jump – catch me!'. On the other hand, *green càr* means 'green car' + 'I'm taking note', 'I'm learning' (mathetic), that is, 'I see (or saw or will see) a green car'; likewise *loud mùsic* means 'that's loud music'; *chuffa stòp* means 'the train's stopped'. Nigel's next move, already implicit however in this scheme of things, is to combine these two modes of meaning so that every act of meaning is both one and the other. This means reinterpreting the concept of function yet again.

By the end of Phase II, near the end of his second year, Nigel's grammatical resources have developed to the extent that he can map grammatical structures one on to another the way the adult language does. For example, he can select the categories **transitive** (in the transitivity system) and **interrogative** (in the mood system) and produce the expression *did you drop the green pen* which encodes both these selections simultaneously. He still does not use this sentence in the adult sense, as a question, because his semantic system is not yet that of the adult language; but he has successfully combined in it an interpersonal meaning, represented by the interrogative structure, and an ideational meaning, represented by the transitivity structure. (The sentence, of course, contains much else besides these two selections.)

The macrofunctions have now become what we might call **metafunctions**. They are no longer just generalizations of the earlier functional categories but reinterpretations of them at another level. They have now become the functional components of the semantic system; and each has its own systems of meaning potential, having as output some specific contribution to the total lexicogrammatical coding. The adult language is structured around these two components of meaning: the ideational and the interpersonal (together with a third, the textual, which I omit from the discussion here for the sake of brevity). They represent the twin themes of reflection and action in the adult semiotic: language as a means of reflecting on reality, and language as a means of acting on reality. The really striking fact about a human infant is that these two modes of meaning are present from the start. In his earliest acts of meaning we find Nigel already engaged in an ongoing conversational process in which the exchange takes these two primary symbolic forms.

1.4 The context of an act of meaning

It is a mistake to suppose that a child's language is ever fully context-bound or that an adult's is ever fully context-free. The principle of semantic continuity and functional evolution means that: (1) an act of meaning always has a context; while (2) the way in which an act of meaning is related to its context changes in the course of development. Equally, the system as a whole (the meaning potential) has a context, and this too changes in the developmental process.

The context for the **meaning system** is the **social system**, as it exists as a semiotic construct for the child at the given time. The context for an **act of meaning** is the **situation**, which is also a semiotic construct, a recognizable configuration of features from the social system. The situation consists essentially of a ***field*** of social process, and a ***tenor*** of social relationships, together with a third element, a ***mode*** of symbolic action – that is, the specific part that is assigned to acts of meaning in the particular context.

Much of the speech a child hears around him is, typically, relatable to its context of situation in recognizable and systematic ways. (It is also, despite a common belief to the contrary, richly structured, grammatically well formed, and fluent.) The meanings reflect the field, tenor, and mode of the situation in which they are expressed; and they do so in a rather systematic way. Typically, ideational meanings, realized in thing-names, transitivity structures and the like, represent the "field", the nature of the social process – what is going on at the time. Interpersonal meanings, realized in moods and modalities, expressions of comment, attitude and so on, represent the "tenor", the social relationships in the situation – who-all are taking part. Textual meanings, realized as patterns of cohesion and the organization of discourse, represent the "mode", the symbolic or rhetorical channel – what part the exchange of meanings is playing in the total unfolding scene. In much adult speech, whether backyard gossip or deliberations in committee, the actual components of the situation are fictions that are construed out of the meanings that are being exchanged: persons and objects are being talked about, and even acted upon, that are not there outside of the talk. But when the child himself is part of the interactive process, the situation is typically such that its features are made manifest to him: the feelings and attitudes of the participants and the objects and actions referred to can be seen or felt or heard.

The child's own acts of meaning relate likewise to his own social constructs. At first, in Phase I, as we have seen, the relation is one in which meaning is goal-directed ('do this', 'I want that', 'let's be together'); the context **is** the goal, and the act of meaning is successful if the goal is achieved. (We should remember that right from the start there are also purely reflexive acts of meaning: 'that's pleasing', 'that's interesting'.) But this relationship changes, by the natural dialectic of development. Nigel's own ability to mean allows him to construe acts of meaning in others, in their relation to the context; but the nature of this relation in adult conversation – or rather in conversation in the Phase III system – is such that the process of understanding it changes the contextual basis of the child's own acts of meaning. Hence what happens in Phase II, when the child makes the transition to the adult system, is that meaning no longer consists in aiming a shaft at a pre-existing target; now, it also involves defining the target. Success criteria here are of two kinds, and with Nigel, as we saw, each act was clearly marked for one or the other. Either success is external (pragmatic acts – rising tone), where Nigel is, or is not, satisfied with the other's response; or it is internal (mathetic acts – falling tone), where Nigel is, or is not, satisfied with his own achievement. In neither case is success a foregone conclusion. It is obvious that, with a pragmatic utterance, such as *more meát*, Nigel may not get an acceptable response: he may get no response at all, or a response that does not accede. But it is just as often the case that, with a mathetic utterance, Nigel recognizes failures of meaning; as he did for example when, holding a toy bus in one hand and a train in the other, he was trying to encode the situation, saying *two . . . two chùffa . . . two . . . two . . .* – finally he admitted defeat and gave up. But in both cases the act of meaning here consists in more than merely specifying a function in context; it involves making explicit the context in which that function is relevant. Nigel has now taken the critical step towards freeing his conversation from the limitations of his immediate surroundings – within which, however, it was never totally confined. Not only can he ask for toast when the toast is not in front of him, he can also recall, or predict, seeing a bus when the bus is no longer, or not yet, in sight.

MEANING AND THE CONSTRUCTION OF REALITY

1.5 Functional continuity and the construction of subjective reality

The functional-semantic continuity not only enables a child to construct a language, it also enables him, at the same time that he is constructing it, to use the language in the construction of a reality.

When Nigel takes the major step of converting his protolanguage into a language, by adding a grammar, which is a new level of coding intermediate between the meanings and the sounds, this is the one major discontinuity in the development of his linguistic system. He takes it against a background of clearly recognizable continuity in the functional-semantic evolution. From his earliest acts of meaning to the complex configurations that mark his entry into the adult mode, there is an unbroken line of development in which the twin themes of action and reflection provide the central thread.

It is this same continuity that allows Nigel to construct a reality, of which the language is both a realization and a part. This is not so much because reality construction is necessarily a continuous process — whether it is or is not is likely to depend on whether or not there are discontinuities in the reality itself. Rather, it is because the continuity of meanings proclaims and symbolizes the permanence of what is "in here" and what is "out there": of the self, and of the social system that defines the self, and of the relation that subsists between the two. The act of meaning, above all others, is what creates and maintains our identity in face of the chaos of things. It is as if, having become self-conscious through learning to mean, we have to go on meaning to keep the self in suspension.

At the very outset of Phase I, around nine to ten and a half months, Nigel has developed a picture of how things are. We know this, because only with some such picture could he mean in the ways he does; we can see the structure of his thinking through our interpretation of the structure of his meaning. By ten months of age Nigel has constructed a subjective reality that we could interpret as being based on the separation of himself from the continuum of things. Given this interpretation, in order to explain the protolanguage that we find him using at that time, we would have to postulate that, at the least, he has constructed a schema of the kind shown in Figure 1. On this same basis, the schema that Nigel has developed by the end of Phase I, six months later, may be represented in Figure 2. (For the data underlying the interpretations in Figures 1 and 2, see Tables 1 and 5 in Appendix 2.) Again, this schema is one which we can recover from observations of Nigel's semantic system; it is implicit in what he is able to mean at the time.

INFANCY AND PROTOLANGUAGE

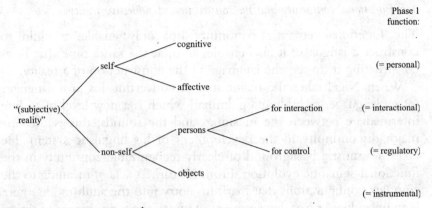

Figure 1 Nigel at 9–10½ months

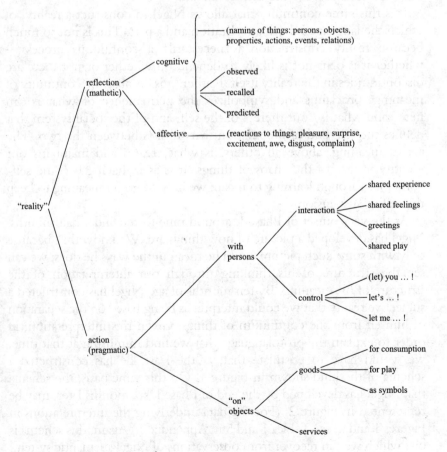

Figure 2 Nigel at 15–16½ months

With any such representation, we are always in fact **behind** the time. These are the minimal structures that we have to recognize as the basis of what Nigel himself can mean – what he can encode in his own speech. Since his understanding is always further developed than his powers of expression, we are seeing things long after they actually happen; as far as his model of reality is concerned, listening to Nigel speak is like observing the light rays from a distant star. And yet we have to be careful here: Nigel has got where he is not by being inducted into adult ways of thinking but by following his own route. Hence, while **his** understanding of what is meant by others (and if we continue to use the word "mean" in this rather un-English way, it is because we are talking not about what is said but about what is meant; saying is merely the outward sign and channel of meaning) shows that he knows more than he himself can mean, we cannot represent what he knows simply by describing what he must know in order to understand the meanings that are addressed to him. This is because we can only express these meanings in the terms of the adult semantic.

When Nigel moved into Phase II, the transition from protolanguage to (adult-like) language, his key functional strategy was, as we saw it, the development of an explicit opposition of pragmatic versus mathetic. It is important to stress at this point that both these modes of meaning are fundamental to the reality-constructing process. Reality, as mediated through a child's semantic system, has a twofold property, namely that it is at once both good to think and good to eat. Just as, when we observe a child using vocal or gestural signs to demand what he wants, we have to remember that he has other signs too, signs that express his pleasure in and curiosity about the surroundings, so also when we are focusing on the child's subjective reality we should not forget that it is something that is acted on as well as thought about. And this is what the pragmatic–mathetic opposition signifies. When Nigel uses a rising tone, he is acting on reality; when he uses a falling tone, he is reflecting on reality; and both action and reflection are mediated by the act of meaning. He achieves by meaning to others, and he learns by meaning to himself. It is the potential to mean – that is, by now, language – that integrates and synthesizes the two modes. Reality can be acted on and reflected on because it can be talked about; and the exchange of talk, ***conversation***, is what makes it one reality not two. When Nigel enters Phase II, a word or a structure belongs to just one mode or the other; by the time he leaves Phase II, each word, and each structure, functions in both. Hence in the transition to the adult mode of meaning we can see rather clearly displayed the empirical foundations of Nigel's theory of what it is all about.

To illustrate the argument, the next section contains a number of short narratives of Nigel's interaction, starting at two and a half years and going back to the first two weeks of life.

2 Examples of conversations

2.1 Two years, six months

"We broke the cot in Mrs Lampeter's house and you licked it and pressed it dòwn," said Nigel. *You* at this stage meant 'I': 'I licked it and pressed it down'.

We have broken the cot – that is, dismantled it for packing. But I didn't remember Nigel licking it. "What did you lick?" I asked.

"The st- . . . the paper-"

"Oh, the label," I guessed. But I was wrong.

"The paper tàpe," he said. I had stuck strips of gummed paper around it, and Nigel had been given some of the pieces to stick on by himself.

Nigel's mother came in.

She had a large sheet of paper in her hand, and a pencil, with which she proceeded to draw an outline of Nigel's foot, explaining that she was going to get a pair of sandals made for him. Nigel recalled the incident later.

"Mummy draw round your fôot," he said.

"Yes, Mummy drew round your foot."

"She didn't draw a lĭon."

"No, she didn't draw a lion."

"She drew a lìne."

"Yes, she drew a line."

"A ràilway line."

"Oh, I didn't know it was a railway line!"

"And then you got off the letter and sat on Daddy's knèe." The piece of paper now had marks on it, so it had become a *letter*.

2.2 Two years, three months

Nigel was sticking pictures in his scrapbook. He could now put the gum on by himself, turn the picture over, and stick it where he wanted it. He had learnt to put the gum on the **back** of the picture; this was difficult, because there was often a picture there too and you had to decide which picture you wanted to be seen and then turn it over, without letting yourself be distracted by the one on the back. He called this the 'second side', as it was like turning over a gramophone record.

"You did put the gum on the sècond side," he said proudly, "but not on the ùnderground train picture."

"That's very good," I said.

"You can put the gum on the bàck of the fast electric underground train pícture," he explained, "but not on the bàck of the fast electric underground train picture." In other words, you can turn it over once to put the gum on, but you have to be careful not to turn it over again.

Another time, we came to a picture of a train that had been stuck in upside down. I pointed to it and looked at Nigel inquiringly.

"Did you stick it wrong way up because it doesn't stick that wáy," he said.

"You stuck it wrong way up because it doesn't stick that wáy."

I looked puzzled.

"No the tràin is not wrong way úp," he explained. "It's the pìcture that's wrong way up. The picture won't fall off the scrăpbook."

In other words: it looks as if the train is going to fall off the rails. But it won't, because the train is really the right way up. The picture is the wrong way up. But being the wrong way up doesn't make the picture fall off the scrapbook. And I stuck it the wrong way up because there wasn't room for it to go in right way up.

2.3 One year, eleven months

"Daddy coming to look at the train has gòne," said Nigel. "It already gone whòosh."

I came to look. It was the picture in his "Trains" book, showing a train which had just sped through a station without stopping. 'Whoosh' (pronounced "whoo'") was the noise the train made as it rushed past when you were standing on the station platform – this being one of Nigel's favourite pastimes.

"Thăt train alrèady gone whoosh," Nigel explained. "Thāt train has alrèady gone whoosh."

A week later, we were in a train, on our way to visit friends for the day.

"There no bùmblebee in thís train," said Nigel. "There was a bumblebee in the wĕt train." This was a reference to a train journey he had made three months previously; it had been raining, and a bee had got inside the train where he was sitting.

Nigel spent the time looking out of the window and talking about what he saw.

"This not an ùnderground train," he said. "Ooh there's a bi-i-ig cràne! There's anòther railway line thére; we're not going on thăt railway line. It not líon," he corrected himself with a growl. "It lĭne ... Fast weel ('diesel') tràin. It gòing nów. But it not say whòosh ... but ... but it not say whòosh ... whòosh ... whòosh," he repeated many times over, thoughtfully to himself.

He was puzzling over a problem. If you were standing on the platform, and the train rushed past you, it made a tremendous noise. Why was it that, when you were inside the train, it didn't make the same noise?

2.4 One year, nine months

We had finished a meal, and were sitting talking about nothing in particular. Nigel was in his high chair.

"eat chúffa," he said.

"You can't eat trains!" I said.

"can't eat blue chùffa"

"No, you can't eat the blue train."

"can't eat rèd chuffa"

"No, you can't eat the red train."

Nigel looked at the little wooden man from his cart. "can't eat màn," he said.

"No, you can't eat the man."

Nigel looked at his book. "can't eat that bòok"

"No, you can't eat that book. You can't eat any book!"

Nigel looked at Pauline. "can't eat Pàuline book"

"No, you can't eat Pauline's book."

Nigel looked thoughtfully at Pauline's hair. "Pauline got èar," he said.

"Yes," I said, moving Pauline's hair aside. "Pauline's got an ear, though you can't usually see it."

Nigel touched his wooden Pinocchio doll. "'nocchio got funny nòse," he said.

"Yes, Pinocchio's got a funny nose, like a —"

"càrrot," Nigel finished off for me.

"Yes, like a carrot."

Some days earlier, Pinocchio's foot had come off, and I had had to mend him. Nigel recalled the incident.

"scrèwdriver," he said. "mend 'nocchio fŏot"

2.5 One year, six months

Nigel was waiting for his lunch. He picked up his fork, and tried the prongs on the palm of his hand. "oôh," he said in a low, breathy voice. It meant 'ooh, it's sharp'.

He dropped the fork on the table. "ōo" It was a short, high-pitched squeak.

"Ooh, dropped it," I said. "Is it sharp?"

Anna came in, with lunch.

"Do you know what it is?" said Anna. "You're having fish."

"lù'," said Nigel. "lù"

"Lunch, yes," said Anna. "It's fish."

"vò" ('fish')

Nigel set himself to eating his lunch. Some fish fell off the fork.

"ōo" It was another very high-pitched squeak.

"Ooh you lost a big bit then," said Anna, "Where did it go?"

"bâiba" Nigel looked up at Anna, inviting her to share a memory. "âiba ... bâiba," he said.

"Yes, all the trains went away, and you said 'byebye,' didn't you?" she said.

"bâiba," said Nigel sadly, waving his hand.

He finished off his lunch. "nōumò ... nōumò"

"Where has it all gone?" Anna asked him.

Nigel turned his attention to the salt. "adīdà," he asked.

"That's salt," said Anna. "Salt and pepper."

"ùh ... ùh" ('I want it')

Anna passed it to him. "That's salt."

Nigel poked the hole in the top with his finger. "lôu! lôu!" ('a hole!')

"Yes, it has a hole in it," she said.

"adīdà"

"It's salt."

"lò"

"Salt."

"lò"

2.6 One year, three months

Nigel was in his high chair; his mother gave him a piece of toast.
"There you are, Bootie," she said. "Toast."
"dòu," said Nigel, picking it up. "dòu"
He looked over at my piece. "dòu," he said again.
"Yes, I've got a piece of toast as well."
Nigel finished his piece.
"dòu," he said firmly.
"Do you want some more?"
"ñ̄" It was a short, very high-pitched squeak, with lips spread, meaning 'yes I do' or 'yes do', in answer to an offer of goods or services.

His mother started to butter another finger of toast. Nigel watched her with growing impatience.
"ùh ... ùh ... mǹg!" ('I want it, I want it. Give it to me!')
"All right, it's coming! You want some butter on it, don't you? See? That's butter."
"bàta"

There was a plop and a miaow, and the neighbour's cat appeared at Nigel's side. She was a regular visitor.
"abâe ... abâe"

It was a greeting to the cat. Apart from Anna, his mother and me, the cat was the one other being with whom Nigel exchanged meanings. They spoke the same kind of language.

2.7 Twelve months

Nigel and I were looking at his book together.
Nigel took hold of my finger, and pressed it lightly against one of the pictures. "èya," he said.

The meaning was clear: 'you say its name'. "It's a ball," I said.
"è – e – eh" Nigel gave his long-drawn-out sigh, meaning 'yes, that's what I wanted you to do.' He was pleased that his meaning had been successful, and he repeated the procedure throughout the book.

Later he was looking at it all by himself.
"dò ... èya ... vèu"

This was Nigel's first complex utterance, and the only one for many months to come. But it made excellent sense. He had picked up the picture book, opened it at the ball page, and pointed at the picture. It was just as if he had said, in so many words, 'Look, a picture! What is it? A ball!'

2.8 Ten and a half months

Nigel was sitting on my knee. On the table in front of us was a fruit bowl with an orange in it. Nigel struggled to reach it.

"nà nà nà nà," he said. It meant 'I want it', 'give it to me'.

I gave him the orange. He made it roll on the table; it fell off.

"nà nà nà nà," he said again.

When the game was over, he got down, crawled away and disappeared along the passage, going boomp-boomp-boomp as he went. Then silence. His mother began to wonder where he was.

"Nigel!" she called.

"è – e – eh" It was his special response to a call: 'Here I am'.

"Where is he?" said his mother. "Nigel!"

She went to look for him. He was standing, precariously, by the divan, looking at his picture cards that were hanging on the wall.

"dòh," he said as she came in. It meant 'hullo – shall we look at these pictures together?' "dòh ... dòh"

"Are you looking at your pictures?" his mother asked him.

"dòh ... dòh"

2.9 Nine months

Nigel had just learnt to sit up on his own, and was now ready to start meaning in earnest.

He had a little floppy rabbit; I was holding it on my hand and stroking it, then making it jump in the air. When I stopped, Nigel put out his hand, and touched the rabbit, firmly but without pushing it. It was a gesture which meant 'go on, do that again' – the same meaning that he was later to express vocally as "ùh".

He had two other gestures. If he meant that he wanted something, he would grasp it firmly in his fist, without pulling it towards him, and then let go. If he meant he did not want it, he would touch it very lightly and momentarily with the tip of his finger.

These gestures were true acts of meaning. Nigel was not acting directly on the objects; he was addressing the other person, enjoining him to act.

In addition to the three meanings conveyed by gesture, Nigel had two other meanings which he expressed vocally. The two expressions were almost the same: one was "èu", the other, slightly higher pitched at its starting point, was "èu". The first meant 'let's be together', and was used in conversation: "Nigel!" – "èu" – "*There's* a woozy woozy woozy" – "èu", and so on ad lib. The other meant 'look – a commotion', and was the successor to " ´ ", the tiny high-pitched squeak. Nigel used it to express interest in his surroundings, especially that part of the surroundings that went into violent movement, like a flock of birds taking off.

This was the opening scene of Nigel's language.

2.10 Six months

We were in the park. Nigel was in his pram, and was lying in his usual posture, on his tummy.

Some pigeons scattered noisily as we went by. Nigel lifted his head. " ´ ", he said, making a tiny squeak on a very high note. It meant 'what's that?' 'what's happening?'

"Those are birds," we told him. "Big birds; pigeons. They flew away."

This was Nigel's first act of meaning, the first time he had used a symbolic expression to communicate with someone. It was a soft high-pitched squeak with what sounded like a note of query in it.

Nigel said this frequently during the next three or four weeks, always with the same meaning. Then he abandoned it. It was as if he had established the principle that he could start the conversation and be responded to. For the moment he was satisfied with that.

2.11 Two months

Nigel greeted me when I came home from work. He gave a long gurgling account of the day's event, always in a cheerful tone, his face breaking into huge smiles. Then he listened while I told him my news.

One day I came into the flat and heard him cooing away with his mother as usual. But as soon as he saw me, his whole expression changed. His face frowned, his tone became mournful, and he was almost starting to cry.

"What happened today?" I asked his mother.

"He had his first injections," she said.

2.12 Twelve days

Nigel had just come home from the hospital, and seemed pleased at the move. But one day he was crying miserably, and his mother was in distress.

The time came to bath him. As she undressed him she noticed a nasty-looking boil in the crook of his elbow.

She called to me. "Look at this," she said.

As soon as she drew attention to it, Nigel stopped crying. The boil must have gone on hurting; it had had nothing done to it. But his mother had found what was wrong, and Nigel didn't cry any more.

3 The social construction of language, and of reality

3.1 The subjective angle: a summary

After a short preview at five months, Nigel's acts of meaning began in earnest at eight months; and by ten and a half months his conversational powers were organized into a system of meaning potential that we have referred to as a protolanguage. Unlike adult language, which is a three-level system (meaning, wording, sound), the protolanguage is a two-level system (meaning, sound), the elements of which are content–expression pairs, corresponding to the classical Saussurean notion of the "sign". These elements have meaning within a small range of semiotic functions; initially we can identify four: an instrumental, a regulatory, an interactional and a personal. These are distinct in two respects: (1) in orientation, towards persons or objects, and (2) in the type of mediation that is involved. In the instrumental function ('I want'), the child is acting on objects through the mediation of other persons; in the regulatory ('do as I say'), the child is acting directly on other persons, in the interactional ('me and you'), the child is interacting with other persons, but through the mediation of shared attention to objects; and in the personal ('here I come'), the child is becoming a self through active attention to, or rejection of, his environment.

From 8 to 17 months, that is, throughout what is referred to as Phase I, Nigel expanded his protolanguage, enlarging his conversational powers until he had a meaning potential of some 50 elements; they were still largely within the same four functions, though a fifth one had been added. This was the imaginative ('let's pretend') function, in which meaning is a mode of play. But up to this point the language had remained a two-level coding system; and, as such, it was subject to certain constraints. The "signs" of such a system are elementary particles, which can be strung together like beads but cannot be dispersed and recombined. Hence Nigel could never mean two things at once.

For this a three-level system is needed, one with an abstract level of **wording** intervening between the meanings and the sounds. This intermediate level (a lexicogrammar, in linguistic terms) is what makes it possible to name, and so to separate meaning as observation of reality from meaning as intrusion into reality. In a two-level system, such as Nigel's protolanguage, it is impossible to name something independently of acting on it. Once given a lexicogrammar, naming something and acting on it become distinct symbolic acts.

Why should Nigel want to separate these two modes of meaning? Because only in this way can conversation evolve along the lines of narrative and dialogue. Narrative and dialogue are the two cornerstones of conversation, prerequisites to the effective functioning of language in the construction of reality.

By the term **narrative** we understand the ability to make meanings context-free: to bring within the scope of conversation things that lie outside the perceptual field – processes in time past and future, states of consciousness, abstract entities, and other non-deictic aspects of subjective reality. To mean '(I see) sticks and stones' is not necessarily a narrative act; it need not imply naming, nor does it require a lexicogrammar in the system. But to mean 'I saw sticks and stones' is a narrative act, one that cannot be performed with a grammarless language; not because it requires grammatical structure (that comes later), but because it requires that the thing-name 'stick' is coded separately from any meaning such as 'I want' or 'I like'. From the moment the child has introduced this intermediate level of coding, his conversation becomes independent of the context of situation. It took Nigel about three weeks (at 17 months) to move from '(I see) sticks and stones' to 'I saw sticks and stones'; and about another three weeks after that to get to 'I will see sticks and stones' (for example, in answer to "Nigel we're going out for a walk"). The form of the utterance did not change – it was simply "stick, stone" in each case – but it now had a different significance as an act of meaning.

By the term **dialogue** we understand conversation of a particular kind, in which the interactants not only exchange meanings but also engage in dynamic role-play, each in turn both adopting a role for himself and assigning a role, or rather a role choice, to the other. Nigel made the discovery that the symbolic system he was constructing for himself as a means of **realizing** a world of meaning simultaneously **created** a world of meaning of its own, a semiotic of social roles and social acts. Since the system creates information, it can be used to exchange this information (that is, to ask and to tell) as well as to exchange goods-and-services in the way the protolanguage does. This in turn means that conversation becomes not merely a symbolic reflection of the sharing of experience but an actual alternative to it. Up to this point, when Nigel's mother suggested he should "tell Daddy what happened" it had made no sense to him. He could tell Mummy, because she had shared the experience, but how could he tell Daddy, when Daddy hadn't been there? Now he adds an ***informative*** function to his functional repertory – and at once becomes its prisoner for life.

Like other major forward leaps in development, this too had had its preview. It was at 15 months that Nigel took his first steps in grammar, when he came to separate the **name-choice** of the three people he conversed with from the **act-choice** of seeking versus finding. The former he expressed by articulation, the latter by intonation. In this way he was able to combine the two systems, so that each name, *ama* ('mummy'), *dada*, *anna*, could be used with either sense, 'where are you? I want you' (mid level + high level) or 'hullo! there you are!' (high falling + mid level). But it is in Phase II, the transition to the adult language, that this distinction between naming and acting becomes his primary semiotic strategy. Naming, as we have seen, is too narrow a concept here, if it is taken to mean merely the creation of a lexicosemantic taxonomy; we are talking about the whole ideational aspect of meaning, of which the assignment of thing-names is only a part. What Nigel did was to generalize, from his Phase I functional repertory, a simple opposition between conversation as a means of learning (a mathetic mode as we called it) and conversation as a means of doing (a pragmatic mode). So fundamental is this opposition to Nigel's construction of reality that at 19 months he took the step of encoding it systematically in prosodic form: from then on, all pragmatic acts of meaning – all utterances of a dialoguic nature, demanding a response – were performed with a rising tone, and all mathetic acts – those of a narrative kind, demanding no response – were performed with a falling tone. In this way Nigel made explicit the fundamental distinction between meaning as reflection and meaning as action, a distinction that lies at the heart of the adult semantic system.

Nigel maintained this opposition intact for about six months; it was the major strategy whereby the concrete functions of his protolanguage were to evolve into the abstract functional components which are the basis of the adult semantic. At the same time, it was more than a strategy of transition; it was itself a form of the schematization of reality. By making this distinction, Nigel represented reality to himself as existing on two planes: as material to be quarried, and as terrain to be explored. Not only objects but also persons figure in this dual role; through dialogue, one person "acts on" the other, and in fact it is only through the intermediary of a person that an act of meaning can be directed onto an object, since objects are not, in principle, affected by symbolic acts.

But from the moment of its inception, Nigel's bimodal strategy, in which each act of meaning is either pragmatic or mathetic, is already breaking down. As soon as the language in which he converses has a lexicogrammar, every utterance in it is inevitably both pragmatic and mathetic at the same time. The cost of being able to mean two things at once is that it becomes impossible not to, except in very limited ways. The intonation signals what continues to be the dominant mode: response demanded (rising tone), or response not demanded (falling tone). But as Nigel moves through Phase II, the other mode becomes more and more prominent as a submotif; until by about 23 months all acts of meaning are in equal measure both pragmatic and mathetic. But in the process, these concepts have changed once again. The original functions first become macrofunctions and then metafunctions

The pragmatic component is now, more often than not, a demand for a verbal response: giving and requesting goods-and-services has been superseded, as the favourite act of meaning, by giving and requesting information. Other elements have been added, including some that would subsequently disappear, such as the very useful distinction Nigel makes, from around 21 months, between telling listeners something he knows they already know and telling them something he knows they do not know. At this point the pragmatic function has evolved into the full interpersonal (sometimes called "socioexpressive") component in the adult semantic system; while the mathetic, meaning as a way of learning, has evolved into the ideational component. Every one of Nigel's conversational acts is now simultaneously both a reflection on and an action on reality.

But Nigel has never lost the essential links between meaning and social context that are what enabled him to make the transition from his own protolanguage to a mother tongue in the first place. Interpersonal meanings – those expressed in the grammar as mood, modality, person, key, and the like – reflect the role relationships in the communication process. Ideational meanings – expressed in transitivity, time and place, lexical taxonomies, and so on – reflect the goings-on around, the phenomenal world of processes and their participants and attendant circumstances.

This is not to say that an act of meaning typically relates directly to its immediate social context; most of them do not. We have already noted that, from the beginning of Phase II, thanks to the introduction of a lexicogrammar, Nigel's conversation has been effectively context-free, not constrained by the situation of speaking. But the meaning potential underlying his acts of meaning has its ultimate frame of reference in Nigel's experience, including, of course, his experience of his own states of consciousness; and it is a fundamental characteristic of acts of meaning that they create their own context out of this past experience. More particularly, what underlies the conversational process is not just the individual's experience of things; it is things as phenomena of intersubjective reality, as bearers of social meaning and social value. Nor is it just the face-to-face interaction of the participants in the dialogue; it is their entire function in the child's social system. Nigel has, after all, been busying himself with all this from birth. The social context of an act of meaning is far more than is made manifest in the sights and sounds around.

3.2 The intersubjective angle

A child's construction of language is at once both a part of and a means of his construction of reality; and it is natural to Western thinking to view both these processes largely from the standpoint of the individual. We tend implicitly to define the aim of the investigation as that of explaining what happens to a child in his development from infancy to maturity.

This preoccupation is embodied in and reinforced by prevailing metaphors such as "language acquisition" and "primary socialization". The former suggests that a child takes possession of a new commodity, that of language; and the latter that he is transformed into a new state, that of being social. In either case he is seen as an individual serving as the locus of external processes; and while we should not make too much of the metaphors themselves, they do perhaps reflect a tendency to think of a child as acquiring language and the rest of reality from somewhere "out there" – as if he was a pre-existing individual who, by a process of learning the rules, achieves conformity with a pre-existing scheme.

Sociolinguistic theorists of language development have attempted to place the developing child in a social context; they have removed the "nativist versus environmentalist" controversy from the agenda and offered instead some version of an "interactionist" approach. A number of investigators have suggested an interpretation in terms of the notion of communicative competence. This leads to what is essentially a socialization model of language development, according to which the child has to master, in addition to the "rules" of language, a set of socially accepted norms of language use. It is open to the objection that learning to mean cannot be reduced to a matter of learning how to behave properly in the contexts in which meanings are exchanged. A more recent interpretation is one based on the notion of the speech act, the speech act being put forward as the structural unit which a child acquires as the simultaneous representation of his conceptual, communicative, and grammatical skills (Dore 1974, 1976). But the speech act is a subjective, not an intersubjective, construct; it is supposed to take account of the fact that people talk to each other, but it represents this fact in terms of the knowledge, the belief structures, and the behaviour patterns of the individual. The consequence of this is that the theory fails to account for the dynamics of dialogue, the ongoing exchange of speech roles through which conversation becomes a reality-generating process.

I think we need to interpret language development more in terms of a conception of social or intersubjective creativity. Learning to mean is a process of creation, whereby a child constructs, in interaction with those around, a semiotic potential that gives access to the edifice of meanings that constitute social reality.

There is ample evidence that children engage in communicative interaction from birth. A newborn infant's orientation towards persons is quite distinct from his orientation towards the objects in his environment; he is aware of being addressed, and can respond. He exchanges attention with the persons who are the "others" in his social system (Bruner 1975; France 1975; Trevarthen 1974b).

In these intersubjective processes lie the foundations of the construction of reality. Reality is created through the exchange of meanings — in other words, through conversation. The exchange of attention which begins at birth already has some of the features of conversation; it has been described by Bateson (1975) as "protoconversation".

But protoconversation does not yet involve an exchange of meanings. If we adopt the distinction made previously in this chapter between an "act of meaning" and other communicative acts, then conversation proper is an exchange of acts of meaning — or, simply, an exchange of meanings; whereas protoconversation consists of communicative exchanges which do not yet take the form of acts of meaning.

MEANING AND THE CONSTRUCTION OF REALITY

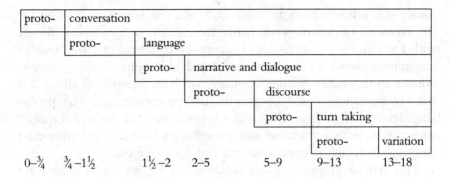

Figure 3 The development of powers of conversation
0–¾ communicative acts (protoconversation), prespeech;
¾–1½, acts of meaning (functional protolanguage);
1½–2, transition to language, macrofunctions mathetic/pragmatic;
2–5, narrative and dialogue, elementary lexicogrammar;
5–9, discourse, intermediate lexicogrammar;
9–13, turn taking, advanced lexicogrammar;
13(–18), variation, register and social dialect.

Protoconversation begins at birth; conversation begins some months later. It begins, in fact, with the beginning of the protolanguage.

At this point it may be helpful to offer a tentative schematic account of the development of a child's powers of conversation (see Figure 3).

The central concept here is that of intersubjectivity (Trevarthen 1974a). The construction of reality depends on conversation – on the exchange of meanings. But the foundations are laid in the protoconversational period when the child is already engaging in intersubjective acts. A child is not born endowed with language. But he is born with the ability to recognize and respond to address; and to communicate with someone who is communicating with him. He even engages, from the age of a few weeks, in what Trevarthen calls "prespeech": the manipulation of the expressive resources that will be put to use in the protolanguage, and eventually in language itself. (It is important to distinguish between prespeech and protolanguage. Prespeech is expression only, whereas protolanguage is expression and content. There is no semantic component in prespeech. But it is significant that it typically accompanies communicative acts of this protoconversational kind.)

Patterns of intersubjective activity are thus well established by the time the child takes the crucial step of starting to mean. An act of meaning is inherently an intersubjective act, one which makes possible the exchange of meanings and hence the construction of reality. Berger and Luckmann (1966) speak in very clear terms of "the reality-generating power of conversation"; and although, as they remark, conversation usually implies language, we have stressed all along that true conversation already begins in the protolanguage. The protolanguage – if Nigel is at all typical – is not organized the way the adult language is, with a grammar and a vocabulary; but it is nevertheless a language in which conversation can and does take place.

The crucial property of conversation in Berger and Luckmann's account is that it is casual. It does not consist of explanations. Nobody instructs the child in the mysteries of things; he would not understand them if they did. Conversation consists of ongoing contextualized chatter. Out of this a child builds an order of things and events, including his own part in them and attitudes towards them.

What makes it possible for the child to do this is the relation of an act of meaning to its context (discussed on pages 121–3). **How** he does it is a different matter. Typically, he organizes his conversation around a limited number of generalized semantic strategies, ways of meaning that are the ontogenetic analogue to, and anticipation of, the speech functions and rhetorical modes of the adult language. Here is a small example from 23 months:

> Nigel's mother and I were planning a visit to the aquarium. Nigel did not know what an aquarium was, but he heard us discussing it.
> "We're not going to see a rào ['lion']," he said to himself. "Vòpa ['fishes']. There will be some wàter."
> In other words, it was not a zoo, but it was something of the same kind, with fishes (and water for them to live in) instead of lions.

The principle of contrast – of seeing things as "same but different" – is a favourite strategy for the representation of experience at this stage. These strategies are not the same as those of an adult, nor can they be understood as unsuccessful approximations to those that an adult employs. A child uses language in different ways; not because he is trying to do what an adult does and failing, but because he is a different person engaged in a different set of tasks.

It is tempting to think of a child's construction of reality as simply his construction of a model of the outside world: of things and their properties, and how they relate and interact. This is, certainly, one important aspect of what he is doing. But it is not the whole story. The child is constructing a social semiotic, a reality in which things are because people are, and people construe them in certain ways. To say that people "construe" things means that they act on them, value them, and interpret them; and it is this construction that is shared through intersubjective acts of meaning. When the child sees things interact, typically he is seeing how people act on them; when he apprehends their significance, typically he is finding out how people value them; and when he builds them into his meaning potential, typically he is learning how people interpret them. He is not taking over a meaning potential, or a reality, that is ready-made for him "out there"; on the contrary, as the interpretation of Nigel's protolanguage makes clear, a child is **creating** meanings, not imitating those he finds around him. But this process of creation is an interactive process, in which the meanings are created in the course of being exchanged between the child and the significant others. The exchange takes place in the context of, and in interpenetration with, the reality that is "out there"; but what is "out there" is a social construct — not a pile of sticks and stones, but a house.

As was said earlier, an act of meaning is a social act, not only in the simple sense that it is a form of interaction between people each of whom is producing meanings of his own and tracking those of others, but also in the deeper sense that the meaning potential from which these meanings derive is itself a social construct; and so is the reality beyond it. The meanings that are embodied in conversation in the protolanguage are, obviously, not very sophisticated; but they are already such that we can see them as the realization of some higher-order semiotic — of a social reality, in fact. Nigel's reality is a social reality and its construction is a social process. It is shared between Nigel and those with whom he exchanges meanings: the significant others, who are significant precisely for this reason, that they are the ones with whom meanings are exchanged.

One of the most remarkable features of the interaction that takes place between a child and his mother — or anyone else with whom the child regularly exchanges meanings — is the extent to which the mother (or other person) knows at each point in time what the child will and what he will not understand. This can be seen (or rather heard) not only in the way in which the mother converses with the child, but also in the way in which she tells him stories and modifies or explains for him anything she is reading aloud. (And we notice it with a shock when we come across someone we feel should have this knowledge and find they have not. One major problem for a child who is cared for in an institution is the lack of anyone who shares his language and his reality.) The phenomenon is all the more astonishing when one takes account of the fact that what the child understands is changing day by day. The mother keeps pace with this development to such an exact degree that it is not unreasonable to say that she is simultaneously building up the same language and the same reality. (I do not mean that she imitates the child's sounds. On the contrary, imitating the sounds a child makes and repeating them back to him nearly always in my experience covers up a failure to track his language adequately; it is an attempt to "con" him into thinking that one is with him in an exchange of meanings. He is never deceived, and usually rejects the attempt as insulting.) Essentially the mother is going through the processes of mental development all over again, but this time in the child's persona; under impetus from the child, the mother is creating a world of meaning along with him. It is for this reason that we call the process an *intersubjective* one.

If one was to attempt to characterize language development in the most general terms, it would be as the process of the intersubjective creation of meanings, and hence of a meaning potential that is a mode of the representation of reality. A child constructs, in interaction with others, a reality that has two parts to it, since it includes within itself a symbolic system – language – through which the rest is mediated. The two parts, language and non-language, are essentially continuous, each influencing and modifying the other. Hence the symbolic system through which reality is mediated is not only a part of reality, but is also, to a certain extent, a determinant of the other part.

The schemata illustrated in Figures 1 and 2 represent reality as apprehended through our understanding of Nigel's protolanguage. There is a direct continuity between the infant's intersubjective experiences of mutual address, shared attention and protoconversation, on the one hand, and the social construction of reality through the natural rhetoric and natural logic of conversation on the other. In Figure 1 we know, from Nigel's ability to mean in the various modes at the outset of the protolanguage, that his subjective reality must contain certain conceptual discontinuities: at the very least, (1) reality distinguished into "out there" (non-self) and "not out there" (self); (2) non-self distinguished into persons and objects; and (3) persons distinguished into two roles, (i) for interaction and (ii) for control. The reality is an intersubjective reality, not only constructed through intersubjective acts of meaning (conversation) but also held in common with the significant others. It is a joint construction; otherwise it could

MEANING AND THE CONSTRUCTION OF REALITY

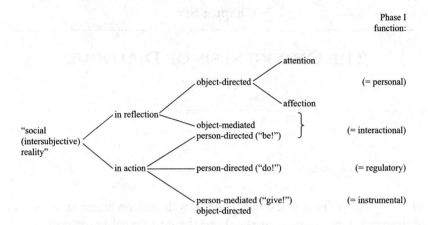

Figure 4 Nigel at nine to ten and a half months (another interpretation)

not get built. The self thus lies, in Meadian fashion, at the intersection of various dimensions of social process – including, critically, processes of a symbolic or **sociosemiotic** kind.

If we then look back at our representation of Nigel's model of reality at ten months, we find in it the same preoccupation with the child as individual that was referred to at the beginning of this section. Reinterpreting in the light of what turned out to be Nigel's primary transition strategy as he moved from protolanguage to language and began to construct an adult-like semantic system, we might arrive at something more like Figure 4. This schema, suggesting an alternative interpretation of Nigel's meaning potential at ten months in terms of the ordering of persons and objects, brings out more clearly the continuity of his transition to the adult language (see Figure 2).

I have tried to outline the nature of the reality that is shared between a child and those with whom he exchanges meanings, with particular attention to the period between nine months and two years. The facts have been taken from the study of Nigel's language, and the results of this study have been used in an interpretation of the language development process. The organizing concept is that of shared meanings. At any one moment, the child has a meaning potential, a semantic system that is shared between himself and the significant others. It has been developed by an ongoing process in which the others first track the child by participating in his acts of meaning, and then reinforce, extend and modify the child's meaning system through the effects of their own responsive acts.

Chapter Six

THE ONTOGENESIS OF DIALOGUE
(1979)

This is a study of how one child, Nigel, developed the linguistic resources of dialogue. First, some remarks about the conceptual framework:

A. **Dialogue** is interpreted as the exchange of meaning through the adoption and assignment of speech roles. A speaker may, for example, take on the initiating role of 'I request information'; in so doing, he assigns to the hearer a responding role that he is to adopt by becoming speaker in his turn, namely 'I give the information requested'. The social–contextual system underlying these roles in the adult language is one of two modes, giving and demanding, with each of two semiotic commodities, goods-and-services and information. These define the four semantic speech functions of:

offer	(giving:	goods-and-services)
command	(demanding:	goods-and-services)
statement	(giving:	information)
question	(demanding:	information)

This is an idealized construct to which we relate the facts of language, and language development, as we find them.

B. The **linguistic system** is interpreted as a resource for meaning, or **meaning potential**, which may be represented in the form of networks of options. The development of dialogue is the gradual creation by a child of a fundamental aspect of his meaning potential, together with the structural, lexical and phonological resources through which the options in meaning are realized.

C. **Language development** is interpreted neither as the working out of

---

First published in *Proceedings of the Twelfth International Congress of Linguistics*, edited by Wolfgang U. Dressler. Innsbruck: Innsbrucker Beiträge zur Sprachwissenschaft, 1979, pp. 539–44.

an innate grammar nor as the imitation of a set of external stimuli. Both these views are rejected here as individualist; they treat the child as an island, an individual *in vacuo*, and language as some ready-made 'thing' which the child has to 'acquire'. The view I take is that of language development as a process of intersubjective creation, whereby a child, in interaction with significant others – mother, family, peer group, teachers – creates in himself the systems of meanings, wordings and expressions that we call language.

What follows is a report of Nigel's progress towards dialogue.

1. In the first few months of life Nigel distinguished two kinds of (pre-linguistic) act: (a) exchanging attention with a person – responding to his mother's address, and addressing her in turn; (b) acting on an object – reaching out to hit a ball on a string, for example. At around the age of six months he took an important new step, that of combining these two modes into a single complex act, acting on an object not directly but by means of addressing a person. By addressing his mother he could get **her** to act on the object (give it to him, throw it up in the air for him, etc.). This new kind of act is a symbolic act, one where the act itself does not constitute the realization of the intent. We shall refer to it as an ***act of meaning***.

2. At eight months Nigel had developed a system of five distinct acts of meaning. Like all acts of meaning, they were addressed to a person, typically his mother; but they differed in orientation, two being instrumental and the others respectively regulatory, interactional and personal. They also differed in the symbolic channel: three were expressed gesturally, the other two vocally. The gestures were iconic; the creation of iconic signs, signs which stand in a non-arbitrary relation to their meaning, is a significant transition point in a child's development of symbolic resources. The elements of Nigel's first linguistic system were as follows:

1	Instrumental, positive 'I want that':	*grasp* object *firmly, and momentarily,* then let go.
2	Instrumental, negative 'I don't …:	*touch* object *lightly, and momentarily,* then let go.
3	Regulatory 'do that (again)':	*touch* object *firmly, steadily.*
4	Interactional 'let's be together':	half-close, front-rounded vowel, *low* falling.
5	Personal 'look, that's interesting':	half-close, front-rounded vowel, *high* falling.

Note that all except the last (which was not addressed anywhere) were addressed to persons; even when the orientation was towards an object (for example, 'you throw that rabbit up in the air for me!'), and the realization involved touching the object, Nigel was looking at the person to whom the act of meaning was addressed.

3. Between nine and ten and a half months Nigel created a **protolanguage** based on these four functions, instrumental, regulatory, interactional and personal ('I want that', 'do that', 'let's be together', and 'I like that' or 'I'm curious about that'); in the course of this process, he abandoned gestures, and created vocal realizations for all the meanings in the system. It is important to stress that none of these meanings has to do with exchange of information; indeed it will be more than another year before Nigel has any concept of information, that is, of telling somebody something they don't know. All the elements in Nigel's protolanguage are language in the service of other functions, functions that can be conceptualized in non-linguistic terms. To express this another way, the intentions that Nigel is carrying out through his protolanguage are intentions that exist independently of the acts of meaning that are used to achieve them. Wanting things, getting people to do things, being 'together' with people, and being pleased or curious about things are all non-linguistic acts or states which Nigel chooses to encode in language. They do embody a distinction of emphasis which turns out later to be fundamental to the move into the mother tongue: the distinction between the more active modes (instrumental and regulatory) and the more reflective modes (interactional and personal). Note that this distinction was already implicit in Nigel's very earliest system at 0;8, where the active meanings were expressed gesturally and the reflective ones vocally.

4. We now come to the difficult point where we have to identify those elements of the system which lead on to the development of dialogue, and to track the steps whereby Nigel built up the conceptual framework of dialogue with which the adult language operates. He is still at this stage constructing his own protolanguage, in interaction with those around him; it is not until nearly 18 months that he abandons his "child tongue" and opts in favour of a mother tongue instead. The expressions he uses in the protolanguage are vocalizations like [ɛ̀ː] and [ˀdɔ̀] and [ʔɜ̀] and [ædædædæd œ̀]. In terms of our original formulation of dialogue as an exchange of meanings there are two aspects of dialogue that need to be accounted for: (i) the mode of exchange – giving or demanding, and also initiating or responding; (ii)

the kind of meaning that is being exchanged – goods-and-services or information. We will follow these through separately, bearing in mind, however, that the processes referred to are going on simultaneously all the time.

4.1. At 0.9, as we saw, Nigel can initiate acts of meaning in four distinct functions. He can respond in just one of these, the interactional function, where he has not only [ˀdɔ̀] (short, high, glottalized and minimum breath) 'nice to see you, hullo – let's look at this!' but also [ɛ::] (long, low and maximum breath) which means 'yes, here I am!', responding to a call 'Nigel!' – [ɛ̀::]. His other meanings are initiating only. By 12 months he is able to respond also in the more active modes: that is, not only can he initiate requests and commands, for example, [nànànànà] 'I want that', [à] or [ʔɜ̌] (high) 'do that!', he can also respond to offers, for example, 'do you want ...?' – [yī] or [â] 'yes I do', with [yī] for an object present, [â] for an object or service mentioned; 'shall I ...?' – [ʔɜ̀] (low, usually repeated) 'yes, do!' and also (his first vocalized negative) [àâà] 'no, don't!'. That is to say, Nigel can respond where the response has the same function as an utterance that he could himself initiate. Up to this time he has had, with very minor exceptions, only generalized meanings: 'I want (that object there, or that service you've just mentioned)'. By 1.4 he is tending to differentiate the objects, services and persons required, for example, [dòᵁba] 'I want some toast'. The system is still, however, of the same protolinguistic kind: [dòᵁba] has what is from the adult point of view a synthetic meaning of 'I want some toast' – it is not yet a word (lexical item) *toast*.

What kind of responses is he himself demanding? Not, of course, verbal responses of a 'question–answer' kind. The person addressed is expected either to act (delivering the goods-and-services, or performing in the game) or to interact, sharing an experience or simply exchanging attention. In other words, the roles that Nigel assigns are those of giving, doing and being – but the assignment is a one-step process: there is not yet a dynamic **exchange** of roles as in true dialogue.

Between 1;4 and 1;7 the system changes its character. It is no longer protolanguage, and by 1½ years Nigel is well launched on the path of transition into the mother tongue. The more active functions have evolved into a generalized pragmatic **macrofunction**, encoded fully systematically by means of a rising tone, which means, always and unambiguously, 'somebody do something!': in other words it demands a response. At first what is demanded is a non-verbal response, in one or other of the same three modes, deriving from the protolinguistic functions, of 'give', 'do' and 'be'. The first, 'give!', is still a request for goods-and-services, for example, *more bréad* [mɔbɹέ] 'I want some more bread', *chuffa 'túck* 'my train's stuck – get it out for me!'. The second, 'do!', now covers the meanings (i) 'I want you to ...', (ii) 'I want us to ..., that is, let's ...' and (iii) 'I want me to ..., that is, I want to be allowed to ..., can I ...?' – not always distinct, of course; for example, (i) *that sóng*, 'sing that song (you were just singing)', *high wáll* 'let me jump off here – and you catch me!'; (ii) *play ráo* 'let's play at lions', *go Abbeywood on tráin* 'let's go to Abbeywood on the train'; (iii) *hit flóor* 'I'm going to hit the floor with the hammer, can I?' and *make cross tíckmatick ... in dada róom* 'I want to be allowed to make a cross on the typewriter in daddy's room'. This 'announcement of intent' is an important component of pragmatic speech in the transition towards the adult mode of dialogue; it may also contain the germ of the meaning 'offer'. The third type of response demanded, 'be with!', includes greetings, sharings and routines of various kinds. By 1;10, when Nigel is, as it were, poised on the threshold of the mother tongue, the pragmatic mode has evolved into a generalized sense of 'I demand'. The response required is still normally non-verbal, that is, 'goods-and-services' of any kind, for example, *dada get knife take skin off ápple*; but now it may also be a verbal response – Nigel is beginning to demand information, for example, *that go thére* 'will that go there – let's see?' and *that very hòt; thát very hot* 'that (pan) is very hot; I wonder if that (pan) is very hot too?'. (We shall see the other source of this in a moment.) Notice that these early 'questions' are really still explorations to be followed up by Nigel himself rather than questions to be answered by others; but they soon become true questions (if only because it is important to be told whether the pan is hot rather than having to find it out for oneself). The meaning 'I demand' is still encoded by a rising tone, so that Nigel's system of intonation is not yet that of adult English, where commands and *Wh*-questions are typically expressed on a falling tone.

Nigel's ability to respond has kept pace with his ability to initiate; that is to say, in whatever functions he can initiate dialogue, he can respond just where the response embodies those same functions, for example, (Do you want the black and the red brush? – N.:) *Yés!* ('I want those'); (Can I brush your hair, Nigel? – N.:) *Nó!* ('I don't want you to do that'). But his ability to respond never exceeds his ability to initiate; so, for example, he cannot answer an information-seeking question (that is, he cannot give information in response) before he can initiate the giving of information himself. We have seen how in a pragmatic context, with language as a mode of action, Nigel learnt to initiate demands and respond to offers, that is, to exchange meanings of the 'goods-and-services' type. For the rest of the story we must go back to the beginning and trace the origin of the other type of commodity that is exchanged in dialogue, namely information. Here we must focus on the non-pragmatic modes: on language as a means not of action but of reflection.

4.2. At the beginning of his protolanguage, at around nine months, Nigel had, as we saw, two non-pragmatic modes of meaning. One was more 'other-oriented'; at first simply [ø] 'let's be together', but soon extending to [ʔdɔ̀] 'let's look at this together' – intimacy achieved through the sharing of a common experience. By 1;0 the shared experience was becoming a mode of intersubjective learning: 'let's attend to this together'; the object was a symbolic object, a picture, so the pattern now became [á:::dà] 'look at this picture – now you say its name' and the other person responded with a name; 'yes – that's a ball'. The name was always one that Nigel already knew and understood very well, though he did not yet use it himself. By the end of the protolanguage (1.5), the form was [ádᵞdà], Nigel's version of the familiar 'what's that?' of all children in all cultures; and now it was a demand for a new, unknown name – and served as one source of the transition to true information-seeking questions when these finally evolved around the age of 1;11. The other early component was self-oriented; it was Nigel's expression of curiosity about his environment. This had begun as early as six months with a high pitched "ʹ", later replaced by [ø], and various other expressions, meaning 'that's interesting – what's going on?'; expressing Nigel's attention to some form of commotion (birds flying, dogs barking, buses roaring) – some form of visual or auditory prominence. The boundary between the two, the other-oriented and the self-oriented, was fairly fluid; they tended to overlap in meaning and in expression; but where the former was interactional, and demanded a response, the latter was a personal experience; no one need respond, no one else need be present. From 1;0 the personal was becoming specific: not simply [ɛ̀ᵞa] 'that's interesting' but [bà] 'a bus!', [œ̀] 'an aeroplane!' and so on; in other words 'that's a ...' or 'I can see a ...' with one of a small class of thing-names, which had reached eight in number by 1;4½. By 1;6, when Nigel was beginning the transition to the mother tongue, the number had reached over 50; more significantly, it was now not only observation 'I see ...' but also recall 'I saw ...' and prediction '(when

I go out) I will see ...', for example ('Nigel, we're going out for a walk' – N.:) [kàkàbàbàtik^{U}tik^U lòulòu] 'there'll be cars, buses, sticks and holes'.

4.2.1 At this point three things begin to happen at once. The meaning 'I see/saw ...' evolves fairly quickly into that of 'I'm telling you what we both saw', a narrative of past experiences such as (1;8) *bird on wàll ... wàlking ... tiny bird flew awày*. These are addressed only to someone who shared the experience with him; they demand no response, and have a falling tone. Nigel can now conceive of language as an expression of shared experience; but he cannot yet conceive of it as an **alternative** to shared experience, a means of telling someone something they don't already know. In other words, he has no concept of information, or of an informative function of language. At about 1;10½, however, he takes this critical step of adding an informative mode – and he does so by adopting a special semantic distinction that is entirely absent from the adult language, a distinction between telling somebody something he knows they know and telling them something he knows they don't know. The former is still the norm for non-pragmatic expressions and is encoded as declarative: for example (1;8–1;11) *red egg hòt; tiny bird flew awày* ('you saw it with me'), *chuffa fell ovèr; hole in toòthbrush; have seen cello in pàrk; they've taken awày that train, it doesn't go any mòre*. The latter is highly marked and is encoded as interrogation – that is, an interrogative structure, as well as a rising tonic: *did the train fall off the tràck* ('you didn't see it, so I'm telling you!'), *did you get síck* ('I got sick'; Nigel regularly refers to himself as *you*), *did the lamp fall óver* ('I knocked the lamp over!'). Not only does he use yes/no interrogatives in this sense, he also uses *Wh*-interrogatives in the same way, for example, *what did Mummy dròp* ('Mummy dropped something'), *where the cràne* ('there's a crane there – you haven't seen it'); and these have a falling tonic. In other words, Nigel is using the grammatical resources of the adult interrogative in English, in their correct (adult) tones – rising for yes/no, falling for Wh- – as the realization of this informative function; compare the following dialogue at 1;11:

N: What did you dròp? (= 'I dropped something!')
F: I don't know – what did you?
N: Did you drop the green pén (= 'I dropped the green pen!')

It is only at this point that we can say that Nigel has added the category of "informative" to his functional potential; he can now 'give information', where the exchange of symbols is not a means towards the exchange of something else (goods-and-services) but actually constitutes, or manifests, the exchange itself.

4.2.2 Simultaneously, but rather more slowly, two other developments take place. The meaning [ádʸdà] 'what is it? give me a name!' gradually evolves into a "true" Wh-question 'who? what? give me an identity!'. This appears to take place through the intermediate stage of the pragmatic form of the indefinite meaning just referred to; at 1;9 we have *what élse put on* meaning 'let's put something else (another record) on', whereas it is not until 2;0 that we get clear non-imitative instances of Wh-questions; *what does thát say?, how did that gone in that little hole thére?* Note that both these meanings, suggestion and question, demand a response; hence the tone here is rising, in contrast both to the norm of Wh-interrogatives in adult English and to his own use of the Wh-interrogative as a form of statement.

4.2.3 Finally we return to a development noted earlier; the example cited was (1;8½) *that very hòt; thát very hot?* These are the beginning of "true" yes/no questions; it was suggested earlier that they arose as a development of the pragmatic 'I want' function, with its rising tone. We interpreted a question as 'demand: information'; we can now suggest more specifically that, with Nigel at least, yes/no questions derived their 'demand' component from the pragmatic mode, and their 'information' component from a blend of (4.2.1) and (4.2.2) above: the meanings 'we shared this experience' and 'I want to know something'. This is the source of *that blue train might brèak; réd train might break?* ('I know one thing; let me see if it applies somewhere else'); compare *blue pin got lòst; white pin got lost?* Even if the premiss is not verbalized, the context in the early instances is always that of trying things out; compare (1;8½) *that go thére?*, fitting shapes into holes. It is not until about 1;11 that these become generalized questions; but when they do, they are still coded as declarative (+ rising tone) and not as interrogative – since, as we have seen, the interrogative is used for giving information, not for demanding it, for example, *did the man give a piece of meat to give to the lion to éat!* So at 1;11 we have *we nearly thére, to the wáll?* ('are we nearly at the wall?'); *Daddy green toothbrush did bréak?* ('did it?'); *the lorry gó, in the house?* ('will the lorry go on the floor (as it does on the plank)?').

In terms of our original idealized model of the social–contextual system of dialogue, Nigel now has the mode 'demand' combined with the semiotic commodity 'information', as well as 'give' × 'information' and 'demand' × 'goods-and-services'. The one he has still not got is 'give' × 'goods-and-services', the one that is semantically typically represented as an 'offer'; that comes later. What I have tried to do is trace the source and ontogenesis of the two basic components of dialogue, the mode of exchange (giving/demanding, including giving in response) and the commodity exchanged (goods-and-services/information). By seeing how a child constructs the system, we may gain a deeper understanding of the system's nature and evolution.

PART TWO

TRANSITION FROM CHILD TONGUE TO MOTHER TONGUE

PART TWO

TRANSITION FROM CHILD TONGUE TO MOTHER TONGUE

Editor's Introduction

The mother tongue is a very natural extension of the child tongue. The chapters in this part focus on the evolution from child to adult language, through transitional Phase II to mastery of the adult system in Phase III. The distinction between the pragmatic and the mathetic – "language as action, and language as reflection" – gradually gives way as utterances become at once both ideational and interpersonal. Both lexicogrammar and texture are added to the system. In Chapter 7, 'Into the Adult Language' (1975), Professor Halliday explains that mastery of the adult system, at about the end of the child's second year, means that the child has successfully "constructed for himself a three-level semiotic system which is organized the way the adult language is". Of course, this is not to say that the child has already mastered the language; but the foundations are now firmly in place.

Chapter 7 also looks at the development of text-forming resources in Nigel's speech. Nigel's control of information structure is evidenced by "his ability to assign a focus of information by locating the tonic prominence". About the second half of his second year, Nigel develops certain semantic patterns for giving cohesion to discourse. His speech, also, exhibits sensitivity to the particular generic structures associated with narrative and dialogue modes.

"Child language studies", writes Professor Halliday in Chapter 8, 'The Contribution of Developmental Linguistics to the Interpretation of Language as a System' (1980), "point strongly to a functional interpretation of the linguistic system; and in doing so, they help to provide a wider context for theories of language". If we follow the route by which the simple contrast of pragmatic/mathetic, which is Nigel's functional setting for the transition from protolanguage to language, develops into the metafunctional framework of the adult semantic system, we can appreciate "exactly how the functional demands that are made on language have shaped the linguistic system". Studies from both linguistic and developmental perspectives are mutually enriched when approached from "an interactional, functional and meaning-oriented, or semiotic, standpoint", argues Professor Halliday in Chapter 9, 'On the Transition from Child Tongue to Mother Tongue' (1983). Having pioneered research into the child's construal of his mother tongue, Professor Halliday had to wait until the early 1980s – when this chapter was first published – before detailed accounts of other participant–observers of children's speech were available for comparison with his own findings. As he notes in this chapter, "the figures are remarkably similar".

Looking at dialogue "as a form of the exchange of social meanings ... as a semiotic process, and therefore as one that is in principle capable of being realized through systems other than language", Professor Halliday presents some examples in Chapter 10, 'A Systemic-Functional Interpretation of the Nature and Ontogenesis of Dialogue', of exchanges between Nigel and his parents, and also discusses how Nigel developed his system of dialogue. Chapter 11, 'The Place of Dialogue in Children's Construction of Meaning', further explores the ontogenesis of dialogue, showing "how the text interacts with its environment, such that meaning is created at the intersection of two contradictions; the experiential one, between the material and the conscious modes of experience, and the interpersonal one, between the different personal histories of the interactants taking part".

Chapter Seven

INTO THE ADULT LANGUAGE
(1975)

1 Reality at nine months (NL 1)

Here we shall try to take further the interpretation of Nigel's progress through Phase II, the transition from his own protolanguage into the mother tongue. In Phase I, Nigel had constructed a semiotic based on the primary distinction between himself and the rest of reality, the environment of people and of things.

This pattern begins to emerge already at NL 1, and underlies the functional system that was discussed in previous chapters. At that stage, Nigel's semiotic universe consists of a self and a non-self, the environment; the environment consists of persons and of objects; and the persons figure in the two contexts of interaction and of control.

I. THE SELF. The meanings that are associated with the self ('personal' function) realize the states and processes of his own consciousness. The orientation may be either inward (withdrawal into the self: 'I'm sleepy') or outward; within the latter there is a distinction between the affect function (pleasure, in general and specifically focused on taste) and the curiosity function (interest, in general and specifically focused on movement).

II. THE ENVIRONMENT: (a) *persons*: (i) *interaction*. The persons in the environment figure in two semiotic roles. In a context of interaction ('interactional' function), the meaning is one of rapport, with the mother or other key person. The first move may be made by the child

---

Two works are combined in this chapter: 'Into the Adult Language', first published in *Learning How to Mean: Explorations in the Development of Language*. London: Edward Arnold, 1975, pp. 82–119.
'On the Development of Texture in Child Language', first published in *The Development of Conversation and Discourse*, edited by Terry Myers. Edinburgh: Edinburgh University Press, 1979, pp. 72–87.

himself (initiation) or by the other party (response); in either case there is an exchange of meanings between them.

II. THE ENVIRONMENT: (a) *persons*: (ii) *control*. In a context of control ('regulatory' function), the meanings express the role of the other as acceding to the will of the self; this is the child's incipient mode of social control.

II. THE ENVIRONMENT: (b) *objects*. The meanings associated with objects ('instrumental' function) realize a demand for possession. There is just one generalized demand, 'I want that'; with the exception that one favourite object is singled out for specific request. This object – in Nigel's case a toy bird, always kept in one spot – stands for the constancy of the environment; it is a symbol of permanence, and it has a request form unique to itself, 'I want my bird'.

At this stage Nigel's semiotic interaction with other persons is channelled through some object; typically an object that is itself symbolic, a picture. There is a kind of natural dialectic here, since it is also true that this effective interaction with objects takes place through symbolic interaction with persons: they give him things, make them jump for him, and so on. Hence the 'other' in the environment enters into all the non-self contexts, but in different guises: as be-er (interactional), as doer (regulatory), and as giver (instrumental). The child himself takes on the complementary roles of, respectively, be-er, causer, and recipient; and this anticipates in an interesting way the roles of persons in the transitivity system of the adult semantic.

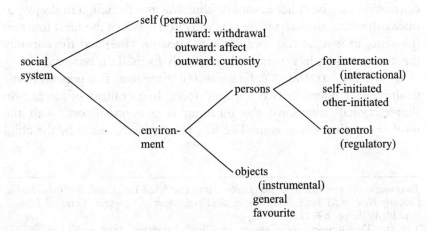

Figure 1

Nigel's model of reality at NL 1 (9 to 10½ months), as we apprehend it from a study of his semantic system, is somewhere along these lines (Figure 1; the semantic functions are shown in parenthesis).

2 Nine to fifteen months (NL 1–5)

This is a socially constructed model of reality. It has been built up in the course of interaction with others, through semiotic exchanges between Nigel and those around him.

Over the next six months, up to NL 5 (15 to 16½ months), the picture is broadened and refined at all points. New meanings are added and details are filled in. But it remains essentially a model of the same kind. The main headings are still the same, though the content of each has significantly expanded.

NL 5 represents the highest point of the Phase I system, when Nigel is about to launch into the transition to the adult language. By NL 5 the picture is as follows:

I. THE SELF. The semiotic projection of the self still takes the forms of reaction to and curiosity about the environment. By NL 4 the affective category, at first restricted to an expression of delight, has specified out into a small number of distinct meanings, of pleasure, excitement, disgust, and impatience. In the same period the curiosity function has extended beyond simple movement to particular classes of objects that are auditorily and visually prominent – aeroplane, dog, ball, bird and bus. The general meaning of curiosity, the outward focusing of the self in the form of attention to a particular object, remains at the forefront of the semantic system throughout this period; it is also closely tied up with interactional meanings in which the self's relationship with another person is realized through **shared** attention to an object – typically, with Nigel at all times, a picture, which is inherently a symbolic object.

II. THE ENVIRONMENT: (a) *persons*: (i) *interaction*. Very early on (NL 2, 10½ to 12 months), Nigel starts to mean individuals – the three that form part of his social system, Anna, Daddy, Mummy (appearing in that order); and he distinguishes these from all other meanings by the use of a clearly marked high level tone – all other meanings are expressed on some kind of falling tone. He can both initiate and respond to greetings, and he develops specific responses in other contexts – to calls, and to reproofs. But the major development here is that of the orientation of interaction, where two distinct emphases emerge. Probably the most frequent of all Nigel's vocalizations in early Phase I is that glossed as 'nice to see you; and shall we look at this together?', interaction with an individual that is channelled through shared attention to an object. From NL 2 onwards, this may focus in either of two ways. It may focus more on the person, with the interaction itself in the forefront, or it may focus more on the object, and this becomes, more and more clearly as time goes on, a demand for a **name**, with a meaning something like 'look at this (picture); now you say the name' (it being understood that the picture is a familiar one and the name of the object already known). The latter meaning is less purely interactional, and is closely linked to the personal meaning of general interest or curiosity, with the sense of 'look: that's interesting' – where, however, the object of attention is not necessarily a picture, and no response is demanded. In this area Nigel also displays his first awareness of 'texture', of meanings in the environment of other meanings: he comes to distinguish the first occurrence 'what's that?' (mid level + mid fall, no upjump) from subsequent occurrences 'and what's *that*?' (mid level + high fall, with upjump).

II. THE ENVIRONMENT: (a) *persons*: (ii) *control*. Nigel's basic system of general regulatory meanings remains in force throughout Phase I, expanding to include responses to offers, both positive and negative ('Shall I ...?' – 'Yes'/'No'), and also one or two specific meanings embodying a request for action, or, more often, for joint action, such as 'pull the curtains', 'let's draw a picture', 'let's go for a walk'. The most frequent control forms, however, are still the general ones whose meaning depends on the situation: 'do that', 'do that again'.

II. THE ENVIRONMENT: (b) *objects*. Requests for objects continue to be mainly dependent on the context; but the specific demand for a favourite object remains and expands into a demand for objects of a ritual kind, having symbolic value with reference to himself or some other person ('pottie', 'powder', 'clock'). Nigel adds a response to offers ('Do you want (me to) ...?' – 'Yes'), distinguishing as always, though with decreasing consistency, between regulatory meanings, demanding behaviour on the part of a specific individual, and instrumental ones, demanding a particular object or service; and in the latter connection he adds another distinction, that between asking for a thing that is visible (goods that are there) and asking for a thing that is not visible (services, and goods that are not there).

3 The picture at the end of Phase I (NL 5)

So when we come to NL 5, at the very end of Phase I, when Nigel is about to launch into the adult system, we find that the pragmatic modes, the instrumental and regulatory, have reached a stage where they embody a number of different kinds of demand: typically, instrumental 'give me', 'show me', 'help me', regulatory 'do this', 'let's do this', and perhaps the first signs of a third, 'let me do this', that is, 'I want to be allowed to ...', 'can I ...?'. The number of different specific demands within each type is, however, quite small, since in most cases of pragmatic speech the context will serve: 'give me that (thing there)', 'show me that (thing you're holding)', 'do that (which you were doing) again', and so on. The specific objects that come to be demanded "by name" are (i) items of food, and (ii) ritual objects.

By contrast, the interactional and personal modes are considerably expanded. In the former, we find (i) generalized greeting 'hullo!' and response 'and hullo to you!'; (ii) shared attention, as before, now contrasting with shared regret 'look it's broken – let's be sad together'; (iii) three responses to verbal interaction, to 'where's ...?', to 'say ...', and to 'look at ...'; and (iv) personalized greetings which are now systemically complex, since two meaning systems intersect: 'Mummy/Daddy/Anna' and 'seeking (where are you?)/finding (there you are!)'. This, as noted earlier, is the first breakaway from the simple semantic taxonomy, and indicates the origin of grammar, the introduction of a level of coding intermediate between context and expression.

In the personal function, the number of thing-names has now increased to eight: five characterized by prominence (movement or noise) and three as simply familiar object (ball, stick, teddy). This is the origin of vocabulary; and it marks the beginning of the stage of observation, recall and prediction which we can interpret as heuristic in function – or, in the terms we have adopted for Phase II, as *mathetic*. At the same time, however, there is a sudden final burst of energy in the Phase I system, with no less than eight distinct "baby words" expressing different kinds of interest and emotion. It is intriguing that this happens just when Nigel is about to begin the transition into the adult semiotic mode, as if it was Nigel's ceremonial farewell to semiotic infancy.

Finally at NL 5 we find a small number of other elements, of the type of games, pretends and jingles, that represent meaning as a form of play. This is the imaginative function in its inception, and it remains a subsidiary but lively motif through Phase II and into the adult language.

The early semiotics of play, verbal and non-verbal, is a rather neglected aspect of language development studies, and one that we have not attempted to cover here; but it is a field which needs to be investigated already at the pre-mother tongue stage.

4 Continuity into Phase II (NL 6)

We have emphasized throughout the twin themes of discontinuity and continuity: discontinuity in the linguistic system, with the major evolutionary change that takes place when the child shifts into the three-level system of the adult language, combined with continuity at the phonetic and semantic ends of the system. With the quite startlingly sudden leap that Nigel took into Phase II, it is all the more striking to find an essential semantic continuity linking the new modes of meaning with those of Phase I. Yet the continuity is clearly there. Nigel does not throw away the meaning potential he has built up for himself in Phase I, nor does he abandon and begin again the definition of the social contexts of language use. He continues along essentially the same path as before, so that the mother tongue comes in as a natural extension of the baby language.

What Nigel does, as we have seen, is to generalize out of the Phase I functional contexts a distinction between two semiotic modes, the pragmatic and the mathetic – language as action, and language as reflection. At first, different words and structures tend to be associated with each, reflecting the two different kinds of meaning that are involved. There is also a third, subsidiary theme of language as creation, or meaning in the imaginative mode.

Nigel expressed the systematic distinction between the two major modes by means of the phonological opposition between falling and rising tone: pragmatic ('response required') as rising tone, mathetic ('response not required') as falling tone. The falling tone was a direct continuation of the dominant intonation pattern of Phase I, where all tones were falling except in one interactional system, that of individualized greetings (personal names), which was first high level and then systematically either mid level stepping up to high level ('where are you?') or high fall followed by low level ('there you are!'). The rising tone evolved in a very striking way in the middle of NL 7, at 19 months, by a progression from falling, through narrow falling, then level, to rising: \ ⌐ ─ / , the whole process taking place within one week. From then on the two tones were in systemic contrast and remained so for the rest of Phase II and into Phase III. In a number of instances Nigel said what was in other respects 'the same thing' on both tones, one after the other, with consequent differences in meaning; we have cited the example of *tell mummy take it òff . . . take it ǒff* ('I'm going to tell Mummy to take it off . . . [running to Mother] take it off!'). The semantics of the system is made explicit by Nigel's imposing on the communication process a formal signal that he does, or else does not, require a response. In time the response that is required comes to be more and more often a verbal one.

At first each utterance is **either** pragmatic **or** mathetic; but gradually, by a reinterpretation of the nature of "function" such that it becomes not just a generalized context of use but the central organizing principle of the entire semantic system, by the end of Phase II a point is reached where every utterance is **both** pragmatic **and** mathetic. But in the process the mathetic/pragmatic opposition has itself disappeared, having created the effective conditions for the emergence of the broad functional components of the adult semantic system. It is largely the mathetic function, that of language as learning, that creates the conditions for the development of ideational meanings, those expressing the speaker's experience of the phenomena around and inside him (processes, quality and quantity, time, etc.); and the pragmatic function, that of language as doing, that creates the conditions for the development of interpersonal meanings, those expressing the speaker's role in and angle on the communication process (mood, modality, intensity, etc.). The third component, the text-forming or textual component, evolves during Phase II in the course of the child's construction of narrative and of dialogue. Every utterance in the Phase III language, which is essentially the adult system, means, and therefore is structured, in terms of these components simultaneously.

The following section presents the details of Nigel's progress through Phase II.

5 NL 6–9: examples

5.1 Specimens of dialogue from NL 6 and 7

24 April

M. Did you tell Daddy what you had for tea? N. (to M., excitedly) a^y ì . . . ȍ . . . a^y ì: a^y ì: ('egg, ooh! egg, egg!') gɔgtgɔgwa ('cockadoodledoo'; =

cornflakes, because of picture on packet; also = weathercock on church spire, so, having returned from walk, continues with inventory of things seen) tıkə ('and sticks') M. You didn't have cornflakes for tea! N. lɔ̄ᵘ ('and holes') M. You didn't have sticks and holes for tea! N. (returning to the subject in hand) dòuba ('and toast')

N. (touching M.'s nose) ⁿdòu ('nose') M. Yes that's my nose. Where's your nose? N. (touching it) dɛ̀ə ('there')

26 April

F. What did you see yesterday? N. kˣà ('car') F. Yes, and you went for a ride in a car, didn't you? and what did you see up there (pointing)? N. t'à ('tower') F. Yes, you saw a tower. And what did you pick in the garden? N. gɣà ('grass') F. And what else? N. dèdı ('daisy')

27 April

M. Take the toothpaste to Daddy and go and get your bib. N. dàda ... nmɔ̀nmɔ̀...t̪'ʉ̂t̪'ʉ̀ ('Daddy ... noddy (toothpaste) ... (bib with) train (on)')

28 April

M. What is it you can't find? Is it something under there? N. (looking under settee) bɔ̀ ('ball')

A. We're going out for a walk, and we'll go and get some fish. N. tıkᵘ ('sticks') A. No, we're not getting any sticks today. N. (plaintively) lɔ̄ᵘ ('holes', = no holes?, what can I put in the holes?)

30 April

N. [ádʸdà] ('what's that?') F. It's a piece of wood. N. m̀ ('I see!')
N. [ádʸdà] ('what's that?') M. That's butter. N. tàbə
N. Gà:ɵGà:ɵ ('ducks') F. You saw some ducks. N. tıkᵘ ('sticks') F. And you saw some sticks? N. lɔ̄ᵘ ('holes)' F. And you saw some holes. Did you put the sticks in the holes? N. bà ('buses') F. And you saw some buses. N. dòubā (?) F. You saw some toast and butter? You didn't see any toast and butter! N. dòubā (?) F. (trying again) Two buses? N. (very distinctly and slowly) dōu bà (?) ḍòuə...ḍòuə... ('tower') F. You saw a tower? N. ḍòuə... bì:ʔ ('tower, big') F. You saw a big tower? N. bì:ʔ ('big!') F. Was it the church? (N. is silent: wrong guess) Did you see the church? N. gɔ̄gtgɔ̄gtgɔ̀ ('weathercock') F. You saw the weather-

cock. N. (with music gesture) gōgtgōgtgò ('sing cockadoodledoo') F. Sing "Cockadoodledoo"? All right. (F. Sings) N. (with music gesture) bì ('bridge') F. Which is that one? "London Bridge"? Shall I sing "London Bridge"? All right.

A. What will you see when you go out for a walk? N. kà bà ('cars, buses')

A. What did you see on your walk? N. ⁰bà⁰kà t'ʉ̀ ('buses, cars, trains')

5 May

N. ɜēɛ̄ɛɛ̄ bɔ̀uwɔ̀u ('hey! dog!': = I want to come and draw with you (originally = 'draw dogs')) F. No I'm working. N. dā:dɪkədà ('you're playing the tabla') F. No I'm not playing dadikeda, I'm writing. N. bɔ̀uwɔ̀u ('then you must be drawing!')

6 May

N. nēnōnēnò ('noddy toothpaste') ɜ̄ɜ̄ɜ̄ɜ̄ɜ̄ ('I want that') M. Can you put it (= the top of the tube) on again? N. (soft; high level, stepping up) ɜ̄ɜ̄ ('I'll try')

F. You went on a train yesterday. N. t'ʉ̈t'ʉ̈ ... bā:bā ('train ... byebye!'; = when I got off, the train went away and I waved to it) F. And you said "byebye" to the train. N. a:n̥ɦ ('another!') F. And you saw another train?

N. (long list of things seen, then:) wlà ('flag') M. Oh you saw some flags? N. (holding out palm) gɣà ('gravel') M. And you had some gravel. N. (touching palm, lips rounded, very quiet) o̰:= ('ooh!') F. And you hurt your hand with the gravel? M. No, that was with the stick, the one with prickles on. N. blà ('blood') M. And there was blood on it, yes.

7 May

M. (pointing) Who's that? N. nā ('Anna') M. (pointing to self) And who's that? N. mā ('Mummy') M. (pointing to N.) And who's that? N. nī.

8 May

F. Are you going out for a walk? N. dōubà ... àiʸ ('toast: eggs': = we're going to buy some bread and some eggs)

9 May

N. mā ('Mummy!') M. be:ta (=sonny) N. āmā M. be:ja etc. etc. ad lib.

5.2 Development of structure in NL 6 and 7

    (NL 2) ᵒdɔ̀ ɛ̀ʸa vœ̀   'look, a picture! what is it? a ball!'
    (NL 5) dādā dòu   (daddy toast) 'Daddy's brought some toast'

(NL 6)

1 co-ordinate strings
    ᵊbà°kà t̢'ʉ̀   'buses, cars and trains'
    kʻàkʻàbàGōGò   'cars, buses and a weathercock'
    kàkàbàtìkʷtìkʷlòulòu   'cars, buses, sticks and holes'
    tìkᵘ tìkᵘlòulòutʉ̀tʉ̀t̢'ʉ̀t̢'ʉ̀bòbòbàbà   'sticks, holes, stones, trains, balls and buses'
    kʻàkʻàbàbàbàuwàgɔ̀gɔ̀ètìkᵘ tìkᵘlòulòu   'cars, buses, dogs, a weathercock, sticks and holes'

2 vocalization + gesture
    ɛ̀   (do that! + *pick me up) 'pick me up'
    ⁿdɔ̀   (star + *negation) 'the star wasn't there any more'
    dā:bɨ̀   (Dvořak + *music) 'I want the Dvořak record on'

3 general + specific element from same functional category
    ʔə̀ʔ bɔ̀kᵊba   (I want! + book) 'I want that book'
    ɛ̀ lòu   (do that! + hole) 'make a hole'
    ɷ̀aʸ ì: (excitement + egg) 'ooh! an egg'

4 others
    dòbɪ nɔ̀nɔ̀   (toothbrush, noddy) 'I want my toothbrush and toothpaste'
    dòə bàuwau   (draw, dog) 'I want to draw – a dog'
    lɛ̀la dà   (letter, there) 'the letters – there they are'
    bʌ̀bʷɷnɔ̄ᵘmɔ̀   (bubble, no-more) 'the bubbles have gone away'

tĭkᵊlòuba (stick, hole) 'I'll put my stick in the hole(?)'

* =gesture

(NL 7)

1 co-ordinate strings: frequent, for example
tìkʷtìkʷlə̀ulə̀udʉ̀dʉ̀kˣàkˣà   'sticks, holes, trains, cars, buses and dogs'

2 vocalization + gesture
lì Φǫ̊   (leaf + *blowing) 'the leaves are blowing in the wind'

3 general + specific element from same functional category
nɒ̀:bənɒ: ... ē ... mā ... əmmā   (banana + I want + mummy) 'I want Mummy's banana'

Structures from 28 May–3 June

28 v 1 àdz ... pʸà:o ... à:ǫ   (Andrew, piano, house) 'Andrew plays the piano in his house'; or 'Andrew plays the piano; so did I, in Anna's house'

2 āpì ... dàda ... āmà ... ān:à   (apple, daddy, mummy, Anna) 'I've got an apple; so has Daddy; so has Mummy; so has Anna'

3 dɔ̀bɪ ... dà: dɔ̀bɪ   'a toothpick, a tiny toothpick'

29 v 4 bīkɛ̀ ... ōdɪə̀ ... mḷʔ ... dàda   (breakfast, oh-dear!, milk, daddy) 'I want my breakfast – I'm hungry – milk! and some for Daddy too'

30 v 5 tʃə̂ya ... là ... gɹī ... lagɹì   (train, light, green; light green) 'the train went and the light turned green'

31 v 6 gɹī: ... gɹī: là   'green, a green light'
7 dâ ... dā: dō:bɪ   'tiny – a tiny toothpick'
8 gɹī: kà   'a green car'
9 əlōʷ tí:ko: 'hullo teacosy!'

1 vi 10 gɹī: kà ... bl:ʉ̄: kà ... a:ṇ̀ɦ: (green car, blue car, another) 'I saw a green car, and a blue car, and lots more'

11 mɔ̀: mìʔ   'more meat!'

167

		12 mɔ̀: mɪ̀ˀ plɪ	'more meat please!'
		13 tʉ̄bɑ̀kʷ	'two books'
2 vi		14 tʉ̄ɛ̀kl̩	'two helicopters' (also *two* + various other things)
		15 gɹī:là	'green light' (also *green car*)
3 vi		16 mɔ̄: ɔ̀blə	'more omelette'
		17 gɹī: pɛ̀ˀ	'green peg'

5.3 NL 7 (18–19½ months): pragmatic and mathetic

Pragmatic

(= Phase I: instrumental, regulatory, some interactional); tone changes to rising

'I want':

dèbɪ	tooth paste	ɪ̀gɔ	cotton-reel	}	to end of
mᵇì	milk	vòba̱	fish	}	May: all
bɑ̀	bone	gà:ɔbʷga:ɔ	cardamom	}	falling tone

nōumɔ̀	'(there's) no more'
ōdì:ə	'sing "Oh dear what can the matter be"'
bi̱ ... nò ... dàlon	'don't sing "London Bridge", sing "The cheese stands alone"'

kēm	'come with me'	}		}
ˀɔ̄fvə	'take it off'	}	very narrow	}
dʸkā	'get down'	}	falling tone	first week in June: transitional
dōu	'sit down'	}	(level	}
ɔɹʷīkēm	'I want my orange'		tone)	}

bɔ̀l̩	'(I want) the ball'	}	
báu	'(I want to) bounce'	}	
bɹɛ́kə	'(I want) breakfast'	}	
mɔ̄bɹɛ́	'(I want) more bread'	}	
kɛ́m	'come with me'	}	second week in
āgǽi	'do it again'	}	June onwards:
ɔ̄ᵘvᵊɹədɛ́@	'come over there'	}	all rising tone
dōu	'sit down'	}	
mēmī kám	'mummy come'	}	
nó	'no (I don't want)'	}	

bē tē ʔɔ́n	'put some butter on'	
kwī: ʔɔ́ɹⁱɪ	'squeeze the orange'	
nɔ̄ω ɹɔ́m	'now (let's go to Daddy's) room'	
mɛn tʃɔ́va	'mend the train'	second week
dā: vɔ́ja	'(draw a) star for you (= for me)'	in June onwards:
ɛ pɪ̀ ... ɛpɪ̀ tʉ́	'help ... help (me with the) juice'	all rising tone
kēm ōᵘvᵊ dɛ́c	'come over there'	
bī:gᵊ bɔ́kωa	'I want my big book'	

Mathetic

(= Phase I: some interactional; personal, heuristic); all falling tone

Observation and recall/things:

ɹɛ: kà	red car	blʉ̄ bɔ̀l̩	blue ball	
ɹɛ: bɹɛ̀la	red umbrella	blʉ̄ kwɛ̀ə	blue square	
gɹī: tɔ̄wəl	green towel	vā: tʃɔ̂va	fast train	
bīʔ tòn	big stone	bī: gᵊbɔ̀k	big book	
t'ʉ̄ àpa	two apples	mēmi bɔ̀kᵊ	Mummy's book	
gɹī ōl tʃɔ̂va	green old train			
tʉ̄ va: tʃɔ̂va	two fast trains			
dā: ɹʷɛ là	tiny red light			

Observation and recall – processes:

bī: bī: làwa	'bee on the flower'
vò tɛ̀ʔ	'foot stuck'
bēbʷ ɹɒuɹɒu	'bubbles (go) round and round'
vòpa ... ɔ̄pēn mɔ̄u	'fishes opening their mouths'

Narrative:

tɔ̄ω tʃɔ̂va ... lēbɹì	(we went to) town (on a) train, to London Bridge
tɹì ... ʔɔ́ ... tìkawè : ... ōgɔ̀ ... bāʸ bāʸ	tree broken, take away, all gone, byebye!
gɹī: tìk ... lòt'ᵊ ... gòn: ... bāʸ bāʸ	green stick, lost, gone byebye!
blāʔ miào ... ɹʷā dɔ̀ᵊ	black cat, (it) ran indoors

Narrative with quoted speech:
qàɪ … qàɪ … māɪn̩tìŋ (there was a) kite; (Daddy said, "there's a) kite; mind the string"

5.4 NL 8 (19½–21 months): (1) Pragmatic

Structures of one and two elements: all rising tone unless otherwise noted:

chuffa stúck	N. calling for help in freeing toy train
find fóryou	'I've lost something; find it for me!'
throw úp	'thrown the rabbit up in the air again'
low wáll	N. about to jump off suitcase, asking to be
high wáll	caught; first used when jumping off walls, low and high, in park
squéeze	'squeeze the orange for me'
gláss	'I want my milk in a glass'
orange lèmon	'sing "Oranges and lemons"'; accompanied by music gesture, which is alternative realization of pragmatic; hence falling tone
turn róund	N. repeating instruction given when fitting shapes into puzzles: 'is that what I have to do?'
play chúffa	'let's play with the train'
open fóryou	(usual form of request for box, etc., to be opened)
back tóothpaste	'put the toothpaste back in the cupboard'
more grávy	also: more ómelette, -léttuce, -tomáto, -bréad, -bún, etc.
bounce táble	'I want to bounce my orange on the table'
cárry	'carry me!'
háve it	(usual form of 'I want that thing')
tóast	'I want some toast'; also *breakfast*, *tomato*, etc.
hit flóor	'I'm going to hit the floor with the hammer'
that sóng	'sing that song you've just sung'
háve that	(same as *have it* above)
hedgehog bóok	'I want the book with the hedgehog picture in it'
play ráo	'I want to play at lions'

Note: Up to the first week of July (that is, half-way through NL 8, which covers the period mid-June to end July), two-element structures predominate; the above examples are taken from throughout NL 8 but mainly from the earlier part. After the first week in July there is a predominance of structures of three or more elements; those in the next list are taken mainly from the later part of NL 8.

Structures of three and more elements; all rising tone unless otherwise noted:

toothpaste ón ... red tòothbrush	'put the toothpaste on the red tooth-brush'; pause for planning second half
train under túnnel ... getit fóryou	both halves rising tone
dówn ... table ... sugar ... spóon	'put the sugar down on the table for me to put my spoon in it'; rising tone on *down* and *spoon*
make cross tíckmatick ... in dada róom	'I want to make crosses on the typewriter in Daddy's room'; both halves rising tone
réd train might break	following *that blue train might brèak*; earliest utterance interpretable as a yes/no question
get stick báll	'I want the stick to get the ball with'; also: *get ball stíck*
bounce big báll	
dada get off coathanger fóryou	'Daddy take the coathanger off for me'
dada squeeze out toothpaste fóryou	
anna help gréenpea	'Anna help me to eat the green peas'
big bubble gòne ... big búbble ... móre big bubble	'the big bubble's burst; I want another one'
butter on knífe	'I want –'
take marmite kítchen	'can I –?'
anna put record on fóryou	
that go thére	'will that go there?'
go abbeywood on tráin	'let's go to Abbey Wood on the train'
have tóothpowder ... nila have tóoth powder	
play highwall mátchstick	'let me jump holding the matchstick'
dada put alltogéther egg	'Daddy put the eggs all together (one inside the other)'
when newworld finish song about bús	'when New World finishes (falling tone), sing me the song about the bus (rising)'

Dialogues involving pragmatic utterances:

F. D'you want the black brush? N. nó F. D'you want the black and the red brush? N. yés
F. Mummy's gone to the shop. N. buy chócolate
N. put bemax down on táble M. It is on the table. N. níla table
N. why that clóck stop F. I don't know: why do you think? N. ménd it

5.5 NL 8 (19½ –21 months): (2) Mathetic

Structures of one and two elements; all falling tone:

molasses nòse	'I've got molasses on my nose' (with accompanying expression of delight)
big bàll	frequent when playing with ball; also: *little ball*
mummy bòok	frequent on picking up book and finding no pictures inside ('it's Mummy's book')
red swèater	on seeing it; also: *red jùmper* (same object)
black brùsh	also *green, red, blue, yellow* with *stick, light, peg, car, train*, etc.
bìg one	applied to goods train, bubble; tonic on *big*, as in adult form
baby dùck	in picture; also: *mummy dùck*
too bìg	frequent; sometimes appropriate, as when trying to push object through wire mesh; sometimes inappropriate, as when trying to reach ball with stick (= 'too far')
that bròke	'that's broken'
loud mùsic	frequent comment as loud passage starts
chuffa stòp	in game (Father bouncing N., N. being 'fast train'; Father stops)

Note: There is also considerable use of single words as holophrases in contexts of observation and recall, for example, fire, chocolate, feather, rhinoceros, bee, cherry. This phenomenon is noticeably less frequent with familiar than with unfamiliar words.

Both one- and two-element utterances become relatively less frequent during the second half of this period. The examples in the next list are typical of the longer utterances that characterize the latter part of NL 8.

Structures of three and four elements; all falling tone except where otherwise indicated:

INTO THE ADULT LANGUAGE

two green pèg	
green stick find	'the green stick's been found'
old green tràin ... green old tràin	both halves falling tone; the second, though less probable, would have been the appropriate one in the context
dada black brùsh	'Daddy's black brush'
no more wàter	
toothpaste ... òn ... tòothbrush	falling tone on *on* and again on *toothbrush*; not fully formed as a single structure
tree fall dòwn	later: 'big tree fall dòwn'
dada got bàll ... nila got bàll	
ball go under càr	compare 'water gone plughole'
one blúe train ... one rèd train	tone and tonicity as in adult language (that is, rising tonic on *blue*, falling tonic on *red*)
glass got hòle	looking at glass with pattern of bubbles
that blue train might brèak	
dada come bàck ... dada come on fast tràin	
man clean càr	'there's a man cleaning a car'
very old trèe	
nila get dada tìn	'Nigel and Daddy will get the tin' (sic)
anna got piano anna hòuse ... very òld one ... (shaking head) very gòod one	(routine) 'Anna's got a piano at home, a very old one, not a very good one'
anna make noise gràss ... that not right kìnd grass	'Anna made a noise with the grass'; second half imitation of what Anna had said
strange man gòne	
red egg hòt	(plastic egg in basin of hot water)
clever boy fix roof on lòrry	
too dàrk ... open cùrtain ... lìght now	'it was too dark; the curtains have been opened, and now it's light'
have clare banàna	'Clare had a banana'
letter fall out mummy bòok	

Dialogues and strings involving mathetic utterances:

N. (holding one train and one bus) two ... two chùffa ... two ... two (puzzled; gives up)

N. two fast chùffa M. Where did you see two fast trains? N. wàlk M. And what else did you see? N. bòwwow

N. dada got scrambled ègg ... mummy get fóryou scrambled egg (second half has rising tonic on *foryou*, marking shift to pragmatic function 'I want', with *scrambled egg* as 'given' element.

N. (getting off train) train go cròss (= Charing Cross) ... go tòwn ... no more tràin ... time go hòme ... have òrange ... squeeze òrange

N. bird on wàll ... wàlking ... tiny bird flew awày. F. Did it? N. ōhyēs

N. big nòise M. Who made a big noise? N. drìll make big noise

N. bùmblebee M. Where was the bumblebee? N. bumblebee on tràin M. What did Mummy do? N. mummy open wìndow M. Where did the bumblebee go? N. bumblebee flew awày

N. (pointing) got nòse ... dada got nòse ... mùmmy got nose ... ànna got nose

5.6 NL 9 (21–22½ months)

Examples in chronological sequence:

N. dear dèar ... chuffa fall òver ... big bàng

N. what élse put in ('what else can I put into the water?')

A. Shall we go for a walk? N. when E-I-O finish (song-on record)

N. why bróken that ('why is that broken?')

N. Pauline went on two fast chùffa ... one fast chuffa hère ... one chuffa ... one fast chuffa brìdge ('one here and one at London Bridge')

N. record back on ráck ... new record back on ráck ... what élse put on ... what élse put on ('put the new record back on the rack and put something else on!')

N. Oh dear dear dèar ... lorry fell òver ... on ... thàt (piece of furniture of which he does not know the name)

N. flỳ ... flỳ ... climbing up tàble ... climbing mummy chàir ... fly clìmbing

M. (looking for lost toy) I can't find the driver's head. N. gone under bèd ... háve it (3) ... ooh dear dèar ... háve it

N. (playing with toy cow) cow eat gráss ('let me make the cow eat grass')

N. dada get knife take skin off ápple (request)

N. eat chúffa F. You can't eat trains! N. can't eat blue chùffa F. No you can't eat the blue train. N. can't eat rèd chuffã F. No you can't eat the red train. N. (looking at wooden man from toy cart) can't eat màn F. No you can't eat the man. N. can't eat that bòok F. No you can't eat that book! You can't eat any book. N. (looking at Pauline) can't eat Pàuline book. F. No you can't eat Pauline's book. N. Pauline got èar F. (moving Pauline's hair aside) Yes Pauline's got an ear, though you can't usually see it. N. dàda got ear ... dada got nòse F. Yes. N. (touching Pinocchio doll) Pinocchio got funny nòse F. Yes Pinocchio's got a funny nose, like a – N. càrrot F. Yes like a carrot. N. screwdriver ... mend Pinocchio fòot (reference to F.'s mending Pinocchio's foot some days earlier)

N. (to F., who has finished shaving, is putting shirt on) put that ón (2) ... dada ready nòw (4) ... put that ón ... dada ready nów (4)

N. (looking at opening in top of packet of Bemax, inside outer cover) hole in bèmax ... (closing outer cover, so that hole is concealed) where hóle

N. (beating time with chopsticks) condùctor ('I'm being a conductor')

F. (on station platform) There are people on the platform. N. waiting chuffa còme

N. chuffa walk on ràilway line (2) ... fast chùffa ... one day might gò on fast chuffa (2) F. Yes we might. N. one day go on blue chùffa ... next chuffa còming ... go on thàt one

N. (looking at pictures) umbrèlla ... bòat ... stìck ... twèet-tweet ... bòwwow

A. Can I brush your hair Nigel? N. nó ... nó

N. lunch back on táble ('I don't want any more')

N. (F. is holding pin in mouth) dada put pin in my mòuth F. No, not in Nigel's mouth; in Daddy's mouth. N. not in nìla mouth ... dada put pin in mòuth

N. (being put to bed) didn't clean your tèeth ('I didn't clean my teeth!')

F. Did you walk on the platform? N. walk on ràilway line F. I don't think you did! N. walk on plàtform ... not walk on ràilway line (routine)

M. Where do the cars go? N. on ròad M. And where do the trains go? N. on ràilway line M. And where does Nigel go? N. on ràilway line (routine)

N. (knocks on F.'s door; F. opens) téatime ... lúnchtime ... nila take lunch on táble ('shall I take my lunch on the table?')

A. What did the baby have in the pram? N. blànket ... not yòur blanket ... bàby blanket ... (pointing to his room) your blanket thère

TRANSITION FROM CHILD TONGUE TO MOTHER TONGUE

N. that very hòt ('that pan is very hot') ... thát very hot ('is that handle very hot?')

N. (trying to stand F.'s book up on end) look at dada bóok ... stand úp ... stand úp F. No it won't stand up. (it did) N. clever bòy

N. dada brùsh ... play dada brúsh ... hòle ... got hòle in it (repeat) ... hole in tòothbrush ... hole in dada tòothbrush (delight)

N. play rao bártok ('I want to play at lions with me holding the sleeve of the Bartok record')

N. anna say go awày nila ('Anna said "go away Nigel"')

N. when music fińish then I sing you dùck song ('when this music's finished you're going to sing me the duck song, aren't you?')

F. (playing lions) This is an eat train lion. N. (picks up engine and gives it to F. to eat)

N. I go shòpping A. Are you going shopping? What are you going to buy? N. ègg A. Where do you buy eggs from? N. Madeline Mòore (The answer is appropriate. It is doubtful whether N.'s first utterance was intended as pretend-play; possibly = 'you're going shopping'.)

F. After breakfast where are we going, do you know? N. àbbeywood F. No not Abbey Wood. N. ólly ('are we going to see Olly?')

N. (at station) chuffa go in mòment ... that chuffa go in mòment ... another chuffa hère ... that train gòing ... that train staying hère ... people want get òff that train M. What a lot of trains! N. two chùffa ... can't see drìver ... can't see drìver in that one

N. (having fallen earlier in the day, touching forehead) ádỹdà ('what's that?') F. That's plaster, sticking plaster N. tell mummy take it òff ... (running to M.) take it óff

N. that tree got no lèaf on ... stìck ('it's all made of sticks') ... thát tree got leaf on but that tree got no lèaf on

N. (finding strand of M.'s hair and stretching it out straight) mummy hair like ràilway line

N. have céllo ('I want the record sleeve with the picture of the cello on') Grandmother. Does he know what a cello looks like? F. I don't think he's ever seen a cello. N. have seen cello in pàrk (in fact he hasn't, but he has often seen brass bands playing in park)

N. have blue pin all ríght ('I can, can't I?') M. The blue pin has got lost. N. under béd M. No it's not under the bed. N. blue pin got lòst ... whíte pin got lost M. No the white pin didn't get lost. N. (pricking pin into vest) that white pin prick your tùmmy ... that white pin prick your knèe ... (sticking it into bedcover) make hòle

N. have nellie élephant bib M. Nellie the elephant bib's being washed;

it may not be dry yet. N. have chúffa bib (goes out to look for it; brings back cat bib) ... that not chuffa bib that miào bib ... put miao bib ón

N. (hearing vacuum cleaner) ȓ-ȓ-ȓ M. What's making that noise? N. chùffa M. No it's not a train. N. àeroplanę M. No it's not an aeroplane. N. càr N. No it's not a car. N. clèaner M. Yes that's right. (All very serious – apparently a genuine search.)

6 Interpretation of Phase II

6.1 *Pragmatic*

Pragmatic contexts are those which evolve out of the instrumental and regulatory functions of Phase I. At the beginning of Phase I, the instrumental take the form of requests for food, for entertainment (music), and for objects as symbols – that is, objects other than his own possessions (which tend not to be explicitly demanded, though it should be remembered that the generalized demand forms of the earlier phase, 'give me that!', remain in use well into Phase II) that are a focus of personal identification or ritual interaction – father's keys, mother's lipstick, certain books, and the like. As Nigel's semantic potential increases, this component expands into a general realm of 'goods-and-services'. The regulatory meanings now extend across the three modes of the adult imperative, first person 'let me', that is, 'I'm going to', second person 'you!', and first and second person 'let's'. These include specific demands for assistance, for movement (places and postures), for objects to be manipulated and so on. There is a close functional relationship among all of these, which we are expressing by the use of the term 'pragmatic', and which Nigel is soon to make explicit by the rising intonation pattern; and also between these and certain meanings deriving from the interactional function – those concerned with the search for other people and the demand for a response from them.

The significant feature that emerges is the steadily increasing content that is associated with pragmatic utterances. The child's requirements can no longer be formulated in terms merely of objects or actions, involving the simple semantic relation of 'object of desire'. They have to be expressed in complex patterns, semantic configurations in which the desired object or service is garnished in some way, for example with the meaning 'more' (*more méat*) or by reference to some relation or process (*Bartok ón, squeeze órange*), including processes which relate the object to himself (*help júice*). If the request is for an action, this comes to involve specification of the kind of action by means of an element expressing the Range (*play tráin; play líons*), or by the addition of circumstantial elements (*bounce táble*, that is, 'I want to bounce my orange on the table'); and including instances where only the circumstances are specified, the action being left unsaid (*now róom*, that is, 'now let's go to (play in) your room'). Furthermore the request may be encoded as a statement of an undesired condition to be relieved (*train stúck, tram under túnnel*). These elements soon come to be combined, so that by NL 8 we get complex request forms such as *make cross tíckmatick ... in dada róom* ('I want to make a cross on the typewriter, in Daddy's room') and *when newworld fìnish song about bús* ('when New World finishes sing me the bus song').

This last request shows for the first time a true integration of the two modes of meaning; and it is one in which the mathetic is operating as a circumstantial qualification of the pragmatic. Hence it happens that the tonal pattern is exactly the reverse of that of the adult language, which typically would have a rise on the first part, signalling its dependence, and a fall on the second, the typical form of the imperative: When the New World finishes, sing me the song about a bùs. But the general significance of the increasing content that comes to be associated with pragmatic utterances is the interactive one: the semantic system is constructed in the process of interaction. The pragmatic mode of meaning, language in action, creates the need for complex semantic configurations; while the effective response to the demands which these express creates the conditions for their continued expression and expansion.

The pragmatic component is the source of the mood system of the adult language. Here we find not only the prototype for the various forms of the imperative mentioned above, but also the origin of questions, which with Nigel seems to lie particularly in the context of trial and error in the manipulation of objects, for example, *that go thére* 'does that go there?', *that blue train might brèak ... réd train might break* 'you told me the blue train might break; now tell me whether the red train might break'. The mood system is an interactive one; in fact it is the semantics of linguistic interaction – a question seeks a response, and once the question has evolved to include "true" questions, searches for information as distinct from requests, the response typically takes the form of a statement – and this, in turn, in the terms of the pragmatic/ mathetic opposition, is mathetic in function, though it is an extension of the mathetic as originally defined, which did not include giving information. True questions of this kind appear in the second half of Phase II, and provide the condition for the shift in the mode of response. Until this time, the typical response to a pragmatic utterance is non-verbal: it is an action, even if that action is accompanied by some verbal signal of accession to the request. So when Nigel says *play chúffa* 'let's play trains', there may be a verbal response to the interpersonal component of the meaning (to the imperative mood) in the form of 'yes let's, shall we? all right' and such like; but the response to the ideational component of the meaning (the content of the request) takes the form of action – the addressee does what the child asks. (He may refuse to do it, of course, but this does not affect the argument.) But if the question is a search for information, the response is entirely verbal: not only the interpersonal component 'yes I will answer your question', which now does not need to be verbalized (since the act of responding is performative in this respect) although it often is, typically by the word 'well' at the beginning of the answer, but also the ideational component which now takes the form of information – the addressee tells what the child wants to know. From the child's point of view, of course, this is turning the developmental process back to front. What the child does is to derive from the semiotic system that he has created for other purposes – not only pragmatic purposes, as we have emphasized, but certainly excluding any conception of an informative function – the concept of information that is inherent in it. A symbolic system that serves to encode other, non-symbolic meanings can also create symbolic meanings of its own, those of 'telling' and 'asking'. (No doubt this is learnt, in part, through the various types of non-responses to requests, disclaimers of various kinds which have to be verbal; for example, 'it is on the table' in the sequence: N. put bemax on táble M. It is on the table. N. nígel table.) Through this route the child comes to master what was the last in the original list of developmental functions, the "informative" function. The use of language to inform is, as we have repeatedly pointed out, a highly complex notion. All the other functions, whether active or reflective – whether concerned with exploiting the environment or with interpreting it – are independent of language; language intervenes as a symbolic means to an end that is defined in non-linguistic terms. But telling and asking are themselves symbolic acts. The use of language to inform depends on conceptualizing the fact that, once the semiotic system has been evolved, it creates its own meanings; the exchange of symbols becomes a function in its own right. All parents are familiar with the typical Phase II sequence of events in which, after the child has shared some interesting experience with his mother, she invites him to 'tell Granny what happened'. The child is tongue-tied. He is perfectly capable of verbalizing the experience, and may even turn to his mother and do so; but he has not yet learnt that language is not just an **expression** of shared experience, it is an **alternative** to it, a means of imparting the experience to the other. For the same reason, when he first learns to answer a Wh-question, he can do so only if he knows that the answer is already known to the person who is asking the question. It is only towards the end of Phase II that Nigel grasps this principle; and when he does, he continues for many months to draw a clear semantic distinction between telling people what they already know (verbalizing shared experience), for which he uses the (unmarked) declarative mood, and telling people what they do not know (verbalizing as a means of sharing experience), for which he uses the (marked) interrogative mood.

6.2 Mathetic

Meanwhile Nigel has developed to a high degree language in its mathetic function, the use of the symbolic system not as a means of acting on reality but as a means of learning about reality. This is the primary context for the evolution of the ideational systems of the adult language: classes of objects, quality and quantity, transitivity and the like. The context in which these systems evolve is that of the observation of how things are. Nigel's experience of how things are is such that it can be represented in terms of processes, of people and things functioning as participants in these processes, and of accompanying circumstances. Not that reality can **only** be represented in this way, but that this is a **possible** semantic interpretation; the fact that Nigel adopts this form of representation rather than another one is because this is the way it is done in the language he hears around him. We readily assume that the semiotics of social interaction – the interpersonal component of the semantic system – is constructed in the course of interaction; but it is no less true that the construction of a semiotic of reality – the ideational component – is also an interactive process. Nigel soon begins to use dialogue as a means of building up complex representations; for example, (NL 9) F. There are people on the platform. N. Waiting chuffa còme. (Compare the many instances of the building up of description and narrative by means of question and answer.)

Nigel goes into Phase II with a set of words for objects, thing-names which are used in observation, recall and prediction; together with a negative which may accompany them in the sense of 'no longer there', and which is expressed by gesture (a shake of the head – it is a long time before he has a verbalized negative in the mathetic mode). The classes of objects are, at first, things in pictures, things seen on walks, small household objects, parts of the body and items of food (the latter being largely different from those found in the pragmatic context, since not valued as items for his own consumption). Then the horizons begin to broaden, first through the introduction of names of properties accompanying the object names; the first to appear are colours and the number two (*green càr, two pèg*). Next circumstantial elements are introduced, typically expressions of place (as with other structures, these are built up step by step, first as semantic constructs and later grammaticalized: *toothpaste òn ... tòothbrush before ball go under càr*). Next come complex processes involving two elements besides the process itself: either two participants, or a participant and a circumstance. By NL 8 Nigel's world extends to complex phenomena such as *dada come on fast tràin* and *anna make noise gràss*.

All these elements, and their combinations, tend to appear in a mathetic context before they appear in a pragmatic one, which is what we might expect. But there is an interesting exception, and one that is right at the heart of the system. The processes themselves – words that will turn into verbs – often appear first in a pragmatic context; and this is particularly true of those that introduce the ergative (causational) element in the semantic system. By and large, Nigel's early process–participant combinations, those that will turn into verb + noun, have the participant as **Medium** – in terms of the adult language, intransitive Actor or transitive Goal. These may appear in either context: 'things happen' or 'I want things to happen'. Soon, however, he introduces agentive constructs; and here the mediating function seems to be the pragmatic one, the meaning being 'let *me* cause things to happen' (*look at dada bóok ... stand úp ... stand úp* 'I am going to stand it up'). Without making too much of this – the evidence is slender – we can suggest that perhaps the pragmatic function contributes to the development of transitivity specifically by creating the conditions for the representation of the causative element in the structure of processes; there is an echo here of Phase I regulatory meanings, where 'do that again!' meant 'make it jump', and of early Phase II demands such as *bounce* meaning 'bounce the ball' or 'bounce me'.

Be that as it may, the general pattern seems to be that the pragmatic function of Phase II creates the conditions for the development of the interpersonal component in the adult semantic system, and the mathetic function creates the conditions for the ideational component. This, essentially, is why the adult language has evolved in the way it has done: it meets the twofold needs of acting on the environment and reflecting on it (the latter, in a developmental context, being interpretable as learning about it). If we have tended to make a great point of this parallel development, it is because there are two mainstream traditions in the interpretation of child language, each emphasizing one component to the exclusion of the other. One tradition derives from cognitive psychology, and assumes that the only function of language is ideational: if the child learns to talk, this is simply to express ideas, and ideas are about things and their relations. The other derives from social anthropology, and assumes that the real function of language is interpersonal: the child learns to talk in order to get what he wants, which means getting other people (or spirits) to give it to him, or do it for him. Obviously, both of these are essential parts of the picture. (So also, we might add, is a third, minor tradition, probably deriving from aesthetics, according to which the child learns language in order to sing and play.) The real interest lies in seeing **how** these functions determine the ontogeny of the system, and how they interpenetrate at various key points in the developmental process.

6.3 Breakdown of the pragmatic/mathetic system

Each function, we are suggesting, carries with it a strong submotif of the other. Pragmatic utterances also concern things and their relations, and some aspects of these – such as, if we are right, the causative element in processes – may actually be verbalized first in a pragmatic context. Similarly, mathetic utterances also involve some kind of a stance *vis-à-vis* the environment; the sort of intensification and evaluation that appear in *very old trèe*, *loud nòise*, *big bàng* and expressions with *too* – *too* is particularly complex, since it is an evaluative element interpretable in terms only of some reference point, and this reference point may be the speaker's opinion. All these appear first in mathetic contexts.

But the point has to be made in more general terms. When we say that the mathetic function creates the conditions for the emergence of the ideational component in the semantic system, and the pragmatic for the interpersonal component, this means that the ideational systems –

transitivity (types of process, participants, circumstances), lexical taxonomy (hierarchy of thing-names), quality and quantity, etc. – evolve first and foremost in mathetic contexts, while the interpersonal systems – mood (indicative, declarative and interrogative, imperative), modality, person, intensity, comment, etc. – evolve first and foremost in pragmatic contexts. We are referring, of course, to these systems in the child's developing semantics; his mood system is very different from that of the adult language, and it is a long time before either the system or its grammatical manifestations take the adult form. What we are describing is the evolution of the concept of function, from its Phase II sense of 'generalized context of language use' to its Phase III sense of 'component of the semantic system'.

But if we then look back at Phase II from the standpoint of the organization of the Phase III system, we can see that this organization is present in prototypic form from the start. In Phase II terms, each utterance is either pragmatic or mathetic; this is attested in Nigel's phonology, in which everything must be either rising or falling tone; and it is the form of continuity from the functional meanings of his Phase I system, each of which is specific and simple – one meaning, in one function, at a time. In Phase III terms, however, all utterances are both ideational and interpersonal at the same time; and this is true – inescapably – from the moment the child builds a lexicogrammar into the system. As soon as the utterance consists of words-in-structure, it has an ideational meaning – a content, in terms of the child's experience; and an interpersonal meaning – an interactional role in the speech situation. (The choice between mathetic and pragmatic is itself an interpersonal system, since it encodes the semiotic role the child is adopting for himself and assigning to the hearer.) This is what we mean by saying that Phase II is transitional. It is not so much a system in its own right, intermediate between baby language and adult language, but rather a period of overlap between the two. The interpretation in terms of the 'Phase II functions', pragmatic and mathetic, an opposition that turns up frequently under different names in language development studies, is one way of explaining the nature of this overlap; but it is also more than that – it is actually Nigel's major strategy for making the transition, as shown by the fact that he clearly assigns every utterance to one mode or the other.

The direction of eventual breakdown of this opposition, as the meaning it expresses evolves and becomes absorbed into the adult mood system, can be seen in two distinct though related processes from about the middle of Phase II onwards. These are the two ways in which mathetic and pragmatic may combine with each other, one linear the other simultaneous. On the one hand, it becomes increasingly common for an utterance to be formed out of a mathetic and a pragmatic component in succession; they may occur in either sequence and, before long, more than one of either may be present. This happens first through changes in the context of the utterance; for example, N. (to F.) *tell mummy take it òff* ('I'm going to ....') ... (running to M.) *take it óff*. But it soon extends beyond this to sequences in which he simply switches from one meaning to the other: *dada got scrambled ègg ... mummy get fóryou scrambled egg* 'Daddy's got some; now get some for me'; and from this it is a short step to complex utterances in which one becomes a condition on the other: *when newworld finish song about bùs*, referred to above. By the end of NL 9 the intonation of these begins to change: *when music finish then I sing you dùck song*. This is the first sign of the breakdown of the rising/falling opposition, perhaps here under strong pressure from the adult system (which in just this context is directly the converse of his own), though it continues to determine the system for some months to come.

On the other hand, it becomes increasingly clear that, while any given utterance or portion of an utterance continues to be explicitly signalled as pragmatic or mathetic, what this expresses is the dominant mode rather than the exclusive mode. It no longer makes sense to interpret the utterances as having meaning exclusively in respect of one function; the function that is assigned (by intonation) is rather the key signature, or prevailing mode for interpretation (compare 'mood' in the adult system). So when Nigel says, coming into his father's study, *téatime ... lúnchtime*, there is obviously an observational ('mathetic') element in the meaning: 'it's teatime – I mean it's lunchtime'; what the selection of pragmatic does is to embed this in a context of action, showing that its real significance is as an instruction 'so come along!' – as is made very clear by the follow-up *nila take lunch on táble*. Similarly there is a pragmatic element in the meaning of *dada ready nòw* 'Daddy's ready now – at least I want him to be', as seen from the fact that, on finding that Daddy was not in fact ready, he repeats the same sentence on a rising tone: *dada ready nów* ('please!').

So by the time the pragmatic/mathetic intonation system does break down, as it has to do in Phase III in order to allow the rising/falling contrast to carry the meanings it has in the adult system, it no longer fits in with Nigel's semantic potential. It is unnecessary, because its role has been taken over by the mood system; and it is also inappropriate, because it imposes a dominance of one mode over the other. The supreme quality of human language is that every semiotic act is a blend of action and reflection. This is what we mean by saying that all utterances are structured on both the ideational and the interpersonal dimensions simultaneously. In order to reach this point, the child has to go through an 'either/or' stage in which each utterance means on one dimension only, as he gradually builds the edifice that allows him to combine them. The functional framework, which has served as the scaffolding, now becomes an obstruction and is dismantled.

6.4 Texture

Meanwhile, in the course of Phase II, and as part of the same general process, Nigel has introduced texture into the system. In terms of the adult language, this represents the third, 'text-forming' component of meaning: it is the potential the system has for being operational in a context, and therefore it is an enabling condition on the other two components – without texture, 'meaning' is a meaningless activity. Texture implies genre, a mode of organization of meaning that relates to function in the other sense of the term that we have now separated off from function interpreted as metafunction – that is, it relates to function in the sense of use: to social context, or situation type. The texture of discourse depends not only on structuring the parts in an appropriate way and joining them together, but also on doing so in a way that relates to the context – as narrative, as dialogue, or whatever generic mode is selected.

In Phase II Nigel recognizes two generic structures: narrative and dialogue. Narrative involves entirely mathetic sequences; dialogue is mixed, but often has a strongly pragmatic component. The two are not, of course, pure categories; narratives occur in dialogue settings, and dialogue is used as a means of constructing narrative. But each has its characteristic forms of organization. Question and answer, for example, is a form of texture that belongs to dialogue, whereas sequences of observations typically occur in narrative. As we saw in Chapter 4, Nigel starts early in Phase II forming sequences that have a semantic structure but not yet a grammatical structure, like 'tree, broken, take-away, all-gone, byebye'; these are early narratives. As time goes on, he learns to represent sequences such as these in a grammatically structured form; but meanwhile his semantic structures have themselves become more complex, so that they are beyond the range of grammatical structure but are structured in the generic sense – they have texture as narrative.

An interesting feature of such sequences is how they are built up through dialogue. The following is an example. Nigel, at 20 months, has been taken to the zoo, and in the children's section has picked up a plastic lid which he is clutching in one hand while stroking a goat with the other. The goat, after the manner of its kind, starts to eat the lid. The keeper intervenes, and says kindly but firmly that the goat must not eat the lid – it would not be good for it. Here is Nigel reviewing the incident after returning home, some hours later:

N: try eat lìd
F: What tried to eat the lid?
N: try eat lìd
F: What tried to eat the lid?
N: gòat ... man said nò ... goat try eat lìd ... man said nò

Then, after a further interval, while being put to bed:

N: goat try eat lìd ... man said nò
M: Why did the man say no?
N: goat shòuldn't eat lid ... (shaking head) gòodfor it
M: The goat shouldn't eat the lid; it's not good for it.
N: goat try eat lìd ... man said nò ... goat shòuldn't eat lid ... (shaking head) gòodfor it

This story is then repeated as a whole, verbatim, at frequent intervals over the next few months.

The outcome of the dialogue is a typical narrative sequence, a set of utterances that are related as parts of a narrative. But as well as having this "generic" structure, they also display texture in the sense of internal structure and cohesion: there is the repetition of the words *goat* and *lid*, the anaphoric *it*, and the marked tonic on *shouldn't* showing that the following *eat lid* is to be interpreted as "Given", as recoverable from what has gone before. In other words Nigel is beginning to build up the third component in the adult semantic system, the textual or text-forming component. In the adult language there are two parts to this: one based on structure, the other based on cohesion. The former consists of the theme and information systems of the clause, expressed through word order, nominalizations of various kinds, and the distribution into **Given** and **New** that is realized by intonation, by the placing of the tonic or primary stress. The latter consists of various anaphoric relations of reference, substitution, ellipsis, conjunction and collocation. Both these forms of texture begin to appear in Nigel's language quite early in Phase II.

Already in Phase I he has used intonation as a text-forming device, when he distinguishes between a̋::dà (mid falling) 'what's that?' and a̋::dà (high falling) 'and what's *that*?'. Perhaps the clearest example came from the "naming game", which Nigel began at about 15 months, with a sign meaning 'look at this picture, let's name it together' — it being understood that he knows the name perfectly well and has heard it in this context before. He opens his little board book, points to a coloured picture in it and says:

adȳdà [mid level + mid fall, no upjump]

This is what is going to evolve at the next stage into the meaning 'what's that?', the demand for a name that is unknown; but at this stage it is simply 'you say the name'. So his mother says "That's a ball". Nigel then turns over to the next page and he says:

adȳdà [mid level + (upjump to) high fall]

'and what's *that*?'. Here we have a clear signal that this is a second move; the upjump and high falling tone show that it is a follow-up to the first exchange. This is already a form of interaction that has texture to it; the relation of this utterance to what preceded it is foregrounded by the use of a special intonation pattern.

Texture is also present, in a special sense, in the kind of reparatory acts that the child engages in, when one of his acts of meaning has failed. We should not be too surprised at the child's early awareness of instances in which the communication process has broken down, when his meaning has not got over. What is interesting is the strategy the child adopts for repairing the breakdown. Nigel developed at an early age (1.6) a strategy that would serve him in such situations for the rest of his life: he learnt to repeat, slowly and clearly, the items that had not been understood. The day after he reached 18 months, he had been out for a walk, and after getting home was rehearsing the things he had seen:

Gà:ɷGɛ̀:ɷ ... tìk^u ... lòu ... bà ...

"(I saw) ducks, sticks, holes, buses". The next item in the list was

dòubā

His father, who was responding as he went along, had followed him up to this point; but this defeated him. The expression usually meant 'toast and butter', but it seemed unlikely that Nigel had seen toast and butter on his walk. He tried various guesses, but they were not right, and finally Nigel repeated, very slowly and deliberately:

dōubà

– just as if he was talking to someone having difficulty with the language. As it happened, the ruse did not work; his father never did understand. But the pattern was established, and represented a significant step in the development of a texture of verbal interaction.

Let me now illustrate the specific stages through which Nigel built up the elementary text-forming resources of the mother tongue. There are certain semantic patterns which serve to give cohesion to a discourse: reference, substitution, conjunction, reiteration. Nigel began to develop these during the transition from protolanguage to mother tongue, roughly the second half of the second year. The first to appear was the demonstrative reference item *that*; and it was used first in a deictic (exophoric) context, referring to the situation, for example, (1;7):

that bròke

meaning 'that thing there'. At the same time, Nigel began regularly using the expressions

háve it [or] háve that [avit, avdát]

accompanied by pointing, meaning 'I want that thing there'. In this period, $19\frac{1}{2}$ to 21 months, *that* and *it* are exophoric, referring to things in the situation; but there is an interesting example at 1;8 which is in a sense intermediate between exophoric and anaphoric references, namely

that sóng

meaning 'sing that song you've just been singing'. The progression to fully anaphoric reference is gradual; in 1;8 we have

train under túnnel ... getit fóryou

where the train is only just out of sight, and

why that clóck stop ... ménd it

where the clock is being remembered from some hours earlier, and the whole utterance may be copied from what his father had said at the time. True anaphoric reference is not established until 1;11.

Meanwhile, however, Nigel had another partly anaphoric element at this stage, which was not a reference item but a substitute. This was the word *one*, as it occurs in English in *give me another one* where *one* is a replacement for some noun that the hearer has to supply from the preceding context: he must be able to tell, another what. Nigel uses the substitute *one* first of all in contexts where it is both exophoric and anaphoric at the same time. He is blowing bubbles; a particularly fine bubble appears, and he says:

    big òne

(with tonic on *one*, not on *big* as in adult speech). Previous to that the world *bubble* had been used, including by Nigel himself:

    bēb^w ɹàuɹəu

'bubbles going round and round'. So when he says *big one*, the bubbles have been mentioned before, and they are also there in the context. The same expression was used when he was watching trains go by at the station and a second train came along which was longer than the one before; this time the tonic was on *big*:

    bìg one

Again the referent is present in the context; there is still a situational as well as a textual component in the meaning of the substitute *one*.

This particular period, $19\frac{1}{2}$ to 21 months, is critical for Nigel's development of text structure. Here is a little interchange with his mother. Nigel is sitting in his high chair and waiting patiently for his breakfast; he says:

    put bemax down on táble

"Put Bemax down on table". But the Bemax is already there, on the big table; his mother says "It is on the table". Nigel says:

    níla table

"Nigel's table", in other words 'put it on my table'. The sequence is:

NIGEL:	Put Bemax down on *table*.
MOTHER:	It *is* on the table.
NIGEL:	*Nigel* table.

Note the intonation pattern, in which the tonic has gone back from its unmarked position on the final lexical item to the lexical item that precedes, thus clearly marking the second occurrence of *table* as related by contrast to the first, exactly as in an adult utterance. Again as in adult speech, the tone is not affected; it remains rising, the tone that Nigel is using at this period for all pragmatic (response-demanding) utterances. Shortly after this, having been warned about the consequences of banging his trains around, Nigel said:

> that blue train might brèak ... réd train might break

"That blue train might break; red train might break?" – in other words, does the rule apply also to the red train? Here the tonic moves right to the beginning and the whole of the rest is post-tonic.

These examples show that Nigel has learnt to contrast different information structures, using a marked form, that with the tonic in pre-final position, to relate what he is saying to the preceding discourse. The same pattern appears again in the following dialogue: Nigel has been out for a walk with his mother, and when he gets back he looks at her and says (1;9):

> big nòise

His mother asks "Who made a big noise?" Nigel answers:

> drìll make big noise

"*Drill* make big noise". The tonic on *drill* signals that what follows is 'given' material.

The systematic placing of the tonic also comes into play when Nigel learns to make lists, for example (1;9):

> One blúe chuffa ... one rèd chuffa

"One *blue* train, one *red* train". This involves not only presupposing what has gone before but also anticipating what is to come; the list must have been planned as a whole.

We have been focusing attention on a stage in language development which is critical because, from a linguistic point of view, it represents a transition. This stage, which corresponds, with Nigel, to the second half of the second year, is the one in which Nigel is moving from the protolanguage into the mother tongue; and as part of the process, at the same time as learning to build up the other components of meaning, and the structures to express them, he is also learning to build up this **textual** or text-forming component.

But the contrastive **location** of tonic prominence cannot arise until there is structure; and instances of it begin to appear around NL 7. Examples are:

> N. put bemax down on **táble** M. It is on the table. N. **níla** table ('on *my* table!')
> N. dada got scrambled **èkg** ... mummy get **fóryou** scrambled egg ('get some for *me*!')
> N. big **nòise** M. What made a big noise? N. **drìll** make big noise

INTO THE ADULT LANGUAGE

About the same time, the first cohesive patterns begin to appear: first substitution (*one*), then reference (*it*, *that*), then conjunction (*but*). The reference items *it* and *that* occur first in what is generally assumed to be their primary meaning, that of reference to the situation: *have it!*, *have that!*, *why broken that?*; their use in text reference follows somewhat later. The substitute *one*, on the other hand, occurs from the start in contexts where it is both situationally and textually relevant – where the object is present **and** the word for which *one* is substituting has already been used, for example, *big one* 'big bubble' while blowing bubbles and talking about them. Conjunction comes a little way behind, the first instance being in NL 9: *that tree got no lèaf on ... thát tree got leaf on but that tree got no lèaf on*, which also has the marked tonic on *that* in the clause immediately preceding the *but*. This *but* is the first instance of a conjunctive in Nigel's speech; its function, as in the adult language, is to link the second clause in a meaningful way to the first. It is the expression of one of a small number of semantic relations – additive, adversative, causal and temporal – which, taken as a whole, provide an interpretation of each step in the discourse in terms of how it relates to what has gone before. As an instance of a number of these patterns coming together, the following is a typical specimen of dialogue from NL 9:

> N. chuffa walk on ràilway line (2) ... fast chùffa ... one day might gò on fast chuffa (2) F. Yes, we might. N. one day go on blue chùffa ... next chuffa còming ... go on thàt one.

6.5 The imaginative function

This last example is in an imaginary setting; the conversation actually takes place in the home. It illustrates the third semiotic mode, the imaginative, which is always present as a subsidiary theme in the development of meaning. Imaginative uses of language tend to have a phonology of their own; we saw in Phase I that the forms of verbal play tended to be distinct both in intonation and in other respects – naturally, since verbal play includes phonological play, with its rhyming and chiming and other types of sound pattern. (The most elaborated form of phonological play is of course singing, which is playing with the intonation and rhythm system.) But the system lends itself to play at all levels, and from this develops the semantic invention that emerges as a feature of Phase II – the use of the meaning potential to create a fictional environment. The recall function plays an essential part in this; when Nigel imagines to himself 'next chuffa coming ... go on that one', he is also recalling past events in which this would have been appropriate discourse and may actually have been said.

In the same way most of a young child's story-telling is a stringing together of recollections, either of past events or of stories told to him. Hence the vehicle for this kind of imaginative use of language is the mathetic mode, and the generic form is that of narrative. So clearly is this so that we tend to use the term "narrative" in ordinary discourse to refer primarily to fictional narrative. But it is worth remembering that narrative develops first as a strategy for learning, and that it is only when the ideational potential comes to be combined with the imaginative function (which has developed independently of it) that fictional narrative is born.

Even when Nigel does begin to use meaning as a form of play, however, it is game-play that predominates rather than pretend-play. Indeed the earliest instance of semantic pretence seems to have been the result of a misunderstanding: Nigel said *I go shòpping*, which probably, in the current state of flux of his person system, meant '(I see) you're going shopping'. It was interpreted, however, as 'I'm (pretending I'm) going shopping', and the response was 'Are you? What are you going to buy?' Nigel thereupon joined in the act and said 'Eggs'. If Nigel's original utterance was pretend-play, it is unique and remains so for some time. Much more typical of the imaginative context is an exchange such as that exemplified from earlier in NL 9, beginning *eat chùffa*, in which Nigel plays a long verbal game – it is a game at every level, phonological, lexicogrammatical and semantic – around the theme of *can't eat chuffa, can't eat man, can't eat book*. It is not long before this sort of thing will make him laugh; the ability to laugh at meanings (as distinct from laughing at things, like the hole in Daddy's toothbrush) seems to be a Phase III accomplishment, dependent on the fully fledged status of the semantic system, but the ability to play with meanings is a noticeable feature of the transition.

The following figures present a summary of the development outlined in this section, arranged under the headings of pragmatic and mathetic. All the examples cited appear in the lists given in section 5. It is hoped that this rather sketchy summary gives some idea of the progress of one child through the transitional stage linking his creation of a first 'infant' language with his mastery of the adult system. It should be emphasized once again that his entry into what we are calling Phase III, at about the end of his second year, does not mean that he has mastered the English language. It means that he has constructed for himself a three-level semiotic system which is organized the way the adult language is. It is English and not any other language, just as a tulip bud is a tulip and not a chrysanthemum or a rose. But it still has a long way to go before it comes into full flower.

INTO THE ADULT LANGUAGE

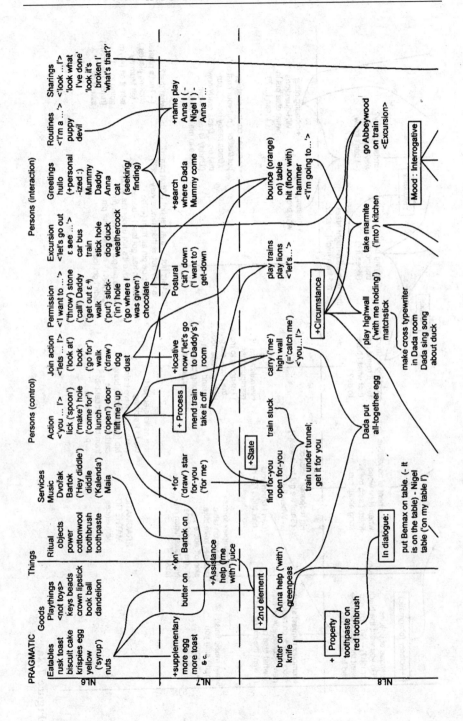

TRANSITION FROM CHILD TONGUE TO MOTHER TONGUE

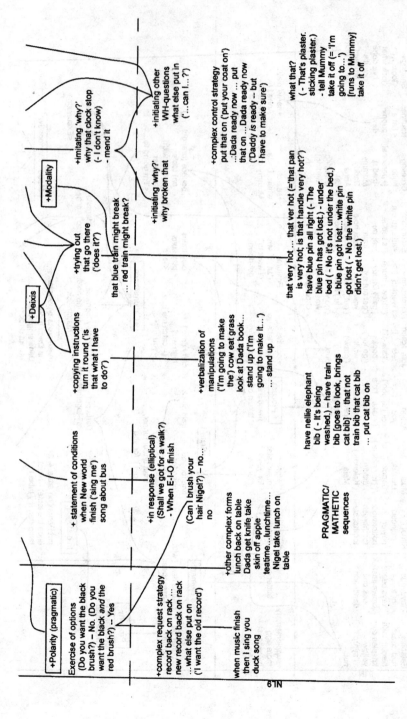

Figure 7.2a

INTO THE ADULT LANGUAGE

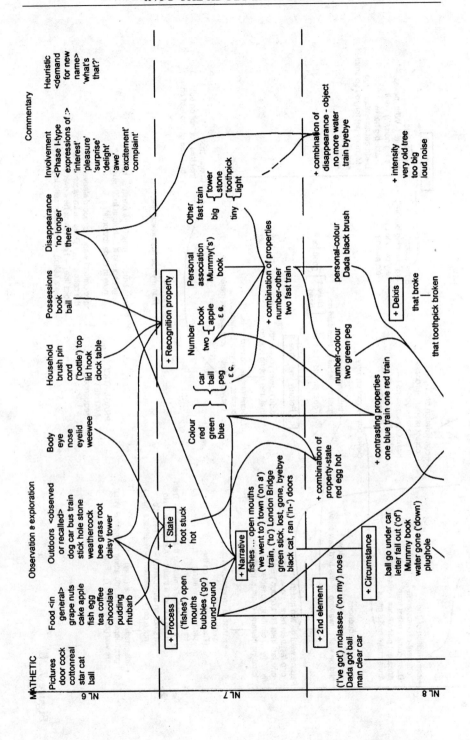

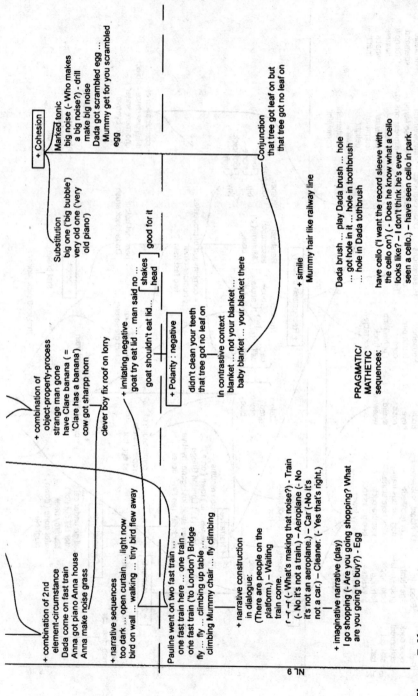

Figure 7.2b

Chapter Eight

THE CONTRIBUTION OF DEVELOPMENTAL LINGUISTICS TO THE INTERPRETATION OF LANGUAGE AS A SYSTEM (1980)

Introduction

Before child development studies could be seriously undertaken, and certainly before they could have a significant impact on intellectual trends, a change had to occur in the interpretation of childhood itself, in society's view of what it means to be a child. Brazelton recalls (1979: 79) that not so long ago infants were considered to be "functioning at a reflex or mid-brain level"; and Margaret Bullowa writes (1979b: 27) "When I was a medical student I was taught that infants were born blind and deaf. ... Even somewhat older infants were not credited with much ability to perceive the world around them. Not only pediatricians but also psychologists consigned them to a world of blurred confusion."

If a child is regarded as an imperfect version of an adult, which is the traditional attitude in Western and some other cultures (compare the representation of children in art as dwarfs with adult facial and bodily proportions), child development, including language development, will be looked on as an advance from imperfection towards perfection; and child behaviour, including language behaviour, as a defective approximation to the adult norm. In such circumstances, neither the behaviour nor the developmental process will have any intrinsic interest for the interpretation of the finished state, whether the adult language or adulthood in general; nor any philosophical interest either.

First published in *The Nordic Language and Modern Linguistics: Proceedings of the Fourth International Conference of Nordic and General Linguistics*. Oslo: Universitesforlaget AS, 1980, pp. 1–18.

Developmental studies can begin to acquire significance when childhood is seen not as imperfection, or even as immaturity in a negative sense (a lack of maturity), but as a distinct facet of the human condition; and growing is seen as a form of being, one that is characterized by positive features of its own.

It requires a mental effort to perceive that, at any moment when a child is construing a system, he also has a system construed. And when we have made this effort we are liable to go to the other extreme, not only recognizing that the child has a system but also so stressing its perfection that we leave ourselves no room for explaining how – still less why – it goes on to evolve into something else. At this point it helps if we remind ourselves that the adult system is not perfect either, but varying and continually evolving; ontogeny is simply one dimension of the system-creating process, and all behavioural systems, including language, are essentially metastable in character, persisting only through adaptation and change.

A child's linguistic system, at any stage in its development, is a system in just the same sense that the adult's is. But it is a system in which we can see not only traces of its past, in the same way that, phylogenetically, language as we know it today carries the traces of its evolutionary past, but also – since we know where it is going – promises of its future. An aim of developmental linguistics is to be able to suggest why the system has developed in just the way it has; and in order to know this we first try to identify what it is that the child has to construe and then ask why this is so, bearing in mind the functions that language serves in the lives both of young and of fully grown members of the human species.

This paper attempts to enumerate some of the significant steps in language development, interpreted in terms abstract enough to suggest why they should be significant; it is an analytic exercise – the steps are not given to us as isolates, nor are they directly recognizable in the forms of language used. The last section summarizes their consequences for our understanding of the nature of language as a system. It should be emphasized that in all of what follows **the object under consideration is language**. We are not using language as instrument, to shed light on child development (or on any other object, such as cognition or the nature of understanding); we are using child development as instrument, to shed light on the nature of the object we call language.

1 The foundations of language: communicative intent and symbolic act

One sign of the revised attitude to childhood is the attention that is now being paid to the behaviour of infants and neonates. From observations of the way they interact with caregivers, it can be asserted that children communicate from birth; that they have an innate predisposition to address, and to recognize that they are being addressed. We hear this assertion couched in general cultural terms: "as any parent knows ...".

It can also be surmised, though not proclaimed with any certainty, that children are born with the ability to act symbolically, to use and recognize symbols. Since they seem to proceed along a path leading from non-symbolic acts, through partially symbolic ones where the symbols are iconic, to reach those that are fully symbolic, it may be that this is something that they have to learn. But the evidence could be interpreted in different ways.

These – the intent to communicate, and the ability to act with symbols (to 'mean') – are the two prerequisites to the construction of language (cf. Bullowa 1979b).

For a time it was hypothesized that a child was 'born with a grammar', an acquisition device specific to language as distinct from other forms of learning. But since one element that is **not** a prerequisite of language is a grammar (there is no grammar in infantile language systems), this hypothesis is difficult to maintain; and in any case it is not necessary.

Whether the ability to act symbolically is innate or not, it cannot develop except through interaction. The language-creating process is an interactive one, shared between child and caregivers; the caregivers not only exchange meanings with the child, they also construe the system along with him. Condon noted some years ago the 'tracking' of speaker by listener in adult speech situations, referring to it as "interactional synchrony" (Condon 1979: 136); later on he observed infants tracking adult speech (Condon and Sander 1974). By the same token, the adult listener tracks the speaking child; child and adult share in the creation of text. Now, when we come to study the infant's language development, we find the concept of tracking is fundamental here too. Not only do the caregivers track the *process*, they also track the *system*. Child and adult share in the creation of language. The mother knows where the child has got to (subconsciously; she is not aware she has this knowledge, as a rule), because she is construing the system along with him; she brings it into play receptively, and stores it alongside her own more highly developed system – which had been construed along similar lines in the first place.

2 The nature of language: pregrammatical (protolinguistic) and grammaticalized (linguistic) systems

The infant begins by construing a *protolanguage* (as discussed in Part 1; cf. Carter 1978a). This has still been surprisingly little studied; but it seems to be a general pattern, compare Newson (1979: 252) "By the final third of the first year normal babies have acquired a number of intonated vocal signals the utterance of which conveys a particular message."

A characteristic of infantile protolanguages is that they are bi-stratal systems, having a semantics and a phonology (or other expressive mode) but no grammar. Their elements are discrete signs, content–expression pairs. The meaning is directly encoded in sound or gesture.

During the second year of life, children construe a tri-stratal system, with a grammar (that is, a lexicogrammar, presented as words and structures) emerging as interface between meaning and sound. I have documented in detail how this step was taken by one particular child (cf. Chapter 7); no doubt there are many possible routes, though perhaps a fairly small number of general strategies.

A tri-stratal system is a prerequisite to the expansion of the meaning potential. Only with a grammar, a purely abstract level of coding between meaning and sound, is it possible to mean more than one thing at once: to map meanings on to one another so that sets of options, each by itself very simple, can combine to form rich and complex paradigms of semantic configurations.

Here is Nigel at age 1;8, reporting on an incident in the street:

blā miào ... ɹʷā dɔ̀ə
'black cat; ran indoors'

The wording conveys the ideational meanings: '(there was) a black cat, (and it) ran indoors'. The intonation signals that the utterance was mathetic not pragmatic – a reflection on the world, not a request for action. As is typical at this stage (as throughout life!), the child's semantic potential was ahead of his grammatical potential; this was a single message, a semantic structure, but he could not yet encode it as a grammatical structure on a single tone contour.

Despite various attempts to demonstrate the contrary, and even to bring it about artificially, it seems likely that species other than humans do not take this critical step of building a grammar, and so turning protolanguage into language. In my opinion this is the criterial distinction between human (adult) and animal communication systems: human languages are tri-stratal systems, having a lexicogrammatical stratum, a linguistic "form", as the interface between meaning and expression. The infantile protolanguage resembles the communication patterns of other species in that it lacks this middle stratum.

3 The content of language: goods-and-services and information

The communication process is a mode of exchange, in which one of two things is being exchanged: either goods-and-services, or information. Language functions in both these modes.

Children first use language – the protolanguage – to exchange goods-and-services. They have no means of conceptualizing the exchange of information until they have language with which to do it. The protolanguage is quite effective for exchanging goods-and-services: a child can use it to **get** what he wants given to him or done for him, to **make** someone behave in the way he wants, or to **give** something to someone; meanings such as 'I want that object given to me', 'I want that service done for me', 'I want you to play with me', 'I'm giving this to you' can be effectively coded in simple signs. But the protolanguage is not well adapted to the exchange of information.

The ability to interact in these two modes is a prerequisite to conversation, and hence to "being socialized" through language. The first steps towards the information mode are taken right at the beginning, at the same time as the first demands for goods-and-services; they are, typically, expressions of pleasure and interest ('I like that', 'I'm curious about that') and signs celebrating the sharing of experience ('let's look at this together'). But the road from here to the information mode is both long and complex.

The act of telling someone something that one knows they do not already know – the paradigm form of the exchange of information, in which language functions as a surrogate for shared experience – is a function that evolves quite late in the developmental process. But it does not arise out of nowhere. There are antecedent steps, as just referred to; and there is an overall functional continuity from protolanguage into language (Griffiths 1979). Table 1 shows the path taken by Nigel in his gradual development of the function of 'I've got something to tell you'.

Table 1 The development of the ability to exchange information: a possible path

Possible age (very variable)	Function of child's utterance	Meaning of child's utterance	Stage
0;8	interaction	'hullo!'	protolanguage
0;10	interaction through shared attention (for example, to picture)	'hullo! – let's look at this together'	protolanguage
1;0	shared attention to object (for example, picture)	'let's look at this together'	protolanguage
1;2	shared attention + naming by other	'let's look at this; you say its name!'	transition
1;4	shared attention + naming by child	'we're both looking at a …'	transition
1;6	shared recall + naming by child	'we both saw a …'	transition
1;8	shared recall + description by child	'… happened (we both saw it)'	language
1;10	recall + description by child of event not shared by other	'… happened (you weren't there to see it)'	language

4 The construal of language: text ('process') and system

In construing language from the representations they hear around them, children seem to adopt a two-pronged strategy.

On the one hand they use the representations as **evidence**, construing the system out of numerous instances; the instances are not only rich in meaning, wording and sound, they are also contextualized – rich in relation to their environment. Thus a child may hear around him instances which include the phonetic representations of ... *bus!*, ... *bus?*, ... *car!*, etc.; these provide evidence for the construal of phonological *systems* of intonation and articulation, a subset of which he is then able to realize productively in his own representations which now come to include forms such as bà, bá, kà, etc. (cf. Crystal 1979).

On the other hand they use the representations as *text*, construing them as integrated pieces and putting them to use in conversation. The child may hear "Look, there's a man cleaning his car." He processes this, represents it as mæ̀ klī: kà, and repeats this text many times over as the narrative of a recalled event.

With these two parallel thrusts he advances in a leapfrog fashion, now one now the other moving ahead. A piece of text is construed, and used appropriately, which includes lexicogrammatical and phonological features that have not yet been processed into the system. The system then catches up and goes ahead, leaving the piece of text still represented in the old way until it is reprocessed and dies a natural death.

The ability to process instances in this way, construing them simultaneously both as system and as text, is a prerequisite to the mastery of all representational systems, including but not limited to language.

The view has been expressed that the instances of language which children hear around them are insufficient as evidence on which to construe the system. This appears to ignore two facts. First, the speech by which a child is typically surrounded is fluent, highly structured and richly contextualized; not at all like the self-conscious, closely monitored and situationally isolated speech that is characteristic of intellectual discussions, on observations of which such a view seems to have been founded. Second, the construal of systems out of observed representations along some such lines as those set out above is a general learning problem that children have to solve for all semiotic systems of the culture; their ability to do so derives from their ability to mean – to recognize and process symbols.

5 The construction of reality through language: action and reflection

As what seems to be a primary strategy for moving from protolanguage into language, some children – possibly a majority – make the systematic distinction already referred to, between pragmatic and mathetic utterances: between talk as a means of **acting on** the world and talk as a means of **learning about** the world. The former is, of course, acting on people, since talk cannot act directly on the world; this derives from the goods-and-services mode.[1] The latter is a stage in the journey towards the information mode (the steps shown as "transition" in Table 1).

Children make this distinction in a variety of ways: typically by some prosodic feature of intonation or voice quality, since it is a feature of the utterance as a whole. But in the initial stage the distinction is not yet integrated into the system: each utterance is **either** one of action **or** one of reflection, so that these functions are functions of the utterance. In the adult language, on the other hand, every utterance has **both** functions. The option of 'goods-and-services or information' is built into the grammar; these become the two primary modes of action, represented by the system of mood in the clause. Here they can be freely mapped on to meanings of the reflection type, represented in the clause by transitivity. In this way action and reflection have become functional components of the linguistic system.

The systematization of these two functions of action and reflection is a prerequisite to using language in the construction of reality. Reality construction is an intersubjective process, and for language to be able to model the world it is necessary for the utterance to select in both systems, having both an ideational content and a rhetorical or interpersonal force (cf. Wells 1974).

At the same time as this, children also construe the context of situation, taking account both of what is happening and of what has been said before, and giving texture to their utterances accordingly. This provides a third strand in the functional fabric of their discourse.

This third component is the source of relevance, and a prerequisite of success in connected discourse. It has still been relatively little studied in developmental linguistic research. But as in so many other aspects, we are continually being surprised at how early children build texture into their speech. One example from Nigel, at 1;9:

NIGEL:	Big **nòise**.
MOTHER:	What made a big noise?
NIGEL:	**Drìll** make big noise.

Nigel's response shows that he has established the principle of information focus. He uses the appropriate marked form, by which *drill* is marked as new information and all the rest as given. He has established it, moreover, in relation to the **linguistic** context: situationally, everything was 'given', since both he and his mother had been watching the drill at work. But textually *drill* was new, the answer to *what?*; and this he signalled, as the adult language does, by the placement of the tonic nucleus. Without this component of texture, language would not be an effective instrument for the child's construal of reality.

6 Implications for language as a system

In the ontogenesis of language, meanings and sounds appear before wordings. The emergence of an organized semantics and phonology precedes that of an organized lexicogrammar, typically by half a year or more. There is thus a basic discontinuity in the evolution of the linguistic system, as it develops from a bi-stratal to a tri-stratal form. But there is no such discontinuity in the meanings themselves (cf. Grieve and Hoegenraad 1979). By the time the grammar begins to be construed, its functions are already defined by reference to the 'outer' levels: its task is to facilitate the representation of meanings in sound. Grammar comes into being with a job already set up for it.

It seems natural, therefore, that we should think of grammar as the derived system, collectively determined by the requirements of meaning and sound. Grammar is as it is because of what it has to do: the kinds of meaning it has to realize, the medium it has to be realized in, and the types of systematic relationship that are possible between the two.

But it is not only the functional organization of the grammar that we can interpret in terms of this continuity from the protolanguage, we can also see in it an explanation of the form of the grammar. Since the meanings were there first – admittedly in an embryonic form, but such as to display clearly the different kinds of meaning the system could generate, with its basic commitment to the twin modes of action and reflection – the grammar is shaped to fit them. It is a 'natural' grammar, in which the active, interpersonal meanings are strung prosodically through the clause, while the reflective, ideational meanings are 'chunked' into clause constituents. For example,

NIGEL (coming into Father's study):   dada ready nòw
    ('Daddy's ready')
(But his father is obviously not ready)
NIGEL: dada ready nów ('Daddy must get ready!')

Nigel's language already displays the essential features of a natural grammar. The ideational meaning is represented by an attribute *ready*, a 'carrier' of this attribute *dada* and a temporal deictic *now*. The interpersonal meaning is represented by a tone contour marking the mood: mathetic (which later evolves into indicative) by falling tone, pragmatic (which evolves into imperative) by rising tone. The textual meaning is signalled, also naturally, at the boundaries: *dada* as theme, *now* as information focus (new).

The relationship of form to meaning here is clearly non-arbitrary; the grammar mediates between the semantics and the phonology but takes its orders from the semantics. No doubt this naturalness of adult grammar is one of the factors that makes it easy for children to learn – and also one that enables adults to communicate linguistically with infants despite the qualitative difference between protolanguage and language (Kaye 1979). The mother can construe the protolinguistic system; and she can respond to protolinguistic text as if it was text in language. And in complementary fashion, the infant can process adult utterances as if they were protolinguistic signs.

Presumably some form of protolanguage is present in the caregiver's own ontogenetic memory. Probably it is also enshrined in the phylogenetic 'memory', in the form of traces in the adult language system: adult languages contain signs which, as it were, bypass the grammar, like intonation contours, and even some which are unifunctional and non-systemic, typically exclamations of various kinds. These represent earlier stages in the evolution of human language; and notably it is often these forms that adults bring into prominence when talking to children. One aspect of the rather elusive "simplicity" that characterizes language that is addressed to young infants is a protolinguistic simplicity; it consists in saying things which, though not part of the child's own protolanguage, could be the output of a system of the same kind.

More significant, however, is the adult's ability to "simplify" in a manner where the simplicity does not lie in the utterance itself but in the response it demands. Adult speech to infants is full of utterances to which the appropriate response is a sign in the infant's protolanguage, like the following exchange with Nigel at age 1;1:

MOTHER: Do you want some orange juice?
NIGEL: Yī! ('(yes) I want (that)')

Text, the language process, is co-created by child and other; each in interaction with the other, and both in interaction with the context of situation (Dore 1979). What the child learns from is not the **product** that comes from out there, but the interactive **process** by which his own resources are playing a part in creating the text. It is not only the pragmatic mode that is interactive in its origin and unfolding; the same is equally true of the mathetic. Here is Nigel at 1;1, in the sort of exchange that occurs dozens of times a day:

NIGEL (looking at picture book): dèə ('look – now you say its name')
MOTHER (looking at book with him): That's a rattle; yes.

It is only later that the mathetic mode evolves into narrative, and then when it does the creation of narrative continues to be an interactive process.

As the grammar develops, the different speech functions evolve with their own grammatical forms. The pragmatic mode expands into a system of command, suggestion and offer: 'I want you to ...', 'I want us to ...', 'I want (me) to ...'. The mathetic becomes a statement; but a statement as **a symbol of** shared experience – the informative function, with its system of statement and question where statement is **in lieu of** shared experience, takes longer to construe. In other words, of the two types of exchange that form the basis of adult dialogue, goods-and-services represents an earlier element in language. The use of symbols to **represent as** acts of meaning (specifically commands, suggestions and offers) acts that are in essence non-symbolic precedes the use of symbols to **create** acts of meaning (statements and questions) that are inherently symbolic in nature. The latter have a complex evolution; but they seem to begin as a blend of the interactive and the personal, a sort of 'let's be interested in this together'.

In the adult grammar, information and goods-and-services are systematically distinguished through the system of mood: imperative for goods-and-services, indicative for information. But since it is only through being encoded as language that information comes into existence, it has to have a 'real' grammar – ***indicative: declarative/ interrogative***, with regular forms of realization. Goods-and-services, on the other hand, exist independently of language, and can be exchanged, up to a point, without benefit of linguistic mediation. Hence the imperative, although it appears early in the genesis of language, remains a marginal category that never fully evolves.

We have stressed that the protolanguage is a repertory of signs; it admits no distinction between system and process. It is only as a child enters the transition from protolanguage to language that it makes sense to separate the two, and then only analytically; as the child construes them, there can be no process without system and no system without process. The meaning of a text resides in its relation to the meaning potential that lies behind it and is instantiated in it. From the ontogenetic point of view, therefore, it is hard to see any justification for having one "theory of language" and another "theory of text". In child language (and I would argue in adult language also) the only way to interpret text is by showing how it derives from the system; and the only way to interpret the system is by showing how it engenders text.

But perhaps the single most salient feature that emerges from a study of linguistic ontogeny is the underpinning of the functional-semantic interpretation of the system. We suggest that the functional contrast of pragmatic/mathetic is a strategy for the transition from protolanguage to language. By observing how this evolves into the semantic system of the adult language, with its interpersonal and ideational components, we can begin to see exactly how the functional demands that are made on language have shaped the linguistic system. There is a clear functional continuity – a continuity that is all the more striking given the changes that take place in the system in the course of its evolution – extending from the earliest instances of protolanguage right through to adulthood.

The study of how children construe language has demonstrated the validity of the claim that a functional theory of language is not a theory of utterance types but a theory about the nature of the linguistic system. More interestingly, developmental linguistic studies show how the functions become incorporated into the system. In the protolanguage, where there is no difference between system and process, functions of the utterance are by definition also functional elements or components of the system. As the two come to be separated, children begin by assigning each utterance to just one of two primary functions, for thinking or for doing; then, passing through an intermediate stage in which each utterance has one function predominating, they reinterpret these two, by means of the grammar, as distinct components in the semantic system. Each is then present in the structure of all utterances: the former as an ideational component, specifying a constituent structure in terms of processes, participants and circumstance; the latter as an interpersonal component specifying the mood, modality and other aspects of the rhetoric of speaker–listener interaction.

Child language studies thus point strongly to a functional interpretation of the linguistic system; and in doing so, they help to provide a wider context for theories of language. One of the interesting byproducts of the last two decades of research in developmental linguistics is that, in the course of throwing new light on child development, it has helped to end the isolation of linguistics itself, creating new links with socialization theory, sociology of knowledge, developmental and cognitive psychology, and other disciplines that are concerned with what it means to be a child.

Note

1. To say this is not to deny the point made many years ago by Malinowski, and taken up recently in child language studies by Strömqvist (1980), that there is an important magical element in the functions of children's speech. In his study of pretend play Strömqvist finds children using language "to create reality by standing in for (and doing the job of) a non-linguistic action or event", thus making "the state of affairs ... conform to the child's conception of how things ought to be" (1980: 59). But this seems to be a linguistic rather than a protolinguistic phenomenon. I have never observed an infant addressing a protolinguistic utterance to an object – though they do frequently address them to animals at this stage.

Chapter Nine

ON THE TRANSITION FROM CHILD TONGUE TO MOTHER TONGUE
(1983)

It is perhaps not too fanciful to say that there has been a revolution in professional thinking about children, and about the nature of childhood, in the last few decades of our culture. Margaret Bullowa, recalling her experience as a student in medical school in the 1930s, wrote (1979b: 27–8):

> When I was a medical student I was taught that infants were born blind and deaf ... Even somewhat older infants were not credited with much ability to perceive the world around them. Not only pediatricians but also psychologists consigned them to a world of blurred confusion ... Not so long ago, infants were hardly credited with having any minds at all, at least in most American academic psychology.

A glance at the chapter headings in her own book will show how different the perspective is today.

How far this reflects a change in the attitudes of the community, and in particular of parents, towards children and towards newborn babies, it is less easy to say. Historians of childhood, such as Philippe Ariès (1962), and Lloyd de Mause (1974), have documented the social distance that lies between our own times and the medieval world; and de Mause, at least, maintains that some of the critical changes in the perception of children by adults are very recent in origin. On the other hand, parental behaviour, especially the communicative interaction of parents with their children, is largely unconscious, and therefore often very different from what it is reported to be; the mother who said to me, with some amazement, "Oh – he can't talk yet!", when I asked her

---

First published in *Australian Journal of Linguistics*. Sydney: Australian Linguistic Society, 1983, 3.2, pp. 201–16.

what her one-year-old son was saying to her, was actually engaged in a lengthy and animated conversation with him – she in her language, he in his protolanguage – in which both parties were actively involved as listener and as speaker by turns. It is not easy to reconstruct the reality of family life in past generations.

Darwin is said to have commented that a human being learns more in the first three years of life than in any subsequent period of comparable length; and his own brief observations on child language suggest that he was a careful and sympathetic observer. In a well-known passage, written in 1877 but based on records made over 30 years earlier, Darwin wrote (Bar-Adon and Leopold 1971: 28–9):

> The wants of an infant are at first made intelligible by instinctive cries, which after a time are modified in part unconsciously, and in part, as I believe, voluntarily as a means of communication, – by the unconscious expression of the features, – by gestures and in a marked manner by different intonations, – lastly by words of a general nature invented by himself, then of a more precise nature imitated from those which he hears;

This is a perceptive and accurate account, one which is conceptually akin to the diary tradition in developmental linguistics, although Darwin's own record as he transmits it is extremely sparse. And it is from the diary studies, in which intensive observations were made of individual children, typically within the family and with the child's behaviour being natural and unelicited, rather than from the academic disciplines, that the message comes through that communicative behaviour begins at a very early stage in life. It begins, we would now say, at birth, and perhaps even before.

Linguists too were slow to take up the message, being constrained by the schemata of their own discipline just as psychologists were by theirs. Developmental linguistics tended, naturally, to follow the theoretical path opened up by general linguistic studies; it began with an emphasis on phonology, represented by Jakobson's (1968) famous work published in 1941, and then moved, following Chomsky, into syntax. As in linguistics, or at least in the established linguistics of the United States and its intellectual allies – NATO linguistics, so to speak – so in the developmental linguistics that derived from it, the 1960s was the syntactic age. Language development was seen as the acquisition of syntactic structures, in line with Chomsky's theory of generative syntax; and from this came the black box view of language acquisition, designed to solve a problem that the theory itself had created – the 'problem' of how a child could construct a grammar on the basis of what was thought to be (quite erroneously, as it happens; cf. Karmiloff-Smith 1979: 5) ill-formed and impoverished data. This purist view of natural speech as something scrappy, formless and unsystematic was itself a product of the same ideology, which idealized the individual speaker, explicitly denied the significance of the social context, and lacked the conception of an underlying semantic system from which the syntax of a natural language is non-arbitrarily derived.

Pre-mother tongue communication has no syntax; so if language development is equated with the acquisition of syntax, everything that happens before the mother tongue is bound to be ignored. Thus Roger Brown's state-of-the-art volume of 1973 was entitled *A First Language*; and despite the fact that Brown argued for a semantic interpretation of the processes of language development, which would inevitably direct attention to the earlier stages, the "first language" referred to in his title was still the mother tongue. This became susceptible of a linguistic interpretation from the point when the mean length of utterance was greater than one; that is, when the child had at least two lexico-grammatical elements (words or morphemes, the two being not yet distinct) and had produced at least one construction of such elements, which typically happens around the middle of the second year (the exact moment differing not only from child to child but also from linguist to linguist, depending on the criteria adopted for recognizing what is a construction). Since an utterance cannot be less than one element, as soon as the child has produced one construction the mean length of utterance will thereafter be in excess of one.

Now there is certainly an important sense in which the mother tongue is a child's "first language". It is the first fully ***stratified*** system he construes: one which has a semantics, a lexicogrammar and a phonology, these strata being linked by the key relationship of ***realization*** (representation, implementation, exponence, projection – it has had many names in post-Saussurean linguistics). But if our concern is with a child's ability to engage in systematic acts of meaning, then the mother tongue is far from being the child's first semiotic ***system***. In the early 1970s a number of factors came together to focus attention on communication before the mother tongue: pressure for applied research in this area, especially teachers' demands for a realistic and useful interpretation (such as is provided in Ede and Williamson 1980); dissatisfaction with the existing interpretations offered in linguistics and psychology, with their emphasis on the individual and their failure to come to terms with language as a social phenomenon and with learning as a social process; the renewal of interest in natural discourse, in language in the family, and in the diary as a basic research method; the concept of "intersubjectivity" in human behaviour; an interest in the boundary, or lack of boundary, between human beings and other species; and, imponderable but no less real, an ideological change towards recognizing cultural "otherness", with the child as one instance of an "other" human being – and hence a readiness to admit (what every parent knows, albeit unconsciously, and displays in daily interaction) that a child is also one who means. All these factors converged in a new consensus, an awareness of meaning as already a feature of infancy. The 1980s thus opened with a very different picture of semiotic ontogenesis, and of the place of the mother tongue in the total developmental linguistic process.

Interpretations of language development are bounded on the one hand by general theories of child development and on the other hand by general theories of language (see Cruttenden 1979 for a linguistically based account). In the past decade these two ideological and disciplinary contexts, the developmental and the linguistic, have tended to remain somewhat distinct; the majority of studies of infant communication, and language before the mother tongue, have dealt with these topics in relation to developmental theory, with relatively little emphasis on their implications for theories of language. In fact, however, the implications are considerable. In Lock's book *Action, Gesture and Symbol* (1978) there are a number of important papers offering interpretations of early language development which contain very positive messages for linguistics: see especially those by Newson, Shotter, Edwards, and Trevarthen and Hubley. From these emerge a number of general ideological principles, which may be summarized in some such terms as the following. "Babies are born as persons"; and what is equally important, they are treated by their caregivers as human beings from the start (Shotter 1978: 55; cf. Newson 1979). There is exchange of meaning "in a richly social-interactional context" (Edwards 1978: 468), in which "the dialogue between a human infant and his regular caretaker represents a 'cultural construction' of the utmost importance to the infant's whole future mental development" (Newson 1978: 41). The construction of language is an intersubjective process (Newson 1978: 35–7), and passes through a salient phase that Trevarthen and Hubley characterize as "secondary intersubjectivity" (1978: passim; this corresponds to the development of the protolanguage – cf. Halliday

1975). An understanding of these processes demands a "hermeneutic approach" – an interpretation "from the inside", in which it is accepted that in the study of human behaviour "observer and participant roles are not and cannot be clearly distinct", so that the task is that "of transforming the vague and perhaps mistaken understandings of **human phenomena** we already possess from an insider's point of view into more precise and effective ones" (Shotter 1978: 50–5).

These are valuable observations, which seem to be in accord with what I would regard as a 'social-semiotic' approach to the understanding of human development (see Rogers 1975 for an excellent historical perspective). At the same time, they do not seek to relate language development explicitly to any coherent overall theory of language. We might accept Lock's formulation that "children discover language through a process of guided reinvention" (1978: 4) – though I find the metaphor in "discover" a little misleading: children construe language rather than discovering it, and I am a little uncertain what is meant by the "re" in "reinvention" – but it does not in any way suggest **how** a linguistic system comes to be discovered or reinvented. There is still a need to ask the many questions that arise when we are seeking explanations of another kind – attempting to interpret the development of language in the context of and as a part of an interpretation of language itself.

Let us trace the steps leading up to the construal of the mother tongue, looking at these primarily from a linguistic point of view; or more exactly from a semiotic point of view, as the development of the ability to mean, which leads eventually to the construal of language in the strict sense of the term – the adult language as we know it and speak it ourselves.

In the first two months of life a child's semiotic acts are of two kinds, both of them pre-symbolic, or at least generally assumed to be so. The one kind are the bodily movements the child performs during the exchange of attention with his mother or other caregiver. These include "pre-reaching" gestures of arm, wrist and hand, anticipating the directed reaching that takes place from around four months onwards; and the oral gestures – tongue and lip movements – that have been designated "pre-speech" because they anticipate vocal articulation in a parallel way (Trevarthen 1979: 327). Functionally, these acts are what has been called "proto-conversation" (Bateson 1979: 65). They embody an exchange of meaning, in the sense that there is shared and reciprocated attention between the interactants; but not yet an exchange of *meanings* – that is, the expression is not yet paired with any content.

Semiotic acts of the other kind are, so to speak, the converse of these; instead of being voluntary acts that are contentless, they are involuntary acts that are contentful – typically, forms of crying, sighing and so on. Later on the child will combine these two elements into a single complex act that I have referred to as an *act of meaning*. It is at least arguable that he may take the first step in this direction already during this neonate period. So for example Nigel, at eight weeks, used to greet his father, when he returned from work every day, with animated gurgles and waving of limbs. One day he was interacting happily with his mother as usual, but as soon as he saw his father come in he burst into cries of distress. Father: *What happened to him today?* Mother: *He had his first injections.* Father expressed appropriate sympathy and the crying stopped. Both Father and Mother had interpreted Nigel's outburst of tears as a communicative act – just as they did the more typical cheerful signals too, to which the father usually responded with some such remark as *Oh, you had a nice time today, did you?* It would be arbitrary to insist that such acts do not realize any "communicative intent".

The next semiotic stage typically occurs at around five to six months, when the child establishes the principle of constructing and using a symbol. This was first noted in 1787 by Tiedemann, who reported *ach!* used as a sign of admiration at five and a half months (he interpreted it, wrongly, as an imitation; and in his record it remains an isolated element up to the age of 14 months). Nigel, also at just under 0;6, used a short high rising tone with oral closure and nasal release [ḿṅ] to mean 'Look, what's that? What's happening?'; he usually said this while lifting his head up and looking around. This sign was used regularly for about three weeks, and after that was heard no more. Reports of a preliminary symbolic act of this kind now figure in various places in the literature; that they were not recognized earlier is probably due to the exaggerated concern that most observers of this age have had with babbling, which is the continuation of pre-speech but has no contextual function – it serves as a form of practising. This single act is important, however, because it is the first true sign; that is, it is an expression paired with a content. One sign is not yet a semiotic system; but it is the critical first step. And, significantly, it is recognized as such by the caregivers, who interpret it as being addressed to them, and respond to it with an answer.

The third semiotic stage again follows on, typically, after a certain gap, a time interval in which from the caregivers' point of view the child is simply resting on his laurels. Then at some time in the period seven to ten months the child proceeds to construe, sign by sign, his first semiotic system. This is Darwin's "invented words", Trevarthen and Hubley's "secondary intersubjectivity"; and it is what I have referred to (1975) as the "protolanguage". By now the child has mastered the principle of creating symbols that will be understood; and although protolanguages themselves are now coming to be rather more fully documented, the way they are arrived at has still not been extensively described. The necessary preconditions are: (i) that the child can now control a range of vocal and gestural movements, that is, he has the potential for creating expressions; (ii) that he has identified a range of interpersonal contexts for acts of meaning, in which the expressions will be recognized and decoded, that is, he has the potential for creating contents; (iii) he has learnt to pair content and expression in a single complex sign; and (iv) he is recognized by the others as a communicator, as being a person and hence someone who means.

Nigel used certain strategies for creating a system of signs.

(a) At 0;7;27 (four days after moving himself forward for the first time) he created a NATURAL symbol, in a context of response. His mother calls: *Nigel!* – Nigel: [ø] – Mother: *Nigel!* – Nigel: [ø] – and so on. The [ø] was a short, mid-low falling to low, front rounded vowel; it was an imitation of his own sigh, a release of tension. He had heard himself make this sound naturally, and he turned it into a semiotic expression.

(b) At 0;8;3 (one day after first deliberately dropping an object on the floor) he created an **iconic** symbol, this time initiating a meaning but in a clearly defined context. His father is throwing up and catching a toy cat, with Nigel on his knee; he stops. Nigel looks at his father; reaches forward and touches that cat firmly for about a second, neither pushing nor grasping, then lets go. Father: *You want me to throw it up again? All right!* This was followed within the same week by two other iconic symbols: (i) Nigel grasps an object firmly, but without pulling it towards him, then lets go, meaning 'I want (to hold) that'; (ii) he touches an object lightly, but likewise without pushing it away from him, meaning 'I don't want that'. These acts are symbolic acts; they are addressed to persons, and they are clearly differentiated from the non-symbolic alternatives of grabbing things and throwing things away. But the symbols themselves are iconic; the expression bears a non-arbitrary relationship to the content. And they are clearly understood; those to whom they are addressed give an appropriate response, for example, *Yes, you can hold it* – or else *No you can't*: the negative response may lead to a fight, but it shows that the sign has been understood; and is no less appropriate as an answer.

Thus the two earliest semiotic abilities that we were able to identify soon after birth now come together in the creation of a linguistic symbol. One is the ability to mean, seen in the exchange of attention that takes place almost from the time the child is born; this provides the input 'I can communicate (with a person)'. The other is the ability to act, the motor control that develops in the first few months of life: this provides the input 'I can act (on an object)'. Putting the two together, we get a sign: 'I can act (on an object) by communicating with a person'. For example, I **address** (look at) mother, I **refer to** (touch) the thing she is holding; she then acts on it for me (gives it to me, or entertains me with it). Once this pattern is established, the expression is free to evolve: it can be any arbitrary act that the child can perform, the mother can perceive, and both parties can understand.

With success having been achieved in these natural and iconic acts of meaning, which gave rise to four distinct signs, one vocal and three gestural, Nigel can now move on to the third strategy, which is the one that makes it possible to create a true protolinguistic system. So:

(c) At 0;8;18 he creates an **arbitrary** symbol. In principle an arbitrary symbol can be either vocal or gestural; Nigel adopts the vocal mode, and uses it first to reintroduce the meaning 'look at that! that's interesting!', this time with a new expression [ø̀] or [bø̀] (the latter possibly incorporating an imitation of the word *bird*, although none of Nigel's subsequent protolinguistic signs is based on imitation for a long time to come). He is now in a position to construe a systematic functioning protolanguage.

This process is working in earnest at nine and a half months, just at the time when Nigel has learnt to stand up; and by ten and a half months he has built up a protolinguistic system consisting of ten to twelve distinct signs. All but one of the expressions are vocal, such as [nà], [ɜ̀], [ʼdɔ̀], [əɲ̊ɲ̊], and [ǧʷɣ̌ʷǧʷɣ̌τ]; the contents are such as might be translated 'give me that!', 'do that again', 'nice to see you', 'here you are at last' and 'I'm sleepy'. I have described this already; but three points need to be brought out explicitly for purposes of the present discussion.

First, it seems highly probable that the development of this kind of semiotic system, the protolanguage, is a general human potential, whether or not it is always actively realized. The latter may depend on a number of external conditions. The particular way the protolanguage potential is realized is no doubt highly variable, across cultures, sub-cultures, family types and families, according to which functions and which meanings are more readily taken up by caregivers and others in the child's "meaning group". In this connection, it is important to insist that the meaning potential is in the child, and the meaning is realized in the child's symbols: it is not put there by the adults around him. When Lock writes (1978: 12) that "action is transformed by interaction into gesture", if he means that an act that is not inherently symbolic is made symbolic by the caregiver's response to it, this is not the general pattern. Children make a rather clear distinction between symbolic and non-symbolic acts. If he means that a child depends on the adult's response for the success of his symbolic acts, this is certainly true. Moreover, the adult's response is selectively determining: only certain of the potential features or aspects of the child's meaning resonate, so to speak, in the adult's interpretation, and these are the ones the child maintains and develops, while others get filtered out, and this is where cultural, sub-cultural and familial variation arises. But if the adult tries, as adults sometimes do, to put in a meaning that is not in consonance with the child's intent, not what he had in mind, the child rejects it; he will have nothing to do with it. You cannot tell a child what he should mean.

Second, the protolanguage is a system, not just an inventory of unrelated signs. It is a semiotic system whose content is interpretable in terms of certain basic developmental functions, contexts of the interaction of a child with the others around him. It is child tongue, not mother tongue: it is constructed, or construed, by the child for his own semiotic purposes. But it is a shared construction, not only in the sense that all symbols are intersubjective – meaning comes into being only in the process of being exchanged – but also in the sense that the child's own intimates, those that make up his meaning group, share in the mental construction. They know that language, as listeners (and readers, if the expressions include gestures), though they do not speak it: they move along with it, interpreting what is new and discarding from memory what has been dropped out; and they contribute to the shaping of it, by interpreting each instance in terms of what they recognize as a content that is possible for an act of meaning. In this way they help to ensure continuity between the child tongue and the mother tongue when the child eventually moves on.

Third, the protolanguage is a system of signs; it is not a language in the adult sense. It has two levels only: a level of content, and a level of expression; and each sign is a pairing of the two. In this respect, it is like non-human communication systems; especially perhaps like those of our domesticated cousins the cats and dogs, since babies, like cats, use the protolanguage to talk to their caregivers and not, in general, to each other. An adult, human language, by contrast, is a three-level or tri-stratal system: in between the content (the semantics) and the expression (the phonology) is a purely abstract level of coding that we call a grammar – or lexicogrammar, to give it its full name: a level of **wording** between the meaning and the sound. Protolinguistic signs are not words, and this remains true even when their **expression** is derived, as it sometimes is, by imitation from an adult word; there is still some confusion caused by reference to them in the literature as words (though perhaps no more than is caused by calling them "sensori-motor vocalizations"). The absence of a grammar is the reason for referring to this semiotic system as protolanguage rather than as language, since the possession of a lexicogrammar is usually taken as the criterion for recognizing any phenomenon as "language".

How large does the protolanguage grow before the child abandons it for the mother tongue? At $10\frac{1}{2}$ months, Nigel had ten to twelve signs; at $16\frac{1}{2}$ months, on the threshold of the mother tongue transition, he had about 50 signs. For some time I had no other accounts with which to compare these findings; then studies such as those of Anne Carter (1978b) and Ronald Scollon (1976) began to suggest something comparable from the observations of other children. Research undertaken by participant–observers in the Department of Linguistics at the University of Sydney produced detailed accounts of other children with which it was possible to make accurate comparisons; and the figures were remarkably similar. Thus Clare Painter, in her study of her son Hal (1982), identifies five signs at 0;9, nine at $0;10\frac{1}{2}$, rising to 38 at $1;4\frac{1}{2}$. Jane Oldenburg-Torr, reporting on her daughter Anne, notes 11 signs at $0;10\frac{1}{2}$ and provisionally 35 at $1;4\frac{1}{2}$. With both Hal and Anne, as with Nigel, the mother tongue transition has begun by 1;6 (18 months), so that at this time words in the true sense have begun to appear.

It should be stressed, perhaps, that the protolanguage is a natural, spontaneously occurring stage in a child's semiotic development. It cannot be taught; it cannot be engendered from outside (as is obvious when one sees an adult attempting to do this); and instances of it cannot be elicited. To observe it comprehensively one has to be in the family, a participant as well as an observer (though not necessarily occupying both roles at the same moment); first, because only a participant understands the language, and second, because a child will not usually speak it in the presence of non-participants. In this respect, the protolanguage is not so very different from language in general. Even in adults, it is only in unelicited natural spontaneous speech that the full richness of the semantic system is deployed and extended; and in the study of a child's language development when he gets to the mother tongue stage, elicited speech gives only a poor indication of his true meaning potential.

A protolanguage is a very effective semiotic instrument; but at the same time it has certain limitations.

(a) It can be used to refer to the environment, for example, [ã] 'that's interesting'; but it cannot serve to interpret experience. For this there has to be a naming function, separated from other functions such as 'I want'. That is to say, there have to be words, for example, a word *ball* as the name of the object, instead of a protolinguistic sign such as [bɔ̀] which might mean 'I want my ball'; and there has to be a grammar, with organic constructions of functionally distinct elements such as *red ball, ball lost, ball under chair*.
(b) A protolanguage can be used to interact with people, to act on them and, through them, on the environment, for example, [ɛ̀:] 'yes? I'm here', [nà] 'give me that'; but it cannot serve to maintain dialogue. For this there has to be a system of speech functions whereby a speaker adopts a role himself and assigns a role choice to the listener, for example, *where ball?, ball there, find ball*, meaning 'you answer!', 'you acknowledge!', 'you act!'.
(c) In a protolanguage, one can **either** refer to the environment **or** act on it, but one cannot do both these things at once. Only with a lexicogrammar is it possible both to exchange speech roles and to represent reality in a single semantically complex construction. All the examples just given in fact do both of these things; thus *find ball* is at once both a command to act and a description of an action.

So a child has to move on, from child tongue to mother tongue, if he is to broaden the functional range of his meaning potential. The adult semiotic — natural language — is organized precisely on these "metafunctional" lines, as a means of both referring and acting simultaneously; together with a third component which organizes meanings as discourse – the ideational, interpersonal and textual metafunctions, in the terminology of systemic theory. How then does a child come to make the transition between these two formally distinct semiotic systems, the transition from protolanguage into language?

Nigel's first strategy in this direction consisted in: (i) separating two components of the expression, namely articulation and intonation; and (ii) assigning a naming (proto-ideational) function to the one and a calling (proto-interpersonal) function to the other. This system generated six utterance types each of which had two simultaneous meanings, one ideational (the name), the other interpersonal (the speech function). Nigel had thus taken the critical step into grammar. But, as with the solitary symbol [m̃m̃] that he had had at six months, there was then a gap before this step was followed up; and once again when Nigel did follow it up he advanced along another route.

I can find no parallel to Nigel's naming and calling systems in other protolinguistic literature. It remains to be seen what other ways in there are to the development of grammar. But for the next step Nigel took there is now a certain amount of evidence suggesting that it is one of the fundamental strategies adopted in the mother tongue transition.

The period of transition from protolanguage to mother tongue is roughly the second half of the second year of life: 1;6 to 2;0. Let us look at the linguistic systems of Hal, Anne and Nigel each at 19 months. Hal by now has a large crop of demand utterances; for example, names of food and household objects which he asks to be given, and requests for services like *up* and *light* and *tower* and *outside*. He also has many words for persons, objects and actions which are used to comment on his environment: personal names, clothes, body parts, evaluative and other adjectives, toys and their parts, locations and so on. There is hardly any overlap between these two contexts: a class of objects is typically **either** demanded (that is, in some way associated with a demand) **or** commented, but not both. Thus *apple* belongs in a demand context; so when his grandmother says *apple* pointing to a picture in a book, Hal interprets this as an offer and toddles off to the kitchen to look for one. And when he comes to form grammatical structure, these too tend to be specialized to one general function or the other.

There are two principles at work here. One is that each **token** (utterance) has one of the two functions only; the other is that each **type** (word or structure) has one of the two functions only. These are tendencies rather than absolute constraints; but with Hal they are clearly marked, and likewise also with Nigel. They are then supported by a third principle, which is that each of the two functions comes to have its own distinct mode of expression. This distinction may not appear right at the start; Nigel introduced it rather suddenly at 1;7, but from then on he maintained it absolutely for the next few months. Up till that time all Nigel's utterances, except for the searching variety of 'call' referred to above, and a separate type having a 'play' (imaginative) function, had been on some variety of falling tone, ending low. During one particular week, however, all his 'demand' utterances shifted, via high-to-mid fall and high level to a rising tone ending high. Thus *mummy come* became, from mʌmī kʌ̀m, via mʌmī kʌ̄m and mʌmī kʌ̄m, finally mʌ̄mī kʌ́m; and all other demand utterances went along with it: būttēr ón, mēnd chúffa ('mend my train'), nōw róom ('now let's go to your room') and so on. Comment utterances, however, remained on a falling tone as before: grēen tòwel, twō àpple, bēe flòwer ('there's a bee on the flower') and so on.

Hal made a phonological distinction between these two functions from the start, though one that was not quite so clearcut as Nigel's: Hal's demand utterances tended to take a high level tone, which was never heard in utterances with a comment function. Anne's transition system has not yet been worked out, since at the time of writing she is still in the transition stage; but it appears that she associates greater length and tonal stretch, plus perhaps a more open vowel quality, with the function of demand – thus, seeing the bread in her mother's shopping basket she said [bɛ̀ ... bɛ̀:ə] 'that's bread ... I want some!' There is still a great deal remaining to be investigated about the functional basis of the mother-tongue transition. But it seems that the systematic distinction of demand and comment functions, which I have referred to respectively as "pragmatic" and "mathetic" (since the former is more general than a demand, while the latter is really the use of language to learn about the environment), is a fairly general strategy; moreover, the child makes the distinction explicit not only by the form of the expression but also by his own criteria of success. Thus with a pragmatic (demand) utterance he will show that he expects a response (in deeds, and later increasingly in words), and he will not be satisfied until he gets one; whereas with a mathetic (comment) utterance he will not worry if no response is forthcoming at all. He **may** back up this semiotic strategy by giving an explicit realization of the distinction in phonological or paraphonological terms; if he does, then the pragmatic, demand function will be encoded as the marked member of the pair. Again, Nigel made this markedness explicit: when, as happened on occasion, he used a gesture to signal the pragmatic component of the meaning (for example, beating time to mean 'sing' or 'put a record on'), the tone of the utterance became falling, showing that the falling tone was the unmarked option.

As the child moves on through the transition, building up the grammar and vocabulary of the mother tongue, the functional grid is, as it were, rotated through 90 degrees: the words and structures become the resources of the transitivity system, while the choice of functions becomes the basis of the mood system. Not that all transitivity structures appear first in a mathetic function; on the contrary, it is clear that both functions provide essential contexts for the child to construct a grammar of representation, the systems and structures with which the language organizes experience of the real world. But it appears that the two basic functional contexts, of language to act and language to learn, may be complementary in that they engender different aspects of, or subdomains within, the transitivity system. Clare Painter's findings have led her to a hypothesis, still very tentative but extremely interesting, that pragmatic utterances evolve an Actor–Goal, or transitive, representation of processes, while mathetic utterances evolve an Agent–Medium, or ergative, representation. This would explain how the two come to coexist in the adult linguistic system.

As the child moves on through the transition, the separation of functions is transformed to become the fundamental organizing principle of the grammar itself. No longer is each utterance token functioning for him just as a demand, or just as a comment; every utterance is simultaneously both action and representation, with both these components combined in all lexicogrammatical sequences. The unit is now a clause; and the clause is the domain both of a transitivity system, for the interpretation of experience, and of a mood system, for the maintenance of dialogue. These are characteristics of an adult language, a mother tongue rather than a child tongue. Let me illustrate the way this transformation may take place.

By the age of 1;10, both Hal and Nigel are coming to adapt any wording to either speech function, as can be seen in the following example. Nigel has fallen and hurt himself earlier in the day; he feels a foreign body attached to his forehead, touches it, and asks his father [ad^{y}dà] 'what's that?' – *That's plaster, sticking plaster.* – *Tell Mummy take it òff*, he says firmly, running to his mother; then, as he sees her. *Take it óff.*

The first *take it off* has a falling tone; it is not a demand, merely a statement of intention. The second, however, is a request; hence the tone is rising. Note that the tone pattern is not that of the adult language, in which imperatives typically have a falling tone. It is not until the very end of the transition that Nigel transfers to the intonation patterns of the adult language.

This step represents the culmination of the process that was foreshadowed in Nigel's naming/calling system eight months earlier. The falling/rising opposition has evolved into a system of modal features that are selected independently with each wording; and so the same wording can switch from one mood to the other, as in the example above. Compare also Nigel's *Dada ready nòw* (statement, 'Daddy's ready now') – *No, I'm not ready; you'll have to wait.* – *Dada ready nów!* (command, 'then get ready!'). The systems themselves are not yet those of the adult language; it is not until the beginning of his third year that Nigel develops the speech functions of statement and question, and the clearly defined grammatical category of indicative mood by which they are realized – this could be considered to mark the end of the transition. But the basic functional framework is there, and in fact can be said to have been there already from the start of the protolinguistic trail.

In these remarks I have tried to maintain a dual focus of attention, on the one hand using evidence from language development to throw light on the linguistic system, and on the other hand using evidence from the linguistic system to throw light on language development. From an understanding of the functional organization of language we can interpret the transition from child tongue to mother tongue; and by understanding how language is construed by children we can gain a greater insight into its essential nature and structure (Chapter 8). The two perspectives are complementary and in a sense inseparable one from the other.

The mutual enrichment of linguistic and developmental studies depends, I think, on the adoption of an interactional, functional and meaning-oriented, or semiotic, standpoint, such as has characterized many recent investigations. In the Bristol project directed by Gordon Wells, which stands out as a major contribution to early language development studies carried out in a broadly educational context, the emphasis throughout has been on language learning in the course of conversational interaction (Wells 1981: Ch. 1). Karmiloff-Smith's study of noun determiners and reference (1979) bridges the gap between (Piagetian) cognitive–psychological and linguistic interpretations through the use of a 'plurifunctional' analysis of the linguistic options involved. And an essential contribution from within linguistics has been the development of text theories and discourse grammars, which has shifted the focus of attention away from isolated sentences towards connected and coherent text, thus showing in a much more convincing way how a young child's basic experience of language, family conversation in the home (and also, subsequently, peer group conversation in the neighbourhood), is a rich source of semiotic material for the listening and participating child, given the symbolic and interactive potential with which he comes into the world endowed.

A child's developing linguistic system can be represented in a systemic grammar as interrelated sets of options in meaning, together with their realizations. This has been done for the protolanguages of Nigel, Hal and Anne, the meaning being interpreted in functional terms and the system redefined at six-week intervals so as to give the clearest account of its growth. For Hal, Clare Painter has continued the systemic interpretation through to the end of the mother-tongue transition, showing how the transitional system founded on the functional opposition of matheic/pragmatic, or comment and demand, is gradually overtaken by the metafunctional system of the adult language. I have tracked Nigel's development of one particular system, that of mood, in a series of 12 networks covering the period from 0;9 to 2;0. Based as it is on the concept of choice, a systemic grammar provides a theoretical interpretation of the child's expanding ability to mean. Now that a systemic grammar of adult English has been implemented on a computer (at the Information Sciences Institute of the University of Southern California; see Matthiessen 1981), a natural subsequent step might be to use the programme to model language development. At some still fairly remote time in the future it might be possible to simulate the mother-tongue transition in the language development process by using as input just the utterances spoken to, and perhaps also in the presence of, one particular child, the computer's task being to construe the system from them, given the child's protolanguage as initial state. More realistically, in the meanwhile, it would be possible with existing resources to model the developing grammar of an individual child (or, if the data from any one diary study was inadequate, a composite grammar based on the records of more than one child) in order to see how — that is, by what routes and through what intervening states — this approximated to the generalized adult grammar as now represented in this format. But — so as not to give the impression that language development studies are now simply a specialized branch of artificial intelligence – let me stress that the most urgent need is for a great deal more direct observational evidence regarding the protolanguage and the mother-tongue transition; and here not even the tape recorder, let alone the computer, has yet displaced the field linguist's traditional equipment in the form of notebook and pencil.

Chapter Ten

A SYSTEMIC-FUNCTIONAL INTERPRETATION OF THE NATURE AND ONTOGENESIS OF DIALOGUE
(1984)

1 A model of dialogue

In the most general terms, at the level of social context, dialogue can be interpreted as a process of exchange. It is an exchange involving two variables: (1) the nature of the commodity that is being exchanged; and (2) the roles that are defined by the exchange process.

1. The commodity may be either (a) goods-and-services or (b) information (cf. Ervin-Tripp 1964). In *Give me a Herald, please!* or *Let me fix it for you!*, what is being exchanged is goods-and-services, and language is functioning simply as a means of furthering the exchange. On the other hand, in *Is it cold inside?* or *I met Colin today*, what is being exchanged is information, and language is both the means of exchange and the manifestation of the commodity being exchanged.

The distinction between information and goods-and-services is theoretically a very fundamental one, despite the fact that there will be many tokens – actual speech events – of an intermediate or a complex kind. Unlike goods-and-services, which are non-verbal commodities, information is a "commodity" which is brought into being only through language (or perhaps other semiotic systems). In the case of goods-and-services, the exchange of symbols helps to **bring about** the exchange; but the two are distinct processes, the one a means to the other. In the case of information, on the other hand, the exchange of symbols actually **constitutes** the exchange; there is only one process,

---

First published in *The Semiotics of Culture and Language*, Vol. 1, Language as Social Semiotic edited by R.P. Fawcett, M.A.K. Halliday, S.M. Lamb and A. Makkai. London: Frances Pinter, 1984, pp. 3–35.

and we are simply looking at two aspects of it – the intention, and the manifestation.

2. The role of speaker taking part in the exchange may be one of either (a) giving or (b) demanding. He may be giving information (*I met Colin today*), or giving goods-and-services (*Let me fix it for you!*); or demanding information (*Is it cold outside?*), or demanding goods-and-services (*Give me a Herald, please!*).

When the speaker takes on a role of giving or demanding, by the same token he assigns a complementary role to the person he is addressing. If I am giving, you are called on to accept; if I am demanding, you are called on to give. There are (a) exchange-initiating roles, those taken on by the speaker himself, and (b) responding roles, those assigned by the speaker to the addressee and taken on by the addressee when he becomes the speaker in his turn. We can take account of this and represent the system for one move as in Figure 1.

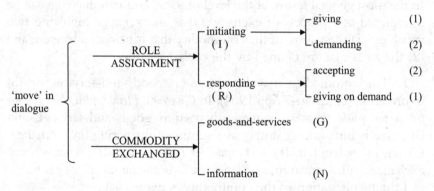

Figure 1 The system of dialogue (a): level of social context – the *move*

In Figure 1, dialogue is being represented at a level that is 'above' the linguistic code: we are interpreting it as a system of the social context. The system network expresses the potential that inheres in one move in the dynamics of personal interaction. When we consider dialogue in this way, as a form of the exchange of social meanings, we are looking at it as a semiotic process, and therefore as one that is in principle capable of being realized through systems other than language. To the extent that other semiotic systems have the facility for encoding the two components of the process (the assignment of roles in the exchange and the nature of the exchange itself), to that extent they can replace language as 'carriers' of dialogue. If no other semiotic system displays these two properties, this will be an instance of a social process that specifically requires language for its realization. This does not mean, of course, that we should therefore not interpret it in terms of the social context: even where a particular function is served only by language, we still seek to explain that function in terms of the social semiotic, and in this way show how it relates to other semiotic processes in which systems other than language do operate as variants (for example, exchange of greetings).

The next step in the interpretation is to move into the linguistic system, at the 'highest' level, the level of semantics; and to show the network of semantic options by which the options in the exchange process are encoded as meanings in language. This will be Lamb's "sememic" stratum. At this level are introduced concepts of the kind traditionally referred to as "speech functions": statement, question, and the like. However, the set of such speech functions that will typically be found in grammar books, namely statement, question, command, and exclamation, is one that is wholly derived from the grammatical system, the next level 'down' in the coding previously defined by the mood system in the grammar. In other words, the interpretation faces only one way. If, on the other hand, the semantic system is being seen as a distinct level of coding that is intermediate between the grammar and the social context, the interpretation will face both ways. In this perspective, the categories of speech function are both (a) *realizing* the social–contextual options of role assignment and commodity exchanged and (b) *realized* by the grammatical options of mood – as well as (c) forming a coherent system in their own right. The basic system for the semantics of dialogue can be represented as in Figure 2.

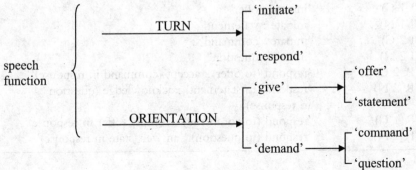

Figure 2 The system of dialogue (b): level of semantics – the *speech function*

Let us now try to show how these semantic options serve to encode the dynamic role-play of dialogue. For this, as for all realization statements, we shall need the concept of **congruence**. A congruent realization is that one which can be regarded as typical – which will be selected in the absence of any good reason for selecting another one. This 'good reason' type of default principle is widely found in the interfacing of semiotic systems. Wherever there is one variant that is congruent, it is this variant that is likely to be taught as a "rule" to foreign learners of a language when they are first presented with the feature in question. In real life, we rarely confine ourselves to congruent realizations for very long; not only because the resulting discourse easily becomes boring but also, and more significantly, because **many of the more delicate distinctions within any system depend for their expression on what in the first instance appear as non-congruent forms**. Nevertheless, as speakers of a language we are aware of what is the congruent mode of encoding of any feature, and we use this as a kind of base line; for example, however rarely we may actually use an imperative in giving orders, we have a feeling that it is in some sense the unmarked way of doing so. By no means all linguistic features display a set of variant realizations such that one of them clearly stands out as congruent; but many do. Table 1 shows the patterns of congruence between the social–contextual system of moves in dialogue and the semantic system of speech functions.

Table 1 Semantic realization of categories of the social context (congruent pattern)

Move in dialogue	Speech function by which typically encoded
(I 1 G)	'initiate : offer'
(I 1 N)	'initiate : statement'
(I 2 G)	'initiate : command'
(I 2 N)	'initiate : question'
(R 2 G)	'respond (to offer) : accept (command in response)'
(R 2 N)	'respond (to statement) : acknowledge (question in response)'
(R 1 G)	'respond (to command) : comply (offer in response)'
(R 1 N)	'respond (to question) : answer (state in response)'

Note that the reciprocity of responses is typical not only of responses to demanding, where a command is responded to by an offer, and a question by a statement, but also of responses to giving: we frequently acknowledge an offer by giving a command, and acknowledge a statement by asking a question. Examples:

1. Give me a Herald, please! – Here!   'command + compliance'
2. Let me fix it for you!   – Yes, do!   'offer + acceptance'
3. Is it cold outside?   – It is.   'question + answer'
4. I met Colin today.   – Did you?   'statement + acknowledgement'

Again, it should be stressed that these are examples of congruent patterns. As ways of expressing the exchange of roles in dialogue, they are typical, but in no sense obligatory.

The meanings are, in turn, coded as **wordings**; that is, as selections of options in the lexicogrammatical system (Lamb's "lexological" stratum). Let us represent this once again as a network, still keeping to the most general features of the system (see Figure 3).

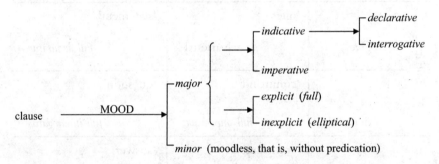

Figure 3 The system of dialogue (c): level of lexicogrammar – the *mood*

Table 2 shows how these grammatical features figure as (congruent) realizations of the semantic options. Table 3 summarizes the principal categories: situational, semantic and lexicogrammatical.

2 Some examples of dialogue between parent and child

We have now set up a three-level interpretation of dialogue based on the principle of congruence, showing the exchange of meaning roles first coded as speech functions (as linguistic meanings of an interpersonal kind) and then recoded as grammatical features, as terms in the mood system. The next step is to ask: what kinds of extension of these patterns of congruence do we find in real-life dialogue?

Table 2 Lexicogrammatical realization of semantic categories (congruent pattern)

Speech function	Mood by which typically encoded
'initiate'	*full*
'respond'	*elliptical* (or *minor*)
'offer'	(various; no congruent form)
'statement'	*declarative*
'command'	*imperative*
'question'	*interrogative*

Table 3 Summary of principal categories

Role assignment		Commodity exchanged	
		Goods-and-services	Information
initiating	give	'offer' [various]	'statement' *full declarative*
	demand	'command' *full imperative*	'question' *full interrogative*
initiating	give on demand	'compliance (response offer)' [various]	'answer (response statement)' *elliptical declarative; minor*
	accept	'acceptance (response command)' *elliptical imperative; minor*	'acknowledgement (response question)' *elliptical interrogative; minor*

The system networks are, of course, idealized constructs; they are a representation of part of the code. However, in setting them up and relating them to each other through the concepts of coding and congruence, we are not treating them as "pure" categories from which instances of living speech are set off as deviant, as in some sort of competence–performance model. The idealization consists in the fact that up to this point the networks (a) have introduced only the most general (least *delicate*) distinctions, and (b) have been shown as related to each other only through their most typical (most congruent) realizations. When they are used in the interpretation of language behaviour they will need to be filled in and extended, so as to show incongruent patterns of relationship, and to introduce more delicate choices.

Let us now consider some examples from real life. Passage A is a dialogue between Nigel, at 1;10, and his mother:

Passage A

NIGEL:	Have blue pin all ríght!	(1)
MOTHER:	The blue pin has got lost.	(2)
NIGEL:	Under béd?	(3)
MOTHER:	No, it's not under the bed.	(4)
NIGEL:	Blue pin got lòst. Whíte pin got lost?	(5)
MOTHER:	No, the white pin didn't get lost.	(6)

In (3–4) and (5–6) we have something very close to an exchange of meanings that is congruent in both dimensions: both in terms of what follows what, and in terms of how each one is realized. Nigel demands information and his mother responds by giving it. This exchange is encoded semantically as: Nigel asks a question and his mother makes a statement which is an answer to it. Grammatically, the encoding on Nigel's part turns out to be congruent once we know what his system is at the time. At this stage, Nigel's primary opposition is one between 'response demanded' and 'response not demanded'. This system is realized by intonation: falling tone realizes 'response not demanded', rising tone realizes 'response demanded'. Hence, what would in adult speech be questions and commands belong to a single semantic category of *pragmatic* utterances realized by the rising intonation contour. His mother's responses are also grammatically congruent, with the proviso that in both instances she used the full and not the elliptical form of the clause.

In (1–2) we have a different situation. Here Nigel is demanding goods-and-services; this is again encoded congruently as a pragmatic utterance, with rising tone, being differentiated from a demand for information by the *have* plus *all right* (the grammatical distinction between command and question is not yet systemic in his language). His mother, however, gives a response that is incongruent: it is a statement, not an offer, and functions as a supplementary response, one which answers by implication – 'so you can't have it'. Here, therefore, the response network needs to be expanded to include features such as those in Figure 4 (cf. Halliday and Hasan 1976: 207).

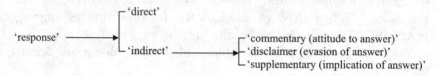

Figure 4 Types of indirect response

The response in Nigel's mother's turn (2) brings out the fact that the only responses considered so far had been of the 'direct' kind. In real life, however, responses are very often indirect; there is no rule requiring a direct answer to a question. A good example of a disclaimer can be seen in this exchange between Nigel, at 4;11, and his father (Passage B):

Passage B

> NIGEL: Why does as plasticine gets longer it gets thìnner?
> FATHER: That's a very good question: why does it?
> NIGEL: Because more of it is getting used ùp.
> FATHER: Well ...
> NIGEL: Because more of it is getting used up to make it lònger, thàt's whý, and so it goes thìnner.

His father's response simply ducks the question, and Nigel goes on to supply an answer for himself – a very appropriate one, as it happens.

Passage C shows the exchange of goods-and-services (offers and commands) taking place largely in minor clauses (Nigel at 3;2):

Passage C

> FATHER: [playing a game called Grrr] One more grrr.
> NIGEL: No, thrèe more.
> FATHER: All right. [They play one.] Now two more.

NIGEL: [thinking he is being cheated] No – thrèe more.
FATHER: Yes, but we've had one of the three, so it's two more now. [Nigel accepts, unconvinced.]

Contrast this with Passage D, where the exchange of goods-and-services takes the form of major declarative clauses (Nigel at 3;3):

Passage D

NIGEL: You can have the box car.
FATHER: But I don't want the box car; I want the diesel engine.
NIGEL: I'm not going to give you the diesel engine.
FATHER: Then I'll have the box car.
NIGEL: But I'm not going to give you one you don't want.

In Passage E (Nigel at 3;3), all instances are congruent throughout:

Passage E

MOTHER: Go and tell Daddy that lunch is ready!
NIGEL: [knocking on study door] Lunch reàdy.
FATHER: Thank you! – I'm coming.
NIGEL: Múmmy, is it reády, or is it stàrting to get ready?
MOTHER: It's ready.
NIGEL: But it's not on the tăble.

Passage D and E illustrate a different point. Both can be interpreted in terms of the general concepts that we started with, without further elaboration; but whereas the realizations in Passage E are congruent (and it is useful to be reminded that congruent patterns do frequently occur!), those in Passage D involve incongruent realization at various points. In this connection it is worth remarking that, as a general feature, languages display a greater tendency to congruence in the exchange of information than in the exchange of goods-and-services. This is hardly surprising. Since information is a commodity that is defined and brought into being only by semiotic systems, with language leading the way, it is no surprise to find that there exist clearly defined categories of declarative and interrogative in the grammar, and that these are typically used as the mode of giving and demanding information. When it comes to exchanging goods-and-services, however, this is a process that takes place independent of the existence of a semiotic in which to encode it; and languages do not display clear-cut categories in the grammar corresponding to offers and commands. The imperative is at best a fringe category, teetering between finite and non-finite (in languages which make this distinction), having either no distinct clause or verb form or else one that is only minimally distinguished; and even when a distinct imperative form does exist, it may be rarely used, with other, non-congruent forms taking over the command function. The position is even clearer with offers: no language seems to have a clearly distinguished grammatical form for offers, the closest perhaps being special types of indicative like the English *shall I . . .?*

This is not to say that offers and commands are not ordinarily verbalized at all. On the contrary, they often are. The difference between information and goods-and-services is that, since information is a semiotic commodity, it is not possible to exchange it except by a semiotic process — in fact a semiotic process can be defined as one through which information is exchanged; so when we exchange information, there are explicit and regular grammatical patterns for doing so, the forms of declarative and interrogative mood, and these are the forms that are typically used. Goods-and-services on the other hand can be exchanged without the intervention of any symbolic acts. Adults, being oriented towards the verbal mode, do typically verbalize offers and commands; for example, *here you are!, would you like a newspaper?, shall I hold the door open for you?, come on — follow me!* But the grammatical system of English does not display any clearly defined pattern of congruence in the realization of offers and commands; and this is true of many other languages, perhaps all. The exchange of goods-and-services, because of its lesser dependence on language, has not brought about the evolution of special modes of expression in the same way that these have evolved for the exchange of information. We shall see in the next section that, in the course of developing the adult pattern of speech functions, Nigel did pass through a stage when he had a relatively clear-cut semantic system of 'let me' (offer), 'let you' (command) and 'let you and me' (suggestion). But this regularity is lost in the adult language.

Passage F (Nigel at 6;5) illustrates a question–answer sequence where the response is direct (unlike those in B and C) but involves a modality:

Passage F

NIGEL: [looking at real estate section of newspaper] Look at that very, very small print! ... Do they always print as small as that in very big bóoks?
FATHER: Not always, no –

A SYSTEMIC-FUNCTIONAL INTERPRETATION

NIGEL: [interrupts; looking at Father's typewriter, a large old-fashioned office machine not yet unpacked after removal]
We've got a printing machine in òur house, hàven't we.
FATHER: We've got a typewriter, yes.

Here, Nigel's father's second response is an indirect one; it answers by implication. His first response, on the other hand, is direct; but it is accompanied by a modality *not always*, echoing the *always* in Nigel's question. To take account of this we shall have to return to the notion of a question, realizing a demand for information, and consider the options open to the person to whom such a demand is addressed. So far we have spoken of dialogue as the assignment of roles by the speaker: the speaker adopts one role for himself, and imposes another complementary role on to the hearer. In fact, however, what he assigns to the hearer is not a role but a choice of roles. The hearer has considerable discretion in the way he chooses to play the part that is assigned to him. We could represent the choice for 'response to question' as in Figure 5. Note that the simple answer 'yes', or 'no', already involves a number of steps or choice points in the logical structure of the decision process.

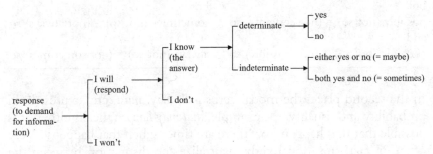

Figure 5 Options open to respondent facing demand for information

The response *not always* in Passage F has the feature 'indeterminate'. An indeterminate response is one that is 'tagged' by the speaker with some assessment of its validity: it is true only with a certain likelihood, or only for a certain proportion of the time. This validity assessment is realized semantically as the system of modality; and there are two dimensions to this, (1) 'maybe', that is, probability, and (2) 'sometimes', which we might refer to as 'usuality' (Figure 6).

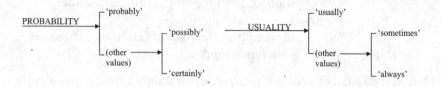

Figure 6 Semantic systems of modality

Various considerations suggest that these two systems are semantically isomorphic. In the first place, in both of them there is a median value in which negation applies without change of meaning either to the modality or to the thesis, contrasting with two outer values in which the negation of one modality is equivalent to the other modality with negation of the thesis (Table 4).

Table 4 Median and outer values of modality

Probability	Usuality
probably (not so) = (not probably) so but	usually (not so) = (not usually) so but
possibly (not so) = (not certainly) so and	sometimes (not so) = (not always) so and
certainly (not so) = (not possibly) so	always (not so) = (not sometimes) so

In the second place, the modal verbs *will, may, must*, etc. express both probability and usuality; for example, *that may happen* means either 'it is possible that that happens' or 'there are times when that happens'. Very often, in fact, the modal verbs neutralize the distinction between the two, suggesting that underlying both is a single system representing the degree of the speaker's commitment to the validity of the statement he is making (Figure 7). More delicately, the 'high' value embodies a further systematic distinction into 'relatively high' (*should*: almost certainly/nearly always) and 'absolutely high' (*must*: certainly/always), which helps to explain negative adverbs like *hardly* (hardly ever/hardly likely = 'nearly always not'/'almost certainly not'). This does not figure in the present illustration.

Modality can be interpreted as an elaboration of the category 'indeterminate'. It is incorporated into the network as in Figure 8.

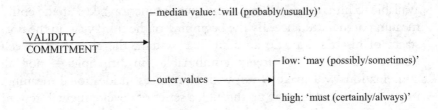

Figure 7 Generalized system of validity commitment (modality)

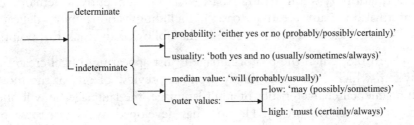

Figure 8 Modality as 'indeterminate' response

Modals do, of course, appear in statements and questions which are not responses, though it could be argued that they are inherently associated with responding rather than initiating. In Passage F, Nigel's question already includes the usuality term *always* ('does this apply to all instances? I know that it applies to at least one'), and the response is both congruent and appropriate. Strictly speaking, in its context the response is not indeterminate, since given the question 'is this always so?' the response 'not always' is equivalent to a determinate 'no'; respondents, however, usually seem to repeat the modality in such instances, perhaps because they feel that a bare *No* might be interpreted as 'it is never so'.

3 The origins of dialogue

In this section we give a brief sketch of how Nigel developed the system of dialogue, starting from the earliest stage of his protolanguage at eight months old.

At the age of eight months, when Nigel has first begun to engage in systematic acts of meaning, the choice of speech function ('give me that', 'do that', etc.) constitutes the only range of semantic choice that is available to him: the signalling of the speech function takes up the entire meaning of the utterance. By the beginning of the third year, in the final stages of his transition to an adult-like system, the choice of speech function is becoming freely combinable (in principle – not all combinations will make sense) with all choices in ideational meaning. Nigel has worked his way up through a series of developmental steps to that highly complex point where, for example, the ideational meaning 'eat + toast' can be mapped on to any of the interpersonal meanings 'demand + goods-and-services' ('I want to eat toast'), 'give + information' ('I am eating toast'), and, incipiently, 'demand + information' ('am I eating toast?'); including various more delicate sub-categories. What is the route he has followed to reach this point?

1. At 0;8, when the protolanguage is just appearing, Nigel creates a system which offers a startlingly accurate preview of one of the most fundamental characteristics of adult language, the language he will one day take over (Figure 9). He now has developed five signs, three of them expressed gesturally and two vocally. The meanings he expresses by gesture are those in the active sphere: 'give me that' and 'do that for me'. The meanings he expresses by voice are those in the reflective sphere: 'let's be together' and 'that's interesting'. Nigel will shortly abandon the gestural mode almost entirely; meanwhile, for a brief five or six weeks he has anticipated what is the central functional distinction of the adult language, that between interpersonal meanings – language as action – which are typically expressed through structures of a prosodic, non-segmental kind, and ideational meanings – language as reflection – which are typically expressed through segmental, constituent-like structures, the sort that are appropriately represented by trees in a structural description.

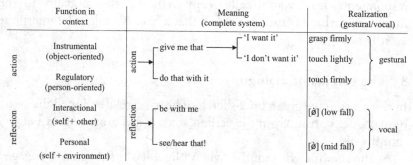

Figure 9 Protolanguage, early (0.8)

2. From here on, and into his second year, Nigel moves on to construct, with the help of the adults around him (since they understand him, and respond with meanings of their own), a protolanguage which serves his four elementary functions: the instrumental, the regulatory, the interactional, and the personal (Figure 10). The last of these functions is 'self'-oriented; it is the expression of Nigel's own cognitive and affective response to his environment. The first three, however, are 'other'-oriented: here Nigel distinguished almost from the start between initiating an exchange of meanings and responding to a meaning that is addressed to him – between, for example, 'give me that!' and 'yes I want that!'. The distinction between active and reflective functions is no longer significant: both kinds of meaning are there, but the systematic distinction between them is (for the time being) lost.

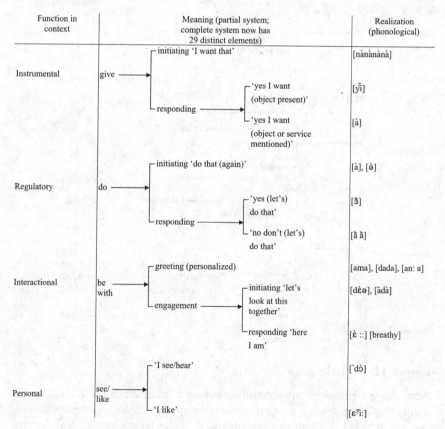

Figure 10 Protolanguage, middle (1;0)

3. Next, at 15 to 16 months, Nigel begins to add content to these generalized meanings (Figure 11). The meaning is no longer just 'I want that', 'that's interesting', but 'I want the clock', 'that's interesting – a bus', and so on. He continues to use the generalized protolinguistic expressions alongside these new forms; in particular, baby signs expressing feelings persist well into the stage when he is already using words and structures.

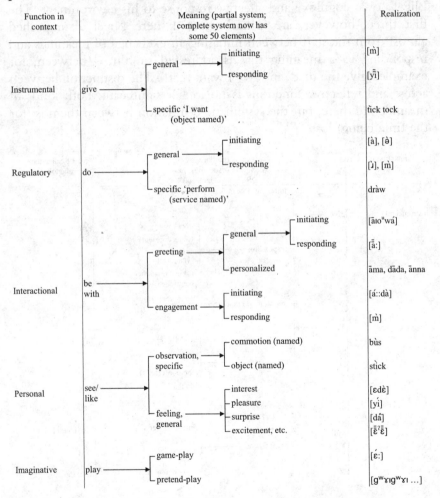

Figure 11 Protolanguage, late (1;4)

Note: the general elements are still protolinguistic, realized phonologically as complexes of articulation and intonation; the specific elements are now names, and so encoded through the intermediary of the lexicogrammatical system. Realizations given in orthography are examples of the categories in question.

4. At 19 months, Nigel reintroduces the active/reflective distinction in a new form; and it serves him as the principal strategy for the transition from protolanguage to language (Figure 12). The distinction is now encoded systematically: a rising tone means 'response demanded', and signals an utterance with a pragmatic function, for example, *play chúffa* 'let's play with the train', *more grávy* 'I want more gravy', while a falling tone means 'no response demanded' – the utterance has a **mathetic** (learning, or reality-constructing) function, for example, *red sweàter* 'that's my red sweater', *loud mùsic* 'that's a loud piece of music'.

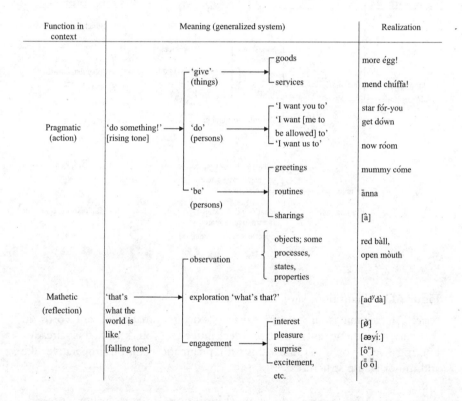

Figure 12 Transition, early (1;7)

Note: The feature 'engagement' is still realized protolinguistically. Other meanings are realized lexicogrammatically, as words, with structures now beginning to appear (for example, *Mummy come! Red ball*); pragmatic on rising tone, mathetic on falling tone. Realizations given in orthography are examples of the categories in question.

Utterances in the mathetic function are self-sufficient; no action is called for. Utterances in the pragmatic function on the other hand carry the general meaning 'do something' – the person addressed is required to give a particular object or service, to engage in some kind of activity ('let you', 'let me', or 'let's') or to interact in some particular way.

5. By 22 months, the pragmatic category has extended to utterances which demand a verbal response; that is to questions (Figure 13).

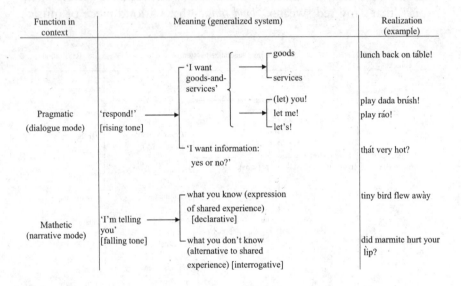

Figure 13 Transition, late (1;10)

Note: All meanings are now realized lexicogrammatically, as words in structures; mathetic as indicative (declarative = 'you know this already', interrogative = 'you don't know this yet'), pragmatic as various imperative-like and minor clause structures.

The pragmatic feature 'do something' now means either 'provide goods-and-services' or 'provide information'. Hence all Nigel's questions, including Wh-questions, have a rising tone. They do not, however, take the interrogative form. The interrogative, which Nigel now introduces into his system, serves instead to encode a new distinction within what was the mathetic function. The meaning of the mathetic has now evolved in the direction of 'I am giving information'; and Nigel develops a systematic distinction which has no counterpart in the adult language: a distinction between 'I'm telling you something which you know already' (that is, you shared with me the experience I'm talking about – declarative) and 'I'm telling you something which you don't know' (that is, my talking about it serves as an alternative to shared experience – interrogative). Hence only the interrogative is strictly 'giving information', in the expected adult sense of something that is not known to the person addressed. Adults, of course, spend much of their time giving information that is already known; but they do not recognize it as a systematic category.

6. At the end of the second year, when Nigel is just on the threshold of entry to the adult language, in the sense of being about to adopt the functional semantic patterns of the mother tongue, he has introduced many more delicate distinctions; but the primary distinctions he is making are now coming to approximate the speech functions of the adult language (Figure 14). It is not difficult to see how this evolves into the adult system as outlined in section 1 above, based on the exchange of meanings of the two kinds that we recognized there: goods-and-services, where language is ancillary to a (non-symbolic) process that itself is independent of language, and information, where the process is itself a symbolic one – the 'commodity' that is being exchanged **is** language, or rather is a semiotic that is realized in the form of language. It is not surprising, when seen in this light, that the concept of information, and the ability to exchange information, is relatively late in developing. By the age of nine months Nigel has a very clearly developed sense of meaning as a mediating process: by addressing another person, and exchanging symbols with that person, he can achieve a variety of intents – but the act of meaning in no way constitutes the realization of those intents. It is not until the very end of his second year that he comes to see the exchange of meanings as a goal, as a process *sui generis*, such that the act of meaning is itself the realization of the intent. We have seen how this awareness of exchanging information has evolved, namely through the convergence of two lines of development, starting from two of the elementary functions of the protolanguage: (1) the interactional – (a) 'let's be together'; (b) shared attention to an external object, as a form of 'togetherness'; (c) the 'naming game' ('look at this picture; now you say its name'); (d) 'what's this called?' (asking for a new name); (e) Wh-questions ('fill in the gap in this account'); and (2) the personal – (a) attention to prominence ('there's a commotion?'); (b) attention to the environ-

ment ('that's interesting'); (c) observation, recall and prediction ('I see/saw/will see ...'); (d) voicing shared experience ('I'm telling you what we both saw/heard'); (e) communicating unshared experience ('I'm telling you what I saw/heard but you didn't').

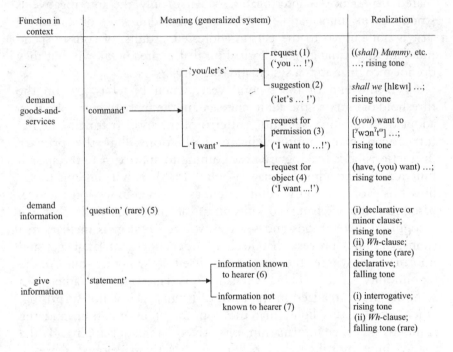

Figure 14 Incipient adult (2.0): Nigel on the threshold of the adult system of dialogue

Note: the systematic distinction between (3) and (4) is disappearing.

At the later stages there is also a third, minor strand in the process, that of 'let's explore this – what will happen?', which plays a part in the development of questions. The process can be represented in tabular form (Table 5). Here finally are some examples of Nigel's utterances in the period 1;11 to 2;0. The numbers relate to the categories in Figure 14.

Table 5 The ontogeny of information

	(interactional function)	(personal function)
0.8	'let's be together'	'there's a commotion'
1.0	'let's look at this together'	'look – that's interesting'
1.4	'look at this picture; you say its name'	'I see a (name of object, for example, stick, bus)'
1.7	'what's this? I want to know its name'	'I'm telling you what we both saw'
	'I know about this; let me try out that'	
1.10	'who? what? I want to know the identity'	'I'm telling you what I saw happen and you didn't'
	'will/does/did this happen?'	
	'I am giving/demanding information'	

1 Daddy carry you on shóulder
   ménd it ... Mummy ménd it
   shall Daddy tell you the chùffa rhýme
   want Daddy to cut the séllotape
   don't wànt the peel taken óff
2 shall we go and get the toást
   shall we look at our fast dièsel train bóok
3 walk on wall by yoursélf
   want to go into the bathroom and put a little bit of toothpaste on these two tóothbrushes
4 y'want a drink of mílk
   want some móre sellotape
   have your púzzle

5 (a) we nearly thére ... to the wáll ('are we?')
Daddy's green toothbrush did breák ('did it?')
gó ... the garbage lorry gó ('does it?')
(b) what does thát say
how did that gone in the little hole thére
6 the machine was making a lot of nòise
the little bird with the long beak sitting on the wire flown awày
James had a tràin
we went in an aèroplane this morning
Mummy put a little bit of bùtter on your arm to feel it bètter[1]
7 (a) did the train fall off the tráck ('the train fell ...')
have you eaten that toast and bútter ('I've eaten ...')
did you get síck ('I got sick')
(b) what did Mummy dròp ('Mummy dropped something')

4 Conclusion

By the time he reaches the end of his second year, Nigel has laid the foundation for the adult system of dialogue. From here on, his meaning potential will develop along adult lines.

What was outlined in section 1 was, of course, the bare bones of the system, the semantic options in their most general form. Deriving from these is the rich network of meaning potential that lies behind the conversational rhetoric of a mature speaker of the language, for whom giving and demanding information and goods-and-services is, at most, the crude raw material of conversation. The conversational process among adults displays a playful variety that, to those whose point of departure was the idealized sentence or isolated speech act of philosophical linguistics, appeared bewilderingly infinite and unstructured. To those in the ethnographic tradition, who had always worked with 'real' data, and never harboured the illusion (but did anyone?) that conversation was like the grammarian's book of rules, to go on being told this as news was simply boring. But in order to understand the system behind the conversational process it is not enough to discover "rules of conversation"; we have to try and understand the relation of conversation to the linguistic system. The magical power of talk derives from the fact that it is, in every instance, the manifestation of a systematic resource, a resource which has been built up through acts of conversation in the first place, and which goes on being modified in each one of us as we talk our way through life.

As a final example, let us look at a very brief specimen of adult interaction; again, one that is taken from real life. A and B have met on a commuter train; they regularly do, but on this occasion they have not seen each other for some days (Passage G):

Passage G

    A: I see yòu're back in circulátion.
    B: Actually I've never been òut.
    A: I haven't šeen you for ages.

In this encounter, A's strategy is: 'We haven't met for some time; this is your fault, because you have failed to be where I was'. The manoeuvre is so blatant that B challenges it; but he does so defensively, by simply denying the implication, and this allows A to return to the attack, this time with a direct accusation of *I haven't seen you* ('so it must be your fault'). In the first, least delicate, analysis, these are all statements; the speakers are giving information, and it is important to recognize this component in their meaning, since without it they would not work. (Note that the interpretation of these as statements is neither 'deeper' nor 'shallower' than other steps in the interpretation. It is simply less delicate, less sharply focused.) But they are also moves in a game, with its strategies of attack and defence; and this is another aspect of the social context, one that is typically realized through the semantics of praise and blame – in other words, through the values that speakers attach to acts of meaning. These values are realized in their turn by various lexicogrammatical features within the interpersonal component; such as, in this example, the adjunct of mild protest *actually*, and the feature 'reservation' realized by the fall-rise tone in A's second turn, meaning 'you claim you haven't been out of circulation, but I haven't seen you, so you have something to explain'.

Interpersonal meanings such as protestation and reservation are just as much part of the linguistic system as are meanings of an ideational kind. The fact that interpersonal meanings often have different modes of expression from ideational ones, being prosodic or 'field'-like in their scope rather than segmental or 'particle'-like, and hence do not lend themselves so readily to representation in a constituency framework, may be one of the reasons why they have usually been treated as unsystematic. We should suggest rather that this is a reason for rejecting constituent structure as the primary organizing concept in linguistics, and for interpreting language in functional and systemic terms. In the explanation of dialogue, whether we are concerned with the most general categories or with the subtlest distinctions, and whether the focus is on the mature system of an adult or on its ontogenesis in a child, we are concerned with meanings of the interpersonal kind; it would be a mistake to adhere rigidly to theories of language which, because they reduce all linguistic organization to one type of structure, one that is typically associated with meanings of a different kind, namely ideational ones, thereby commit themselves to treating all interpersonal meanings as something secondary or tangential.

The organization of dialogue is a systematic feature of language; it is linguistically coded behaviour. It is built up by a child as part of his total semiotic potential. Neither the system nor its evolution can be satisfactorily explained in terms of a competence–performance dichotomy in which the code is so highly idealized that it cannot be used to explain what people do. Dialogue is not just a matter of "performance" (whatever that might mean). Nor, however, is it a matter of a special kind of competence ("communicative competence") that is somehow distinct from the ability to construct ideationally well-formed sentences. Taking part in dialogue is a dynamic process of selecting within a whole range of interrelated networks of interpersonal meanings. Interpersonal meanings are not 'uses of' ideational ones, or optional extras that sometimes get tacked on to them as an afterthought. The two constitute distinct but parallel components of the semantic system, and every act of meaning is the product of selections in both.

Note

1. All those in (6) are addressed to a person who had also witnessed the event; all those in (7) are addressed to a person who had not witnessed the event.

Chapter Eleven

THE PLACE OF DIALOGUE IN CHILDREN'S CONSTRUCTION OF MEANING
(1991)

1 Meaning as a social phenomenon

Much of the discussion of children's language development in the last quarter of a century, especially in educational contexts, has been permeated by a particular ideological construction of childhood. This view combines individualism, romanticism, and what Martin calls "childism": the disneyfied vision of a child that is constructed in the media and in certain kinds of "kiddielit".[1] Each child is presented as a free-standing autonomous being; and learning consists in releasing and bringing into flower the latent awareness that is already there in the bud. This is the view that was embodied in the "creativity" and "personal growth" models of education by James Britton, John Dixon and David Holbrook in Great Britain; and more recently, from another standpoint, in the United States in Donald Graves' conception of children's writing as process and of their text as property to be individually owned.[2] It has been supported theoretically first by Chomskyan innatism and latterly by cognitive science models which interpret learning as the acquisition of ready-made information by some kind of independent processing device (cf. Kintsch 1988).

What these various discourses have in common is that they are all essentially antisocial – or perhaps 'asocial', to be more accurate. In this they contrast with interpretations of development and learning that would make reference to Vygotsky, to Bernstein and, in linguistics, to the functional, social-semantic tradition that derives from European

---

First published in *Dialoganalyse III. Referate der 3, Arbeitstagung*, edited by Sorin Stati, Edda Weigand and Franz Hundsnurscher. Tübingen: Max Niemeyer Verlag GmbH, 1991, pp. 417–30.

scholarship, especially the Prague and London schools, from glossematics, and from the American anthropological linguists.[3] In this view meaning is a social and cultural phenomenon and all construction of meaning is a social process. We can use the term "intersubjective" for it provided we do not take this to imply that the "subject" comes into existence first and then proceeds to interact with other subjects. There is no subject until construed by social meaning-making practices (see Thibault 1991).

2 Developmental stages

In studying child language development some 20 years ago, I was struck by how clearly this social-semantic perspective stands out once you observe how children begin to communicate – especially if you observe it from birth and in a natural form, without eliciting or experimenting and without using too many technical aids. These practices tend to obscure the social nature of semiotic development, whereas the traditional diary method of child language studies brings it out. In this context, some fairly clearly defined developmental stages seemed to me to emerge:[4]

(1)	pre-symbolic ('primary intersubjectivity')	typically	birth–0;5
(1/2)	transition to:	"	0;5–0;8
(2)	symbolic: protolinguistic ('secondary intersubjectivity')	"	0;8–1;4
(2/3)	transition to:	"	1;4–2;0
(3)	symbolic: linguistic	"	2;0 –

Since I was focusing specifically on the development of language I concentrated on the last three, referring to them as 'phases':

(2)	symbolic: protolinguistic	= Phase I,	***protolanguage***
(2/3)	transition	= Phase II,	***transition***
(3)	symbolic: linguistic	= Phase III,	***language***

Since then detailed studies of early language development have been carried out in comparable terms, based on intensive observation of children in their home, by Clare Painter and by Jane Oldenburg-Torr; and Qiu Shijin has observed a population of Chinese children living in Shanghai, over a short period but covering different ages within the range. All have used the same theoretical framework for their interpretations (see Oldenburg-Torr 1990; Painter 1984; Qiu 1985).

From the beginning of life a child's acts of meaning are joint constructions, dialogically enacted between himself and some "significant other" by reference to whom he is achieving a personal identity. Colwyn Trevarthen documented this process for the pre-symbolic stage many years ago when he showed that a newborn infant within two or three weeks of birth takes part in exchanging attention.[5] This exchange of attention is the beginning of language. It has no "content", in the adult sense; but it has meaning. For the child, the meaning is 'we are together, and in communication; there is a "you" – and "me"'. 'You' and 'me' are, of course, mutually defining; neither can exist without the other. I shall not dwell on this stage here; but I have found it fascinating to take part in, and been amazed by the semogenic potential of these early microencounters. They are not entirely without content, as a matter of fact; but there is as yet no **systematic** construing of experience.

When the child begins to control his material environment, typically at round about four to five months, he begins the transition to **systematic** symbolic construction. He can reach out and grasp an object that is in view; and this coincides with his first **symbolic** encounter with the environment, which takes the form of an act of meaning that is something like 'that's interesting! – what is it?'. This introduces a 'third person' into the protoconversation alongside the 'you' and 'me'. The act itself may take any accessible form (my own subject, Nigel, produced a high-pitched squeak) – anything which can engage the child and the other in shared attention to some third party. This third party, that is construed as 'neither you nor me', is typically not, in fact, an object but a happening – a commotion of some kind like a sudden noise or a bright light coming in to the child's attention. But the act of meaning is clearly *addressed*; the meaning is jointly constructed, and the material phenomenon is construed as experience only through the shared act of exchanging a symbol. The mother, of course, or whoever is sharing in the act, responds in her own tongue; she says "yes, those were pigeons", or "that's a bus", or "see, they've put the lights on". But the semogenic process is dialogic, in two distinct respects; on the one hand *interpersonally*, in that the two acts define each other as question and answer, and on the other hand *experientially*, in that some kind of perturbation in the environment is construed dialogically as a phenomenon of experience. In other words it is through language that this 'third party' acquires the status of reality.

The child is also at the same time construing his own body; the first **symbolic** construction of self versus environment coincides more or less with the first construction of this same opposition in **material** terms. What is 'out there' is what can be grasped, 'grasping' being both a material process and a process of consciousness. But is has to be actively explored, on both these planes; and the transition to the systematic symbolic stage, that of the protolanguage, takes place only after the child has learnt that he can detach himself from the material environment (by rolling over). This protolanguage phase, that of "secondary intersubjectivity", is then reached, typically at somewhere between seven and ten months of age, through a change in both forms of his dialogue with the environment. On the one hand, in his **bodily** engagement the child learns to propel himself from one place to another, by some form of crawling. He now has the freedom of space–time; and at the same time he achieves the semiotic freedom of construing meanings into systems – that is, on both planes he achieves paradigmatic choice. This choice of meaning is the essential characteristic of protolanguage.

Protolanguage is the form of language that we humans share with what we think of as the "higher" mammals: mainly primates and cetaceans, but it also appears in our two most favoured pets, cats and dogs, at least when they interact with us. All these are of course different languages; but all have the same formal structure, as systems of simple signs. In the process of his symbolic activity, the child construes meaning into **systems**; and the systems are functional in different contexts – I referred to these as **microfunctions** in my analysis. The process is of course dialogic; the others share in construing the meaning potential. In this protolinguistic phase we can see clearly how meaning is created at the point of impact of the material and the conscious, in the dialectic engagement between these two domains of experience. Consider a typical protolinguistic dialogue such as the following:

[Mother is holding child in her lap, throwing his toy rabbit in air and catching it. The child is watching attentively.]

CHILD:	[ə̀ ə̀]
MOTHER:	There he goes!
CHILD:	[ə̀ ə̀ ə̀]
MOTHER:	Oh you want me to throw him up again do you? – all right.
CHILD:	[loudly] [m̀ng]
MOTHER:	No, that's enough. Let's find something else to do.

Here the material processes taking place in space-time (the mother throwing up the rabbit and catching it) impact on the conscious processes whereby both parties are attending, with shared positive affect, both to the other and to the third party, the rabbit-commotion. It is the interpenetration of these two that generates a ***meaning***, such as 'that's fun; I want you to do it again'; and also a contrasting meaning of 'I **insist** that you do it again!'. These evolve dialogically as part of a shared ***system*** of meanings in different microcontexts, which includes others such as 'I want / don't want that object', 'let's be (you and me) together/ let's attend to this (third party) together', 'I like / am curious about that' and so on.

It is in protolanguage, then, that the activity of ***meaning*** comes to be construed in the form of a system, such that there is an ongoing dialectic relationship between the ***system*** and the ***instance***. The system is the potential for generating instances; and by the same token each new instance perturbs the system.[6] The system is a dynamic open system, metastable in character, that persists only through constantly changing in interaction with its environment; and each new instance constitutes an incursion from the environment, since the material conditions that engender it are never totally identical. (We may note that this impacting of the conscious with the material takes place at both 'ends' of the symbolic process, the semantic and the phonetic; so that the system is evolving at both these interfaces, both in the construction of content and in the construction of expression. In the latter, the material conditions are those of the child's own body, his physiological potential – which also, of course, is constantly changing.)

The second major transition is that from protolanguage into language – into the distinctively human semiotic that is not, as far as we know, shared by other species. In the course of this transition the resource for making meaning is further transformed, this time into a system of another, significantly different kind. In the context of overall development, while protolanguage goes with crawling, language goes with walking; and both these activities are carried out by specialized organs – mouth and legs – leaving arms and hands free for other purposes. But the criterial, and critical, difference between protolanguage and language is that language is ***stratified***; that is, it has a ***grammar***. A grammar (strictly, ***lexicogrammar***: syntax, vocabulary, morphology if any) is a purely symbolic system that is introduced 'in between' the content and the expression; that is, it is a distinct level of semiotic organization located between the two material interfaces. Unlike a protolanguage, a language cannot be described as a system of signs; it is a system based on the more complex principle of *realization*, which cannot be reduced to pairs of 'signifiant/signifié'. The grammar thus does not interface directly with either material environment. But at the same time it is not neutral between the two; it is biased towards the content plane. The grammar is a 'natural' grammar which has evolved as the primary means for construing experience and enacting social processes – still, of course, in dialogic contexts.

Only a system that is stratified in this way can construe meaning in the form of 'information' – as a specifically linguistic commodity that can be **exchanged**, on the model of the exchange of goods-and-services that evolves with protolanguage. Without a grammar there can be no information. Once a grammar has evolved, I can tell you things and we can argue about them. The critical final step leading to the joint construction of information is the complex one of **arguing about**: the combination of mood with transitivity, in grammatical terms. But the child cannot reach this point in one giant leap. Let us try to enumerate the main steps in his progress.

3 Dialogic construction of meaning

It seems that children have a favourite strategy for achieving the transition from child tongue to mother tongue. It may be universal, or some aspects of it may be, and it may well have been the course taken by language in its evolution. The grammar makes it possible to construe experience, through the system of transitivity and its lexical counterpart in naming.[7] But at the same time, because the grammar is a purely abstract system at one remove from the material interfaces, it also makes it possible simultaneously to construe two contrasting dialogic modes (when they become grammaticalized we know them as "moods"): the imperative, or *pragmatic* mode, meaning 'this is how things **should** be; you bring them about!', and the declarative, or *mathetic* mode, meaning 'this is how things **are**; you can check whether you agree'. Early examples of pragmatic utterances from my records were:

1 water ón   'turn the water on!'   squeeze órange   'squeeze an orange!'
   get dówn   'I want to get down!'   play tráin   'let's play with the train!'

All had rising tone, and demanded a response. Contrast these with mathetic utterances such as the following, all on falling tone:

2	big bàll	'that's a big ball'	new rècord	'here's a new record'
	red sweàter	'I've got a red sweater'	two hàmmer	'I'm holding two hammers'

These were from 1;7. A later example shows the two modes in syntagmatic sequence (1;9):

3 no room walk on wàll ... walk on óther wall 'There's no room to walk on (this) wall; I want to walk on the other wall!'

The three English-speaking children who were recorded intensively by natural language diaries all made this distinction systematically as the primary semantic option in the protolanguage – language transition. All three expressed it prosodically, by intonation and/or voice quality; and in all three the pragmatic was the marked option. The Chinese-speaking children also made it, and also expressed it prosodically; however, there were not enough data to establish the markedness pattern.[8]

The pragmatic is a demand for goods-and-services; it seeks a response, in the form of action, and the 'others' involved in the dialogue recognize and construe it as such (unconsciously of course). That does not mean that they always accede to the request; but they show that they have got the message, and in that respect 'no' is as effective as 'yes'. Gradually, during the course of the transition, the pragmatic evolves into a demand for information; thus ontogenetically (and perhaps also phylogenetically) the interrogative, although in the adult grammar it pairs with the declarative, is derived by splitting off from the imperative – a demand for action becomes a demand for verbal action. The mathetic, on the other hand, does not demand any action. What it does do is invite confirmation: 'yes that's a big ball', 'it's not a big ball; it's a little ball', 'it's not a ball; it's a melon', and so on. And here an important question arises: what is the essential condition for entering into a dialogue of this kind, in which one interactant corroborates, or disputes, what the other one has just said. It is that the experience must have been **shared**. You cannot corroborate or dispute what happened unless you also were there to see it.

Thus the basic form of information is **turning shared experience into meaning**; that is, telling someone something that they already know. I can construe an experience semiotically, and offer the construction to you, provided I know that you have shared the experience; and you then share in construing it. Thus the construction is again dialogic: meaning is created by the impact between a material phenomenon and the shared processes of consciousness of those who participated in it.

Every parent is familiar with the situation where their child is asked to give information to someone about an experience that person has not shared, and the child is unable to do it. Mother has taken the child to the zoo; when she comes home she says 'Tell Daddy what you saw at the zoo today'. Daddy is attending; but the child cannot oblige – either he remains silent, or he turns back to Mummy and tells her. Why? Because she was the one with whom he shared the experience. How can he tell Daddy about it, when Daddy wasn't there?

Conversation, then, evolved as the joint construal of shared experience, whereby phenomena that are accessible to the consciousness of both parties – things both can see, events both have experienced – are turned dialogically into meanings. This is how conversation begins; and how it continues, with a child, until he is well on the way from protolanguage to mother tongue. No doubt conversation continued in that way for many generations in the history of the human species, before its further potential was taken up. But the potential is there once the *system* of meaning-making is in place: this is what enables the listener to construe phenomena that only the speaker has actually witnessed. And in the course of time each child makes this same discovery: that language can **create** information – it can take the place of shared experience. It is not necessary for the listener to have been there and seen the thing too; the experience can be ***reconstrued*** out of the language. This is such a major discovery that Nigel, at least, consistently used a different grammar for the two situations: he had one form for 'I'm telling you something we shared', which was his original context for giving information, and another form for 'I'm telling you something that happened, even though you weren't there to see it'. This grammatical distinction is not made in the adult language, so after a few months Nigel gave it up. We do not distinguish between telling people what (we think) they know and telling them what (we think) they don't know; the declarative covers both. But at the same time, we do not stop using language in the earlier way. In communication models the concept of information is usually taken to imply that knowledge is being transmitted from a knower to a non-knower: 'I know something which you don't know; I "mean" it, and as a result you now know it'. Where this happens, language is operating as a surrogate for shared experience: a way sharing semiotically what has not been shared materially. Prototypically this is monologic, since only the knower takes part in transforming it into meaning. But it is mainly in rather specialized uses of language, like an academic lecture, that information is constructed and imparted in this monologic way. Most of the time when we are in the indicative mood we are construing meanings interactively on the basis of shared experience. The prototypical form of this process is the dialogic one, in which the construction proceeds by argument. Arguing is the shared construction of experiential meaning; it occupies the space from consensus to conflict, and interactants will typically move between the two as they extend their dialogue into conversation.[9]

In Chapter 7 I gave an example of the joint construction of narrative in a dialogue between Nigel (at 20 months) and his parents about a goat eating a plastic lid (p. 186).

We tend to think of narrative and dialogue as opposed forms of discourse; but this type of text suggests that in its early development narrative itself is dialogic. The material experience had been shared between child and parents; the child then takes the initiative in verbalizing it so that it becomes part of a shared construction of reality. The parents join in, their turns taking the form of questions; but these are not simply interpersonal prompts – since they are Wh-type questions, they contain experiential information:

> "What tried to eat the lid?" – there was a doer (grammatically an Actor); you identify it.
> "Why did the man say no?" – there was a reason (grammatically some expression of cause); you identify it.

Thus there is joint participation in the construing of this experience.

We may compare this with the accompanying sequence of texts (A1–A9, see below) taken from the record of conversations over a period of about eight months, when Nigel is 2.10 to 3.6. These are not narratives of events, but rather the ongoing construction of a general concept, in this case that of 'cats'. The child is older now, and in these instances he is asking the questions; many of these are yes/no questions, but there are also Wh-questions of 'how?' and 'why?'. In both types, of course, the child is also **contributing** information:

> "Do cats like meat/bones/marrow?" – constructing and testing out a taxonomy of potential foods.
> "How do the cat's claws come out?" – they come out and go in again.

"Does it go with (= walk on) its claws?" – they come out and go in in different contexts and functions.

But the conversations achieve much more than that. Experientially, for example, the dialogue constructs the general taxonomy of plants and animals ('things that grow' versus 'things that go'); compare the complex argument around a four-way distinction of cats, puppets, people and trains at 3;6. Interpersonally, it evolves into a dynamic modelling of question, answer, challenge, contradiction and the like, that is the essential component of the resources out of which all conversation is constructed.

I have given various examples elsewhere from my own records (Part 1 of this Volume); many more will be found in the writings of Oldenburg-Torr and Painter, as well as throughout the now extensive literature on child language (but note that very little of this takes any account of protolanguage). It is instructive both to examine single instances and to track conversational motifs through time, as in the cat extracts just cited. For example, in wondering how Nigel had construed his experience of time and space I was able to put together conversational fragments extending over several years, while Joy Phillips, from intensive study of the earlier data, showed how he had developed the fundamental semantic strategies of comparison and contrast. And the extraordinarily rich body of natural conversation between mothers and their children of three to four that Ruqaiya Hasan has assembled adds a significant new dimension to our understanding of the development of dialogue. In all these early discourses we see clearly how the text interacts with its environment, such that meaning is created at the intersection of two contradictions: the experiential one, between the material and the conscious modes of experience, and the interpersonal one, between the different personal histories of the interactants taking part. Thus from the ontogenesis of conversation we can gain insight into human learning and human understanding.

The construction of 'cats' (Nigel from 2.10 to 3.6) from Halliday (1984)

Text A1: Nigel at 2;10;22

NIGEL:	And you (= 'I') saw a cat in Chania Falls.
MOTHER:	Yes, you saw a cat in Chania Falls.
NIGEL:	And you picked the cat up. Mummy, do cats like meat?
MOTHER:	Yes, they do.
NIGEL:	Do cats like bones? Do cats like marrow?

Text A2: Nigel at 2;10;26

NIGEL: Can I stroke the cat? You (= 'I') want to stroke the cat ... you want to scratch it ... it's drinking its milk ... it's moving its tail out ... it's moving its tail outside ... it's scratching ... it's putting its tail up ... what's this?
MOTHER: I don't know; I suppose it's its elbow.
NIGEL: It's wagging its tail ... it's lapping it with its tongue ... you can go near its elbow ... you **can** go near its elbow ... but you can't go too near its face ... because it thinks you might take away its milk ... it was just a bit frightened ... it thinked that you might take away its milk ... has it finished its milk?

Text A3: Nigel at 2;11;5

NIGEL: (thinking about "The house that Jack built") What is a rat?
FATHER: It's a sort of big mouse.
NIGEL: Does the rat go when the cat has killed it?
FATHER: No, it doesn't go any more then.
NIGEL: Why did the cat kill the rat?
FATHER: Cats do kill rats.
NIGEL: Why do they?
FATHER: (formula) You'll have to wait to understand that till you're a bit bigger.
NIGEL: No, I can understand it now.
FATHER: Well, cats just like to eat rats and mice.
NIGEL: Why do they like to eat them?
FATHER: They just do.

Text A4: Nigel at 2;11;15

NIGEL: Why did the cat go out? Mummy, why did the cat go out?
MOTHER: It gets fed up, having its tail squashed.

Text A5: Nigel at 3;0;26

NIGEL: How do the cat's claws come out?
FATHER: They come out from inside its paws. Look, I'll show you.
NIGEL: Does it go with its claws?
FATHER: Not if it's going along the ground.

| NIGEL: | And not if it's climbing up a tree. |
| FATHER: | Yes, if it's climbing up a tree it does go with its claws. |

Text A6: Nigel at 3;2;7

| NIGEL: | Will the cat eat the grape? |
| FATHER: | I don't think so. Cats like things that go, not things that grow. |

Text A7: Nigel at 3;5;12

| NIGEL: | Cats have no else to stop you from trossing them ... cats have no other way to stop children from hitting them ... so they bite. Cat, don't go away! When I come back I'll tell you a story. (He does so.) |

Text A8: Nigel at 3;6;12

NIGEL:	Can I give the cat some artichoke?
MOTHER:	Well she won't like it.
NIGEL:	Cats like things that go; they don't like things that grow.

Text A9: Nigel at 3;6;14

NIGEL:	I wish I was a puppet so that I could go out into the snow in the night. Do puppets like going out in the snow?
FATHER:	I don't know. I don't think they mind.
NIGEL:	Do cats like going out in the snow?
FATHER:	Cats don't like snow.
NIGEL:	Do they die? (He knows that some plants do.)
FATHER:	No they don't die; they just don't like it.
NIGEL:	Why don't puppets mind snow?
FATHER:	Well (hesitating) ... puppets aren't people.
NIGEL:	Yes but ... cats also aren't people.
FATHER:	No, but cats are alive; they go. Puppets don't go.
NIGEL:	Puppets do go.
FATHER:	Yes, but you have to make them go; like trains.
NIGEL:	Trains have wheels. Puppets have legs.
FATHER:	Yes, they have legs; but the legs don't go all by themselves. You have to make them go.

Notes

1. This ideology is particularly characteristic of what has been called the "manipulative capitalist" society (see Martin 1989: especially Chapter 4, passim).
2. See for example Dixon (1967), Graves (1983). For an excellent critique see Rothery (forthcoming).
3. Among contemporary linguists an outstanding contributor to the development of this tradition is Claude Hagège (see for example Hagège 1985).
4. The initial interpretation of my observations is contained in Halliday (1975). The data to age 2.7 is available in Halliday (1984). See also Bullowa (1979a).
5. Colwyn Trevarthen's important work in this field in presented in a number of his papers; see especially 1979 and 1980. For his work on the protolanguage phase see Thevarthen and Hubley (1978). Bruner's work provides a valuable general theoretical underpinning from a psychological standpoint; compare 1977.
6. Contrast genetically transmitted communication systems (like the dances of bees), where instances do not perturb the system. This fundamental feature of semiotic systems is obscured in adult language by the massive quantitative effects to which it contributes (cf. Halliday 1987); but it is seen very clearly at the protolanguage phase of development.

    For language as dynamic open system, see Lemke's three articles 'Towards a model of the instructional process', 'The formal analysis of instruction' and 'Action, context and meaning', in Lemke (1984).
7. Naming (lexicalized denotation) and transitivity are the cornerstones of the potential of language for construing experience (the experiential metafunction, in the terms of systemic theory). They were first explicitly linked in this way by Mathesius (see for example 1936). For naming in the development of conversation see Chapter 10.
8. It may seem surprising that, with children learning a tone language, a major distinction such as this could be realized by intonation. In fact, of course, Chinese uses intonation (grammatical tone) as well as lexical tone; but this is irrelevant. The protolanguage is 'child tongue', not mother tongue; you cannot tell, when a child is speaking protolanguage, what language his mother tongue is going to be, and although by the time children introduce this distinction they are already launched into the mother tongue, this particular contrast is still their own invention.

    In some instances, in fact, their system runs counter to the pattern of the mother tongue. Thus in Nigel's grammar proto-imperatives, being pragmatic, were rising in tone, whereas in English the informal imperative is typically falling; while when he first used dependent clauses, which have no macrofunction, he gave them the unmarked (falling) tone. Thus when, at just under 1;9, he said "When New-World finish, song about bús!" ('When the New World [symphony] is finished, sing me the song about a bus') the first clause was falling, the second rising; whereas in adult English the tones would have been the other way round.

9. From her study of long conversations among groups of adults, Suzanne Eggins postulates that it is in fact the periodicity of consensus and conflict that is the major factor in keeping conversation going (see Eggins forthcoming).

Part Three

Early Language and Learning

Editor's Introduction

Providing a perspective on language that is educationally relevant is the subject of Chapter 12, 'Relevant Models of Language' (1969). Professor Halliday describes two components of an educationally relevant approach to language. One of which "is that it takes account of the child's own linguistic experience, defining this experience in terms of its richest potential and noting where there may be gaps, with certain children, which could be educationally and developmentally harmful". The other "is the relevance to the experiences that the child will have later on: to the linguistic demands that society will eventually make of him, and, in the intermediate stage, to the demands on language which the school is going to make and which he must meet if he is to succeed in the classroom". The models referred to here as being educationally relevant are not models of language acquisition, but rather 'images' of language at work realizing the intentions of its users. Language is what language does. Among the child's models of language discussed are the instrumental ("I want"), regulatory ("do as I tell you"), interactional ("me and him"), personal ("here I come"), heuristic ("tell me why"), imaginative ("let's pretend"), and representational ("I've got something to tell you").

Along with his developing awareness of the uses of language, the child is becoming a member of the species 'social man', or "'socio-semiotic man', man as a repository of social meanings". Those around the child, interacting with the child – whether parents, caregivers, or teachers – are active participants with the child in his own construction of both a linguistic and a social semiotic. In Chapter 13 'The Social Context of Language Development' (1975), Professor Halliday describes how as the child learns the social semiotic – the culture – simultaneously "he is learning the means of learning it" – the language. An essential condition of learning is the systematic link between the components of meaning – "different aspects of the meaner's ability to mean" – and the semiotic properties of the situation. Nigel's interaction with his mother is used to illustrate how linguistic features of the text are determined by situational features specified in terms of field ("the ongoing activity"), tenor ("the role relationships involved") and mode ("the symbolic or rhetorical channel").

Coinciding with the launch of the Language Development Project in Australia in 1977, Professor Halliday proposed adopting the following threefold perspective: learning language, learning through language, learning about language. The idea is that language development is a continuous process of learning to mean with two dimensions of continuity: "not only a developmental continuity right through from birth to adult life, with language in home, neighbourhood, primary school, secondary school, and place of work, but also a structural continuity running through all components and processes of learning". From birth, the child is developing an unconscious awareness of "what [he] can do with language". Education needs to build on this awareness if it is to succeed in strengthening and extending the child's language development. Chapter 14, 'Three Aspects of Children's Language Development: Learning Language, Learning Through Language, Learning About Language' (1980), suggests "relating the language work in the classroom to what he already knows about language from his own experience". Chapter 15, 'Towards a Language-Based Theory of Learning' (1993), suggests grounding learning theory in what is known about 'learning language'. Based on the direct observation of children's use of language at home and at school, Professor Halliday identifies 21 features of child language development which "are critical to a language-based theory of learning". Both teachers and students stand to benefit from the insights into the processes of language development obtained from investigations – such as are reported on in the final chapter in this section, 'Grammar and the Construction of Educational Knowledge' (1999) – into "how certain children were learning their language or, more accurately, of how they were learning *through* their language; that is, how they were using language, as they learnt it, in learning everything else to do with their world".

Chapter Twelve

RELEVANT MODELS OF LANGUAGE (1969)

The teacher of English who, when seeking an adequate definition of language to guide him in his work, meets with a cautious "well, it depends on how you look at it" is likely to share the natural impatience felt by anyone who finds himself unable to elicit "a straight answer to a straight question". But the very frequency of this complaint may suggest that, perhaps, questions are seldom as straight as they seem. The question "what is language?", in whatever guise it appears, is as diffuse and, at times, disingenuous as other formulations of its kind, for example "what is literature?". Such questions, which are wisely excluded from examinations, demand the privilege of a qualified and perhaps circuitous answer.

In a sense the only satisfactory response is "why do you want to know?", since unless we know what lies beneath the question we cannot hope to answer it in a way which will suit the questioner. Is he interested in language planning in multilingual communities? Or in aphasia and language disorders? Or in words and their histories? Or in dialects and those who speak them? Or in how one language differs from another? Or in the formal properties of language as a system? Or in the functions of language and the demands that we make on it? Or in language as an art medium? Or in the information and redundancy of writing systems? Each one of these and other such questions is a possible context for a definition of language. In each case language "is" something different.

The criterion is one of relevance; we want to understand, and to highlight, those facets of language which bear on the investigation or

---

First published in *The State of Language, Educational Review.* 22.1, pp. 26–37.

the task in hand. In an educational context the problem for linguistics is to elaborate some account of language that is relevant to the work of the English teacher. What constitutes a relevant notion of language from his point of view, and by what criteria can this be decided? Much of what has been objected to, among the attitudes and approaches to language in the profession, arouses criticism not so much because it is false as because it is irrelevant. When, for example, the authors of *The Linguistic Sciences and Language Teaching* (Halliday *et al.* 1964) suggested that teaching the dos and don'ts of grammar to a child who is linguistically unsuccessful is like teaching a starving man how to hold a knife and fork, they were not denying that there is a ritual element in our use of language, with rules of conduct to which everyone is expected to conform; they were simply asserting that the view of language as primarily good manners was of little relevance to educational needs. Probably very few people ever held this view explicitly; but it was implicit in a substantial body of teaching practices, and if it has now largely been discarded, this is because its irrelevance became obvious in the course of some rather unhappy experience.

It is not necessary, however, to sacrifice a generation of children, or even one classroomful, in order to demonstrate that particular preconceptions of language are inadequate or irrelevant. In place of a negative and somewhat hit-and-miss approach, a more fruitful procedure is to seek to establish certain general, positive criteria of relevance. These will relate, ultimately, to the demands that we make of language in the course of our lives. We need, therefore, to have some idea of the nature of these demands, and we shall ask, in effect, about the child's image of language: what is the **model** of language that he internalizes as a result of his own experience? This will help us to decide what is relevant to the teacher, since the teacher's own view of language must at the very least encompass all that the child knows language to be.

The child knows what language is because he knows what language does. The determining elements in the young child's experience are the successful demands on language that he himself has made, the particular needs that have been satisfied by language for him. He has used language in many ways – for the satisfaction of material and intellectual needs, for the mediation of personal relationships, the expression of feelings and so on. Language in all these uses has come within his own direct experience, and because of this he is subconsciously aware that language has many functions that affect him personally. Language is, for the child, a rich and adaptable instrument for the realization of his intentions; there is hardly any limit to what he can do with it.

As a result, the child's internal **model** of language is a highly complex one; and most adult notions of language fail to match up to it. The adult's ideas about language may be externalized and consciously formulated, but they are nearly always much too simple. In fact it may be more helpful, in this connection, to speak of the child's **models** of language, in the plural, in order to emphasise the many-sidedness of his linguistic experience. We shall try to identify the models of language with which the normal child is endowed by the time he comes to school at the age of five; the assumption being that if the teacher's own **received** conception of language is in some ways less rich or less diversified, it will be irrelevant to the educational task.

We tend to underestimate both the total extent and the functional diversity of the part played by language in the life of the child. His interaction with others, which begins at birth, is gradually given form by language, through the process whereby at a very early age language already begins to mediate in every aspect of his experience. It is not only as the child comes to act on and to learn about his environment that language comes in, but it is also there from the start in his achievement of intimacy and in the expression of his individuality. The rhythmic recitation of nursery rhymes and jingles is still language, as we can see from the fact that children's spells and chants differ from one language to another: English nonsense is quite distinct from French nonsense, because the one is English and the other French. All these contribute to the child's total picture of language "at work".

Through such experiences, the child builds up a very positive impression – one that cannot be verbalized, but is nonetheless real for that – of what language is and what it is for. Much of his difficulty with language in school arises because he is required to accept a stereotype of language that is contrary to the insights he has gained from his own experience. The traditional first "reading and writing" tasks are a case in point, since they fail to coincide with his own convictions about the nature and uses of language.

★ ★ ★

Perhaps the simplest of the child's models of language, and one of the first to be evolved, is what we may call the *instrumental* model. The child becomes aware that language is used as a means of getting things done. About a generation ago, zoologists were finding out about the highly developed mental powers of chimpanzees; and one of the observations described was of the animal that constructed a long stick out of three short ones and used it to dislodge a bunch of bananas from the roof of its cage. The human child, faced with the same problem, constructs a sentence. He says "I want a banana"; and the effect is the more impressive because it does not depend on the immediate presence of the bananas. Language is brought in to serve the function of 'I want', the satisfaction of material needs. Success in this use of language does not in any way depend on the production of well-formed adult sentences; a carefully contextualized yell may have substantially the same effect, and although this may not be language, there is no very clear dividing line between, say, a noise made on a commanding tone and a full-dress imperative clause.

The old *See Spot run. Run, Spot, run!* type of first reader bore no relation whatsoever to this instrumental function of language. This by itself does not condemn it, since language has many other functions besides that of manipulating and controlling the environment. But it bore little apparent relation to any use of language, at least to any with which the young child is familiar. It is not recognizable as language in terms of the child's own intentions, of the meanings that he has reason to express and to understand. Children have a very broad concept of the meaningfulness of language, in addition to their immense tolerance of inexplicable tasks; but they are not accustomed to being faced with language which, in their own functional terms, has no meaning at all, and the old-style reader was not seen by them as language. It made no connection with language in use.

Language as an instrument of control has another side to it, since the child is well aware that language is also a means whereby others exercise control over him. Closely related to the instrumental model, therefore, is the ***regulatory*** model of language. This refers to the use of language to regulate the behaviour of others. Bernstein and his colleagues (1970) have studied different types of regulatory behaviour by parents in relation to the process of socialization of the child, and their work provides important clues concerning what the child may be expected to derive from this experience in constructing his own model of language. To adapt one of Bernstein's examples, as described by Turner (1969), the mother who finds that her small child has carried out of the supermarket, unnoticed by herself or by the cashier, some object that was not paid for, may exploit the power of language in various ways, each of which will leave a slightly different trace or after-image of this role of language in the mind of the child. For example, she may say *you mustn't take things that don't belong to you* (control through conditional prohibition based on a categorization of objects in terms of a particular social institution, that of ownership); *that was very naughty* (control through categorization of behaviour in terms of opposition approved/ disapproved); *if you do that again I'll smack you* (control through threat of reprisal linked to repetition of behaviour); *you'll make Mummy very unhappy if you do that* (control through emotional blackmail); *that's not allowed* (control through categorization of behaviour as governed by rule), and so on. A single incident of this type by itself has little significance; but such general types of regulatory behaviour, through repetition and reinforcement, determine the child's specific awareness of language as a means of behavioural control.

The child applies this awareness, in his own attempts to control his peers and siblings; and this in turn provides the basis for an essential component in his range of linguistic skills, the language of rules and instructions. Whereas at first he can make only simple unstructured demands, he learns as time goes on to give ordered sequences of instructions, and then progresses to the further stage where he can convert sets of instructions into rules, including conditional rules, as in explaining the principles of a game. Thus his regulatory model of language continues to be elaborated, and his experience of the potentialities of language in this use further increases the value of the model.

Closely related to the regulatory function of language is its function in social interaction, and the third of the models that we may postulate as forming part of the child's image of language is the **interactional** model. This refers to the use of language in the interaction between the self and others. Even the closest of the child's personal relationships, that with his mother, is partly and, in time, largely mediated through language; his interaction with other people, adults and children, is very obviously maintained linguistically. (Those who come nearest to achieving a personal relationship that is not linguistically mediated, apparently, are twins.)

Aside, however, from his experience of language in the maintenance of permanent relationships, the neighbourhood and the activities of the peer group provide the context for complex and rapidly changing interactional patterns which make extensive and subtle demands on the individual's linguistic resources. Language is used to define and consolidate the group, to include and to exclude, showing who is 'one of us' and who is not; to impose status, and to contest status that is imposed; and humour, ridicule, deception, persuasion, all the forensic and theatrical arts of language are brought into play. Moreover, the young child, still primarily a learner, can do what very few adults can do in such situations: he can be internalizing language while listening and talking. He can be, effectively, both a participant and an observer at the same time, so that his own critical involvement in this complex interaction does not prevent him from profiting linguistically from it.

Again there is a natural link here with another use of language, from which the child derives what we may call the *personal* model. This refers to his awareness of language as a form of his own individuality. In the process whereby the child becomes aware of himself, and in particular in the higher stages of that process, the development of his personality, language plays an essential role. We are not talking here merely of "expressive" language – language used for the direct expression of feelings and attitudes – but also of the personal element in the interactional function of language, since the shaping of the self through interaction with others is very much a language-mediated process. The child is enabled to offer to someone else that which is unique to himself, to make public his own individuality; and this in turn reinforces and creates this individuality. With the normal child, his awareness of himself is closely bound up with speech: both with hearing himself speak, and with having at his disposal the range of behavioural options that constitute language. Within the concept of the self as an actor, having discretion, or freedom of choice, the "self as a speaker" is an important component.

Thus, for the child, language is very much a part of himself, and the *personal* model is his intuitive awareness of this, and of the way in which his individuality is identified and realized through language. The other side of the coin, in this process, is the child's growing understanding of his environment, since the environment is, first of all, the "non-self", that which is separated out in the course of establishing where he himself begins and ends. So, fifthly, the child has a *heuristic* model of language, derived from his knowledge of how language has enabled him to explore his environment.

The heuristic model refers to language as a means of investigating reality, a way of learning about things. This scarcely needs comment, since every child makes it quite obvious that this is what language is for by his habit of constantly asking questions. When he is questioning, he is seeking not merely facts but explanations of facts, the generalizations about reality that language makes it possible to explore. Again,

Bernstein (1970) has shown the importance of the question-and-answer routine in the total setting of parent–child communication and the significance of the latter, in turn, in relation to the child's success in formal education: his research has demonstrated a significant correlation between the mother's linguistic attention to the child and the teacher's assessment of the child's success in the first year of school.

The young child is very well aware of how to use language to learn, and may be quite conscious of this aspect of language before he reaches school; many children already control a metalanguage for the heuristic function of language, in that they know what a 'question' is, what an 'answer' is, what 'knowing' and 'understanding' mean, and they can talk about these things without difficulty. Mackay and Thompson (1968) have shown the importance of helping the child who is learning to read and write to build up a language for talking about language; and it is the heuristic function which provides one of the foundations for this, since the child can readily conceptualize and verbalize the basic categories of the heuristic model. To put this more concretely, the normal five-year-old either already uses words such as *question*, *answer* in their correct meanings or, if he does not, is capable of learning to do so.

The other foundation for the child's "language about language" is to be found in the imaginative function. This also relates the child to his environment, but in a rather different way. Here, the child is using language to create his own environment; not to learn about how things are but to make them as he feels inclined. From his ability to create, through language, a world of his own making he derives the ***imaginative*** model of language; and this provides some further elements of the metalanguage, with words like *story*, *make up* and *pretend*.

Language in its imaginative function is not necessarily 'about' anything at all: the child's linguistically created environment does not have to be a make-believe copy of the world of experience, occupied by people and things and events. It may be a world of pure sound, made up of rhythmic sequences of rhyming or chiming syllables; or an edifice of words in which semantics has no part, like a house built of playing cards in which face values are irrelevant. Poems, rhymes, riddles and much of the child's own linguistic play reinforce this model of language, and here too the meaning of what is said is not primarily a matter of content. In stories and dramatic games, the imaginative function is, to a large extent, based on content; but the ability to express such content is still, for the child, only one of the interesting facets of language, one which for many purposes is no more than an optional extra.

So we come finally to the ***representational*** model. Language is, in addition to all its other guises, a means of communicating about something, of expressing propositions. The child is aware that he can convey a message in language, a message which has specific reference to the processes, persons, objects, abstractions, qualities, states and relations of the real world around him.

This is the only model of language that many adults have; and a very inadequate model it is, from the point of view of the child. There is no need to go so far as to suggest that the transmission of content is, for the child, the least important function of language; we have no way of evaluating the various functions relative to one another. It is certainly not, however, one of the earliest to come into prominence; and it does not become a dominant function until a much later stage in the development towards maturity. Perhaps it never becomes in any real sense the dominant function; but it does, in later years, tend to become the dominant **model**. It is very easy for the adult, when he attempts to formulate his ideas about the nature of language, to be simply unaware of most of what language means to the child; this is not because he no longer uses language in the same variety of different functions (one or two may have atrophied, but not all), but because only one of these functions, in general, is the subject of conscious attention, so that the corresponding model is the only one to be externalized. But this presents what is, for the child, a quite unrealistic picture of language, since it accounts for only a small fragment of his total awareness of what language is about.

The representational model at least does not conflict with the child's experience. It relates to one significant part of it; rather a small part, at first, but nevertheless real. In this it contrasts sharply with another view of language which we have not mentioned because it plays no part in the child's experience at all, but which might be called the "ritual" model of language. This is the image of language internalized by those for whom language is a means of showing how well one was brought up; it downgrades language to the level of table manners. The ritual element in the use of language is probably derived from the interactional, since language in its ritual function also serves to define and delimit a social group; but it has none of the positive aspects of linguistic interaction, those which impinge on the child, and is thus very partial and one-sided. The view of language as manners is a needless complication, in the present context, since this function of language has no counterpart in the child's experience.

Our conception of language, if it is to be adequate for meeting the needs of the child, will need to be exhaustive. It must incorporate all the child's own **models**, to take account of the varied demands on language that he himself makes. The child's understanding of what language is is derived from his own experience of language in situations of use. It thus embodies all of the images we have described: the instrumental, the regulatory, the interactional, the personal, the heuristic, the imaginative and the representational. Each of these is his interpretation of a function of language with which he is familiar. Doughty (1969) has shown, in a very suggestive paper, how different concepts of the role of the English teacher tend to incorporate and to emphasize different functions, or groups of functions, from among those here enumerated.

★ ★ ★

Let us summarize the models in terms of the child's intentions, since different uses of language may be seen as realizing different intentions. In its instrumental function, language is used for the satisfaction of material need; this is the 'I want' function. The regulatory is the 'do as I tell you' function, language in the 'me and him' function (including 'me and my mummy'). The personal is related to this: it is the expression of identity, of the self, which develops largely **through** linguistic interaction; the 'here I come' function, perhaps. The heuristic is the use of language to learn, to explore reality: the function of 'tell me why'. The imaginative is that of 'let's pretend', whereby the reality is created, and what is being explored is the child's own mind, including language itself. The representational is the 'I've got something to tell you' function, that of the communication of content.

What we have called "models" are the images that we have of language arising out of these functions. Language is defined for the child by its uses; it is something that serves this set of needs. These are not models of language acquisition; they are not procedures whereby the child learns his language, nor do they define the part played by different types of linguistic activity in the learning process. Hence no mention has been made of the chanting and repeating and rehearsing by which the child practises his language. The techniques of mastering language do not constitute a "use", nor do they enter into the making of the image of language; a child, at least, does not learn for the luxury of being a learner. For the child, all language is doing something: in other words, it has meaning. It has meaning in a very broad sense, including here a range of functions which the adult does not normally think of as meaningful, such as the personal and the interactional and probably most of those listed above – all except the last, in fact. But it is precisely in relation to the child's conception of language that it is most vital for us to redefine our notion of meaning; not restricting it to the narrow limits of representational meaning (that is, "content") but including within it all the functions that language has as purposive, non-random, contextualized activity.

Bernstein (1970) has shown that educational failure is often, in a very general and rather deep sense, language failure. The child who does not succeed in the school system is one who has not mastered certain essential aspects of language ability. In its immediate interpretation, this could refer to the simple fact that a child cannot read or write or express himself adequately in speech. But these are, as it were, the externals of linguistic success, and it is likely that underlying the failure to master these skills is a deeper and more general failure of language, some fundamental gap in the child's linguistic capabilities.

This is not a lack of words; vocabulary seems to be learnt very easily in response to opportunity combined with motivation. Nor is it, by and large, an impoverishment of the grammar: there is no real evidence to show that the unsuccessful child uses or disposes of a narrower range of syntactic options. (I hope it is unnecessary to add that it has also nothing to do with dialect or accent.) Rather it would appear that the child who, in Bernstein's terms, has only a "restricted code" is one who is deficient in respect of the set of linguistic models that we have outlined above, because some of the functions of language have not been accessible to him. The "restriction" is a restriction on the range of uses of language. In particular, it is likely that he has not learnt to operate with language in the two functions which are crucial to his success in school: the personal function, and the heuristic function.

In order to be taught successfully, it is necessary to know how to use language to learn; and also, how to use language to participate **as an individual** in the learning situation. These requirements are probably not a feature of any particular school system, but rather are inherent in the very concept of education. The ability to operate effectively in the personal and heuristic modes is, however, something that has to be learnt; it does not follow automatically from the acquisition of the grammar and vocabulary of the mother tongue. It is not, that is to say, a question of which words and structures the child knows or uses, but of their functional significance and interpretation. In Bernstein's formulation, the child may not be oriented towards the meanings realized by the personal and heuristic functions of language. Restricted and elaborated code are in effect, as Ruqaiya Hasan (1969) suggests, varieties of language function, determining the meanings that syntactic patterns and the lexical items have for the child who hears or uses them.

To say that educational failure is linguistic failure is merely to take the first step in explaining it: it means that the most immediately accessible cause of educational failure is to be sought in language. Beyond this, and underlying the linguistic failure, is a complex pattern of social and familial factors whose significance has been revealed by Bernstein's work. But while the limitations of a child's linguistic experience may ultimately be ascribed – though not in any simple or obvious way – to features of the social background, the problem as it faces the teacher is essentially a linguistic problem. It is a failure in the child's effective mastery of the use of language, in his adaptation of language to meet certain basic demands. Whether one calls it a failure in language or a failure in the use of language is immaterial; the distinction between knowing language and knowing how to use it is merely one of terminology. This situation is not easy even to diagnose; it is much more difficult to treat. We have tried here to shed some light on it by relating it to the total set of demands, in terms of the needs of the child, that language is called upon to serve.

The implication for a teacher is that his own model of language should at least not fall short of that of the child. If the teacher's image of language is narrower and less rich than that which is already present in the minds of those he is teaching (or which needs to be present, if they are to succeed), it will be irrelevant to him as a teacher. A minimum requirement for an educationally relevant approach to language is that it should take account of the child's own linguistic experience, defining this experience in terms of its richest potential and noting where there may be gaps, with certain children, which could be educationally and developmentally harmful. This is one component. The other component of relevance is the relevance to the experiences that the child will have later on: to the linguistic demands that society will eventually make of him, and, in the intermediate stage, to the demands on language which the school is going to make and which he must meet if he is to succeed in the classroom.

We are still very ignorant of many aspects of the part language plays in our lives. But it is clear that language serves a wide range of human needs, and the richness and variety of its functions is reflected in the nature of language itself, in its organization as a system: within the grammatical structure of a language, certain areas are primarily associated with the heuristic and representational functions, others with the personal and interactional functions. Different bits of the system, as it were, do different jobs; and this in turn helps us to interpret and make more precise the notion of uses of language. What is common to every use of language is that it is meaningful, contextualized, and in the broadest sense social; this is brought home very clearly to the child, in the course of his day-to-day experience. The child is surrounded by language, but not in the form of grammars and dictionaries, or of randomly chosen words and sentences, or of undirected monologue. What he encounters is "text", or language in use: sequences of language articulated each within itself and with the situation in which it occurs. Such sequences are purposive – though very varied in purpose – and have an evident social significance. The child's awareness of language cannot be isolated from his awareness of language function, and this conceptual unity offers a useful vantage point from which language may be seen in a perspective that is educationally relevant.

Chapter Thirteen

THE SOCIAL CONTEXT OF LANGUAGE DEVELOPMENT (1975)

1 Learning the language and learning the culture

In the present chapter we shall focus attention on the question of how a child learns the culture. How does he construct a social system, an interpretative model of the environment in which he finds himself? In other words, how does he construct reality?

It is commonplace that the child's construction of reality is achieved largely through the medium of language. But to say this does not resolve the puzzle: if anything, it enhances it. It is not as if anyone teaches a child the mysteries of the social system – the social structure, systems of knowledge, systems of values and the like. Yet before he ever comes to school he has accumulated a vast store of information about these things; and he has done so not only without instruction but also without those from whom he has learnt it being aware that they know it themselves. And he has learnt it largely through language: through the small change of everyday speech, the casual linguistic interaction of the home, the street and the neighbourhood.

The learning of language and the learning of culture are obviously two different things. At the same time, they are closely interdependent. This is true not only in the sense that a child constructs a reality for himself largely through language, but also in the more fundamental sense that language is itself a part of this reality. The linguistic system is a part of the social system. Neither can be learnt without the other.

In Chapter 4 we suggested a way of conceptualizing the social system and the linguistic system that would enable the two to be brought into

---

First published in *Learning How to Mean: Explorations in the Development of Language*. London: Edward Arnold, 1975, pp. 120–45.

some sort of relevant relationship with one another in a developmental context. We took the view of the social system as a semiotic, a system of meanings that is **realized through** (*inter alia*) the linguistic system. The linguistic semiotic – that is, semantics – is one form of the realization of the social semiotic. There are many other symbolic systems through which the meanings of the culture are expressed: art forms, social structures and social institutions, educational and legal systems, and the like. But in the developmental process language is the primary one. A child's construction of a semantic system and his construction of a social system take place side by side, as two aspects of a single unitary process.

In the process of building up the social semiotic, the network of meanings that constitutes the culture, the child is becoming a member of the species 'social man'. This carries all the same implications as are present in our characterization of the social system as a semiotic. Social man is, effectively, 'sociosemiotic man', man as a repository of social meanings. The child builds up a potential for exchanging the meanings that are engendered by the system (and, so, in the long run, for modifying the system – since the social system is a system of meanings, it is constituted out of innumerable acts of meaning which shape and determine the system). We can watch this process taking place at all stages in the child's development of a language.

Consider the following examples, all taken from Nigel at 2;11 in verbal exchanges with his mother:

1 MOTHER [having fetched Nigel home from school]: How on earth did you get all that sand in your hair?
    NIGEL: I was just standing up and I threw the sand to it [= 'at it'; referent unspecified] and it got in my hair.
    MOTHER: And what did the teacher say?
    NIGEL: No ... because it was time to go home and have your [= 'my'] pieces of meat.

2 NIGEL [from playroom]: Mummy where are the ones with green in?
    MOTHER: The what?
    NIGEL: The all green ones.
    MOTHER: But I don't know what it is you're talking about.
    NIGEL [patiently]: The ones I had in Nairobi. [Mother gives up.]

3 NIGEL [at teatime]: What day is it today?
    MOTHER: It's Thursday.
    NIGEL: There's no school on Thursday.
    MOTHER: There is – you've already been to school.

NIGEL: I mean ... what comes after Thursday?
MOTHER: Friday. There's school on Friday too.
NIGEL: But you can't [= 'I can't'] go to school on Friday yet.
MOTHER: No, it hasn't started being Friday yet.

Specimens such as these, at a first glance, show the gulf between the child's world of meaning and that of the adult. Nigel's concept of the relations between events is not that of the adult. The sand got in his hair because that's the way things happen, not as you plan them; and he was told not to throw sand because it was time for lunch ('time to go home and have your pieces of meat'). His working out of divisions of time is far from complete: he knows that days succeed one another and have different names, but is not very clear just when the changeover takes place ('But you can't go to school on Friday yet' – that is, Friday, on which I go to school next, hasn't started yet?). He cannot conceive that the person he is talking to is unable to identify an object that is in his own focus of attention ('Mummy where are the ones with green in?', with no clue given as to what is presupposed by the substitute *ones*; compare *it* in 'threw the sand to it'). At the same time, on closer inspection, the examples show how the linguistic interaction in which the child takes part, while it reveals semiotic incompatibilities of all kinds, also provides him with the means of learning the semiotic of the adult culture. It is very clear to Nigel that his own meanings fail to get across in example 2; and he is himself clearly searching for meanings in 3. Even in example 1 the cultural concept of rational action is present, and is in fact foregrounded by Nigel himself, although his own attempts at applying it are not quite what the adult semiotic prescribes.

We can see all the time, if we pay attention to what is said by, to and in the presence of a small child, how in the course of the most ordinary linguistic interaction he is constantly learning the structure of the environment in which he is growing up, in all its aspects – material, logical, institutional and social. He is also, at the same time, developing his own unique personality, which is being formed at the intersection of a whole number of role relationships which are themselves likewise part of the semiotic structure of his universe. It is one thing, of course, to recognize that all this is taking place, and that it is taking place through the medium of language. It is quite another thing to explain how it happens, and how the linguistic system is endowed with the potential for making it happen.

In principle, a child is learning one semiotic system, the culture, and simultaneously he is learning the means of learning it – a second semiotic system, the language, which is the intermediary in which the first one is encoded. This is a very complex situation. In order to sort it out, let us first identify the various components which make up the total picture of language as social interaction, as expression of the social semiotic. Having considered each of these separate components in turn, we shall then try to integrate them into some sort of a composite pattern.

2 Text and meaning

Let us first consider the language people produce and react to, what they say and write, and read and listen to, in the course of daily life. This we shall refer to as text. Any instance of language that is operational, as distinct from citational (like sentences in a grammar book, or words listed in a dictionary), is *text*. The term covers both speech and writing, and is quite neutral as regards style and content: it may be language in action, conversation, telephone talk, debate, dramatic dialogue, narrative fiction, poetry, prayer, inscriptions, public notices, legal proceedings, communing with animals, intimate monologue or anything else.

From birth onwards, a child is surrounded by text. There is a constant exchange of meanings going on all around him, in which he is in one way or another involved. It should not be forgotten, in this regard, that he listens to a vast quantity of text in the form of dialogue in which he is not himself a participant. It was at 3;1 that Nigel began formulating to himself the difference between being a participant in an exchange and being an onlooker; he used to ask, very frequently over just a few weeks until he was satisfied he understood the principle, 'Were you saying that to me?'. Where the child is a participant he is, of course, a co-author of the text.

What are the essential properties of text? It is meaning, and it is choice. In the first place, text is meaning. We think of text first of all as words and sentences; and it is, certainly, encoded in words and sentences – in just the same way as those words and sentences are further encoded in sounds, or in letters. But text is not made of sounds or letters; and in the same way it is not made of words and phrases and clauses and sentences. It is made of meanings, and encoded in wordings, soundings and spellings. In other words, we are locating text at the semantic level. A text is a semantic unit, realized as (encoded in) lexicogrammatical units which are further realized as (recoded in) phonological or orthographic units.

Second, text is choice. A text represents a selection within numerous sets of options; everything that is said presupposes a background of what might have been said but was not. In linguistic terms, each decision of the speaker – each microlinguistic act, as it were – presupposes a paradigmatic environment, a set of options that have the potentiality of being selected under the given conditions. This is the background of what might have been. Since we have defined the text in semantic terms, however, we should replace **say** by **mean**. Text is 'what is meant' – presupposing a background of what might have been meant but was not. The microlinguistic acts, or countless small choices that the speaker makes as he goes along, are actually microsemantic acts; what the speaker is doing is meaning. Hence a text is a semantic structure that is formed out of a continuous process of choice among innumerable interrelated sets of semantic options.

We are referring to the total set of such semantic options as the *meaning potential*. The meaning potential is what can be meant – the potential of the semantic system. This is what we have been following through in its earliest phases in previous chapters, asking how Nigel started building up a meaning potential and what it looked like at different stages in its construction, in the course of its development. Text represents the actualization of this meaning potential. So everything the child says is interpreted – not just by a linguist, but by those who interact with the child in daily life – as a pattern of selection within the meanings that make up his semantic system at that time. This is what we mean by referring to text as semantic choice; and it explains why the mother understands everything the child says, much of which is unintelligible to those outside the circuit of his daily life. They do not know the child's meaning potential.

There are two ways of looking at the meaning potential. We may interpret it in the context of the situation, or we may interpret it in the context of the culture (still using Malinowski's all-important distinction). We may choose to think of the meaning potential as being the whole semantic system of the language; or we may choose to think of it in the form of specific sub-systems each of which (or each set of which) is associated with a particular class of situations. The former is a fiction; we cannot describe the whole semantic system. The latter is also, of course, a fiction; but it may be a more accessible one. It may be possible to represent the meaning potential in the form of sets of options that are specific to a given situation type.

This is in fact what we have been doing from the start. The headings "instrumental", "regulatory" and so on are the headings, the points of entry, of semantic systems that are associated with specific social contexts. A child constructs his meaning potential just in this way, by building up context-specific micro-paradigms, small sets of options that are his resource for each of the types of situation that serve, for him, as environments of symbolic action. At first, as we have pointed out, these are insulated one from another; the system allows just one meaning at a time. But later they come to be combined; and, as we saw, it is the combination of meanings from different functions that leads to the reinterpretation of the notion of "function" itself, first as a generalized context of use (the "macrofunctions" of pragmatic and mathetic) and subsequently as an abstract component of the system (the "metafunctions" of ideational and interpersonal).

3 Other components of the social semiotic

Meanwhile the meanings by which the child is surrounded are, as always, meanings in context. They relate to their environment, and are interpreted in relation to their environment – to the context of situation, in other words. The ***situation*** is the medium in which text lives and breathes. This, as we have seen, is the Malinowskian concept of "context of situation" as made explicit and modified by Firth, who pointed out that it had to be seen not as an aggregate of concrete spatio-temporal goings-on, a sort of ornamental backdrop of sights and sounds, but as an abstract representation of the relevant environment of the text. In modern jargon, it is the ecology of the text. It is a characteristic of the adult language system that the text it engenders is not tied to the immediate scenario as its relevant environment. The context of situation of a text may be entirely remote from what is happening around the act of speaking or writing.

Consider a traditional story as it is told by a mother to her child at bedtime. Here the context of situation is on two levels. On the one hand there is the immediate environment, the interaction of mother and child under particular circumstances that are associated with intimacy and relaxation. On the other hand there is the fictive environment conjured by the text itself, the imaginary world of wolves and woodcutters in which the events described take place. It is only in very strictly pragmatic contexts, those of language in action as it has been called, where the text is simply an ancillary to some activity that the participants are engaged in, that the context of situation can be identified with the visible and tangible phenomena surrounding the text; and even here, these phenomena are likely to be endowed with social values.

For this reason we are interpreting the concept of "situation" in still more abstract terms, as a semiotic structure deriving from the totality of meaning relations that constitutes the social system. This makes it possible to talk not so much about the particulars of this or that actual context of situation in which a given text is located but rather about the set of general features that characterizes a certain ***situation type***. The way in which a generalized context of situation, or situation type, might be represented as a semiotic construct will be discussed in the next section.

The first two of the concepts to be brought into relation, therefore, are those of text and situation: text as semantic choice, and situation as the semiotic environment of text. The third to be added to these is the concept of ***register***. The register is the semantic variety of which a text is an instance.

A register can be defined as a particular configuration of meanings that is associated with a particular situation type. In any social context, certain semantic resources are characteristically employed; certain sets of options are, as it were, 'at risk' in the given semiotic environment. These define the register. Considered in terms of the notion of meaning potential, the register is the range of meaning potential that is activated by the semiotic properties of the situation.

To return to the same example, there are certain types of meanings that are typically associated with traditional stories as told to children. These are not simply thing-meanings, names of persons and animals and objects and events that typically figure in such stories, though these are a part of the picture, but also characteristic role relationships, chains of events, patterns of dialogue, and special types of complex semantic structures such as are represented in expressions like *and she was so (frightened,* etc.) *that she (ran and ran,* etc.); *but the third time he tried, he (managed to reach,* etc.). The set of such typical meanings and combinations of meanings constitutes the register of traditional children's narratives in very many cultures and sub-cultures.

The fourth major component of the sociolinguistic universe is the ***linguistic system*** itself. The difficulty with notions like text and situation lies not so much in their own definition and interpretation as in the relating of them to the linguistic system as a whole. In what way does a particular text draw on the resources of the linguistic system?

How can we see the meanings that the child encodes on any particular occasion in relation to the potential that lies behind them? This is a perspective that it is easy to lose sight of if one is focusing attention on the text, on what a child has actually said or had said to him. But it is of great importance in our understanding of the developmental picture. We are interested in the potential of the system, and in how the child constructs the system. This means not merely being able to analyse a particular piece of text so as to reveal what are the structures underlying it, but also being able to show what are the options that are expressed by those structures and what is the total set of options that the child has at his disposal in that part of his semantic system. So, for example, we might recognize from something the child says that he can form a structure made up of the elements Actor + Process + Goal, as in Nigel's *man clean car* at 1;8. But we want to know what semantic option this represents, in the sense of what is the type of process that he encodes in this way; and what other types of process does he recognize – in other words, what is the semantic system that he has at this stage for the representation of the processes of action, thought, feeling and so on that come within the realm of his experience? The concept of register becomes especially important here, as the system expands, because it forms a bridge between the system and the text.

In the present context, what concerns us most within the linguistic system is the semantic system. We are considering the semantic system not from a conceptual but from a functional point of view, as a potential in respect of certain semiotic operations; and in particular we are considering its organization into basic components which are of a functional kind. In the language of a small child, these components are specific to the social context, or situation type: they are the instrumental, regulatory and other components of the Phase I system. In the adult language, however, the functional components of the semantics are no longer specific to the context; they are general to all contexts. Whatever the particular situation type, the meanings that are expressed are of three kinds, which we have called **ideational**, **interpersonal** and **textual**.

The infinitely varied properties of different situations, the types of activity, the role relationships, and the symbolic channels, are all realized through selections in these three areas of meaning potential. The ideational represents the potential of the system for the speaker as an observer: it is the content function of language, language as about something. The interpersonal is the potential of the system for the speaker as an intruder: it is the participatory function of language, language as doing something. The textual is the potential of the system for the creation of text: it is the relevance function of language, whereby the meanings derived from the other functional components relate to the environment and thus become operational.

These are the functional components of the adult semantic system; with only trivial exceptions (such as *Hi!* as a greeting, which presumably has no ideational element in its make-up), any adult exchange of meanings involves all three components. Whatever the particular use of language on this or that occasion, whatever the subject-matter and the genre and the purpose of the communication, there will be a choice of content, a choice of interaction type, and a choice of texture. These are the different kinds of meaning potential of the system. But they are also the formally definable components of the lexicogrammatical system; these different semantic realms appear as clearly defined, mutually independent sets of options at the formal level. It is this that enables, and disposes, the child to learn the lexicogrammar: since the system is organized along functional lines, it relates closely to what the child can see language doing as he observes it going on around him.

The fifth and final element in the sociolinguistic universe is the ***social structure***. This term is being used in a way which is not synonymous with "social system". The social system is the broader term; it encompasses all the elements that make up the picture, and much else besides – it is more or less equivalent to 'the culture'. The social structure refers specifically to the organization of society. This permeates all forms of interaction and exchange of meanings by the members; but it enters into the picture that we are building up here in two significant ways. In the first place it is a part of the environment; hence it is a part of what is being transmitted to the child through language. In the second place it is a determinant of the transmission process, since it determines the types of role relationship in the "primary socializing agencies", the social groups through which a child takes out his membership of the culture – the family, the young children's peer group, and the school – and so creates the conditions in which the child lives and learns. Our understanding of how this happens is very largely due to Bernstein. Bernstein's work demonstrates that the social structure is not just a kind of incidental appendage to linguistic interaction, as linguists have tended to think of it, but is an integral element in the deeper processes that such interaction involves.

If a child learns the culture from ordinary everyday linguistic interaction, as he certainly does, we must suppose not only that he decodes what he hears correctly in a way that is specifically relevant to the context of situation but also that he interprets it correctly in a way that is generally relevant to the context of culture. In other words if his mother tells him off, he not only knows that he is being told off but also learns something in the process about the value systems of the culture he is participating in. This presupposes that the linguistic system must be coherent not only within itself but also with the culture; not only are the semantic options which make up the meaning potential *realized* explicitly in the lexicogrammar – they are also themselves *realizing* the higher-order meanings of the social semiotic. All the elements mentioned above play some part in the total picture.

4 Structure of the social context

From a sociological point of view a text is meaningful not so much because we do not know what the speaker is going to say, as in a mathematical model of communication, as because we do know. Given certain facts, we can predict a good deal of what is coming with a significantly high probability of being right. This is not, of course, to deny the creative aspect of language and of text. The speaker can always prove us wrong; and in any case, his behaviour is nonetheless creative even if our predictions are fulfilled to the letter.

What are these 'certain facts'? They are the general properties of the situation, in the abstract sense in which the term is being used here. Essentially what we need to know is the semiotic structure of the situation.

A number of linguists, notably Firth, Pike and Hymes, have suggested interesting ways of characterizing the context of situation. Hymes' list of categories could be summarized as follows: form and content of the message, setting, participants, ends (intent and effect), key, medium, genre and interactional norms. The problem is, however, to know what kind of status and validity to accord to a conceptual framework such as this one. Are these to be thought of as descriptive categories providing a framework for the interpretation of text in particular situation instances, as conceived of by Malinowski? Or are they predictive concepts providing a means for the determination of text in generalized situation types?

Either of these would be of interest; but in the present context, in which we are trying to see how a child constructs the social system out of text instances, and are therefore concerned to relate text, situation and linguistic system, it is the second of these perspectives which we need to adopt. We are thinking not in terms of this or that situation but of a situation type, a generalized social context in which text is created; and of the situational factors not merely as descriptive but as constitutive of the text. The semiotic properties of the situation specify the register, the semantic configurations that characterize text associated with that type of situation – the meaning potential that the speaker will typically draw on.

So if we set up a conceptual framework for the representation of situation types, we do so in order that the categories we use will serve to predict features of the text. But this is not enough. Such categories are two-faced; they not only related "downwards" to the text but also "upwards" to some higher order of abstraction – in this case, two such higher orders, the social and the linguistic. In other words the concepts that we use in describing a situation type, or social context, whatever concepts they are, have to be interpretable both in terms of the culture and in terms of the linguistic system.

The second of these requirements is particularly strong, since it is not immediately obvious how situational factors like the setting, the statuses and roles of the participants, and the like, can relate to linguistic categories. But it is this requirement which may lead us to select one from among the number of existing and possible schemes; and we shall return to one proposed by Halliday, McIntosh and Strevens (1964), which was a threefold analysis in terms of the concepts of *field*, *tenor* and *mode*. It was not entirely clear at the time why such a scheme should be preferred, except that intuitively it seemed simpler than most others. But it can now be seen to offer a means of making an essential link between the linguistic system and the text.

A framework of this general kind has been discussed subsequently by a number of writers on the subject; for example, Spencer and Gregory in *Linguistics and Style* (1964). Doughty, Pearce and Thornton in *Exploring Language* (1971), Halliday in *Language and Social Man*, and Ure and Ellis in 'Register in descriptive linguistics and descriptive sociology' (1972). We can relate the general concepts of field, tenor and mode to the categories set out by Hymes in 'Models of interaction of language and social setting' as these were summarized above. A situation type, or social context, as we understand it, is characterized by a particular semiotic structure, a complex of features which sets it apart from other situation types. This structure can then be interpreted on three dimensions: in terms of the ongoing activity (field), the role relationships involved (tenor), and the symbolic or rhetorical channel (mode). The first of these, the field, corresponds roughly to Hymes' "setting" and "ends"; it is the field of action, including symbolic action, in which the text has its meaning. It therefore includes what we usually call "subject-matter", which is not an independent feature but is a function of the type of activity. The second, the tenor, which corresponds in general terms to Hymes' "participants" and "key", refers to the role relationships that are embodied in the situation, which determine levels of formality and speech styles but also very much else besides. The third heading, that of mode, is roughly Hymes' "instrumentalities" and "genre"; this refers to the symbolic channel or wavelength selected, which is really the semiotic function or functions assigned to language in the situation. Hence this includes the distinction between speech and writing as a special case.

Field, tenor and mode are not kinds of language use; still less are they varieties of language. Nor are they, however, simply generalized components of the speech situation. They are, rather, the environmental determinants of text. Given an adequate specification of the situation in terms of field, tenor and mode, we ought to be able to make certain predictions about the linguistic properties of the text that is associated with it; that is, about the register, the configurations of semantic options that typically feature in this environment, and hence also about the grammar and vocabulary, which are the realizations of the semantic options. The participants in the situation themselves make just such predictions. It is one of the features of the social system, as a semiotic system, that the members can and do make significant predictions about the meanings that are being exchanged, predictions which depend on their interpretation of the semiotics of the situation type in which they find themselves. This is an important aspect of the potential of the system, and it is this that we are trying to characterize.

The possibility of making such predictions appears to arise because the categories of field, tenor and mode, which we are using to describe the semiotics of the situation, are in their turn associated in a systematic way with the functional components of the semantic system. This is not, of course, a coincidence. The semantic system evolved, we assume, operationally, as a form of symbolic interaction in social contexts; so there is every reason that it should reflect the structure of such contexts in its own internal organization.

We referred above to the tripartite functional composition of the adult semantic system, with its components of ideational, interpersonal and textual. It was mentioned that this scheme was not something that is arrived at from the outside; this organization is clearly present in the lexicogrammatical system – as seen, for example, in the threefold structuring of the clause in English in terms of transitivity (ideational), mood (interpersonal) and theme (textual). Now it appears that each of these different components of meaning is typically activated by a corresponding component in the semiotic structure of the situation. Thus, the *field* is associated with the **ideational** component, the **tenor** with the **interpersonal** component, and the **mode** with the **textual** component.

Let us see how this works, using another example from Nigel's interaction with his mother, this time at age 1;11.

Text – Nigel at age 1;11:

> MOTHER [in bathroom, Nigel sitting on chair]: Now you wait there till I get your facecloth. Keep sitting there. [But Nigel is already standing up on the chair.]
> NIGEL [in exact imitation of mother's intonation pattern, not in a correcting intonation]: Keep standing thére. Put the mug on the flóor.
> MOTHER: Put the mug on the floor? What do you want?
> NIGEL: Daddy tòothbrush.
> MOTHER: Oh you want Daddy's toothbrush do you?
> NIGEL: Yés ... you (= 'I') want to put the fròg in the múg.
> MOTHER: I think the frog is too big for the mug.
> NIGEL: Yes you can put dùck in the múg ... make búbble ... make búbble.
> MOTHER: Tomorrow. Nearly all the water's run out.
> NIGEL: You want Mummy red tóothbrush ... yes you can have Mummy old red tóothbrush.

Situational features:

> *Field*: Personal toilet, assisted (mother washing child); concurrently (child) exploring (i) container principle (that is, putting things in things) and (ii) ownership and acquisition of property (that is, getting things that belong to other people).
> *Tenor*: Mother and small child interaction; mother determining course of action; child pursuing own interests, seeking permission;

mother granting permission and sharing child's interests, but keeping her own course in view.

Mode: Spoken dialogue; pragmatic speech ('language-in-action') the mother's guiding, the child's furthering (accompanying or immediately preceding) the actions to which it is appropriate; cooperative, without conflict of goals.

Determination of linguistic features by situational features:

- Field determines:
  - transitivity patterns – the types of process, for example, relational clauses, possessive (*get*, *have*) and circumstantial:locative (*put*);
  - material process clauses, spatial:posture (*sit*, *stand*);
  - the minor processes, for example, circumstantial:locative (*in*);
  - perhaps the tenses (simple present);
  - the content aspect of the vocabulary, for example, naming of objects.

  All these belong to the ***ideational*** component of the semantic system.

- Tenor determines: patterns of m*oo*d, for example, [mother] imperative *(you wait, keep sitting)*;
  - of modality, for example, [child] permission *(want to, can)*;
  - non-finite forms such as *make bubble* meaning 'I want to be allowed to ...');
  - of person, for example, [mother] "second person" *(you)*, [child] "first person" *(you* = 'I'), and of key, represented by the system of intonation (pitch contour, for example, child's systematic opposition of rising tone, demanding a response, versus falling tone, not demanding a response).

  All these belong to the ***interpersonal*** component of the semantic system.

- Mode determines: forms of cohesion, for example, question-and-answer with the associated type of ellipsis (*What do you want?* – *Daddy toothbrush*);
  - the patterns of voice and theme, for example, active voice with child as subject/theme;
  - the forms of deixis, for example, exophoric (situation-referring) *the* (*the mug*, etc.);
  - the lexical continuity, for example, repetition of *mug*, *toothbrush*, *put in*.

  All these belong to the ***textual*** component of the semantic system.

5 Semiotic strategies

What this example suggests is that there is a general tendency whereby different elements in the context of situation call for different components of the semantics — different aspects of the meaner's ability to mean. The situation is a semiotic structure, consisting essentially of a doing part and a being part: a social process (things going on), and associated role relationships and role interaction (persons taking part). The nature of the social process tends to be expressed through ideational meanings, and the nature of the role relationships through interpersonal meanings. Meanings of the third kind, the textual, express the particular semiotic mode that is being adopted. The meanings are expressed, in their turn, through the medium of the lexicogrammatical system; and hence there is a systematic, though indirect, link between grammatical structure and the social context. This is the central feature of the environment in which a child learns language. Since everything that he hears is text — language that is operational in a context of situation — the fact that it is systematically related to this context is the guarantee of its significance for the learning process. It is this that makes language learnable.

We shall return to this point briefly in a final discussion below. Meanwhile we should remember that from the child's point of view learning how to mean is like learning any other form of activity. It is something he has to master, and it has to be broken down into manageable tasks. This breaking down process is at once both cognitive and social. We know from the work of Piaget (1926, 1957) and Sinclair de Zwart (1969) that the meaning potential is cognitively ordered; certain meanings will be learnt before others, and this is an aspect of the biological processes of maturation. But there is an environmental aspect to this too. The functional system with which the child is operating at any given moment acts as a filter on the semantic input, so that he processes just those elements which are consonant, or resonant, with his semiotic potential at that time.

It is not easy to illustrate this except by inspection of large quantities of data, in which whatever is said to and around the child has been incorporated, together with relevant situational information. But the following short illustration will perhaps suggest what is meant. Nigel at 21 months (NL 8) had been for a walk with his father in Greenwich Park; they had paused, as often, to look at the Meridian Clock mounted in the Observatory wall. Unprecedentedly, it had stopped.

> F. I wonder why that clòck's stopped? I've never known it stopped befóre. Perhaps they're clèaning it, or mènding it.

They return home. Some hours later, on the same day, Nigel returns to the subject:

> N. why that clóck stop
> F. I don't know. Why do you think?
> N. ménd it

Nigel's utterances are both on the rising, pragmatic tone. Now, many features of the text-in-situation constituted by the father's first remark are relevant as potential input: the mood of *I wonder*, the modality of *perhaps*, the temporal relation *before*, the collocation *clean + clock*, and so on. Looking at Nigel's later utterance, we see what he has in fact processed in the intervening period. The mood of *I wonder* has been translated into the pragmatic, response-demanding mode (note that none of the father's utterances was on a rising tone) – resulting in what is in fact the first Wh-question recorded in Nigel's speech. The meaning 'response demanded' carries the potential of being extended to include 'verbal response demanded', the process being perhaps furthered by the open-ended modality of *perhaps* meaning 'supply "yes" or "no"'. He cannot, of course, answer a why question; but he retains the *why* from his father's utterance because it does chime in with a recognizable semiotic function. In *mend it*, mending has been reinterpreted in terms of this pragmatic function, which is the only context Nigel knows for *mend* ('I want this to be mended'): cleaning has, however, been filtered out as irrelevant, presumably because although it is a word he knows – he had said *man clean car* some days previously – it has occurred only in mathetic contexts and is therefore functionally incompatible with mending. The result is an utterance which in terms of his pre-existing system would be interpreted as 'I want the clock to be mended', but which has the potentiality also for meaning 'will they mend it?' and even 'are they mending it?'. The point is not that we are called on to decide which of these it actually meant; that question is undecidable, because those are not alternative meanings in Nigel's system. The point is that this little interchange plays its part in providing the conditions for the emergence of new meanings, in this case the yes/no question as a possible form of response-seeking semiotic act.

Such delayed reactions are often very suggestive indicators of the selective processing of meanings into the system. There is a clear functional limitation on the input; though rather than seeing it as a limitation, we should see it as an interpretative device, a means of assimilating what comes in to what is already there in a way which also allows it to change what is already there. The functional organization of the existing meaning potential acts as a kind of semantic resonator capturing just those components of the input which are near enough to its own frequencies to be able to modify and expand it further.

For the child the overall context is one of survival, and he develops semiotic strategies such that he can use his meaning potential as he is building it and build it as he is using it. These are highly valued patterns of meaning that play a significant part in the developmental process. They can be found at all levels in the system. A number of Nigel's general patterns already referred to could be included in this category; here is a summary of some of the more important ones in Phases I and II:

1. PHONOLOGICAL. The most obvious strategy here is the opposition of falling and rising tone, the realization of the mathetic/pragmatic opposition (which is itself the key semantic strategy for Phase II). The fall/rise opposition is the heart of the adult intonation system; all the complex tones, and all the meanings of the tones, can be explained on the basis of this simple system, in which falling means 'decided' (certain, complete, etc.) and rising means 'undecided'. Nigel's Phase II system is not that of the adult language, naturally, since he has not learnt the various grammatical systems which determine its specific significance (for example, he has no mood system, and so cannot use falling/rising as the realization of sub-categories of indicative (declarative and interrogative) and imperative the way the adult does). But Nigel's use does reflect the basic meaning that the opposition between falling and rising has in English: falling means complete (no response demanded) and rising means incomplete – moreover rising, as in the adult language, is the marked term.

2. GRAMMATICAL. The fundamental grammatical strategy is structure, the combining of variables. At the beginning of Phase II, Nigel learns that new meaning results from the combination of elements one with another. He also learns that such combinations take two forms:

(i) Univariate structures: combinations of variables each having the same value in the resulting configuration. The adult language has a number of such types of combination (for example co-ordination, apposition, subclassification); Nigel's only one at this stage is co-ordination, as in 'cars, buses, trains, stones, sticks and holes'. It is noticeable that for a time there is a minor but distinct phonological strategy associated with these: each element in a co-ordination must have two syllables (so *bus*, ordinarily ba, becomes baba; *dog*, ordinarily bɒuwɒu, does not change).

(ii) Multivariate structures: combinations of elements having different values in the resulting configuration. Examples in early Phase II are: Supplementation + Desired object (*more meat*), Property + Class of object (*green car*), Process + Medium of process (*open mouth*). These are the prototypes of the multivariate structures that make up the nominal group and the clause of the adult language.

3. SEMANTIC. Phase II semantic strategies are the specific functional meanings of the mathetic and pragmatic modes. An example is the pragmatic strategies deriving from the Phase I regulatory function: requests for permission, requests for action, suggestions for joint action ('can I?', 'will you?', 'shall we?'). But in fact the entire functional interpretation that we are putting on the picture of Nigel's language development is nothing other than an interpretation of the semantic strategies that appear to be critical for his success in learning how to mean.

4. SEMIOTIC. All those listed above are, in fact, semiotic strategies, since the term encompasses all aspects of the organization of meaning. But there are more general strategies which are strategies for the use of the linguistic system, ways of deploying the meaning potential, so to speak – sometimes with alternative, or accompanying, non-linguistic modes of realization. The child's aim is to be good at meaning, and from the start he locates himself in symbolic contexts in which semiotic success is significantly at risk. He undertakes meaning tasks which may fail, but which typically are rewarded if successful. Here are some examples:

(i) *Reparatory strategies.* What to do when meaning breaks down. The fundamental semiotic strategy of repeating loudly and slowly when not understood, which involves recognizing that meaning has not been successful, that this may result from a failure in the expression, and that the expression can be foregrounded as a way of overcoming the failure, develops remarkably early. A clear example is found in the material in Chapter 7, section 5.1, from the beginning of NL 7 when Nigel has just reached 18 months. In the context of a list of things seen on a walk, Nigel says *douba*, which usually means 'toast'; his father tries that interpretation, but Nigel rejects it, repeating the word very slowly and distinctly. It happens that his father never does get the meaning on this occasion, and now never will; but the principle is established and Nigel does not abandon it.

(ii) *Interaction strategies*. Semiotic interaction with others through shared attention to objects. This strategy appears at the very outset of the system, in NL 1; but it is a major motif in the evolution of the Phase II mathetic function. It has been discussed in the earlier chapters and need not be repeated here.

(iii) *Development of instrumental forms*. The semiotics of getting what one wants goes through a number of strategic moments: Phase I nànànànà 'I want that'; Phase II, specific, for example, *more méat*; general, *háve it, háve that*; Phase III, introduction of a mood system as in *you want your meat* 'I want my meat'. Those of Phases II and III may be accompanied by politeness forms, for example, Phase II *plɪmeyaya* 'please may I have?', which make their function explicit.

(iv) *Development of simile and metaphor*. A fundamental semiotic strategy is the use of likeness as a mode of meaning, likeness between things that are essentially different. Recognizing a picture – identifying it as a representation – exemplifies the receptive form of this strategy. In its productive form it appears from NL 7 onwards; examples are 'Uncle's pipe blows smoke like a train' (note that this itself depends on the symbolic representation of a train, since Nigel has never seen a steam train except in pictures) and *Mummy hair like railway line* (NL 9; see Chapter 7, section 5.6). Such metaphorical meanings characteristically relate to highly coded realms of experience – in Nigel's case, trains.

The interest of these and other semiotic strategies lies not only in the contribution they make to the learning of the language and the culture but also in the way in which they anticipate the adult communicative style. An adult, in his various registers (the semantic configurations that he typically associates with given social contexts), tends especially in those well-tried social contexts that make up much of his daily semiotic activity to adopt various more or less routinized semiotic strategies, some of them being simply rules for the particular type of discourse and others more individual paths through the network of sociosemiotic interaction. In their extreme form, these are the 'games people play', mechanisms for mediating between the individual and social reality. But all exchange of meanings involves semiotic strategies. Thanks to the work of Sacks (1973) and Schegloff (1968), we are gaining significant insights into the nature of these and their place in the social process. It is interesting to see them evolving in the developmental context, and an important question for current investigation is how far and in what specific ways they are a necessary component of learning.

6 Language development as an interactive process

We referred in Chapter 2 to the different emphases and contrasts in perspective that characterized the renewed interest in language development studies from the mid-1960s onwards, in particular the rather artificial polarization between two conceptions of language and language learning, one as genetically endowed and ready-made, the other as environmentally fashioned and evolving. It is refreshing to find language development studies in the 1970s moving away from this rather sterile debate, in a direction which puts language in a less insulated and more relevant perspective. Language is no longer being thought of as an autonomous object; nor is language development seen any longer as a kind of spontaneous once-for-all happening resting on a given biological foundation, to be achieved by a certain maturational stage or not at all. This is not to deny, of course, the fact that there is a biological foundation to language; but simply to assert that language development is an aspect and a concomitant of ongoing developmental processes of a more general kind. As Lois Bloom (1975) put it, "The beginning of the 1970s marked a major shift in research in language development, away from the description of child language in terms of linguistic theory and towards the explanation of language development in terms of cognitive theory"; and her own work provides a convincing illustration.

In other words, the direction of movement has been up the levels of the linguistic system and out at the top. The focus of attention has gone from the phonological system, to the lexicogrammatical system (syntax), to the semantic system, and is now moving out to the cognitive system. In the latest analysis, the learning process is a process of cognitive development and the learning of the mother tongue is an aspect of it and is conditioned by it.

The present discussion shares this non-autonomous approach to language. It seems sensible to assume that neither the linguistic system itself, nor the learning of it by a child, can be adequately understood except by reference to some higher level of semiotic organization. But we have adopted the alternative perspective – one that is complementary to the cognitive one, not contradictory to it – of locating this higher-level semiotic not in the cognitive system but in the social system. The social semiotic is the system of meanings that defines or constitutes the culture; and the linguistic system is one mode of realization of these meanings. The child's task is to construct the system of meanings that represents his own model of social reality. This process takes place inside his own head; it is a cognitive process. But it takes place in contexts of social interaction, and there is no way it can take place except in these contexts. As well as being a cognitive process, the learning of the mother tongue is also an interactive process. It takes the form of the continued exchange of meanings between the self and others. The act of meaning is a social act.

The social context is, therefore, not so much an external condition on the learning of meanings as a generator of the meanings that are learnt. And part of the social context is the language that is used by the interactants – the language the child hears around him. It has been concluded from semantic interpretations of language development, in the work of Bever (1970), Osgood (1971), Bowerman (1973), and others, that a child learns ideational meanings that reflect the world around him; for example, the distinction between things, on the one hand, and relations between things on the other. One theory is that the whole inventory of transitivity functions is recoverable from the extralinguistic environment; this is suggested for example by Greenfield and Smith's (forthcoming) interesting application of Fillmore's 'case theory' to one-word utterances of Phase II. But the structure of the environment, as apprehended by the child, is coded in the mother tongue. Even in Phase I, the semantics of the mother tongue determines the meanings that the mother and others respond to, thus helping to shape the child's social reality. By Phase II, when the child is building a lexicogrammatical system, things and the relations between them are entirely interpreted through the mother tongue; this is an inevitable consequence of having a lexicogrammar – the child is no longer free to code as he likes. (In case this appears as a Whorfian conception, let it be said at once that it is – but in terms of what Whorf said, not of what he is often assumed to have said. We are not the prisoners of our cultural semiotic; we can all learn to move outside it. But this requires a positive act of semiotic reconstruction. We are socialized within it, and our meaning potential is derived from it.) What makes learning possible is that the coding imposed by the mother tongue corresponds to a **possible** mode of perception and interpretation of the environment. A green car **can** be analysed experientially as carness qualified by greenness, if that is the way the system works.

Important though this is, however, it is still only an aspect of a more significant fact about language and the social system, that which we illustrated in section 3. The essential condition of learning is the systematic link between semantic categories and the semiotic properties of the situation. The child can learn to mean because the linguistic features in some sense relate to features of the environment. But the environment is a social construct. It does not consist of things, or even of processes and relations; it consists of human interaction, from which the things derive their meaning. The fact that a bus moves is by no means its only or even its most obvious perceptual quality, as compared, say, with its size, its shininess, or the noise it makes; but it is its most important semiotic property, the meaning with which it is endowed in the social system, and it is this that determines its semantic status in English. Things have to be interpreted in their social contexts. More relevant, perhaps, they have to be interpreted in their social **proportion**; they are not that important, so to speak, compared with the processes of interaction themselves.

This is, of course, deliberately to overstate the case. The point being made is that the reality in which meaning takes place is a social reality into which the external environment enters through its significance for interaction, and is embedded in contexts of evaluation, argument, manipulation, and other social acts. Nor is it suggested that the child does not perform his own interpretations of reality and adapt the linguistic system to them; he certainly does. Nigel, for example, like many other children, had in Phase II some meaning such as 'capable of moving by itself', and used the form *gó* as a general question 'is it alive?' (in the early stages also applied to vehicles); some form of 'animal, vegetable or mineral?' seems to be very generally adopted as a learning strategy. But the semantics of things is only a part of the total semantic system; most of the time when we are talking about things we are relating them to ourselves; and whether we are or not, they have been coded into the system in a way which reflects their relation to, and value for, the social process.

So when we stress the fact that language takes place in a context of situation, and say that a child is able to learn from what he hears because there is a systematic relation between what he hears and what is going on around him, this is not primarily because our talk is focused on the objects and events of the external world. Much of the time it is not; and even when it is, it does not reflect their structure in any unprocessed or "objective" way, but as it is processed by the culture. The relation of talk to environment lies in the total semiotic structure of the interaction: the significant ongoing activity (and it is only through this that 'things' enter into the picture, in a very indirect way), and the social matrix within which meanings are being exchanged. The "situation" of discourse is made up of these two elements, together with a third, the semiotic modes that are being adopted – in other words, the field, tenor, and mode of section 4 above.

The point has been developed by Lois Bloom that the speech of a young child can be understood only by reference to the context of situation, and it can be maintained that language development consists in progressively freeing the system from dependence on situational constraints. But we find that the major step has already been taken by Nigel at the very beginning of Phase II, when he moves from observation to recall (from 'I see cars, buses ...' to 'I saw cars, buses ...' said when they are no longer in sight), and from 'I want what is there in front of me' to 'I want (something which I can't see, for example) a rusk'. The direct dependence of a speech instance on the perceptual environment disappears the moment he introduces the third level into his system, the lexicogrammatical level of words and structures, since this provides him with an abstract ("formal") level of coding which intervenes between content (the level of reference to the situation) and output. From the time when the child enters the transition to the adult mode, his individual speech acts are no longer constrained by features of the immediate situation. But this does not mean, on the other hand, that there is no systematic link between the meanings the child expresses and the environment in which the act of meaning takes place. There is – but so there is also with the adult. The conception of language development as the freeing of the meaning potential from the confines of 'here and now' is a valid one provided we interpret it not in absolute terms but as a *change* in the nature of the relation of meaning to environment. We have in fact already identified the conditions for this change, when we show the progressive evolution of the concept of 'function' from a stage (Phase I) where it is synonymous with 'use', at which, therefore, meaning relates directly to the immediate situation, to a stage (Phase III) where it is equivalent to 'component of the semantic system', at which meaning relates to the situation only indirectly, through the social semiotic – the socially constructed reality and the place accorded to language within it. Note that the former is a characterization of Phase I, before the child has embarked on learning what we recognize as language – that is, an adult-like system. At the beginning of Phase II, when 'function' is becoming generalized and conventional linguistic forms – words and structures – are starting to appear, 'constraint' by, or dependence on, the situation already takes the more abstract form of the selective association of meanings with the different social values accorded to the environment, either as terrain to be explored (mathetic) or as mineral to be quarried (pragmatic). There is no restriction such that words and structures can be used to name only what is in sight; what there is, as we have seen, is a tendency for each word, and each structure, to be activated in one function only – certain words and structures in a pragmatic function, other words and structures in a mathetic function. By the time we reach Phase III, the dependence of meaning on context has been reinterpreted at a still more abstract level, although it is still the same general principle at work. In Phase III, and in adult language generally, there is a tendency for each functional component in the meaning potential to be activated by a corresponding component in the context of situation. At no stage is meaning totally context-bound, and equally, at no stage is it totally unrelated to the context; but 'context' means different things at different stages. The Phase I functional headings specify meaning and context undifferentially: a term like 'instrumental' covers both. In Phase III the 'functions' are ways of meaning, and we have to find other frames of reference to characterize the situation as a social construct. It is worth observing, however, that even at Phase I the context of situation is a social construct and its elements are defined by social value: an object is a favourite object, a person is a mother. At no time does the environment in which meaning takes place consist solely of 'props', of the uninterpreted sights and sounds of the material world. Even at nine months, the 'things' to which the child's meanings relate realize values in his social system.

Meaning is at the same time both a component of social action and a symbolic representation of the structure of social action. The semiotic structure of the environment – the ongoing social activity, the roles and statuses, and the interactional channels – both determines the meanings exchanged and is created by and formed out of them. This is why we understand what is said, and are able to fill out the condensations and unpeel the layers of projection. It is also why the system is permeable, and the process of meaning subject to pressures from the social structure. The particular modes and patterns of meaning that tend to be associated with different types of social context are determined by the culture, through a process that Bernstein has interpreted and referred to by the term 'codes'. The reality that the child constructs is that of his culture and sub-culture, and the ways in which he learns to mean and to build up registers — configurations of meanings associated with features of the social context — are also those of his culture and sub-culture. He builds the semiotic of his own society, through interaction in family, in peer group, and, later, in school — as well as in a host of other microsemiotic encounters which, though outside the main socializing agencies, may for that very reason be relatively even more foregrounded in their effects. But at this point we must leave the story, to take it up from another vantagepoint elsewhere. We conclude with a final section showing Nigel on the eve of his second birthday, busily meaning from the moment he wakes up.

7 Over the threshold: Nigel at the end of NL 10

` falling tonic (adult tone 1)
´ rising tonic (adult tone 2 or 3)
ˇ falling-rising tonic (adult tone 4)

(Early morning. N. comes into F.'s study)
N. Where the little chùffa ... you want the little green chuffa that you found on the pàvement

(Garbage lorry draws up outside)
F. Do you want to see the garbage lorry?
N. Find the little green chúffa

(N. runs out to M.)

N. Have your big chúffa (M. gives it to him) ... it got bènt ... it not bent nŏw ... it was broken yĕsterday but Daddy had to mend it with a screwdriver ... We must rèady to go on a tràin (repet.)
M. No, we're not going on a train, not today. When we go to Claremont, first we're going on a train and then on an aeroplane.
N. Not going on tràin ... (starts looking at book) ... That was a big tràin ... that was an òld train ... they've taken awày that train ... it doesn't go any mòre ... it got a tall chìmney ... that was a very òld train ... might go and see that tràin one dáy ... and we might go and see that old tràin one dáy (repet.) ... we will walk on the

ràilway line (2) ... look at the train with the tiny tiny stàr on ... now that is the light shining out of the train on to the plàtform ... now that is a very fast tràin and it say whòosh ... if that train coming past (whispers) and 'it say whòosh ... that a fast whòosh train ... the train say whòosh (2) ... (finishes the book) ... But first on to the tráin ... first on to the blue tráin ... and then on an àeroplane ... but we don't go thăt way

(N. comes back into F.'s study)
N. Gárbage lorry (4) (looking out of window)
F. Has it gone?
N. Want your green pén (2) ... when Daddy finished writing with that pen and thèn you can have Daddy green pén ... Daddy wòrking ... make cross on týpewriter ... we have to put some pàper ín it

(F. puts paper in typewriter. N. strikes keys)

F. What did you make?
N. A dòt ... (several characters come up together and stick) ... Put that dówn ... yes you will put that dówn

(N. presses down, gets fingers inky; is taken to have fingers wiped, returns to typewriter)
N. (strikes key; indicating mark on paper) What thàt
F. That's called a caret.
N. 'm putting them all dòwn ... that one make a tìkuwa ('stick') ... a ràilway line ... want to have your green pén

(N. strikes keys again; two characters stick)
N. That twò (3)

(N. listens to F.'s watch)
N. Daddy clock going ticktockticktòck ... shall we – ... shall we make a church spíre (2) ... with a goglgò ('weathercock') ón it ... have you màde a church spíre (2) ('look I've made a church spire!') ... thère the gogogogó ... have the red pén (2) ... have Daddy red pén ... (drops green pen) what did you dròp?
F. I don't know; what did you?
N. Did you drop the green pén ('I dropped the green pen')
(F. picks it up) ... chúffa ... draw a chúffa ... put it báck ... shall we make a railway line with the red pén ... shall we make a railway line with the chùffa ón it

F. All right, let's make a railway line.
N. Shall we make a fast train which say whóosh, sháll we ... (F. and N. drawing) ... Daddy said I wonder that penguin will dive in the wàter ... shall we make a pénguin ... (F. draws penguin) ... it gó ... gó ... gó ('is it alive?') ...? we drawn a? fast weel tràin ('fast diesel train')
F. No it's an electric train; it's got a pantograph.
N. It an elèctric train ... it got a pàntograph

Chapter Fourteen

THREE ASPECTS OF CHILDREN'S LANGUAGE DEVELOPMENT: LEARNING LANGUAGE, LEARNING THROUGH LANGUAGE, LEARNING ABOUT LANGUAGE (1980)

I would like to share with you some thoughts on the subject of language development; taking as my point of departure the fact that language development is something which is taking place naturally, with every child, long before the processes of his education begin.

There are, I think, three facets to language development: learning language, learning through language, and learning about language. In a sense, and from a child's point of view, these three are all the same thing. But in order to understand them properly, we need to consider them apart; this will enable us to see where each comes in in the overall growth and development of a child.

First, then: "learning language". A child starts learning language from the moment he is born; newborn babies are very attentive listeners. No doubt, in fact, the baby has already started learning language before he was born, picking up the rhythms of speech from their source in his mother's diaphragm. But from birth onwards he is actively involved in communication, exchanging signals with the other human beings around him. For this purpose he has to construct a language; and we are now beginning to understand something of how he does it.

In London in the 1960s I directed, for the British Schools Council, a research and development programme in the teaching of the mother

---

First published in *Oral and Written Language Development: Impact on Schools*, edited by Yetta M. Goodman, Myna M. Haussler and Dorothy Strickland. Newark, DE: International Reading Association, 1980, pp. 7–19.

tongue. The team consisted of primary, secondary and tertiary teachers, all working together, and we produced educational materials such as *Breakthrough to Literacy* and *Language in Use*. During this period we were regularly involved in in-service courses of one kind and another, and I was often asked by the teachers taking part if I could say something about the language experience that children had had before they came to school. How much of language had they already learnt, and how had they come to learn it? So I tried to build up a picture of what was known about this at the time.

That was the mid-1960s, when mainstream linguistics was in what is now known as its syntactic age: everything was seen in terms of syntactic structures, and child language development was no exception. The child's learning of language was primarily thought of, and frequently referred to, as the acquisition of syntax. Now I found both of these terms misleading; I was unhappy with both the "acquisition" and the "syntax". It seemed to me that language development was essentially a process of construction, not acquisition; and that it was based on semantics, not on syntax.

There were at the time two prevailing views of language "acquisition", set up as being in direct opposition to each other but in fact, as is often the case with what are seen as competing theories, having many features and assumptions in common. One was labelled "behaviourist", or sometimes (the two being presented by their opponents as if they were synonymous) "environmentalist"; the second was labelled "nativist". The former stressed learning by imitation from without, the latter stressed learning by predisposition from within.

In both these accounts of the learning process the child is treated as an island. Here is the child, an individual entity; here is language, a ready-made thing-in-itself, and the child's task is to reach out, or reach in, and acquire it. In the behaviourist version, language is "out there" and its structure has to be inferred from the experience of listening to it; in the nativist version, although instances of language are out there, its structure exists as a ready-made blueprint "in here", a specific language programme with which the child is genetically endowed. Both these views were based on essentially the same metaphor, that of the child as an individual possessor and language as a commodity to be possessed.

As I saw it, a child is not an isolated individual, and learning language is not a process of acquiring some commodity that is already there. Learning language is a process of construction. More accurately, perhaps, we should use a term expressing mental construction, such as "construal" and "construing"; this would avoid the pitfalls of yet another kind of metaphor suggesting a product that is static and a process that could still be seen as located within the individual. Mental construction is not and cannot be an individual process. A child has to construct language, but he does not do this alone – he does it in interaction with others; and the others are not simply providing a model – they are actively engaged in the construction process along with him.

Language learning is an intersubjective and inherently social phenomenon. So much for the "learning" part of it; but what do we understand by the "language" part? Here again we were faced with two rather unsatisfactory interpretations, this time coexisting in mutual ignorance rather than actively competing, one drawn from psychology and the other from linguistics. In psychological studies, language was generally seen as consisting of expressions and meanings, in the form of sensori-motor and cognitive schemata. In the framework of linguistics, language was seen to consist of expressions and structures, or phonology and syntax. Each recognized two components, but a different two: psychologists left out the abstract system of grammar that serves (at least in adult languages) to translate between meanings and sounds; while linguists left out the realm of meaning that lay (for them) beyond that abstract system. Neither model offered a rich enough interpretation of the language-creating process in which a child is engaged.

To understand this process we have to put these two accounts together, producing a model in which language is a three-level construct; that is, there are three stages in the coding process, not two. Essentially, language is made of meanings: humans talk because they have something to say, not because they have clever tongues and brains. But the meanings have to be encoded in order to be communicated; and this is where the extra step comes in. Meanings are 'first' coded in **wordings** – that is, lexicogrammatical constructs, or words-in-structures (grammar and vocabulary, in traditional terminology) – and these wordings are 'then' recoded in expressions, which can be transmitted. An expression may be anything that another human being can recognize; but there are three main kinds of expression – gestures, sounds and writing. Gestures are used in infancy, and for limited purposes throughout life; and with a deaf child they come to be developed into a fully fledged system of expressions (the outward manifestation of a language known as "sign" which has systematic wordings and meanings of its own). With a hearing child, sound takes over as the principal means of expression; and after a time, in some cultures such as our own, it comes to be supplemented by a third medium, that of writing, which in turn affects the organization of the middle level of the code — the wordings of written language are significantly different from those of speech.

The fundamental task of a child in learning language is to construct a three-level system of this kind. And he does it, naturally, in stages, but always, I remind you, in interaction with others. He starts by construing what I have called a "protolanguage". If my own observations, and the few others that I know of, are at all typical, the pattern of its development is something like the following. By five to seven months he has learnt to construct a symbol, some sound or gesture intentionally addressed to another person which that person will decode. He experiments with this for a month or two, and then at some time about nine months begins to construct a system of such signs organized around a small range of different functions, different kinds of meaning that he wants to put across. You know the sort of thing I have in mind. Maybe you are playing with him, bouncing him up and down on your knee, and you stop, for a rest. He looks you in the eye and goes "Uh! uh!". This means "Go on! Do it some more!". Or you go into his room when he's woken up and he points to a picture on the wall, looks up at you and says "Doh! doh! doh!". This means something like "Where've you been all this time? — now let's look at this together". It's a request for interaction through the sharing of a common experience. These symbols are part of the child's protolanguage.

In the terms just referred to, the protolanguage consists of two levels only. It has meanings and expressions — each symbol is a meaning/expression complex, a *sign* in the Saussurean sense — but it has no wordings, no grammar or vocabulary. The child's next task, having built up a protolanguage that is effective for his original purposes but limiting in that it does not allow different kinds of meaning to be combined, is to turn it into a language of the adult kind, a three-level system in which the meanings are first coded into wordings and the wordings then recoded into sound.

If we want to observe how children do this, one approach is to use structured observations and sampling techniques, with audio and video records of the same child for so much time each week, or of large numbers of children in particular experimental situations. These techniques have contributed an essential part of the picture. At the same time, they do not tell the whole story. We also need very intensive records of natural interaction, records which are best obtained by means of the oldest of the traditional methods used in developmental linguistics, the language diary method. We can learn a great deal from records kept by parents of their children's speech, particularly if the parent is trained in linguistics and has mastered the skills of observing and recording natural language. Yet there is a real dearth of detailed, informed and informative case studies, of children whose language has been followed through from birth. It used to be considered that a child had no language at all until he had, or had begun to develop, a mother tongue; that is, until he had words, recognizable as words of English or whatever language was used around him, and even one or two incipient structures where the words appeared in combination. This typically happens somewhere between 12 and 21 months of age. My own systematic observations began when my child was about seven months old; at the time it seemed almost absurdly young, although subsequently I realized I should have started seven months earlier. Of course, the interaction that takes place during the very first months of life is not yet language; it is not even protolanguage, since the child is not yet exchanging symbols. But he is engaged in interaction, even if it is not yet symbolic; and it is important to investigate the nature of this "pre-protolanguage" communication and to understand how it evolves into communication of a linguistic kind.

The importance of case studies and of the naturalistic data they produce is that only through these do we get a full picture of a child learning "how to mean" – of language development as a semantic or perhaps *semogenic* process. The child is building up a resource, and it is a resource for meaning: a meaning potential, together with the wordings and the sounds through which these meanings can be expressed. And, of course, the resource is a two-way resource, since it also includes the potential for decoding the meanings of others: meaning is an interactive process, not something you do on your own. This in turn implies an environment in which to mean; meaning takes place in social contexts that are shared with the "significant others" that are part of the child's meaning group. These are the ones who are intimate with the child; they are usually quite a small group, mother, father perhaps, maybe one or two older brothers and sisters, sometimes grandparents if they live in the same household – people who are around for a significant part of the child's waking life. By "being there" they share in the language-creating process along with the child.

Now it is important to make clear what it means to say that they are sharing in the child's construction of the language. It does not mean that they are making the same noises, serving the child's own expressions back to him. They are addressing him in their own tongue, the mother tongue. But they are also there on the inside of the child's head, so to speak; not only do they know what he means, but they also know what he understands. They are creating the system along with him. But, surprisingly perhaps, this *tracking* by the others of the child's language development is entirely unconscious on their part. If you ask a mother, one who is actively and attentively conversing with a typically communicative 12-month-old, what that child can say and understand, she cannot tell you; and if you ask her three months later to recall what went on between them at the time, she has totally forgotten – because she too has moved on, as the child has moved on, to a new and more highly developed stage.

The child himself recognizes, also unconsciously of course, that he and the others are in it together; and he learns very early to help the process along (see Chapter 13). Once when my child was just 18 months we had been out for a walk together, and when we came back he was going through with me the things he had just seen outside: "*ba*" (buses), "*tiku*" (sticks), "*gaaugaau*" (ducks) and so on. Next in the list came "*douba*", which usually meant toast and butter. "Toast and butter?" I said. "We didn't see any toast and butter!" He looked me in the eye as if I was really stupid and said, very slowly and distinctly, "*d-o-u-b-a*". As it happens, his strategy didn't work; on that occasion I never got what he meant. But he knew that I hadn't understood, and he knew what there was that he could do about it.

As a child moves out beyond the home into the wider social groups of neighbourhood and school, his linguistic resources have to meet new and greatly extended demands; and the resources themselves expand accordingly. No one is teaching him to listen and to talk; he learns because he needs to in order to succeed. Then, in our culture, there comes a time when his language development is taken over by an institution created for the purpose, namely a school; and he is suddenly required to become conscious of language – first, because he has to master a new medium, writing, and adapt his existing potential to it; second, because from now on language itself is going to be treated as educational knowledge, rather than just common-sense knowledge, and the school is going to take over responsibility for extending his linguistic resources. The reason for these changes lies in the demands that will now be made on his capacity for "learning through language", which was the second of our main headings and which I shall come to in just a moment. Linguistically, the teacher is now in *loco parentis*; he – mostly she, at the beginning of the school career – will now be the one doing the tracking. But tracking the language development of 30 children in a classroom is, obviously, an entirely different matter from tracking the language development of one small child in the home; not only because it is impossible to do it, in anything like the same sense, but also because for the new caregiver, the teacher – as also for the child himself – language development has now become the object of conscious attention. And there is an inherent contradiction between this and the essentially unconscious nature of linguistic processes, a contradiction which many people never entirely resolve.

Of course, the greater part of a child's language development, even after he has started school, in most circumstances continues to take place unconsciously outside the school, in the family and in the peer group. The leading edge of the development of his meaning potential continues to be in informal, natural, unself-conscious speech. But the school takes charge of a particular and essential part of it, something that can only develop in an educational context. From now on language must function for the child as a means of learning all the other things that are learnt in school. As well as reading and writing, and the range of new **linguistic** achievements that are associated with these, from spelling and punctuation to versifying and story-telling, a large part of all his other learning tasks, in mathematics, social studies and the rest, consists in mastering the requisite language resources. This does not mean simply new vocabulary, with terms to be defined; it means new ways of organizing discourse, new ways of meaning in the construction of a test.

It would take too long to illustrate this in detail. But a minimal requirement that this imposes on the child is the ability to vary the kind of language used according to the context of its use; so to round off this section I would like to cite three examples of the spoken language of nine-year-olds, in order to show both the complexity of meanings and structures that children control by this age and the way their language varies as we move from a structured interview to a more natural and spontaneous dialogue. These extracts are taken from a large corpus of recordings of children made in England in the mid-1960s by the Nuffield Foreign Languages Teaching Materials Project, a sister project to the one I was directing at the time. In passage A, the child is talking to an adult interviewer and is listening to herself carefully as she goes along; it is rather self-conscious, monitored speech. In passage B, the child is still talking to the interviewer; but she launches into a personal narrative and becomes more absorbed, and so more casual, as the story progresses. Passage C has the children talking to each other; there was still an interviewer present, but they had forgotten all about her and were responding unself-consciously and naturally to each other's turns in the dialogue.

Example 1

Text A

ADULT: Now, er – what did you do in your holidays? I hope not spotting another burglary or anything?

CHILD: No! We went to the Isle of Man for our holidays last year. Er – we went by boat and it was called the "Manx Maid"; and, er – we, erm, – stayed at a place called Port St Mary, erm – stayed in a boarding house which was just over the – well, the cliff was in front of us and then the sea. And from the bedroom we had a lovely view of the harbour. It was very nice there; not very crowded. We didn't have any real events; we just used to sunbathe every day, and went back for our lunch, then went down on the beach and sunbathed. We visited many places: Laxey Wheel, and the Witch's Castle I think it was.

ADULT: What is the Witch's Castle?

CHILD: Erm, – oh, it's just a very old castle and it's just got that name, and there's – by the side of it there's, erm – a little tea-shop, and upstairs there's lots of ornaments and things.

ADULT: There are no witches around?

CHILD: No; there – there are ornaments of witches and things and there's a circle on the grass and it says that that is a Witch's Circle.

Text B

CHILD: Well, last year my mother and father had gone out to see an open-air theatre, and it was late at night; and when they'd come home Mummy had got a tummy-ache and she couldn't go to sleep, and so she'd been just prancing up and down the kitchen. Anyway, at about – ooh, about quarter to one, somewhere round there, she heard these men who kept walking up and down, and ... they kept coming up the gangway and sometimes they tried the door – luckily it was locked. Anyway at about one o'clock I heard this terrible crashing sound and I woke up and I wondered what was happening. I was scared stiff and – you know how you are when you're scared stiff, so I thought it was somebody under the bed. Anyway Grandma was sleeping in the same room; she went to look out of the window, but we couldn't see anything. Then Mummy and Daddy came in, and they said they'd heard it as well and they didn't know what had happened. And I suggested it could have been a robber, but they said it w – you know: 'no'. Anyway, so they went down with the owners of the flat – anyway, it had been a robbery, and there were some cameras stolen, and the chairs were all ...

Text C

ADULT: Do you – when you have a small baby in the house, do you call it 'it' or do you call it 'she' or 'he'?

CHILD 1: Well, if it's just – if you don't know what it is, I think you ought to call it 'it', because you don't know whether you're calling it a boy or a girl, and if it gets on, and if you start calling it 'she' then you find out it's a boy, you can't stop yourself, 'cause you've got so used to calling it 'she'.

CHILD 2: Erm – Mrs Siddons says that it – if some neighbour has a new baby next door and you don't know whether it's a he or a she, if you refer to it as 'it' well then the neighbour will be very offended.

CHILD 1: Well if it's in your family I think you should call it either 'he' or 'she', or else the poor thing when it grows up won't know what it is.

ADULT: Well what did Mrs Siddons suggest you should do if your neighbour has a baby and you don't know whether it's a boy or a girl?

CHILD 2: She didn't. I don't suppose she knew.

CHILD 1: Call it 'the'.

CHILD 2: Hello, the!
CHILD 1: Oh, I know. Call it 'baby'.

(recorded by Ruqaiya Hasan for Nuffield Foreign Languages Teaching Materials Project, Leeds and York, England)

The first example, being the most self-conscious, is most like the written language we would expect to get from a child that age. The second is a little further away; while the third differs most of all from what we usually find in writing. For one thing, the grammatical structure of the third passage is too complex to be easily tolerated in a written text, whereas in casual speech it trips off the tongue of the speaker, and into the ears of the listeners, without any of them noticing its quite remarkable structural complexity. But the point I want to draw attention to here is merely the range of variation that the children are beginning to control, in adapting their language to the different functions it is now being called upon to fulfil.

This leads me into the second heading, learning through language. It turns out we have already been talking about this for some time; we need hardly be surprised at that, since it is just another facet of the same basic phenomenon of language development.

"Learning through language" refers to language in the construction of reality: how we use language to build up a picture of the world in which we live. This means the world that is around us and also the world that is inside us, the world of our consciousness and our imagination. The great American anthropological linguists of the first half of the twentieth century, Boas, Sapir and Whorf, gave us a deep insight into the part played by language in shaping and transmitting the world view of each and every human culture.

From the start language is the main instrument we have for interpreting and organizing our experience. Not everything we perceive is "processed" by language, but most of it is; language is far and away the most significant instrument for building up our model of the universe and of our own place in it.

What is the origin of this process in a young child's developing language system? Our understanding of this is still very tentative and incomplete; but it appears that, as a child begins the transition from protolanguage to language – from child tongue to mother tongue – he comes to make a rather systematic distinction between two basic functions of language, which I have referred to as the "pragmatic" and the "mathetic", the doing function and the learning function. I have described this in earlier chapters, showing how my own child made the distinction explicit by his intonation pattern, expressing pragmatic by a rising tone and mathetic by a falling tone. The striking thing about this was that not only did he introduce into his own speech, more or less overnight at the age of 19 months, a fundamental semantic distinction which has nothing corresponding to it in the mother tongue, but also that his mother and those around him understood straight away what this opposition meant. Not consciously, of course; they were not aware of what was happening, and nor was I until I got to that point in my analysis. But they responded immediately to the different meanings he was expressing. This is how it happened.

When Nigel was using language for pragmatic purposes, in the sense of 'I want', for example "more meat!", "butter on!" (put some butter on my toast), "train stuck!" (get it out for me), he used a rising intonation. The meaning of this intonation pattern was 'somebody *do* something!'; and the significant observation was that somebody always did. Not that they immediately jumped up to do whatever he asked or give him whatever he wanted; the answer would often be "You can't have any more", or "I'm busy; try and get it out yourself". But they responded – thereby unconsciously acknowledging the fact that the meaning had been a request for action, and making it clear to the child that they recognized it as such.

When he was using language in a "mathetic" function, saying things like "green light" (there's a green light there), "Mummy book" (that's Mummy's book) or "two buses", the intonation was falling. And I noticed that on these occasions nobody felt it necessary to say or do anything. Sometimes they acknowledged, saying things like "yes, that's a green light", or they corrected him, "no, that's blue, not green"; but often they said nothing at all. And whereas if he got no response to a pragmatic utterance Nigel was clearly dissatisfied, and went on saying it until he did, if he got no response to a mathetic utterance, he was not in the least concerned: he didn't really expect one. The meaning was: this is how things are; you can confirm (or deny) it if you like, but I'm really sorting things out just for myself. Nigel maintained this distinction between language as a means of doing and language as a means of learning consistently for about six months, until the time came when the grammar of speech functions of the adult language was well established in his own system; then he abandoned it.

Nobody was setting out to teach him anything. Nigel's learning, his construction of reality, was taking place through these little micro-encounters in which he decided what he wanted to talk about. Usually – always, at first – the experience he was representing in words was one that was being or had been shared with someone else; and that person might correct him if they thought he'd got things wrong. But the knowledge he was storing up was common-sense everyday knowledge which the others could not have imparted to him consciously because they were not aware of having it themselves.

Learning through language typically proceeds by way of such "innumerable small momenta", to use one of my favourite expressions from Benjamin Lee Whorf; this is precisely what makes it so difficult to document and to illustrate in any very satisfactory way. I decided that I would try to illustrate by picking out a set of instances that were grouped around a single theme; and I chose the theme of 'relativity in time and space' because it shows clearly how the child's picture of reality is different from ours. We can see from this how much mental adaptation he has to go through, as well as how much simple accumulation of experience, in order to achieve something like our adult view of the time–space continuum in which we live.

Example 2

10;6   N: (looking in a mirror) Sometimes I wonder which side of the mirror I'm on – whether they're the reflection or I am.

10;0   N: (watching a bubble that floated for a long time without bursting) In germ time, how many years d'you think that would have lasted?

9;8   N: Daddy, if something is a mile long and half a mile thick you don't call it long. But if it's a mile long and only a centimetre thick, you do call it long.

8;4   N: (arguing with friend) You can't see, in your sleep.
       F: I do. I had a dream last night; I saw in that.
       N: Well, you see with your backwards eyes, that go in, to the fantasyland, the other way, in a dream.

7;10   N: (making a complicated space vehicle) In the future, when I invent these gadgets, then in the future **future** they'll be dumped on rubbish heaps.

7;0   N: How do you see what happened long ago, before you were born?
      F: You read about it in books?

	N:	No; use a microscope to look back.
	F:	How do you do that?
	N:	Well. If you're in a car, or in an observation coach, you look back and then you see what happened before. And you need a microscope to see what happened long ago, because it's very far away.
6;4	N:	How old are you?
	F:	Fifty.
	N:	Then you weren't born when the Blackheath Hill track was taken up. When you're eighty, how old will I be?
	F:	Thirty-six.
	N:	Thirty-six! Ooh! When you're eighty, then you **will** have been born before the track was taken up.
5;5	N:	If you started from Chicago instead of Glenview would you get to Minneapolis later? Cos it's further.
	F:	No, you'd get there at the same time. You'd just start earlier.
	N:	No, you wouldn't ... but ... (unable to work it out)
4;4	N:	How do mummies and daddies get born?
	N:	Well they all start as babies.
	N:	How do they get to grow people when there aren't anybody around? How do you get your **big** birthdays, when I'm as big as you? How do I get my birthday then?
3;5	N:	Wednesday Tuesday Thursday Friday Monday ... Monday Tuesday Wednesday Thursday Friday ... why does Friday come before Saturday?
	F:	Well I don't know; I suppose that's where they put it.
	N:	Yes but **I** put it in the middle of Wednesday.
	F:	Is that where you put Friday?
	N:	Yes ... (looking up at sky) is it way up in the clouds?
	F:	You mean that's where the days are? That's a nice idea.
	N:	Yes but **are** they way up in the clouds?
2;6	N:	(looking for plasticine (modelling clay)): Why did Daddy put the brown plasticine away before breakfast?
	F:	I didn't.
	N:	It wasn't crumbly ... the old plasticine was crumbly ... we have to wait till the old plasticine gets new again and **then** we can use it to make a diesel train.

Starting with the latest one, we find Nigel at ten and a half years old looking in a mirror and wondering which is the reflection: them or us?

At ten, he watches a soap bubble floating for a long time in the air before it bursts, and asks, if one had the point of view of a microorganism, how many years on that time scale it would have lasted. At nine years eight months he is considering the relative nature of values on one dimension when another dimension is made to vary: if two objects are the same length but differ in breadth, one will be called long and the other not. At eight years four months he is describing the nature of inner experience: seeing in a dream. At seven years ten months it is the relative nature of time: what is novel in the next age will be old-fashioned in the one after. At seven years, he is thinking about movement through time and space; and so on.

From one point of view, these could be thought of as failed attempts to construct the adult world. But each stage in that construction process represents a world view on its own, and makes sense to him in as much as the world ever makes sense to anyone. It is also, like the construction of the language itself, an interactive process – though in a somewhat different way. The child's construction of reality similarly takes place through interaction with others; but it seems unlikely that the others are tracking the process in the way that they are unconsciously tracking his early language learning. In other words, whereas a mother who is close to her child may have an accurate, though subconscious, mental representation of his language, she probably has not got, to anything like the same extent, a mental representation of his world view. The construct that is shared is that of the meaning **potential**, the language. How the child uses that meaning potential to structure his experience is something that cannot be shared, since that would imply nothing less than the sharing of all his experience, including the inner experience of his thoughts, feelings and perceptions.

There will, of course, be conflicts and tensions between the various different realities; this is where learning takes place, when there is some kind of tension between the child's world and that of the adult's, or between different aspects of his own world, and the child attempts to resolve it. There may also be tension between the language and the reality it is being used to encode. I became aware of an example of this happening at a very early age when my own child, at 19 months, was just learning to control the meaning 'two'. One day he was sitting on the floor playing with his toys, and he held up a bus in one hand and a train in the other. "Two chuffa", he said, using his word for a train. Then he looked at the two objects again, rather perplexed, and hesitated: "two... two...". Finally he gave up, puzzled and defeated;

the problem was beyond him. The point is, however, that he clearly recognized that it was beyond him; he knew there was no way of interpreting the situation within his linguistic system. As it happens, there is no way of interpreting it in everyday English either; we learn to get by without a general term for 'wheeled vehicle'. There is a mismatch here between language and reality; or rather – since language is also part of reality – between the child's experience and the symbolic system that is used to encode it. Such conflict, far from being destructive, may in fact contribute positively towards his understanding of both.

My third heading was "learning about language"; in other words, coming to understand the nature and functions of language itself. In one sense, every human being **knows about** language simply because he talks and listens. But this is unconscious understanding, in the same way that our **knowledge of** language is unconscious knowledge. It is knowledge stored in the gut, so to speak (which is where many cultures locate true understanding), rather than knowledge stored in the head.

How do we know such knowledge is really there? Perhaps the clearest demonstration of it may be found in the evolution of writing. Writing evolved very slowly over long periods by innumerable small progressions. There was no conscious analysis of language behind it. Yet every writing system embodies a deep insight into the nature of language, its semantics, lexicogrammar and phonology. Such insight is brought to the surface only with the greatest difficulty; much of the history of linguistics has been a struggle to make explicit an understanding of language that is no more than must be present for writing to have evolved at all – and it is ironical that the main barrier to making it explicit has been writing itself, which having once evolved gets in the way and prevents one from seeing through to the language that lies behind it. (The nature of writing, and its relationship to language, remains to this day one of the least well explored and documented branches of linguistics.)

It is important, however, to make a distinction between this kind of understanding about language, which is very difficult to bring to consciousness, and the explicit folk linguistics of the community and the classroom. This, like most folk wisdom, is a mixture of scholarly insights and old wives' tales. (The same distinction arises in other spheres of knowledge. In medicine, for example, there is the unconscious "instinct" for what is good and bad for us, going back no doubt to the period in our evolution when we could tell the molecular structure of a substance simply by sniffing at it; and the explicit "folk medicine", likewise compounded out of a mixture of fact and myth.) The medieval grammatical tradition that found its way eventually into our classrooms was scholarly and perceptive; it was unfortunate, however, that it represented the philosophical rather than the rhetorical strand in Western thinking about language, which made it less relevant to education and everyday life. Hence its impact has usually been minimal, and it tends to be stored in people's consciousness in the form of misremembered precepts about linguistic trivia, its more important insights (for example, into the nature of syntactic dependence) being ignored. A friend of mine who was a property surveyor in the public service once sent up a letter for the head of his department to sign, ending with the words "as soon as the lease has been drawn up we will send you a copy of it". Back came the letter with the word "it" crossed out and the wording amended to "we will send you a copy of same". My friend was incensed by this barbarism and complained to his superior, who said, in shocked reproof, "But you can't end a sentence with a proposition!".

The reason why this sort of nonsense is often all that remains from the study of language in school is that the kind of knowledge about language that is embodied in it bears little relation to educational needs. This is not to say that there is no place in language development for this third component: there is. Quite apart from its intrinsic value, it is necessary as a source of support to the other two. But there are two points to be made about it. The first is that much of the learning about language that is relevant to education is not concerned with grammar at all, but with other things such as register variation, language and society, different media of expression in language and so on. Out of the 110 units making up *Language in Use* for secondary schools, not one was concerned with grammar; this was certainly going too far, but the reason for the decision lay in the second point, namely that the grammar that was familiar to teachers was a grammar of the wrong kind. For educational purposes we need a grammar that is functional rather than formal, semantic rather than syntactic in focus, oriented towards discourse rather than towards sentences, and represents language as a flexible resource rather than as a rigid set of rules.

When children first recognize that language itself is part of the world they live in, and that it can be talked about like everything else, the metalinguistic terms they use are words such as *say* and *call* and *mean*. (Note that these are verbs, not nouns; to a small child language is a process, not a thing.) A very young child can in fact report that something was said even before he has the word *say* with which to do it. When Nigel was 19 months he and I were walking across an open field where some boys were flying a kite; the kite fell to the ground and the string lay stretched out across our path. "There's a kite there," I said. "Mind the string!" Sometime later, after we got home, Nigel said to me "Kite. 'Kite. Mind string' ". There was a marked change of tone and voice quality between the first "kite" and the next; and I suspect that it was this that led me, quite without thinking, to interpret his little narrative as including a report of what I had said: "There was a kite. And Daddy said, 'There's a kite. Mind the string!'".

We still know relatively little about how children build up this unconscious awareness of language. It begins with the awareness that things have names; and from very early on – the end of the protolanguage stage – a child can ask for a name, 'what's that?'. This is soon perceived as a two-way relationship; once the concept of 'what is that thing called?' is built into the child's semantics, it is soon followed by the concept of 'what does that word mean?'. Nigel at 20 months would play a meaning game, chanting a string of nonsense syllables and then asking (but without inviting an answer) "what that mean!".

It was not until much later – four years old – that Nigel began using nouns for exploring language. By then he could play the rhyming game, "I'm thinking of a word that rhymes with ...", with the word *word* as part of the formula; but when I was guessing and he wanted to give a hint, he would say "No, daddy, it's not a word, it's a thing". This distinction between words and things, which he made for himself, was in fact that between grammatical items (function words) and lexical items (content words); the hint "it's not a word, it's a thing" was what he said if I had guessed, say, "she" where the correct answer was "tree". This distinction between grammatical and lexical elements in the vocabulary is one of the basic ingredients in our unconscious awareness of language; it is also one that is incorporated in the English writing system, in the principle that a lexical item must have at least three letters in it whereas a grammatical item may have only two (hence *by the bye, he is in the inn* and so on).

A child's unconscious awareness of language is largely determined by functional considerations; and at the heart of his understanding is the awareness that 'this is what I can do with language'. From birth he has been building up a picture of what language is for; he knows that it is his lifeline to the others that interact with him and that, through such interaction, it is a means of doing and of learning. When we come to strengthen and extend his language development through education, we need to build on this awareness, relating the language work in the classroom to what he already knows about language from his own experience. It often happens that the two bear little relation to each other, with the result that the child never realizes that what the teacher is on about is just an extension of something he already knows and already does. There is no need to impose an artificial discontinuity on his learning experience, in any of the three aspects of language development I have been talking about.

Language development is a continuous process. Even the move into written language, which is often made to seem as if it was a totally new experience unrelated to what the child has already learnt, is simply part of the same massive project in which every child is engaged, the construction of the ability to mean. This is not to imply that written language is just spoken language written down; as I pointed out earlier, the difference in the two media leads to significant differences in the forms that they serve to express. But the essential relationship between the two is a functional one. Writing evolved in the history of the human race in response to certain new and extended demands that people were making on language. It was being required to function in contexts that had not existed before; and these new contexts – commercial, religious, scientific – needed new forms of communication for the exchange of meanings. There was no **logical** necessity for the new symbolic systems to be mapped on to language, and at first, it seems, they were not; but it was not long before they came to be, since it was still the same cultural reality that lay behind them. The age at which we put a child in school is the age at which we judge him to have reached this point, where he too is making new functional demands on his language – or at least where he can understand the nature of such demands if others make them. He also has to learn that writing maps on to the words and structures that by this time are already embedded deeply in his unconscious knowledge of the world.

I hope that these three headings, learning language, learning through language and learning about language, may help to clarify some of the early learning experience that forms the background to a child's encounter with language in school. When we think of language development, it helps, I feel, to see it as a complex process in which all these components are present. As I stressed at the beginning, they are not three things that happen separately; they are three aspects of a single complex happening. But if we are aware of all three we can perhaps understand the process more perceptively and take part in it in more richly varied ways.

Chapter Fifteen

TOWARDS A LANGUAGE-BASED THEORY OF LEARNING
(1993)

When children learn language, they are not simply engaging in one kind of learning among many; rather they are learning the foundation of learning itself. The distinctive characteristic of human learning is that it is a process of making meaning – a semiotic process; and the prototypical form of human semiotic is language. Hence the ontogenesis of language is at the same time the ontogenesis of learning.

Whatever the culture they are born into, in learning to speak children are learning a semiotic that has been evolving for at least ten thousand generations. But in some cultures, including those comprising the Eurasian culture band, during the past hundred generations or so the nature of this semiotic has been changing: a new form of expression has evolved, that we call ***writing***, and following on from this a new, institutionalized form of learning that we call ***education***. Children now learn language not only in home and neighbourhood but also in school; and with new modes of language development come new forms of knowledge, educational knowledge as distinct from what we call common sense. At the same time, the process of language development is still a continuous learning process, one that goes on from birth, through infancy and childhood, and on through adolescence into adult life.

Most theories of learning, including those that take account of language learning, come from outside the study of language. They tend either to ignore language development, or to treat it as just one learning domain; and sometimes they take on board preconceptions about the nature and history of language that are quite remote from reality. If we

---

First published in *Linguistics and Education*. London: Elsevier Science, 1993, 5.2, pp. 93–116.

try to translate such theories into practice, into activities in which language is involved (and these include all educational activities), we may seriously miss the mark. Language is not a **domain** of human knowledge (except in the special context of linguistics, where it becomes an object of scientific study); language is the essential condition of knowing, the process by which experience **becomes** knowledge.

With this in mind, I would like to suggest an alternative: that we might explore approaches to learning theory that are based on consideration of language. In other words, we might interpret learning as something that is inherently a semiotic process. And this in my opinion imposes certain constraints. One is that the theory should be based on natural data rather than experimental data – that is, on language that is unconscious, not self-monitored; in context, not in a vacuum; observed, not elicited. The reason for this is that, of all forms of human activity, language is perhaps the one that is most perturbed by being performed under attention – not surprisingly, because all other learning depends on the learner not having constantly to attend to the way experience is being construed. Another constraint is that the theory would not dissociate the *system* from the *instance*: language from text, *langue* from *parole*, competence from performance, or other related oppositional pairs.

I am not presuming to offer any general theory, but I would like to offer certain considerations that such a theory would have to address. These come from the study of children's language development. It seems clearer if these could be enumerated one by one; so in the remainder of this article I have listed a total of 21 features, aspects of child language development that I think are critical to a language-based theory of learning (a summary of these features is provided at the end of this paper). They are drawn from my research and that of colleagues in the field, and they derive largely from direct observations of: (1) children's spontaneous language in the home and neighbourhood, (2) their use of language in construing common-sense knowledge and enacting interpersonal relationships, (3) their move into primary school, and the transition into literacy and educational knowledge, and (4) their subsequent move into secondary school and into the technical knowledge of the disciplines. Where possible I have given specific references; but many of the points raised are generalizations made from various sources among the items listed in the references, especially those of Halliday, Hasan, Martin, Oldenburg-Torr, and Painter.

Features of child language development

Feature 1

A human infant engages in symbolic acts, which I have referred to as **acts of meaning**. Children are predisposed, from birth: (a) to address others, and be addressed by them (that is, to interact communicatively); and (b) to construe their experience (that is, to interpret experience by organizing it into meanings). **Signs** are created at the intersection of these two modes of activity. Signs evolve (a) in mediating – or, better, in enacting – interaction with others, and (b) in construing experience into meaning; specifically, in exploring the contradiction between inner and outer experience (between what is perceived as going on "out there" and what is perceived as going on "in here", within the child's own consciousness) (cf. Trevarthen 1980).

Thus, typically, at 0;3 to 0;5 babies are "reaching and grasping", trying to get hold of objects in the exterior domain and to reconcile this with their awareness of the interior domain (they can see the objects). Such an effort provokes the use of a sign, which is then interpreted by the adult caregiver, or an older child, as a demand for explanation; the other responds in turn with an act of meaning. There has been "conversation" before; but this is a different kind of conversation, in which both parties are acting symbolically. A typical example from my own data would be the following, with the child at just under 0;6 (See Chapter 5 and also accompanying CD):

> There is a sudden loud noise from pigeons scattering.
> Child [lifts head, looks around, gives high-pitched squeak]
> Mother: Yes, those are birds. Pigeons. Aren't they noisy!

Feature 2

When symbols begin to be established as regular signs, typically at about 0;6 to 0;10, they are characteristically **iconic**: they embody a natural relationship between expression and meaning. Such symbols are created by the child in interactive contexts. Examples from my own data (Halliday 1979: 173) are:

> [grasp object and release] 'I want (to hold) that'
> [touch object lightly, momentarily] 'I don't want that'
> [touch object firmly for measurable time] 'go on doing (what you were doing) with that (for example, throwing it up in the air)'.

There seems to be a clear distinction between these and non-symbolic acts (for example, grabbing and pulling, or hitting out of the way); moreover the symbolic acts are clearly addressed to a person, and again the caregivers are tracking and responding: "Oh, you want to hold that yourself, do you?", "Shall I do that again? all right!".

These particular signs were gestural in expression; others may be vocal, for example, a high tone expressing 'curiosity' (construing experience), a low tone 'togetherness' (enacting interpersonal relationship). What emerges is a varied repertory of signs, fluid both in meaning and in expression but by no means randomly variable, so that the caregivers continue to track and also to respond. The child creates the symbols, using vocal and gestural resources in acting out the role of learner, and by the same token enabling the "others" to act out their roles as teachers (Oldenburg-Torr 1990; Trevarthen 1987).

Feature 3

These sets of symbolic acts develop into **systems**. An act of meaning implies a certain choice: If there is a meaning 'I want', then there can be a meaning 'I don't want', perhaps also 'I want very much', as alternatives. If there is a meaning 'I'm content', this can contrast with other states of being: 'I'm cross', 'I'm excited', and so on. Sets of alternative meanings of this kind form semiotic paradigms called "systems": each term in a system excludes, and hence presupposes, the other(s).

This stage when children are construing their signs into sign systems, the protolanguage, typically extends somewhere in the range of 0;8 to 1;4, and it is associated with freedom of movement. Semantically, the systems develop around certain recognizable functions (the **microfunctions**, as I have called them): instrumental and regulatory, where the sign mediates in some other, non-symbolic act (for example, 'give me that!', 'sing to me!'); interactional, where the sign sets up and maintains an intimate relationship ('let's be together'); and personal, where the sign expresses the child's own cognitive and affective states (for example, 'I like that', 'I'm curious about that'). There may also be the beginnings of an imaginative or play function, a 'let's pretend!' sign, often accompanied with laughter.

Although some protolanguage signs may be imitations of adult words, the protolanguage is not yet mother tongue; I have referred to it as "child tongue" (Chapter 9; Oldenburg-Torr 1987). Hearing it, one could not yet tell what the mother tongue was going to be (cf. Qiu

1985, on Chinese children's protolanguage). Studies by Painter (1984) and Oldenburg-Torr (1987) reveal the significance of the protolanguage as a stage in human learning. At the same time, they show its limitations: it cannot create information, and it cannot construct discourse. To do these things it has to be transformed into something else.

Feature 4

The system as a whole is now deconstructed, and reconstructed as a stratified semiotic, that is, with a **grammar** (or, better, because this concept includes vocabulary, a **lexicogrammar**) as intermediary between meaning and expression. The grammar interfaces with a semantics at one edge and with a phonetics, or phonology, at the other. In other words, the protolanguage becomes a language, in the prototypical, adult sense.

This process no doubt took many hundreds or even thousands of generations in the course of linguistic evolution. Children take the step quickly, so that those around are aware of the discontinuity; they say "now he's beginning to talk!". They have been conversing at length with the child already for six months or more, but they do not recognize the protolanguage as "talk".

The change is highly complex, and needs to be broken down into a number of analytic components. The grammar opens the way to naming and reference, and hence can function as a theory of human experience. It allows for an ongoing exchange of roles between speaker and listener, and hence can function as the enactment of human relationships. It makes it possible to create discourse (text that is operational in its environment), and hence brings into being the commodity we call "information". It opens up a universe of meaning, a multidimensional semantic space that can be indefinitely expanded and projected. In other words, the grammar brings into being a semiotic that has unlimited potential for learning with. The next six features relate to this "explosion into grammar", beginning with one or two localized (but still general) principles and strategies.

Feature 5

The symbols now become **conventional**, or "arbitrary": typically, there will no longer be any natural relationship between expression (sound) and meaning. Two conditions were necessary for this step to be taken:

(a) that the principle of symbolic action (acts of meaning) should already have been established; and (b) that there was now a level of purely abstract coding – the grammar – mediating between meaning and expression. Only with this step can it become possible to separate reference from analogy (for example, *quack* is no longer the imitation of the noise of a duck, it is the name of that noise, so we say *it quacked*), and hence to construe all experience as meaning. Of course there will continue to be iconic symbols in language (and deaf sign, being a visual semiotic, makes very positive use of this resource in its construal of experience). What is important is that the fundamental principle of conventionality has been established.

Feature 6

One of the strategies that children seem to adopt in learning language is that of the ***trailer***: a kind of preview of what is going to come. Children take a new step forward, and leave a footprint as it were, showing that they have been there; but then back off for a while before consolidating this step and building it into the overall learning process. It is as if they are satisfying themselves that they will be able to cope with this new demand on their semiotic powers when they need to.

There is often a gap of this kind between the very first acts of meaning, referred to under feature 1, and the beginning of the protolanguage proper. More noticeably, in the middle of the protolanguage period, a child will suddenly use an expression in a context which seems clearly referential; yet it will be another two or three months before that same child starts building a system based on referential meaning. Instances of this kind continue through early language development (cf. the example under feature 7).

When we observe an occurrence of this type we have a name for it: we call it a "fluke", meaning by that that it is a purely chance event. There is no doubt that there are such things as flukes, and that they can happen in the course of learning. But the trailer seems to be a more consistent feature, perhaps having to do especially with the construction of a semiotic system.

Feature 7

The trailer is also perhaps related to another learning strategy, that which I call the ***magic gateway***. This is the strategy of finding a special way in, a magic gateway to a different world of meaning. In a sense the magic gateway may be complementary to the trailer: the learner may sense where he or she has to go next, but have to find a route by which to pass.

One example may be found in what I have discussed already; the iconic sign, as a magic gateway between non-symbolic and symbolic modes of action. But let me give a more specific example from the present context, that of the move into grammar: where is the magic gateway into the grammar? This is again from my own data, when Nigel was 1.3. He was beginning to incorporate names (Mummy, Daddy, Anna) into his protolanguage, but they were not yet referential; they were still microfunctional signs meaning 'play with me', 'I'm giving this to you', and so on. Then, within three consecutive days he constructed the system shown in Table 1. By separating articulatory from prosodic features in the expression, Nigel had deconstructed the sign; in doing so, he had succeeded in varying one dimension of meaning (one system, in the technical sense) while keeping the other one constant, and in the process marked out one of the two meaning systems as referential. Thus, the combination of "proper name" (Mummy/Daddy/Anna) with mood, or protomood (seeking/finding), provided the magic gateway into this new stratum of lexicogrammar; it enabled him to mean two things at once, so that one of the two meanings became a name. Then (on the trailer principle) he stayed content with that, not following it up until another ten weeks had gone by.

Table 1 Dimensions of meaning in a protolanguage system

	Expressed by Prosody	
expressed by articulation	"Where are you?" (mid level + high level)	"There you are!" (high falling + low level)
"Mummy" [ama]	[ā m ā]	[à m ā]
"Daddy" [dada]	[d ā d ā]	[d à d ā]
"Anna" [an:a]	[ā n: ā]	[à n: ā]

Feature 8

The next step is that of ***generalization***, whereby the principle of naming evolves from "proper name", which is not yet a sufficient condition for a grammar, to "common name", which is the name of a class: of entities, of processes, or of properties (noun, verb, or adjective in a typical early stage of transition into English mother tongue). This is the origin of words, in the technical sense of the word as a lexical item, or lexeme. A "common" (that is, class-naming) word functions first of all as an *annotation* of experience; when the child uses it, it is frequently checked out by the "other" acting as a consultant. For example, the child sees a large object moving along the road on wheels and says "bus". The caregiver responds, saying "Yes, that's a bus"; or "No, that's not a bus, it's a van". The second kind of response shows that annotating also involves *classifying*.

The problem is that the phenomena of experience tend to be paradigmatically unbounded; there is no obvious distinction between one class and another. (They may also be syntagmatically unbounded, in that it is not clear where they begin and end, although that does not apply to objects like buses!) The lines between 'car ... bus ... van ... lorry' are hardly clearer than those between 'purple ... blue ... green ... yellow'. There may indeed be **objects** of intermediate or mixed class, half van and half lorry, for example; but the name has to be one or the other; since the sign is conventional, we cannot create an intermediate expression between *van* and *lorry*. (As Tigger did, when he was accused of bouncing. "All I did was I coughed," said Tigger. "He bounced," said Eeyore. "Well, I sort of boffed," said Tigger (from A. A. Milne, *The House at Pooh Corner*).) We do, of course, play with the system in this way, as A. A. Milne was doing, using a mixed expression as metaphor for a mixed class in the content. But even where a new word is created by mixing two expressions, as with *smog* (smoke + fog), it still classifies; the classification has merely become more delicate.)

A class name is therefore several steps away from a protolinguistic sign. In protolanguage, *mamamama* ... may mean 'I want (that)', then 'I want mummy to (do/give me that)', then 'I want mummy!'. Then, by some such gateway as described previously, it becomes 'Mummy'; it now refers, so beginning the transition from protolanguage into language. But since 'Mummy' is a unique member of a class, this "proper name" annotates but does not yet classify. Only when "common names" emerge, like *bus* or *run* or *green*, does annotating come to involve classifying; and, by the same token, it also implies *outclassifying*, as in "That's not a bus, it's a van", "That's not green, it's blue", or "Walk, don't run!".

The system now has the potential for creating information; the more so because one class may include several other classes, thus creating a *taxonomy*. Fruit is a kind of food; berries are a kind of fruit; raspberry is a kind of berry. Early investigations of language development tended to foreground problems of classification; it takes time, of course, for young children to sort out the details, but they have no problem with the taxonomic principle. Words are learnt not as in a dictionary but as in a thesaurus, each one being progressively located in the expanding topological space by reference to the "others" to which it is taxonomically related. (It should perhaps be made explicit, however, that the vocabulary of a natural language does not constitute a strict taxonomy. Rather, a word is the intersection of features from different sets of options, or **systems**; the systems form a network, in which words appear as the realization of various features combined. These may include interpersonal features as well as experiential ones; children soon learn that *dawdle* means 'walk' + 'slow' + 'I want you to hurry up!'.)

Feature 9

Perhaps the most important single principle that is involved in the move from protolanguage into mother tongue is the ***metafunctional*** principle: that meaning is at once both doing and understanding. The transition begins with an opposition between utterance as action (doing) and utterance as reflection (understanding); I have referred to this as the opposition of two ***macrofunctions***, "pragmatic/mathetic". This is transformed, in the course of the transition, into a combination whereby every utterance involves both choice of speech function (that is, among different kinds of doing) and choice of content (that is, among different realms of understanding). In the grammar of the mother tongue, each clause is a mapping of a "doing" component (the ***interpersonal*** metafunction) and an "understanding" component (the ***experiential*** metafunction) (see Chapter 9; Oldenburg-Torr 1987; Painter 1984, 1989).

We can summarize this as shown in Table 2. In stage 1, content$_x$ and content$_y$ do not overlap and there are no combinations of prosody$_a$ with content$_y$ or prosody$_b$ with content$_x$. Stage 2 shows the beginning of clause and group structures, the grammar's construction of processes and entities. In Stage 3 the mood is now also grammaticalized, the non-declarative then evolving into imperative versus interrogative.

The child has now established the metafunctional principle, that meaning consists in simultaneously construing experience and enacting interpersonal relationships. The mood system is part of the interpersonal grammar: here the meaning is 'what relationship am I setting up between myself and the listener?'. The transitivity system is part of

Table 2 Stages in development of the metafunctional principle

Stage	Examples			
1 (early transition)				
Either:	Doing ("pragmatic") $\downarrow [\text{prosody}_a + \text{content}_x]$		more meat	"I want more meat!"
Or:	Understanding ("mathetic") $\downarrow [\text{prosody}_b + \text{content}_y]$		green car	"That's a green car."
2 (mid-transition)				
	$\left\{ \begin{array}{l} \text{Doing} \\ \text{Understanding} \end{array} \right.$	$\left. \begin{array}{l} \downarrow \text{prosody}_a \\ \downarrow \text{prosody}_b \end{array} \right\} + \begin{array}{l} \text{any} \\ \text{content} \end{array}$	mummy book mummy book	"I want mummy's book!" "That's mummy's book."
3 (late transition)				
	Mood system (speech functions) $\left\{ \begin{array}{l} \text{Non-declarative} \\ \text{Declarative} \end{array} \right.$	Transitivity system (Process types)	$\left\{ \begin{array}{l} \text{Material} \\ \text{Mental} \\ \text{Relational} \end{array} \right\}$	

the experiential grammar; here, the meaning is 'what aspect of experience am I representing?'. From now on (subject, obviously, to specific localized constraints), any content can combine with any speech function. But the more significant aspect of the metafunctional principle, for learning theory, is that in language (as distinct from protolanguage) it is the **combination of the experiential and the interpersonal** that constitutes an act of meaning. All meaning – and hence all learning – is at once both action and reflection.

We shall see later (feature 16) that the metafunctional principle also implies a third component of meaning, simultaneous with the other two.

Feature 10

With a semiotic system of this kind, one that is stratified, having a distinct stratum of lexicogrammar as its core, children now have a range of strategies available for expanding their meaning potential; let us call them ***semogenic strategies***. Such a grammar defines a multidimensional semantic space, highly elastic, which can be expanded (if we follow the usual representational metaphor) horizontally, vertically, or by a combination of the two.

First, children who have construed a system of this kind can refine further the meanings they have already built up, introducing more delicate distinctions within the same topological region. For example, they can interpose 'it may be' between 'it is' and 'it isn't'; or elaborate 'go' into 'walk, jump, run, climb' and so on.

Second, they can extend their meaning potential into new semantic domains, areas of experience or forms of interpersonal relationship that were not previously accessible. (They are now moving around freely on two legs, from home to neighbourhood and from family to peer group.) They will use the grammar to explore any field that interests them, and to establish their own *personae* in interaction with others. Much new vocabulary is added on "vertically" in this way; an example from grammar is the move into logical–semantic relations of 'when' and 'if and 'because' (see Phillips 1985 for a detailed account of the development of comparison and contrast at this stage in children's grammar).

The third strategy is really the intersection of these two, which is why it is a very powerful way of expanding a semiotic system; this is the strategy of dissociating associated variables, or deconstructing and recombining, like demanding iced coffee when the alternatives offered are hot coffee and iced tea. We saw under feature 8 that it was with this strategy that Nigel opened up the road to grammar in the first place. An example from the subsequent phase was his gradual dissociation of polarity from modality: at first certain modals were always positive (for example, *might*), others always negative (for example, *can't*), then at a later stage the two systems became independent.

Feature 11

The last of the effects of grammatical stratification to be mentioned here is the emergence of **information**, that is, imparting meanings that are not already shared by the person addressed. At the beginning of the transition from protolanguage, when children are first using language to annotate and classify experience, the particular experience that is being construed in any utterance is one that the addressee is known to have shared. When the child says *green bus*, the context is 'that's a green bus; you saw it too (and can check my wording)'. What children cannot do at this stage is impart the experience to someone who has not shared it. Parents often notice how, if they ask their child after an outing to "tell Granny what you saw", the child is unable to do this. He may look at Granny and remain tongue-tied, or else turn back and tell the parent what they had seen together. But he cannot tell it to Granny; she had not been there to see (Painter 1989: 52–7).

As they approach the end of the transition, children learn to create information: to use language not just as a rehearsal of shared experience but as a surrogate. They learn to tell people things they do not already know. This is a complex operation, because it involves using language to "give" a commodity that is itself made of language (as distinct from using language to make an offer, where what is being "given" is a non-linguistic commodity, some object or service that is independent of the language being used to offer it). Some children actually construe such "telling" with a different grammar: in my own data, from about 1;9 to 2;4, Nigel consistently distinguished between rehearsing an experience that had been shared and imparting an experience to someone who had not shared it with him (Halliday 1975: 105–6).

Once children can impart information, they also learn to ask for it. The generalized meaning of 'demand', as originally embodied in utterances of the "pragmatic" type, now splits into two: a demand for goods-and-services, which is how it first evolved, and a demand for information. This distinction is grammaticized as the distinction between imperative and interrogative (where previously there had been a single non-declarative form). Of course, children have begun asking questions long before they develop an interrogative category of mood; but only of a limited kind, typically asking what something is called, and with limited potential for dialogic learning. Now for the first time learning becomes a two-way semiotic process, based on the reciprocity of learning and teaching. And just as children are predisposed to learn, so parents, and other "others", are predisposed to teach (cf. Hasan and Cloran 1990, especially Section 5). Lemke (1984) has shown that a theory of learning must take account of the human predisposition to teach – as well as of the teaching function, in a broader sense, that is a feature of the environment as a whole.

Feature 12

Let us return to the notion of a learning gateway. Under feature 7 I referred to what is undoubtedly the single most critical step in learning language, and arguably the most critical step in the entire experience of learning, namely, the move into grammar, and suggested that, since this step involves leaping over many generations of semiotic evolution, children have to find a magic gateway through which to pass.

This move into grammar is a unique event in the life of any individual. But the evidence suggests that the gateway principle has a more general application in language learning. There are numerous smaller steps that have to be taken; and it seems to be the case that, most typically, each critical step in learning language is taken first of all in the interpersonal metafunction – even if its eventual semiotic contexts are going to be primarily experiential.

These terms are being used here in their technical sense in systemic theory, as outlined under feature 9: the interpersonal is the "active" principle, whereby language enacts interpersonal relationships; the experiential is the "reflective" principle, whereby language construes experience. Here, in fact, it would be appropriate to introduce the more general term **ideational**, encompassing the **logical** as well as the **experiential** mode of meaning. It appears that we can recognize a generalized **interpersonal gateway**, whereby new meanings are first construed in interpersonal contexts and only later transferred to ideational ones, experiential and/or logical.

We can identify a number of such "interpersonal occasions" when the meaning potential has been extended in this way, as shown in the following five examples: (1) imparting unknown information, (2) extending into new experiential domains, (3) developing logical–semantic relations, (4) learning abstract terms, and (5) moving into grammatical metaphor.

Imparting unknown information

This is the step discussed in the previous section, that of learning to "tell". Painter (1989: 52) recorded the context in which Hal first learnt to impart unshared experience (that is, give information previously unknown to the listener): she heard a noise from the next room, after which the child ran up to her crying "Bump! Bump!": 'you weren't there to see, but I hurt myself, and I need your sympathy'. We naturally think of information as something inherently experiential, and so, eventually, it will turn out to be, but its origins seem to be interpersonal.

Extending into new experiential domains

Oldenburg-Torr (1990) described how Anna, at 2;0, learnt about the principle of sharing. Hasan (1986) cited part of an extended text in which Kristy's mother talks to Kristy, 3;9, about dying. In the first instance the semantic domain is itself largely interpersonal; in the second, however, it is entirely experiential, but the way in is through interpersonal meanings – Kristy has been upset by observing the death of a moth, and she needs new knowledge for comfort and reassurance.

Developing logical–semantic relations

The logical component of natural languages included, as a central motif, the grammar's construal of logical–semantic relations, among which cause and condition play a critical part. Such logical–semantic relations are part of the ideational grammar, but, again, they are first built up, it seems, in interpersonal contexts. Phillips (1986) showed how Nigel, at 1;7 to 2;7, developed the potential for hypothetical meanings; examples such as *if you walk on the railway line the train would come and go boomp! and knock you over* (you = 'I, me'), *if you* (= 'I') *make it fall on the floor how will Daddy be able to cut it?* are typical of the warnings and threats in which these meanings first appear – modelled for children by adults saying such things to them, like 'don't touch that because it's hot', 'if you don't stop that ...!', and so on. Hasan's (1992) exploration of rationality in everyday talk shows the same principle at work in the age range 3;6 to 4;0.

Learning abstract terms

It seems likely that abstract meanings are first understood when children come to terms with strongly interpersonally oriented expressions such as 'you're a nuisance', 'that's not fair'. Thus, Nigel at 1;10 learnt to use *right* and *wrong* in expressions such as *that not right* (when someone misquoted a verse he knew), *that the wrong way to put your bib* (when it kept falling off the chair), *that not the right record to put on* (when he wanted a different one) (Halliday 1984; see accompanying CD). Cloran's (1989) account of the social construction of gender contains many instances of interpersonal abstractions being foregrounded in discussions between parents and children aged 3;6 to 4;0. The abstract conceptualization of experience is still a source of difficulty at this age, but it is necessary for the move into literacy (cf. feature 18), and once again, the gateway seems to be through the interpersonal metafunction.

Moving into grammatical metaphor

Likewise, when at a later stage children begin to develop the principle of grammatical metaphor, this appears to have been first construed in interpersonal contexts. Children learn to "unpack" expressions such as *if you'd just keep quiet for a moment* (= 'keep quiet!'); compare examples in

Cloran (1989: 135) such as *"I don't think Nana wants her blind cord chewed"*. Butt (1989) showed that rhetorical strategies of this kind may themselves become the object of discussion with the child concerned. Such exchanges probably serve as models for subsequent unpacking of ideational metaphors based on nominalization, for example, *in times of engine failure* 'whenever an engine fails' (see feature 20).

Feature 13

By the **dialectic of system and process** I mean the principle whereby (a) from **acts of meaning** children construe the **system** of language, while at the same time, (b) from the **system** they engender **acts of meaning**. When children learn language, they are simultaneously processing text into language and activating language into text.

The effect of this ongoing dialectic is a kind of leapfrogging movement: sometimes an instance will appear to be extending the system, sometimes to be lagging behind. So, for example, when Nigel at 1;8 built up a story about one of the day's events (a goat in the zoo had tried to eat a plastic lid he was clutching), this was frontier text, going beyond his previous powers of meaning (for example, the clauses *goat try eat lid, goat shouldn't eat lid*). He then routinized this story, repeating it at frequent intervals over a long period with identical phonology and grammar; meanwhile, however, the system had moved on, so that the text had become fossilized at an earlier stage of development (Halliday 1975: 111–12; Chapter 8).

Firth (1950; cf. Pawley 1985) pointed out many years ago how much of what we say as adults is similarly routinized, stored in ready-coded form, as what he called our "lines": it does not emerge each time freshly processed from the system. This is a natural consequence of the way language has been learnt. A language is not a mechanism for producing and understanding text. A language is a system–text continuum, a meaning potential in which ready-coded instances of meaning are complemented by principles for coding what has not been meant before.

Feature 14

The principle of **filtering**, and the "challenge" zone, is that whereby learners decide what is and what is not on their agenda, identifying which aspects of the ongoing phenomena may appropriately be tackled for learning.

Children will attend to text that is ahead of their current semiotic potential, provided it is not too far ahead. They will tackle something that is far enough beyond their reach to be recognized as a challenge, if they have a reasonable chance of succeeding (cf. Vygotsky's "zone of proximal development"). Whatever is too far beyond their powers of meaning they will simply filter out. It is impossible to illustrate this point without locating the example text in the total context of the child's meaning potential at the time; I have given a fairly detailed account of one such example (Chapter 13) in which Nigel, at 1;8, returns to something his father had said to him earlier in the day. They were looking at a museum clock, often seen before, and his father said: "I wonder why that clock's stopped? I've never known it stopped before. Perhaps they're cleaning it, or mending it." Later in the day, Nigel asked: *Why that clock stop?* "I don't know," his father said. "Why do you think?" Nigel said: *Mend it!* It is possible to recognize, in this brief dialogue, a number of features that Nigel has taken up from the earlier discourse and built into his own grammar, and other features, still beyond his reach, that he has effectively filtered out.

Here the learning energy is being concentrated, so to speak, to attack at points that are accessible and ready to yield. The importance of this strategy is that, once a new semiotic quantum is brought into the meaning potential, not only is it available for instantiation in text, but it is also immediately transformed into a resource for further learning.

Feature 15

Learning a semiotic system means learning its options **together with their relative probabilities**, and so building up a quantitative profile of the whole. This concept is familiar in linguistics with regard to word frequencies: it is accepted that speakers have a rather clear sense of the relative frequency of the words in their mother tongue; for example, in English, that *go* is more frequent than *walk*, and *walk*, in its turn, is more frequent than *stroll*. But remarkably little attention has been paid to probabilities in the grammar.

Grammatical probabilities are no less part of the system of a language; and they are more powerful than lexical probabilities because of their greater generality. Children construe both kinds from the very rich evidence they have around them. By five years of age, a child is likely to have heard between half a million and a million clauses, so that, as an inherent aspect of learning the principal grammatical systems of the language, he has learnt the relative probabilities of each of their terms.

An important corollary of this is that children are able to sequence their learning of the grammar, beginning with those options that stand out as being the more frequent. The longitudinal data suggest clearly that this is what they do, and examples will be found throughout.

It is necessary here to distinguish between quantitatively unmarked (more frequent) and formally unmarked (simpler). In most cases, the two coincide; thus in polarity (positive/negative), positive is unmarked in both respects, so if children learn the positive first (as they do) this might have to do as much with its formal simplicity as with its frequency. A case where the two are reversed is the system of mood in questions: here the interrogative is quantitatively unmarked while the declarative is formally unmarked – **as a question** (both on rising tone), *do you like it?* is very much more frequent in adult speech than *you like it?*, as can be attested from Svartvik and Quirk (1980). There is a time, of course, when children have not yet developed the 'question' feature at all; but when they do, they use the interrogative form for some time before introducing the declarative as a marked alternative to it.

It is conceivable that grammatical frequencies in natural languages follow a fairly regular pattern, such that the options in the most general grammatical systems display one or the other of two probability profiles: either equiprobable (for example, number: singular/plural), or noticeably skew, perhaps by about one order of magnitude (for example, polarity: positive/negative; Halliday and James 1993). This would be the quantitative analogue of the distinction between systems having no unmarked term and those having one term unmarked. If this was so, it would have significant consequences for a learner, because a semiotic of this kind would be learner-friendly in a way that one displaying all possible probability profiles would not.

Feature 16

We now return to the metafunctional principle (cf. features 9 and 12) and consider a third metafunction, the ***textual***, which is the resource for creating discourse. I have suggested that learning consists in expanding one's meaning potential, and up to this point, meaning potential has been defined in terms of the ideational (experiential plus logical) and interpersonal metafunctions. The interpersonal component of the grammar is that of "language as action"; this builds up into a rich array of speech functions, modalities, personal forms, keys, and various dimensions of force and attitude by which the speaker enacts immediate social relationships and, more broadly, the whole pattern of the social system with its complexity of roles, statuses, voices, and the like. The experiential component of the grammar is that of "language as reflection"; this expands into a theory of human experience, construing the processes of the "outside world", as well as those of inner consciousness, and (in a related but distinct "logical" component) the logical–semantic relations that may obtain between one process and another. Together these make up a semiotic resource for doing and for understanding **as an integrated mode of activity**.

The intersection of these metafunctions defines a multidimensional semantic space. This becomes operational through being combined with a further component, the ***textual***. From about mid-way through the transition from protolanguage to mother tongue, children begin to create discourse; that is, text that is open-ended and functional in some context of situation. This means that they develop a further set of grammatical resources, learning to structure the clause as a piece of information (a "message"), and also learning to construct semantic relationships above and beyond those construed by the grammatical structure – but still using lexicogrammatical resources: patterns of conjunction, ellipsis, coreference, synonymy, and the like (for an informative case study, see Nelson and Levy 1987). An early example of a child learning to structure the clause as a message is the following from Nigel at 1;8 (Chapter 7). Walking past some road repair work, his mother had exclaimed at the noise made by the pneumatic drill. "Big **noise**", said Nigel when they reached home. He often said this as a comment on one of his own raucous yells. "Who makes a big noise?" his mother asked. But this time Nigel was not talking about himself. "**Drill** make big noise", he said, giving a marked intonation prominence on the appropriate word *drill*.

These resources constitute a distinct metafunctional component, by which the language creates a semiotic world of its own: a parallel universe, or "virtual reality" in modern terms, that exists only at the level of meaning but serves both as means and as model, or metaphor, for the world of action and experience (see Matthiessen 1992 for the source of this important insight). Children learn to navigate in this universe, producing and understanding discourse that "hangs together" (coheres with itself) as well as being contextualized by events on the non-symbolic plane. This step is a prerequisite for construing any kind of theoretical knowledge, because all theories are themselves semiotic constructs, and theory building is a semiotic process.

Feature 17

Related to the last point is the principle of **complementarity** in the grammar. In its ideational metafunction, a natural language is a theory of human experience. But natural language grammars do not present experience in rigid, monosystemic terms. Rather, they frame up a highly elastic space, within which the phenomena of experience can be construed from different angles of vision. I am not talking here about elaborated scientific metalanguages – these do tend to be somewhat rigidified – but about the common-sense grammars of daily life. They embody complementarities of many kinds, contradictory interpretations of some aspect of experience, each illuminating one facet of it, such that the whole is construed in terms of the tension between them. Different languages exploit this potential in different ways; these are some examples drawn from English:

- Number (countable) versus mass (uncountable) as different models of matter and substance (for example, *a stone/stones* vs. *stone*).
- Aspect (manifesting: realis/irrealis) versus tense (eventuating: past/present/future) as different models of time (for example, *doing/to do* vs. *did/does/will do*).
- Transitive (action: +/– goal) versus ergative (realization: +/– agency) as different models of material processes (for example, *they're building/what are they building?* vs. *they're breaking/what's breaking them?*).
- Active versus middle as different models of mental processes (for example, *it didn't strike me* vs. *I didn't notice it*).

In construing these complementarities children come to see their own experience in depth. Note how Nigel (just 7;0) is playing with transitivity in the following.

> "I wish I lived in a caravan with a horse to drive like a pedlar man." Roger thinks it's a horse to **ride**. He thinks you can't drive horses. But horses can drive caravans. He thinks you can't drive horses – well you can't, really; but horses can drive caravans – you know, pull them: you can call that driving, can't you? Roger thinks it's a horse to ride; but pedlars don't ride horses – they ride in the caravans, and the horse drives the caravan.

Nigel is interpreting *with a horse to drive* in the original verse both ergatively 'a horse for me to drive' and transitively 'a horse to drive it'. The grammar of daily life is rich in multiple perspectives of this kind.

Feature 18

The next heading concerns **abstractness**, which has particular significance for the development of **literacy**. In making the transition from protolanguage to mother tongue (cf. feature 8) children learn to generalize: to construe "common" terms, which make reference to a class. This used to be seen as a major problem in learning language; as noted earlier, children have to work at defining class boundaries – but they have no problem with the classifying principle itself, or with that of constructing such classes into taxonomies. It is important to distinguish here, however, between generalization and abstraction, that is, between the opposition of general/specific and that of abstract/concrete. To follow up the example used earlier, *fruit* is more general than *raspberry*, but it is no more abstract. What children cannot cope with, in the early stages of learning language, is abstractness; that is, words of which the referents are abstract entities.

It appears that this threshold is typically crossed at around the age of four or five. As mentioned under feature 12, it may be that the "magic gateway" is via the interpersonal metafunction, with words such as *fair* in *that's not fair*; such words have an evaluative feature that is readily associated with concrete actions and behaviour. For example, at 5;2, Nigel was watching a shadow on the wall, and said "That looks like a person, carrying something which is very precious, the shadow." "Why precious?" his father asked. "Well look," said Nigel, "he's got his hands like this", and he cupped his hands together to make it clear. However that may be, until they learn to exchange abstract meanings, children cannot gain entry to education, because without this one cannot become literate. Writing is learnt as a second-order symbolic system, with symbols standing for other symbols; hence the learner has to recognize two sets of abstract entities, and also the abstract relation between them (for example, *word, letter, stand for, spell*, or analogous terms in other languages and writing systems).

So when children learn to read and write, they have to enter a new phase in their language development, moving on from the general to the abstract. This then enables them to attend to language itself, a necessary condition for becoming a reader and writer (see Rothery 1989). In the process of becoming literate, they learn to reconstitute language itself into a new, more abstract mode.

Feature 19

Reconstituting language means reconstituting reality: children have to reinterpret their experience in the new mode of written language. This is not just a matter of mastering a new medium, one made up of marks on paper or screen instead of sound waves in the air, it is mastering a new form of knowledge: written, educational knowledge as against the spoken knowledge of common sense. Because this knowledge is construed in a different kind of language, building it up involves ***reconstruction*** and ***regression***.

Consider the following example of written knowledge from a primary school science text (Vickery *et al.* 1978):

> Animal protection. Most animals have natural enemies that prey upon them. To survive, these animals need some protection from their enemies. Animals protect themselves in many ways.
> Some animals rely on their great speed to escape from danger ... Animals like snakes and spiders protect themselves with bites and stings, some of which are poisonous. These bites and stings can also help the animals capture food.

Now children know very well by the time they go to school that some animals bite and sting, although they may not think of the stinging ones, mainly insects, as "animals". But they have to learn it over again, in a different context: as systematic, educational knowledge. They may not even recognize that it is something they know already; partly because of the grammatical metaphor in which it is presented (see feature 20), but partly also because they have to reconstrue it in the new medium of writing. They have to be able to recall it, in a purely semiotic context (that is, as classroom knowledge, rather than bush knowledge), and to reproduce it in an acceptable form.

In the first years of schooling these two factors come together: children have to struggle with the written medium, and they have to monitor their own learning process. The result is that when they have to present their knowledge in written form, they typically regress in semiotic age by anything up to three years. A teacher may get a class of seven-year-olds, in preparation for a writing task, talking on some topic with a high level of fluency and common-sense understanding; yet, when they come to write about the topic, their text is in the language of a child of three; for example, *I am a dinosaur. I was hatched out of an egg. Today I was hungry. I ate some leaves.* This kind of semiotic regression may make it easier for children to *reconstrue* their experience in the form of systematic knowledge (Hammond 1990).

Feature 20

But there is yet another reconstruction still to come: that in terms of **grammatical metaphor**. Children know very well, as already remarked, that animals bite and sting. They also know why. Nigel himself said this, quite unprompted, at age 3;5:

> Cats have no else to stop you from trossing them — cats have no other way to stop children from hitting them; so they bite.

Notice how he said it first of all in his own lexicogrammar and then translated it into adult speech. But he could not have expressed it in the way that it is presented in the book. For one thing, children would say *by biting and stinging*, using a verb instead of a noun to name these actions. In the classroom text, meanings that would typically be expressed by verbs, because they are construed as actions, have been represented instead by nouns: *with bites and stings*. The experience has been reconstrued, in metaphorical terms, but with the metaphor being in the grammar, instead of in the vocabulary like metaphor in its traditional sense (Halliday and Martin 1993).

A written text is itself a static object (or has been until the advent of computers): it is language to be processed synoptically. Hence it projects a synoptic perspective onto reality: it tells us to view experience like a text, so to speak. In this way writing changed the analogy between language and other domains of experience; it foregrounded the synoptic aspect, reality as object, rather than the dynamic aspect, reality as process, as the spoken language does. This synoptic perspective is then built into the grammar of the written language, in the form of grammatical metaphor: processes and properties are construed as nouns, instead of as verbs and adjectives. Where the spoken language says *whenever an engine fails, because they can move very fast, ... happens if people smoke more*, the written language writes *in times of engine failure, rely on their great speed, ... is caused by increased smoking*.

Pairs of this kind are not synonymous. Each of the two wordings is representing the same phenomenon, but because the prototypical meaning of a noun is a *thing*, when you construe a process or property as a noun you objectify it: endow it with a kind of "thinginess". It is this particular feature which is at the centre of grammatical metaphor; while numerous other, concomitant changes take place, they combine to form a syndrome around such nominalizations. If there was no natural relationship between the semantics and the grammar, the difference between the two kinds of wording would be purely formal and ritualized; but there **is** such a natural relationship, and so the metaphor brings about a reconstrual of experience, in which reality comes to consist of things rather than doing and happening.

Children apparently do not normally come to grips with grammatical metaphor until they are approaching the age of puberty, say round about the age of nine. We thus have to postulate a three-step model of human semiotic development:

(protolanguage →) generalization → abstractness → metaphor

with a three- to five-year gap between the three post-infancy steps. As grammatical generalization is the key for entering into language, and to systematic common-sense knowledge, and grammatical abstractness is the key for entering into literacy, and to primary educational knowledge, so grammatical metaphor is the key for entering into the next level, that of secondary education, and of knowledge that is discipline-based and technical. As Martin (1990) has shown, specialized technical discourse cannot be created without deploying grammatical metaphor. Such discourse evolved as the language of technology and science, and was moulded by the demands of the physical sciences into its modern form; but today it invades almost every register of adult English that is typically written rather than spoken, especially the institutionalized registers of government, industry, finance, commerce, and the like. We are so familiar with wordings like *prolonged exposure will result in rapid deterioration of the item* (from a care label), *he also credits his former big size with much of his career success* (from a television magazine), that we forget how far these are from the language of daily life – or how far the language of daily life has had to evolve for these to become a part of it.

Feature 21

This leads to the final heading, which is that of *synoptic/dynamic complementarity*. All learning – whether learning **language**, learning **through** language, or learning **about** language – involves learning to understand things in more than one way. In a written culture, in which education is part of life, children learn to construe their experience in two complementary modes: the dynamic mode of the everyday common-sense grammar and the synoptic mode of the elaborated written grammar. Any particular **instance**, of any kind of phenomenon, may be interpreted as some product of the two – once the adolescent has transcended the semiotic barrier between them. Modern scientists have become increasingly dissatisfied with their own predominantly "written", objectified models and often talk of trying to restore the balance, the better to accommodate the dynamic, fluid, and indeterminate aspects of reality (cf. Lemke 1990: especially Chapter 7). They do not know how to do this (I have commented elsewhere on Bohm's 1980 search for the "rheomode"; cf. Halliday and Martin 1993: Chapter 6). One suggestion we might make, as linguists, is that they should go back and replenish their meaning potential at the fountain of everyday speech.

Teachers often have a powerful intuitive understanding that their pupils need to learn multimodally, using a wide variety of linguistic registers: both those of the written language, which locate them in the metaphorical world of things, and those of the spoken language, which relate what they are learning to the everyday world of doing and happening. The one foregrounds structure and stasis, the other foregrounds function and flow. The kind of complementarity that we have already seen in the grammar (cf. feature 17) exists also between these two grammatical modes, the congruent common-sense grammar of daily life and the metaphorical grammar of education and of the workplace. This dynamic/synoptic complementarity adds a final critical dimension to the adolescent learner's semantic space.

Summary

It seems to me that, when we are seeking to understand and to model how children learn, we should not isolate learning **language** (especially using the very inappropriate metaphor of "language acquisition") from all other aspects of learning. When the Language Development Project was launched as a national curriculum project in Australia in 1977, I proposed adopting a threefold perspective of "learning language, learning through language, learning about language". With this formulation I was trying to establish two unifying principles: that we should recognize not only a developmental continuity right through from birth to adult life, with language in home, neighbourhood, primary school, secondary school, and place of work, but also a structural continuity running through all components and processes of learning. The expression "learning through language" was designed to bring out this structural continuity and to locate it with respect to those contexts where the learning is actually focused on language (cf. Christie 1989; Cloran 1989; Rothery 1989).

It should be possible to capture these two continuities in a theory of learning by seeing learning itself as a semiotic process: learning **is learning to mean**, and to expand one's meaning potential. The important initiatives which have taken place in language education in Australia (see, for example, Christie *et al.* 1992) exploited these two dimensions of continuity. The notion of learning as a semiotic process is obviously consistent with verbal learning, which includes all learning in educational contexts and much common-sense learning as well (cf. Hasan 1992). But even non-verbal learning is learning systems of meaning, whether we envisage learning the rights and duties of kinship or learning to swim or play a musical instrument. This is a characteristic of the human species: once having evolved the power of semiosis, we encode all of our experience in semiotic terms.

The prototypical resource for making meaning is language. Language also functions as the "signifier" for higher-level systems of meaning such as scientific theories (Lemke 1990; Martin 1991). In this perspective it seems appropriate that a general theory of learning, interpreted as "learning through language", should be grounded in whatever is known about "learning language". I have tried in this article to set out some of the salient features of what happens when children learn language, which could be taken account of within the framework of a language-based theory of learning.

Summary of features

1 Symbolic Acts ("Acts of Meaning"): starting to construct signs.
2 Iconic (Natural) Symbols: constructing signs that resemble what they mean.
3 Systems of Symbolic Acts: organizing signs into paradigms (protolanguage).
4 The Lexicogrammatical Stratum: constructing a three-level semiotic system (language).
5 Non-Iconic (Conventional) Symbols: taking up signs that do not resemble their meanings.
6 "Trailer" Strategy: anticipating a developmental step that is to come.
7 "Magic Gateway" Strategy: finding a way in to a new activity or to a new understanding.

8   Generalization (Classifying, Taxonomizing): naming classes ("common" terms) and classes of classes.
9   The "Metafunctional" Principle: experiential and interpersonal meanings (from single function utterances, either pragmatic (doing) or mathetic (learning), to multifunctional ones, both experiential and interpersonal).
10 Semogenic Strategies: expanding the meaning potential (refining distinctions, moving into new domains, deconstructing linked variables).
11 Construal of "Information": from rehearsing shared experience to imparting unshared experience.
12 The Interpersonal "Gateway": developing new meanings first in interpersonal contexts.
13 Dialectic of System and Process: constructing language from text, constructing text from language.
14 Filtering and the "Challenge" Zone: rejecting what is out of range and working on what is accessible.
15 Probability – The Quantitative Foundation: construing relative frequencies.
16 Discourse – The Third Metafunction: construing a parallel world of semiosis.
17 Complementarities: construing experience from different angles of vision.
18 Abstraction and Literacy: understanding abstract meanings and moving into the written mode.
19 Reconstruction and Regression: backing off to an earlier semiotic "moment" while reconstruing both content and expression.
20 Grammatical Metaphor (Nominalizing, Technologizing): from common-sense grammar to the grammar of objects and technical hierarchies
21 Synoptic/Dynamic Complementarity: reconciling two semiotic models of human experience.

Chapter Sixteen

GRAMMAR AND THE CONSTRUCTION OF EDUCATIONAL KNOWLEDGE (1999)

1 Introduction

When I first began working in language education with teachers from primary and secondary schools, a couple of questions that were always being raised were: "What is the students' previous experience of language?" "How have they arrived where they are?". These questions become especially pertinent at the two major transition points in their personal history and experience of language: at the beginning of primary school, and at the transition from primary to secondary. So I began investigating language development, to discover something about the linguistic biography of an individual human child. What I will try to say about this is based mainly on four sets of data, direct observations of how certain children were learning their language – or, more accurately, of how they were learning **through** their language; that is, how they were using language, as they learnt it, in learning everything else to do with their world. I shall refer to this learning through language as *construing experience*. The four data sets are my own and those of Clare Painter, Ruqaiya Hasan and Beverly Derewianka. References to the relevant publications are given throughout the text.

2 Early infancy

Learning language is learning how to mean; and learning how to mean

---

First published in *Language Analysis, Description and Pedagogy*, edited by Barry Asker, Ken Hyland and Martha Lam. Hong Kong: Language Centre, Hong Kong University of Science and Technology, 1999, pp. 70–87.

is also learning how to learn. How does a human child set about this process? Let me first take the story right back to early infancy. A baby is aware of what is going on around him. He is also aware of something going on inside himself – his perceptions, and emotions. There is a clash: a tension is set up between the two orders of experience, the outer and the inner, which the infant tries to resolve by developing a new form of behaviour, symbolic behaviour – interacting with others by dint of meaning. The two complementary motifs with which he breaks through the meaning barrier are those of curiosity (the urge to know about the world) and control (the urge to act on the world); and we can hear these first 'utterances' in the form of squeaks and grunts at around 0;4 to 0;7. His meaning potential develops alongside his physical development: these first acts of meaning appear when the baby is beginning to control his own body – rolling over, and sitting up so that he sees the world as landscape.[1]

From here the infant goes on to develop his first system of meanings, typically around age 0;8 to 1;4. This takes the form of a ***protolanguage***, a system of primary consciousness (like the communication systems of other higher animal species) that develops along with locomotion when the child begins to crawl. The protolanguage is organized functionally around these same motifs of curiosity and control ('I think' and 'I want'); each in two orientations, either towards 'me and you' or towards 'others' (the persons and objects around). The central meanings of protolinguistic expressions, if we try to gloss them in adult terms, are something like 'here's you and me together', 'what's happening out there?', 'do for me (for example, play with me)' and 'give me that (thing there)'. The protolanguage is not dependent on adult language, and you cannot tell from the child's sounds and gestures whether he's Chinese or English or what.[2]

The child's protolanguage is a shared language, in the sense that the parents and close siblings understand it, although they respond to the child in their own mother tongue. But the protolanguage has no words, and no grammar; you cannot use it to name things, or to 'make sense' of what it is that you are experiencing. So already while he is using it the child wants to go beyond it, to understand and to master his environment. As he stands up and starts to walk on two feet, he begins the transition to language proper – to the "mother tongue" that he's been hearing all around him; this transition typically takes place from around 1;4 to 2;0. In terms of brain development, this is when primary consciousness is overtaken by higher-order consciousness, something that is unique (as far as we know) to the human species. With a meaning system of this kind, the child can understand, or construe, his experience, and at the same time enact his interpersonal relationships – interact with, and act on, the persons that live in his world.

Let me comment on this notion of **construing experience**. The human species had to make sense of the complex world in which it evolved: to classify, or group into categories, the objects and events within its awareness. Such categories are not 'given' to us by our senses; they have to be construed, and it was in the process of construing human experience that language evolved. But it is construed as experience which is shared: language is always simultaneously both construing experience and enacting the social process. With language, we understand and we act: understand the world, and act on the other people in it (you cannot use symbols to act directly on things!). And each human individual comes to develop this same resource. For the child at this age, before two years old, experience is always that which is shared by the person he is talking to; he cannot yet use language to inform, only to rehearse what they – he and his interlocutor – are both aware of. He has yet to learn that you can use language in order to give information. When he has mastered that very difficult principle (and like most major steps in language learning, it is mastered through situations of strong emotional pressure – pain, distress, anxiety), he has effectively made the transition out of infancy into the post-infancy mode of meaning, the "mother tongue" with which he will achieve his knowledge and his power.

Thus a language – every human language – is a resource for understanding and for acting: construing experience, and enacting social relationships. What enables a language to do both these things (and to do them both at once) is that it has a grammar: systems of words and grammatical features, realized as hierarchies of structures. In what follows I will try to bring out some of the salient aspects of the way children come to master language: foregrounding the experiential component, because that is what dominates in educational learning, but taking note of the interpersonal wherever it stands out (Chapter 15).

3 First step

The first step in construing experience is naming things. "Proper names", like *Mummy* or *Daddy*, are transitional, since they name individuals not classes; but as soon as the child uses "common names", like *bus, green, run*, he has started categorizing – these are names of classes. Very soon, children learn a grammar for assigning things to classes: 'that's a bus', 'that's green', and so on. They then try to fit classes into other classes – to create taxonomies; and they look for superordinate terms, like *animal* to include both *cats* and *dogs*. They are thinking analogically, using the strategies of comparing and contrasting (where "comparing" means finding likenesses among things that are different, and "contrasting" means finding differences among things that are alike).

Joy Phillips (1985) has worked out a typical pattern of the development of comparison and contrast from an intensive study of Nigel's language from 1;6 onwards; I will draw on her account and present it as a plausible general picture. Like almost all new developments, comparing begins in contexts of action: *more* ...! 'I want some more (of the same thing)', *again!* 'do that (same thing) again'. This is a way of classifying by simple addition; it is then transferred from contexts of action to contexts of understanding, with expressions like *another* or the number *two: another bus, two buses*. Soon the child moves on to expressing comparison and contrast explicitly, distinguishing two degrees of each, one absolute ('sameness' and 'opposition'), one relative ('likeness' and 'difference'); and these are applied to things, to qualities and to processes (actions and events), for example (JP = Phillips 1985; LN = Halliday 1984; CP = Painter 1984. Numbers refer to pages.)

1. [N 1;10] Cello like big big violin (JP 231)
2. [N 1;10] Our train was coming and the other train was going (JP 247)
3. [N 1;10] That wall too high, but that wall not too high (JP 243)

Table 1 shows the order in which Nigel introduced these different types of comparison and contrast; including comparison by evaluation, with 'too ...', and then 'not ... enough', as the generalizing concepts.

Thus comparing and contrasting are strategies for categorizing experience. They extend the power of simple naming so that every phenomenon has a place in the total scheme of things. But naming is only one part of the total meaning potential. Names are only potent because they enter in as **elements** of larger constructions of experience, namely **figures**, like *train go on railway line* or *that tree got no leaf on*; and figures, in turn, can be construed into logical **sequences**. Grammatically, the elements (names) are **words** – or rather, **word groups**, expanded

Table 1 One child's way into comparing and contrasting (Phillips 1985)

1;6–1;7½	1;7½–1;9	1;9–1;10½	1;10½–2;0	2;0–2;6
'SAMENESS' of object →	of process →	of attribute, circumstance, time		
		'SIMILARITY' of object →	of process, circumstance	
	'EVALUATION' 'excessive'	⟶	'satisfactory', 'inappropriate', 'appropriate'	'insufficient'
'ADDITION' of object ⟶	⟶	of process →	of attribute	
	'OPPOSITION' of attribute →	of object, process →	of circumstance →	of condition
	'DIFFERENCE' of object, attribute, person →	of circumstance, time	⟶	of condition, real vs. hypothetical time

from nouns (for things: persons, animals and objects) and from verbs (for processes: actions, events, etc.). Since things, especially man-made things, are highly organized, the **nominal groups** soon get very long, for example:

4. [N 1;11] That big old Russian steam train with a cowcatcher (LN 85)

Processes (**verbal groups**) are less highly organized; but they are located somewhere in time–space, and are classified into different types, or domains of experience: those of 'outer' experience (doing and happening), those of consciousness ('inner' experience: sensing and saying), and those of existence and order (being and having). The figures are grammatical **clauses**; and the sequences are **clause complexes** (compound, complex, and compound–complex sentences). The grammar differs, of course, from language to language; but these are the sorts of principles that languages generally follow.

What is the central thread, the directive that guides children's explorations as they build up these rich resources? It is often said, after Piaget, that the child's mental world starts off as egocentric, and then gradually develops towards a sociocentric model. But when we look at the child's development linguistically we can see that this is not quite right. The centre of meaning is not 'me', it is 'me-and-you'; or, more explicitly, it is 'you-and-me, here, now' – what we call the *deictic centre* from which the child takes his perspective in construing experience. The construction of meaning is dialogic: it is the shared construction of experience which is also shared. As the child learns, he moves out of this complex centre in various directions: from 'now' to the past and the future, to all times (including imaginary time); from 'here' to there and everywhere (again, to places that exist in imagination); and from 'you-and-me' as vantage point – what we can see, what we know and think – to the vantage point of other parties. It is these moves outwards from the deictic centre that enable the child to shift in orientation between the interpersonal and the experiential, and later on between the common-sense knowledge of daily life and the systematic educational knowledge of the school.

4 From two to five

At around the age of two years, children have made the transition into the mother tongue. (Physically, they can not only walk and run, hop, skip and jump, but they can also sit on wheeled vehicles and propel themselves along the ground.) They have mastered the basic lexicogrammatical resources: the clause, with some systems of transitivity, of mood, and of thematic (or rhetorical) organization; the clause complex; and a wide variety of phrases and groups. For the next phase I shall draw on Clare Painter's findings in her study of Hal's (Painter 1984) and, more especially, Stephen's (Painter 1993, 1996) learning experiences, again generalizing from these as an account of what typically happens. During the third year of life, children like to organize 'things' into common-sense taxonomies, based on the principles of hyponymy ('one thing is a **kind** of another') and meronymy ('one thing is a **part** of another'); they have learnt to make class membership explicit, by using a figure of 'being' (grammatically, a relational clause, for example, *is a monkey an animal?*), but without making explicit the shared features by which the classes are defined. (Assignment to a class may, of course, conflict with what they will learn later on; at this early stage, a whale is likely to be a fish and spider an insect, while neither fishes nor insects will be accepted into the class of animals.) Children at this age will talk about what they themselves do, and what they see happening or being done by others, construing these actions and events as figures – grammatically, as clausal configurations of a process, participants, and circumstances; and they will make temporal and causal–conditional links between one such figure and another – typically to make predictions associated with threats, warnings and promises, or to seek permission or explanation of a command, for example:

5. [N 1;11] If there a lion hiding in the long grass and then you must not bump your head! (LN 102) [playing 'lions' under the table]
6. [N 2;2] If you [= 'I'] make it fall on the floor how will Daddy be able to cut it? (LN 143)
7. [N 2;5] No you can't eat the tomatoes when they're green. But you can eat the chives when they're green. (JP 260)
8. [S 2;8] We don't want a big dog, 'cause he would lick on my tongue. (CP 285)

In other words, these logical sequences are first construed in contexts of interpersonal negotiation; but they drift towards the experiential (that is, towards generalized reasoning about experience) through intermediate cases where the consequences are still likely to be dire, for example, *won't touch it 'cause it might sting you*. It is in this period that children start asking 'why?' questions, demanding to be given a reason; again these are, as a rule, interpersonally oriented to begin with – when they are told to do something, or refused permission to do what they want, for example:

9. [S 2;10] MOTHER: You can't have chips every day.
            STEPHEN: Why can't we have chips?
            MOTHER: Because it's not good for you. ... I haven't got any chips.
            STEPHEN: Why? No, but at the chip shop. (CP 278)

These also shift towards the experiential, when they are arguing or challenging a generalization (for example, *why don't animals wear clothes?*). They already talk about all the major process types (doing and happening, sensing, saying, being and having); but those of sensing (inner experience) are largely confined to 'me' and 'you' as the Senser (*I think, I wonder, do you know?*, etc.), and they function more as modalities (opinions attached to some other propositions) than as propositions in their own right. And while children of this age often report what they have heard someone say, they seldom impute it to a Sayer – being told something is just an alternative way of observing it oneself.

In the fourth year of life (age three), sayings come to be construed in the prototypical adult fashion: they are **projected** through an explicit Sayer, for example:

10. [S 3;9] Only animals bite people because they don't know. [Mother: What don't they know?] Because the teacher says 'You don't bite'. (CP 236)

This means that they can be questioned and disbelieved; and also that the child's own sayings can be used to 'trick' others – raising the familiar moral problem of the difference between pretending and lying! Figures of saying are used as requests for information ('you tell me ...'); but also, the Sayer can now be any informational source, for example, *the book says* ... This last step is an essential precondition for learning to read and write; it allows for 'what does that say?', referring to a piece of written text, 'that letter says ...' and so on. Processes of sensing now come to be imputed to persons other than 'you' and 'me'; this seems to come about through the intermediary of behavioural processes which are observable manifestations of sensing, like *watch* and *think*, for example, *don't interrupt Mummy; she's thinking*. Children also learn at this stage that their own observations are fallible: what you see and hear are not always reliable as sources of knowledge.

Conditionals (*if*), causals (*because, so*) and 'why?' questions now come to be used for exchanging information, not just for negotiating action; and by the same token they become fully monologic, developing from '(a) – Why? – Because (x)' [two speakers], via '(a), because (x)' [one speaker, reason added], to '(x), so (a)' [one speaker, cause given first]. Children of this age increasingly appeal to facts in giving reasons: past events, or else general properties '(a) hasn't got this attribute, so (a) doesn't do (x), whereas (b) does'; and such generalized causes may not be directly observable, hence there can be purely imaginative reasoning as in:

11. [S 3;6] If a dragon bites you your bones will go crunch; if you fall down [Mother: What will happen?] you'll just hurt yourself (CP 310)

Likewise, time is also extended, beyond 'past' and 'future', to include 'at all times (generalized)' and hence 'hypothetical (alternative or imaginary) time'. Time and cause come together when prior causes are used to explain observed states; and here children develop a clear sense of a norm, what generally is (and so should always be) the case – and what, by contrast, is anomalous and exceptional, for example:

12. [S 3.8] I was standing there and the water was getting hot and [indignantly] it didn't get hot! (CP 181)

As far as the categories of element are concerned, children now explicitly work from a series of instances to a class, and formulate criteria of class membership so that they can use them to explore further; and they try to fill out their taxonomies by seeking superordinate terms (compare Stephen's *What's a bus?* meaning 'what higher category does it belong to?').[3]

Ruqaiya Hasan and her colleagues conducted an intensive study of conversational interactions between children within this age group (all between 3;6 and 4;0) and their mothers, all in real-life, natural settings in the home (Hasan 1988, 1991, 1992; Hasan and Cloran 1990). From a total of 24 such mother–child dyads, they collected altogether over 100 hours of talk; of this, they analysed 45 minutes of conversation from each dyad, amounting to nearly a thousand clauses from each. Their aim was to find out to what extent, and in what ways, the spontaneous dialogue that went on inside the family was preparing children for education in school. The researchers analysed the mothers' speech as well as that of the children, so taking account of what the children heard as well as what they said. One of the studies deriving from this body of data concerned questions and answers. Altogether the mothers asked just over two thousand questions, the children about two-thirds this total; the children were thus fully aware of how questions functioned as a mode of learning, and their own questions and answers were modelled on those of their mothers. This modelling became clear because there turned out to be significant differences within the mothers between two groups, in the kinds of questions they asked and the kinds of answers they gave; and the children followed the pattern of their own mothers in each case. Thus, one group of mothers prefaced a lot of their questions by clauses of projection, like *I'm going to ask her, did Dad say, do you remember I told you*, and qualified them with an added feature such as a temporal clause, whereas they asked very few questions of the type that made assumptions about what 'ought to be' or 'was sure to be' the case; their answers were generally appropriate to the question, and often contained further elaboration where they thought it relevant. With the other group of mothers, the pattern was reversed. And the same tendencies were found in each group of the children.

Hasan also studied the modes of reasoning that were used by the same mothers and their children; and here likewise the children modelled their reasoning on that of the mothers. All mothers gave reasons on many occasions, particularly when the children challenged what they were being told to do, or not to do; and the reasoning formed an ordered chain which Hasan characterized as 'claim + reason + principle + grounding', of which the first two were present in every instance. Beyond that, however, there was variation; and here again the mothers tended to fall into two groups: one group used longer chains of reasoning, typically adding elaborations at various points, and they grounded their reasoning in some physical (in Hasan's term, 'logical') necessity; the other group used shorter chains, with less elaboration, and grounded their reasons in what she refers to as a 'social' necessity ('it's the law', 'it's what everyone does'), or else gave no grounding other than 'my authority'. (With the latter group, as Hasan points out, the reasoning forms part of a more visible system of control.) Again, the children favoured the patterns that were favoured by their mothers. The point that emerges from these studies is that children of this age group clearly know how to use language to learn – although they have different access to knowledge, depending on their different modes of reasoning and of asking (and answering) questions.

In the fifth year of their lives (age four), children are becoming aware of different types of text, and the fact that these text types have names (they have already met "stories", "rhymes", "jokes", "riddles" and so on). And this is one aspect of what is, from an educational point of view, the most critical feature of this age group: for the first time they are including abstract 'things', and institutions, among the categories of their experience (such as *size, speed, electricity, the Council*); critical because they must recognize such things, and admit them as participants in figures, if they are to succeed in learning to read and write, since they will have to be aware of features of language which are precisely of his abstract kind, like *writing, spelling, sound* (in speech), *sentence* and so on. They also become aware, at this stage, of both themselves and others as 'knowers', particularly with reference to the kind of 'uncommon-sense' knowledge that these abstract entities embody (where, again, symbols appear as a central category); for example:

13. [S 4;4] I know how to do an 's' now. I knew all the time how you do an 's' ... except when I was three. (CP 243)

In the light of this, they now like to check on the sources of their knowledge, for example by referring to earlier texts (*I didn't know ...*, *you said ...*); and also on the reality of phenomena that are presented to them as images, such as photographs and pictures on television. They want to know how things come to be known; and how it is that something that is not factual, or not real, can be made to seem so, for example:

14. [S 4;3] Is there such thing as ghosts? [Mother: No.] But a person can dress up as a ghost. [Mother: Yes] How can you be dressed up as a ghost if there's no such thing as a ghost? (CP 248)

All persons are now recongnized as conscious beings, so one can discuss what they see and feel, what they know and what they think. Reasoning about causes and conditions can now involve processes of all types, and can be entirely distanced from the deictic centre; Painter (1993) refers to "factual generalization as an obligatory conclusion from known facts", and cites examples of reasoning such as 'cars go faster than bikes; vans are as powerful as cars; so vans can go faster than bikes'. So children of this age can seek explanation through reasoning, and verify conclusions from premises; and now for the first time they start to use **internal** causal relations, those of evidence and proof ('I know this is so, because ...'), and can switch their perspective from themselves to that of other conscious beings ('he doesn't know ...'). In other words, at age four children can construe processes of knowing and learning, the participants that engage in these processes (including those of an abstract kind), and the 'facts' that enter in as reasons or as conclusions. It is not surprising, therefore, that this is the moment when we decide they are ready for school – one of the few things on which all literate cultures seem to agree!

5 Learning in school

All these resources are in place – or may be in place – when the child is ready to enter primary school, to be initiated into the magic of the written word and embark on the transition from common-sense knowledge to educational knowledge. The critical moves that the child has made, in the years since starting on the mother tongue, can perhaps be summed up as follows:

- from interpersonal orientation (language as action) to include experiential orientation (language as understanding)

- from dialogic mode to include monologic mode
- from the deictic centre ('you-and-me, here, now') outwards to include 'other persons and objects', 'other times', 'other places'
- from entities that are concrete and perceptual to include entities that are institutional or abstract
- from simple categories ('common' terms) to include taxonomies of categories
- from generalization to include prediction, reasoning and explanation.

These are preconditions for learning to read and write and for acquiring systematic knowledge under instruction.

Children have been using language to construe experience ever since some time during the second year of life. The primary school will assume that they can learn by using language, and that they can do this at a fairly high level of understanding. The teachers will expect them to master abstract terms organized into systematic, mutually defining taxonomies: exact ones for numeracy, rather fuzzy ones for literacy. They will expect them to master fairly strict (if often implicit) generic structures for different kinds of text: for stories, reports, expositions and other classroom varieties. They will expect them to process new knowledge that comes to them in written form; and to construe new meanings directly in experiential terms, without going through an interpersonal staging first. And sooner or later they will expect them to handle metaphor.

This last item, metaphor, is the most difficult hurdle of all. Let me try to suggest what it involves. The way children learn their mother tongue is the way that language itself first evolved. Grammar evolved, in one of its aspects, in the construing of human experience; the framework of clauses, clause complexes, and groups of words sorted out the phenomena of experience into figures, with the figures organized into sequences and made up of various kinds of elements. The categories of verbal, nominal and other types of group or phrase sorted out the elements, in turn, into processes, participants in these processes, and various kinds of circumstantial element like times and places. The details of the grammar vary, of course, from language to language, with considerable differences between major cultural types; but the principles are general to all. Let me refer to this pattern of construal as the *congruent* pattern.

However, as technology advances, knowledge comes to be restructured; so experience is **reconstrued** by the grammar in significantly different ways. When the human condition was materially altered with the technology of the iron age, it also underwent certain semiotic transformations. In particular, new resources evolved which gave theoretical status and power to certain types of category: (1) properties of substances, like 'heat', 'density', 'porousness'; (2) general processes, like 'motion', 'impact', 'fusion'; (3) measurements, like 'length', 'distance', 'speed'; (4) complex relational concepts like 'sum', 'ratio', 'angle'. Many of the terms for these had started out as adjectives or verbs: *length* as *how long* (something is), *motion* as *how* (something) *moves*; but they typically ended up as nouns, taking on the category meaning that was already associated with a noun, namely 'thingness'. When this happens, a new metaphorical entity has been created, one that is **both** thing **and** quality or process at one and the same time.

These words are what we call "technical terms". Over the course of time, they lose their metaphorical quality (they become "dead metaphors", in the terminology of rhetoric); but they remain as abstract theoretical concepts. You can see something moving; you can perhaps see **that** it is moving; but you cannot see motion, as such. Similarly you can't perceive speed, density, ratio. The educational discourse of the primary school contains a lot of these abstract technical terms. As we have seen, children come to master such elements at the age of four or five, though they still cause them a certain amount of difficulty. What they cannot master at this age, but will need when they get into secondary school, is the kind of grammatical metaphor that is not "dead" – that is still alive, and retains its metaphorical character. This is the sort of language that we find in science textbooks, for example:

15. Accessiblity has changed since settlements began. . . . The arrival of the railway reduced the journey time to less than one day.

I will come back to these in a final section; let me first, however, say a little about the situation where a second language is involved.

Even if the language used in school is their mother tongue, children have a lot of new language to learn; and in many parts of the world they have to move into a new language altogether.[4] (The old distinction between "second language" and "foreign language" was useful here. A second language is one which you are going to use to construe new knowledge; a foreign language is one into which you simply take over knowledge you already have – you may have to modify it to fit in with the grammar, but you are not using the language to learn new things.) For a second-language teacher at the primary level, Phillips (1985) stresses four aspects of preschool language development that are particularly relevant.

1 Children's learning strategies, such as comparing and contrasting, predicting from generalization, etc., are important for the *organization of discourse*; they can be taught not as isolated grammatical patterns but as the means of realizing semantic principles which the children already control – so that they are going from the known (the meanings) to the unknown (the grammar) rather than the other way round.
2 These same strategies have an important place in real-life *negotiations and decisions*, so such activities can be built in to their language learning tasks.
3 These strategies are put in place in the first language on certain *ordering principles*; for example, positive comes before negative ('more than' before 'less than', 'too ...' before 'not ... enough'); similarity and difference (that is, partial likeness and unlikeness) have more general application than sameness and opposition (that is, absolute likeness and unlikeness).
4 The semantic categories involved are *systemic*: that is, the meanings are defined both by what they are and by what they are not (what they contrast with); this is a fundamental language learning strategy which can be closely modelled on the way children learn their mother tongue.

When they get to the upper primary classes, children embark on yet another reconstrual of experience, in preparation for the way in which learning is organized at the secondary level. They encounter passages like the following:

16. Try to explain your observations by using your hypothesis about the movement of water through plant walls.

Mastering this kind of language is the final phase of children's language development – the move out of childhood into, and through, adolescence.

6 Into the secondary school

As students at the secondary level, they will be exploring a different structure of knowledge, the specialized knowledge structure of the disciplines. The discourse becomes highly technical, with more layers of abstraction: in the case of the humanities, often with associated value judgements; and in the case of the sciences, including the technological disciplines and also mathematics, more reliance on grammatical metaphor. This technical language does not consist solely of technical *terms*; rather, whole figures and sequences are reconstrued in an entirely new mode of meaning. (See examples at the end of this chapter.) It is a characteristic of this mode of construal that the wording can be 'unpacked' – one can take the metaphor out, because it is still a living metaphor. To show what this means, I have given a congruent 'translation' of each of the passages cited. Note that each one embodies some logical relation between happenings, such as time or cause.

Let me summarize the transformations that take place between the congruent and the metaphorical variants. Here is the congruent pattern (Figure 1):

Semantic units	Grammatical units	Types of elements	Classes of head word
sequence →	clause complex	relator	→ conjunction
figure →	clause	process	→ verb
element →	word group	quality	→ adjective
		thing	→ noun

Figure 1   Congruent pattern

(The directed arrow means 'is construed by'.) In the metaphorical variant, the typical pattern of construal is as follows (Figure 2):

Semantic units	Grammatical units	Types of elements	Classes of head word
sequence	clause complex	relator	conjunction
figure	clause	process	verb
element	word group	quality	adjective
	word/part of group	thing	noun

Figure 2   A typical pattern of construal in the metaphorical variant

In other words, the whole of the grammar has taken on a technical character, through the processes of grammatical metaphor (Halliday

1985, 1998; Halliday and Martin 1993; see also Volume 5, *The Language of Science*).

This requires a certain degree of maturity. Just as, in general, children are not able to master abstract entities until age four or five, so they are not able to master metaphorical modes of construal until around age eight or nine. This highly complex linguistic resource is typically being developed throughout the middle years of schooling, when they are about 9 to 13 years of age. So just as there is a good reason for starting primary school when they do, so also there is a good reason for moving up to the secondary level when they do, approximately six years later. Beverly Derewianka (1995) has provided a detailed account of one child's linguistic development from childhood to adolescence, with the emergence of grammatical metaphor as the main focus of attention. Since grammatical metaphor is largely associated with the written mode, she has used her subject's writing, and the issues that arose in the course of his reading and writing in school, as the main source for her findings. It is not until the age of nine that.the child is able to control the experiential patterns of grammatical metaphor, especially the nominalizing metaphors (processes and qualities construed as nouns) which are the mainstay of the metaphoric shift. Derewianka brings out the various 'precursors' of grammatical metaphor that pave the way: forms of word-play which explore the frontier between semantics and grammar; lexical forms of metaphor; rank shift and class shift as devices in the grammar; the 'faded metaphors' of the everyday spoken language; and the kinds of abstract technical terms that I have already discussed. All these are prior resources that the child has accumulated along the way; so that he readily becomes aware of grammatical metaphor as a phenomenon of adult language, and consciously tries to engage with it in some of his writing tasks.

Teachers of the upper primary and lower secondary classes are well aware of the problem that children have with the transition from primary to secondary education. My point is that these are linguistic problems: problems of meaning, and of learning how to mean in new ways that go with technical, discipline-based knowledge.[5] An important resource for the learner is to be able to range over the full variety of the registers available for learning: both written sources (textbooks; teachers' notes; library books; students' writing, both notes and essays, reports, etc.; and non-verbal semiotics such as maps, charts and diagrams) and spoken sources (teachers' lecturing; teacher–student talk; students' talk among themselves, both in and out of class; radio and television lessons, if available; even students' talk with parents and siblings at homework time). This familiarity with different registers helps them to switch between more and less metaphorical variants of the subject language. In a multilingual situation, of course, it is an advantage if they can also switch between the two languages; in many cases there is likely to be some measure of functional complementarity between them.

It is sometimes thought that linguistic features of the kind I have been talking about under the heading of ***grammatical metaphor*** are specifically features of English, and perhaps other languages besides; but that Chinese is somehow different. Chinese is, of course, different from English in many respects, but not in this respect. It may be that these nominalized forms have not penetrated so far into other, more informal registers of Chinese as they have done in English;[6] but as far as Chinese science is concerned, it has at least as much grammatical metaphor as English, and the distance between the discourses of common-sense knowledge and those of educational knowledge is every bit as great. Here is an example from a Chinese secondary science textbook:

17. 兩電子的靜電斥力勢能爲正值，且與兩者的間距成反比．

['The electrostatic repulsion potential of two electrons is a positive value, and is in inverse proportion to the distance between them.']

7 Conclusion

I think that some awareness of the processes of language development, from infancy right through to the end of schooling, is a valuable resource for teachers at any level. ***Common-sense*** knowledge is **largely** construed in language, as children transform their experience into meaning using the system that their forebears evolved in just this same context. ***Educational*** knowledge is **almost entirely** construed in language; even when it is presented in other forms, like scientific diagrams or mathematical formulas, these are given verbal equivalents during the learning process. In a bilingual situation, there may be a clear functional complementarity between the languages – first language in home and neighbourhood, interpersonally oriented; second language in school, experientially oriented; but nowadays there is likely to be rather more interpenetration between the two. It is not clear (to me, at least) what kind of complementarity there will be between Chinese and

English (or between Cantonese and Mandarin) in Hong Kong at any time in the future. But this is perhaps all the more reason for paying attention to the language of education, so that in a period of uncertainty and change one has some idea of what the problems – and the possibilities – really are.

I also think (more controversially, perhaps) that it is a source of great strength for the students themselves to learn about the **language** of the subjects that they are studying. Australian experience is very convincing on this point.[7] Students learn about variation in register, and they learn the structures of the particular genres that they are reading and that they are being required to write. Then through this they learn about the grammar: the types of construction that go with particular parts of the discourse – not only that mathematics has a different grammar from science but that, within science, explanations have a different grammar from descriptions of experiments. Thus they learn about language in the context of using language to learn, not as an isolated exercise the way it usually is. And at a higher level, they can reflect on the languages of learning: on how they relate (or fail to relate) to the language of everyday life, and how they may need to be modified for the educated democratic societies of the twenty-first century.

Examples

15. (lower secondary text)
    Accessibility has changed since settlements began at Boulder.... The time taken to travel 100 kilometres today is much less than it was one hundred ... years ago. The first settlers who came to Boulder in 1858 made difficult journeys over rough tracks. A speed of 4 kilometres per hour (kph) would have been good travelling by horse-drawn wagon. ... Stage coaches later made the journey at least four times faster. The arrival of the railway reduced the journey time to less than one day.

    (congruent 'translation' of 15)
    Places can be reached more easily now than when people first began settling at Boulder.... One can travel 100 kilometres much more quickly today than one hundred ... years ago. The first settlers who came to Boulder in 1958 travelled with difficulty over rough tracks. If you travelled 4 kilometres in an hour by horse-drawn wagon it would have been good. Stage coaches later travelled (?there/that far)

at least four times faster. When the railway arrived it became possible to reach there in less than one day.

16. (upper primary text)
    Here is an experiment to set up. This experiment will let you make some more observations about the direction in which water moves through a thin plant wall. ... In your note book, record your observations and try to explain them. Then try to explain your observations by using your hypothesis about the movement of water through plant walls.

    (congruent 'translation' of 16)
    Here is an experiment to set up. If you do this experiment you will be able to make some more observations about which way water moves through a thin plant wall. In your notebook, record your observations and try to explain them. Then try to explain your observations by using your hypothesis about how water moves through plant walls.
    (*Note*: I have treated *experiment*, *observation* and *hypothesis* as technical terms.)

Notes

1. It should be stressed that all references to the age at which children develop their linguistic resources are merely approximations. Children vary greatly in the age at which they take any particular step.
2. Compare Qiu Shijin's study of the early language development of children growing up in families speaking the dialect of Shanghai (Qiu 1985).
3. There is a problem with this question in English, since there is no everyday word for 'wheeled vehicle'. For a Chinese child, the answer is clear: it's a *che*!
4. If they live in cities, or in a technically advanced countryside, they will have embarked on this kind of knowledge already in the home and in the neighbourhood. But it is often those who have not had this experience who also have to move into a second language.
5. During the present century the theoretical discourses of the sciences and mathematics have been gradually penetrating into the secondary school, working their way down from the top; so that today pupils in years 11 to 12 are often studying things that would have been undergraduate or even postgraduate studies two or three generations ago.
6. Answering a query about how large or small some particular products are, an English-speaking shopkeeper might say "They come in all sizes";

whereas one speaking Chinese might answer "大的小的都有" [there are bigger ones and smaller ones].
7. See, for example, Hasan and Martin (1989); Williams (1995); Martin (1998), and references therein.

BIBLIOGRAPHY

Allerton, D. J., Carney, E. and Holdcroft, D. (eds) (1979) *Function and Context in Linguistic Analysis: Essays Offered to William Haas*. Cambridge: Cambridge University Press.
Ariès, P. (1962) *Centuries of Childhood*. London: Cape.
Bar-Adon, A. and Leopold, W. F. (eds) (1971) *Child Language: A Book of Readings*. Englewood Cliffs, NJ: Prentice-Hall.
Bateson, M. C. (1975) 'Mother-infant exchange: the epigenesis of conversational interaction', in D. Aaronson and R. W. Rieber (eds), *Developmental Psycholinguistics and Communication Disorders*. New York (Annals of the New York Academy of Sciences 163).
Bateson, M. C. (1979) 'The epigenesis of conversational interaction, a personal account of research devlopment', in M. Bullowa (ed.), 1979.
Berger, P. L. and Kellner, H. (1970) 'Marriage and the construction of reality', in H. P. Dreitzel (ed.), *Recent Sociology. II: Patterns of Communicative Behaviour*. New York: Macmillan.
Berger, P. L. and Luckmann, T. (1966) *The Social Construction of Reality: A Treatise in the Sociology of Knowledge*. London: Allen Lane (Penguin Press).
Bernstein, B. (1970) 'A critique of the concept "compensatory education"', in S. Williams (ed.), *Language and Poverty: Perspectives on a Theme*. Madison: University of Wisconsin Press.
Bernstein, B. (1971) *Class, Codes and Control*, Vol. 1: Theoretical Studies Towards a Sociology of Language. London: Routledge and Kegan Paul (Primary Socialization, Language and Education).
Bever, T. G. (1970) 'The cognitive basis of linguistic structure', in J. R. Hayes (ed.), *Cognition and the Development of Language*. New York: Wiley.
Bloom, L. (1970) *Language Development: Form and Function in Emerging Grammars*. Cambridge, MA: MIT Press.
Bloom, L. (1975) 'Language development review', in F. Horowitz (ed.), *Review of Child Development Research*, vol. 4. Chicago: University of Chicago Press.
Bowerman, M. (1973) *Learning to Talk: A Cross-linguistic Study of Early Syntactic Development, with Special Reference to Finnish*. Cambridge: Cambridge University Press.

Braine, M. D. S. (1963) 'The ontogeny of English phrase structure: the first phase', *Language* 39.

Braine, M. D. S. (1971) 'The acquisition of language in infant and child', in C. E. Reed (ed.), *The Learning of Language*. New York: Appleton.

Brazelton, T. B. (1979) 'Evidence of communication during neonatal behavioral assessment', in M. Bullowa (ed.),.

Britton, J. N. (1970) *Language and Learning*. London: Allen Lane (Penguin).

Brown, R. (1973) *A First Language: The Early Stages*. Cambridge, MA: Harvard University Press.

Bruner, J. (1975) 'The ontogenesis of speech acts', *Journal of Child Language* 2.

Bruner, J. S. (1977) 'Early social interaction and language acquisition', in H. R. Shaffer (ed.), *Studies in Mother-Infant Interaction*. London: Academic Press.

Bühler, K. (1934) *Sprachtheorie: die Darstellungsfunktion der Sprache*. Jena: Fischer.

Bullowa, M. (1979a) 'Infants as conversational partners', in T. Myers (ed.), *The Development of Conversation and Discourse*. Edinburgh.

Bullowa, M. (1979b) 'Prelinguistic communication: a field for scientific research', in M. Bullowa (ed.),.

Bullowa, M. (ed.) (1979) *Before Speech: The Beginning of Interpersonal Communication*. Cambridge: Cambridge University Press.

Butt, D. G. (1989) 'The object of language', in R. Hasan and J. R. Martin (eds), 1989.

Carter, A. (1978a) 'The development of systematic vocalizations prior to words', in N. Waterson and C. E. Snow (eds), 1978.

Carter, A. L. (1978b) 'From sensori-motor vocalization to words: a case study of the evolution of attention-directing communication in the first year', in A. Lock (ed.), 1978.

Christie, F. (1989) 'Language development in education', in R. Hasan and J. R. Martin (eds), 1989.

Christie, F., Gray, B., Gray, P., Macken, M., Martin, J. and Rothery, J. (1992) *Exploring Explanations: Teacher's Book; Students' Books Levels 1–4*. Sydney: Harcourt Brace Jovanovich (Language: A Resource for Meaning).

Cloran, C. (1989) 'Learning through language: the social construction of gender', in R. Hasan and J. R. Martin (eds), 1989.

Condon, W. S. (1979) 'Neonatal entrainment and enculturation', in M. Bullowa (ed.), 1979.

Condon, W. S. and Sander, L. W. (1974) 'Synchrony demonstrated between movements of the neonate and adult speech', *Child Development*, 45.

Cruttenden, A. (1979) *Language in Infancy and Childhood: A Linguistic Introduction to Language Acquisition*. Manchester: University Press.

Crystal, D. (1979) 'Prosodic development', in P. Fletcher and M. Garman (eds), 1979.

de Mause, L. (ed.) (1974) *The History of Childhood*. New York: Psychohistory Press.

Derewianka, B. (1995) 'Language Development in the Transition from

Childhood to Adolescence: The Role of Grammatical Metaphor'. Macquarie University: PhD thesis.
Dixon, J. (1967) *Growth through English*. London: National Council of Teachers.
Donaldson, M. (1978) *Children's Minds*. Glasgow: Collins.
Dore, J. (1974) 'A pragmatic approach to early language development', *Journal of Psycholinguistic Research*, 4.
Dore, J. (1976) 'Conditions on the acquisition of speech acts', in I. Markov (ed.), *The Social Context of Language*. New York: Wiley.
Dore, J. (1979) 'Conversation and pre-school language development', in P. Fletcher and M. Garman (eds), 1979.
Doughty, P. S. (1969) 'Current practice in English teaching', paper presented to Conference of Teachers in Approved Schools "Language, Life and Learning", Sunningdale, May.
Doughty, P., Pearce, J. and Thornton, G. (1971) *Language in Use*. London: Arnold (Schools Council Programme in Linguistics and English Teaching).
Ede, J. and Williamson, J. (1980) *Talking, Listening and Learning: The Development of Children's Language*. London: Longman.
Edelman, G. (1992) *Bright Air, Brilliant Fire: On the Matter of the Mind*. New York: Harper Collins (Basic Books).
Edwards, D. (1978) 'Social relations and early language', in A. Lock (ed.), 1978.
Eggins, S. (forthcoming) *Keeping the Conversation Going: The Dynamics of Sustained Talk and the Definition of Conversation*.
Ervin, S. M. and Miller, W. R. (1963) 'Language Development', *Yearbook of the National Society for the Study of Education*, 62.
Ervin-Tripp, S. M. (1964) 'An analysis of the interaction of language, topic and listener', in J. J. Gumperz and D. H. Hymes (eds), *The Ethnography of Communication (American Anthropologist*, 66(6), Part 2).
Fillmore, C. J. (1968) 'The case for case', in E. Bach and R. Harms (eds), *Universals in Linguistic Theory*. New York: Holt.
Firth, J. R. (1950) 'Personality and language in society', *Sociological Review*, 42(2). Reprinted in J. R. Firth, *Papers in Linguistics 1934–1951*. London and New York: Oxford University Press, 1957.
Firth, J. R. (1957) 'A synopsis of linguistic theory', *Studies in Linguistic Analysis*. Oxford: Blackwell (Special Volume of the Philological Society). Reprinted in F. R. Palmer (ed.), *Selected Papers of J. R. Firth 1952–1959*. London: Longmans, 1968.
Fletcher, P. and Garman, M. (eds) (1979) *Language Acquisition: Studies in First Language Development*. Cambridge: Cambridge University Press.
France, M. N. (1975) 'The Generation of the Self: A Study of the Construction of Categories in Infancy'. University of Essex PhD thesis.
Graves, D. (1983) *Writing: Teachers and Children at Work*. Portsmouth, NH: Heinemann Educational Books.

Greenfield, P. M. and Smith, J. H. (forthcoming) *Communication and the Beginnings of Language: The Development of Semantic Structure in One-word Speech and Beyond*. New York: Academic Press.

Grieve, R. and Hoegenraad, R. (1979) 'First words', in P. Fletcher and M. Garman (eds), 1979.

Griffiths, P. (1979) 'Speech acts and early sentences', in P. Fletcher and M. Garman (eds), 1979.

Gruber, J. S. (1967) 'Topicalization in child language', *Foundations of Language*, 3.

Hagège, C. (1985) *L'homme de paroles: contribution linguistique aux sciences humaines*. Paris: Fayard.

Halliday, M. A. K. (1967) *Intonation and Grammar in British English*. The Hague: Mouton (Janua Linguarum Series Practica 48).

Halliday M. A. K. (1970) 'Language structure and language function', in J. Lyons (ed.), *New Horizons in Linguistics*. Harmondsworth: Penguin Books. See also *On Grammar*, Volume 1 in the Collected Works of M. A. K. Halliday.

Halliday, M. A. K. (1973) *Explorations in the Functions of Language*. London: Edward Arnold (Explorations in Language Study Series).

Halliday, M. A. K. (1975) *Learning How to Mean: explorations in the development of language*. London: Edward Arnold (Explorations in Language Study); New York: American Elsevier. See also Chapter 2 of this Volume.

Halliday, M. A. K. (1979) 'One child's protolanguage', in M. Bullowa (ed.), 1979. See also Chapters 3 and 4 of this Volume.

Halliday, M. A. K. (1984) 'Listening to Nigel: Conversations of a Very Small Child'. Unpublished manuscript, University of Sydney, Linguistics Department, Sydney, Australia. (The data is on an accompanying CD to this Volume)

Halliday, M. A. K. (1985) *An Introduction to Functional Grammar*. London: Edward Arnold.

Halliday, M. A. K. (1987) 'Language and the order of nature', in N. Fabb *et al.* (eds), *The Linguistics of Writing*. Manchester: University Press.

Halliday, M. A. K. (1993) 'Towards a language-based theory of learning', *Linguistics and Education*, 5.2, 93–116. See also Chapter 15 of this Volume.

Halliday, M. A. K. and Hasan, R. (1976) *Cohesion in English*. London: Longman (English Language Series 9).

Halliday, M. A. K. and James, Z. L. (1993) 'A quantitative study of polarity and primary tense in the English finite clause', in J. M. Sinclair, M. Hoey, and G. Fox (eds), *Techniques of Description: Spoken and Written Discourse*. London: Routledge.

Halliday, M. A. K. and Martin, J. R. (1993) *Writing Science: Literacy and Discursive Power*. London: Falmer Press.

Halliday, M. A. K., McIntosh, A. and Strevens, P. (1964) *The Linguistic Sciences and Language Teaching*. London: Longmans: Longmans (Longmans' Linguistics Library).

Halliday, M. A. K. (1998) 'Things and Relations; Regrammaticising experience as technical knowledge' in J. R. Martin and R. Veel (eds) *Reading Science: Critical and Functional Perspectives on Discourse of Science* (pp. 185–235). London: Routledge.

Hammond, J. (1990) 'Is learning to read and write the same as learning to speak?', in F. Christie (ed.), *Literacy for a Changing World*. Hawthorn: Australian Council for Educational Research.

Hasan, R. (1973) 'Code, register and social dialect', in B. Bernstein (ed.), *Class, Codes and Control, Vol. 2: Applied Studies towards a Sociology of Language*. London: Routledge and Kegan Paul (Primary Socialization, Language and Education).

Hasan, R. (1986) 'The ontogenesis of ideology: an interpretation of mother-child talk', in T. Threadgold *et al.* (eds), *Semiotics, Ideology, Language*. Sydney: Sydney Association for Studies in Society and Culture (Sydney Studies in Society and Culture, vol. 3).

Hasan, R. (1988) 'Language in the process of socialisation: home and school', in J. Oldenburg, T. van Leeuwen and L. Gerot (eds), *Language and Socialisation: Home and School* (Proceedings from the Working Conference on Language in Education, 17–21 November, 1986). North Ryde, NSW: Macquarie University.

Hasan, R. (1991) 'Questions as a mode of learning in everyday talk', in T. Le and M. McCausland (eds), *Language Education: Interaction and Development*. Launceston: University of Tasmania.

Hasan, R. (1992) 'Rationality in everyday talk: from process to system', in J. Svartvik (ed.), *Directions in Corpus Linguistics: Proceedings of Nobel Symposium 82, Stockholm, 4–8 August 1991*. Berlin: de Gruyter.

Hasan, R. and Cloran, C. (1990) 'A sociolinguistic interpretation of everyday talk between mothers and children', in M. A. K. Halliday, J. Gibbons and H. Nicholas (eds), *Learning, Keeping and Using Language: Selected Papers from the Eighth World Congress of Applied Linguistics, Sydney, 16–21 August 1987*. Philadelphia: John Benjamins.

Hasan, R. and Martin, J. R. (eds) (1989) *Language Development: Learning Language, Learning Culture*. (*Meaning and Choice in Language*, vol. 1.) Norwood, NJ: Ablex.

Ingram, D. (1971) 'Transitivity in child language', *Language*, 47.

Jakobson, R. (1968) *Child Language, Aphasia and Phonological Universals* (trans. A. R. Keiler). The Hague: Mouton (German original published 1941).

Karmiloff-Smith, A. (1979) *A Functional Approach to Child Language: A Study of Determiners and Reference*. Cambridge: Cambridge University Press.

Kaye, K. (1979) 'Thickening thin data: the maternal role in developing communication and language', in M. Bullowa (ed.), 1979.

Kelley, K. L. (1967) 'Early syntactic acquisition', Santa Monica, CA: Rand Corp.

Kintsch, W. (1988) 'The role of knowledge in discourse comprehension: a construction-integration model', *Psychological Review*, 95. 2.

Lamb, S. M. (1970) 'Linguistic and cognitive networks', in P. Garvin (ed.), *Cognition: A Multiple View*. New York: Spartan Books.

Lemke, J. L. (1984) 'Towards a model of the instructional process' and 'The formal analysis of instruction', in J. L. Lemke, *Semiotics and Education*. Toronto, Canada: Toronto Semiotic Circle Monograph 1984. 2.

Lemke, J. L. (1990) *Talking Science: Language, Learning, and Values*. Norwood, NJ: Ablex.

Leopold, W. F. (1939–49) *Speech Development of a Bilingual Child: A Linguist's Record*. Evanston and Chicago: North-Western University Press.

Lévi-Strauss, C. (1966) *The Savage Mind*. London: Weidenfeld and Nicolson.

Lewis, M. M. (1936) *Infant Speech: A Study of the Beginning of Language*. London: Routledge and Kegan Paul. (International Library of Psychology, Philosophy and Scientific Method) (2nd edn, enlarged, 1951).

Lewis, M. M. (1957) *How Children Learn to Speak*. London: Harrap.

Lock, A. (1978) 'The emergence of language', in A. Lock (ed.), 1978.

Lock, A. (ed.) (1978) *Action, Gesture and Symbol: The Emergence of Language*. New York: Academic Press.

Mackay, D. and Thompson, B. (1968) *The Initial Teaching of Reading and Writing*. Programme in Linguistics and English Teaching, Paper 3, London: Longmans.

Mackay, D., Thompson, B. and Schaub, P. (1970) *Breakthrough to Literacy: Teacher's Manual*. London: Longmans (Schools Council Programme in Linguistics and English Teaching).

Malinowski, B. (1923) 'The problem of meaning in primitive languages', Supplement I to C. K. Ogden and I. A. Richards, *The Meaning of Meaning*. London: Kegan Paul (International Library of Psychology, Philosophy and Scientific Method).

Martin, J. R. (1989) *Factual Writing: Exploring and Challenging Social Reality*. Oxford: Oxford University Press.

Martin, J. R. (1990) 'Literacy in science: learning to handle text as technology', in F. Christie (ed.), *Literacy for a Changing World*. Hawthorn: Australian Council for Educational Research.

Martin, J. R. (1991) 'Nominalization in science and humanities: distilling knowledge and scaffolding text', in E. Ventola (ed.), *Functional and Systemic Linguistics: Approaches and Uses*. Berlin: de Gruyter (Trends in linguistics studies and monographs 55).

Martin, J. (1998) 'Mentoring semogenesis: 'genre-based' literacy pedagogy', in F. Christie (ed.), *Pedagogy and the Shaping of Consciousness: Linguistics and Social Processes*. London: Cassell.

Mathesius, V. (1936) 'On some problems of the systematic analysis of grammar', *Travaux du Cercle Linguistique de Prague*, 6.

Matthiessen, C. M. I. M. (1981) *A Grammar and a Lexicon for a Text-Production System*. Marina del Rey, CA: University of Southern California Information Sciences Institute. Report no. ISI/RR-82-102.

Matthiessen, C. (1992) 'Interpreting the textual metafunction', in M. Davies and L. Ravelli (eds), *Advances in Systemic Linguistics: Recent Theory and Practice*. London: Frances Pinter.

Morris, D. (1967) *The Naked Ape*. London: Jonathan Cape.

Nelson, K. and Levy, E. (1987) 'Development of referential cohesion in a child's monologues', in R. Steele and T. Threadgold (eds), *Language Topics*, vol. 1. Philadelphia: John Benjamins.

Newson, J. (1978) 'Dialogue and development', in A. Lock (ed.), (1978).

Newson, J. (1979) 'The growth of shared understandings between infant and caregiver', in M. Bullowa (ed.), 1979.

Oldenburg-Torr, J. (1990) 'Learning the language and learning through language in early childhood', in M. A. K. Halliday, J. Gibbons and H. Nicholas (eds), *Learning, Keeping and Using Language: Selected Papers from the 8th World Congress of Applied Linguistics, Sydney, 16–21 August 1987*. Amsterdam: John Benjamins, pp. 27–38.

Oldenburg-Torr, J. (1997) *From Child Tongue to Mother Tongue: A Case Study of Language Development in the First Two and a Half Years*. University of Nottingham: Department of English Studies (Monographs in Systemic Linguistics 9).

Osgood, C. (1971) 'Where do sentences come from?', in D. D. Steinberg and L. A. Jakobovits (eds), *Semantics: An Interdisciplinary Reader in Philosophy, Linguistics and Psychology*. Cambridge: Cambridge University Press.

Osser, H. (1970) 'Three approaches to the acquisition of language', in F. Williams (ed.), *Language and Poverty: Perspectives on a Theme*. Chicago: Markham.

Painter, C. (1984) *Into the Mother Tongue: A Case Study in Early Language Development*. London: Frances Pinter.

Painter, C. (1989) 'Learning language: a functional view of language development', in R. Hasan and J. R. Martin (eds), 1989.

Painter, C. (1993) *Learning Through Language: A Case Study in the Development of Language as a Resource for Learning $2\frac{1}{2}-5$*. London: Cassell.

Painter, C. (1996) 'Learning about language: construing semiosis in the pre-school years', *Functions of Language*, 3.1, 95–125.

Pawley, A. (1985) 'On speech formulas and linguistic competence', *Lenguas Modernas* (Universidad de Chile) 12.

Phillips, J. (1985) 'The Development of Comparisons and Contrasts in Young Children's Language'. Masters thesis, University of Sydney, Australia.

Phillips, J. (1986) 'The development of modality and hypothetical meaning: Nigel $1;7\frac{1}{2}-2;7\frac{1}{2}$', *Working Papers in Linguistics*, 3, Linguistics Department, University of Sydney.

Piaget, J. (1926) *Language and Thought of the Child*, trans. M. Gabain. London: Routledge and Kegan Paul (3rd edition, revised and enlarged, 1959).

Piaget, J. (1957) *Construction of Reality in the Child*. London: Routledge and Kegan Paul.

Qiu, S. (1985) 'Transition period in Chinese language development', *Australian Review of Applied Linguistics*, 8.1
Reich, P. A. (1970) 'Relational networks', *Canadian Journal of Liniguistics*, 15.
Rogers, S. (ed.) (1975) *Children and Language: Readings in Early Language and Socialization*. London: Oxford University Press.
Rothery, J. (1989) 'Learning about language', in R. Hasan and J. R. Martin (eds), 1989.
Rothery, J. (forthcoming) *The Pedagogies of Traditional School Grammar, Creativity, Personal Growth, and Process*.
Schlesinger, I. M. (1971) 'Production of utterances and language acquisition', in D. I. Slobin (ed.), *The Ontogenesis of Grammar: A Theoretical Symposium*. New York: Academic Press.
Scollon, R. (1976) *Conversations with a One Year Old: A Case Study of the Developmental Foundation of Syntax*. Honolulu: University of Hawaii Press.
Shotter, J. (1978) 'The cultural context of communication studies: theoretical and methodological issues', in A. Lock (ed.), 1978.
Sinclair de Zwart, H. (1969) Developmental psycholinguistics', in D. Elkand and J. Favell (eds), *Studies in Cognitive Development*. New York: Oxford University Press.
Spencer, J. and Gregory, M. (1964) 'An approach to the study of style', in J. Spencer (ed.), *Linguistics and Style*. London: Oxford University Press.
Strömqvist, S. (1980) *Speech as Action in the Play of Swedish Three-Year-Olds*. Stockholm: Stockholm University, Department of Scandinavian Languages (Child Language Research Institute Paper no. 3).
Svartvik, J. and Quirk, R. (eds) (1980) *A Corpus of English Conversation*. Lund, Sweden: C. W. K. Gleerup (Lund Studies in English).
Thibault, P. (1991) *Social Semiotics as Praxis: Text, Social Meaning Making and Nabokow's "Ada"*. Minneapolis: University of Minneapolis Press.
Thibault, P. (in press) *Brain, Mind, and the Signifying Body*, London and New York: Continuum.
Trevarthen, C. (1974a) 'Conversation with a two-month-old', *New Scientist*, 62 (2 May).
Trevarthen, C. (1974b) 'The psychobiology of speech development', in E. H. Lenneberg (ed.), *Language and Brain: Developmental Aspects* (Neuroscience Research Program Bulletin 12).
Trevarthen, C. (1979) 'Communication and cooperation in early infancy: a description of primary intersubjectivity', in M. Bullowa (ed.), 1979.
Trevarthen, C. (1980) 'The foundations of intersubjectivity: development of interpersonal and cooperative understanding in infants', in D. Olson (ed.), *The Social Foundations of Language and Thought*. New York: Norton.
Trevarthen, C. (1987) 'Sharing makes sense: intersubjectivity and the making of an infant's meaning', in R. Steele and T. Threadgold (eds), *Language Topics*, vol. 1. Philadelphia: John Benjamins.

Trevarthen, C. and Hubley, P. (1978) 'Secondary intersubjectivity: confidence, confiding and acts of meaning in the first year', in A. Lock (ed.), 1978.

Turner, G. J. (1969) *Social Class Differences in Regulatory Language*. Report prepared for Sociological Research Unit, University of London Institute of Education.

Turner, G. J. (1973) 'Social class and children's language at age five and age seven', in B. Bernstein (ed.), *Class, Codes and Control, Vol. 2: Applied Studies Towards a Sociology of Language*. London: Routledge and Kegan Paul (Primary Socialization, Language and Education Series).

Ure, J. and Ellis, J. (1972) 'Register in descriptive linguistics and linguistic sociology', in O. U. Villegas (ed.), *Las concepciones y problemas actuales de las sociolinguistica*. Mexico City: University of Mexico Press.

Vickery, R. L., Lake, J. H., McKenna, L. N. and Ryan, A. S. (1978) *The Process Way to Science, Book C* (rev. ed.). Milton, Queensland: The Jacaranda Press.

Waterson, N. and Snow, C. E. (eds) (1978) *The Development of Communication: Social and Pragmatic Factors in Language Acquisition* (Papers presented to the Third International Child Language Symposium). New York: Wiley.

Wells, C. G. (1974) 'Learning to code experience through language', *Journal of Child Language*, vol. 1.

Wells, G. et al. (1981) *Learning through Interaction: The Study of Language Development*. Cambridge: Cambridge University Press (Language at Home and School I).

Williams, G. C. (1992) *Natural Selection: Domains, Levels, and Challenges*. New York: Oxford University Press.

Williams, G. (1995) 'Functional grammar in primary schools', in P. H. Fries (ed.), *Australian English in a Pluralist Australia: Proceedings of Style Council 95*. Sydney: Macquarie University, for the Dictionary Research Centre.

Appendix 1

DEVELOPMENT OF NIGEL'S PROTOLANGUAGE

This narrative showing Nigel at twelve months is from 'One child's protolanguage', see Chapter 3.

1 To nine months

Nigel's first clearly identifiable act of meaning was in the last week of April at just under six months.

He was lying face downwards in his pram. Some pigeons took off noisily into the air. Nigel lifted his head, looked at his mother and said " ́ ".

"Those are birds," she said to him. "Big birds. Pigeons. They all flew away."

Nigel's " ́ " was a small sound, with no articulation, just a short high rising note. He used this expression frequently over the next three or four weeks, always when there was some kind of commotion around; and the three adults with whom he was in daily contact, his mother, his father and Anna, all took notice – they attended, and they responded. In other words, they interpreted it as an act of meaning. Since it was Nigel's first act of this kind, they were conscious of it and commented on it to each other; moreover they were in agreement as to 'what he meant' – that it could be translated into adult as 'what's that? What's going on?'. Considering the nature of the signal this might seem surprising, until one takes account of the fact that, given the assumption that the meaning is contextually relevant (an assumption which they never questioned), there was not much choice. Since Nigel was not 'speaking adult', the question 'was that what he really meant?' does not arise. He made it clear that he was satisfied with the response.

After a few weeks, Nigel stopped saying " ́ ". He had found that he could 'mean' successfully – he could initiate an exchange, and be responded to. He now put meaning aside for a while, to be returned to later. Meanwhile, at six and three-quarter months (24 May) for the first time he laughed at something, the fluttering of a toy bird twirled on a stick; and at seven and a quarter months, just when he had learnt to sit up on his own, he gave his first response: his mother was saying a jingle to him, and Nigel responded by making rhythmic movements with his hands (hands clasped, bending alternate wrists). His first response in the form of an act of meaning came at just under eight months (in the interval on 21 June he had moved himself forward for the first time), when he took part in a conversation; his part was a short, half-close, front-rounded vowel falling mid-low to low, [ø̀]. The conversation went something along these lines: "Nigel!" – "eu" – "Hello bootie!" – "eu" – "There's my bootie!" – "eu", and so on. We could translate Nigel's part as 'yes, we're together', which is more or less the meaning of his mother's part also. Here for the first time Nigel was exchanging meanings; the function of the exchange was interpersonal, a symbolic expression of togetherness.

It was shortly after this that Nigel first carried out a verbal instruction ("Clap hands!"); and at eight months, on the day after he learnt to play the 'dropping' game, he first acted symbolically on an external object. I was making his toy cat jump in the air. I stopped; Nigel leant forward, and touched the cat steadily for a second with his finger, looking at me as he did so. The meaning was clear: 'do that again'. I did, and Nigel showed he was satisfied. His act of meaning had succeeded.

This was the first instance of a little language that Nigel used for about six weeks, from eight months (the beginning of July) to around nine and a half months (the middle of August). The language consisted of five meanings, of which three were expressed gesturally and two vocally. We could perhaps refer to these elements as **signs**. A sign is a content–expression pair, remaining constant over a period of time, where the expression is some bodily act (which may but need not be a vocal act) and the content is functional in respect of the child's intent; it forms part of a systemic set of signs, and its execution constitutes an act of meaning. At this stage, then, Nigel's language consisted of five signs.

The second to appear was the 'I want' sign, expressed by grasping an object firmly but momentarily, and then letting go; and this was followed almost immediately by a contrasting sign 'I don't want', expressed by touching the object lightly with outstretched finger and then taking the finger away. The contrast between these two was unmistakable. The expressions were, very clearly, iconic; they were related to the meanings in a non-arbitrary way. Nevertheless the act was a symbolic act. Nigel was not acting directly on the object itself – he did not pull it towards him or push it away; he was addressing a person, and he looked not at the object but at the person he was addressing. On other occasions, of course, he did grab at objects or push them away, and then he looked at the objects. What was noticeable was the sharp distinction between the two kinds of act: the act of meaning, symbolic and person-directed (even though in the case of 'I want' and 'I don't want' it is object-oriented), and the act projected directly on to the object. It is interesting that the day on which Nigel first used the 'I don't want' sign was also the day on which he learnt to demolish, repeatedly knocking down a tower of beakers that was being built for him.

The fifth of the signs to emerge in this period was one that was expressed vocally; it was oriented towards the environment, picking up the thread of the " ́ " of two months earlier. There were a number of what might be seen as preparatory steps leading up to this. On 9 July, Nigel first pulled himself up to a standing position; on 14 July he went on his first voyage of exploration, and on 17 July he first got his knees and tummy off the ground and managed to creep forward on forearms and toes. It was on that day that he first used this new exploratory sign: watching birds in flight, when their wheeling movement reached its peak of prominence, he said [ø̀] – a short, half-close, front-rounded vowel falling mid to low. The expression differed only marginally from the 'togetherness' sign, perhaps starting on a slightly higher pitch. But the context, and the function, were distinct; moreover this sign was addressed partly to himself – sometimes he switched his gaze between the commotion and the person being addressed, and sometimes he did not look at another person at all.

In the same week Nigel began playing with a ball, pushing it away from him, and also trying to put it into a beaker. His language was now as follows:

Meaning	**Expression**	**Function**	**Orientation**
'give me that'	grasping firmly	instrumental	object
'don't give me that'	touching lightly	instrumental	object
'do that (with it)'	touching firmly	regulatory	other person
'yes, we're together'	[ø̀] mid-low to low	interactional	other and self
'look, that's interesting'	[ø̀] mid to low	personal	self and object

It is interesting to note that the distinction between the vocal and the gestural modes of expression anticipates the semantic contrast which will be Nigel's primary strategy for making the transition from protolanguage to adult language (second half of second year). In this later, transitional phase Nigel makes a systematic distinction between utterances of the 'do something' type, demanding a response, and those of the 'I'm learning' type which require no response; the distinction is expressed as an opposition of rising and falling tone:

| | Mode of meaning | |
	active	reflective
Age (months)	Mode of expression	
9	gestural	vocal
19-24	rising tone	falling tone

Figure 1

The distinction is lost in the intervening period; there is no trace of it in the developed protolanguage (10 to 18 months). But it is interesting to see as early as nine months a glimpse of what is to become the primary functional contrast not only in Nigel's language-creating strategy but also, eventually, in the adult linguistic system.

2 Nine to ten and a half months

Nigel could now pull himself up to a standing position; in the week in which he reached nine months he began putting things on things, and one week later made his first (and unsuccessful) attempt at standing one beaker on top of another. At this time his protolanguage underwent a significant change. Around nine and a half months he abandoned the three gestures, replacing them with vocal expressions; and he added a number of new signs, so that by ten and a half months the total had increased to twelve.

The 'I want' sign was now [nã], usually repeated about four times; but it was never very frequently used. 'I don't want' had disappeared altogether. The 'do that' sign had two variants, a regular [ʒ̃] or [n̂ŋ], very frequent from ten months, and an intensified form [mnŋ]ᶠ meaning 'do that – I insist!'. The general sign of attention to surroundings was still [ò], [œ̀]; but this now became symbiotic with other expressions [bò], [ᵒdɔ̀]; also on low falling tone, which may have originated as imitations of *bird* and *dog* and which were particularly associated with attention to rapid movement: 'look, a commotion'. Two new signs were added, also in the 'personal' realm of meaning but signalling pleasure rather than interest: [à] 'that's nice', and [n̑n̑] 'that tastes good', both again on low falling tone.

In the interactional realm Nigel still had his sign for responding to address, 'yes? here I am'; this tended now to have the lips spread, [ɛ̀], so that it sounded distinct from the expression of interest, which had the lips rounded. He now added two more. One, which was variously [ʔɔ̀], [ʔɔ̀], [ᵒdɔ̀] (always glottalized), meant 'nice to see you, and shall we look at this together?'; a favourite utterance, it was used to greet someone, especially someone coming in to see him when he had just woken up, and to create a bond of shared attention, either looking out of the window as the curtains were drawn back, or focusing on a picture, a symbolic object whose only function is to be attended to. The other was an intensified variant of the same thing, a repeated [ən̑n̑n̑]ᶠ, loud and high falling in pitch, meaning 'nice to see you – and why didn't you get here before?'.

Meanwhile Nigel added one more sign of an 'instrumental' kind, [bò] meaning 'I want my bird'. This was Nigel's favourite possession, the same fluttering bird on a stick that he had laughed at some months earlier. It was kept high up on the wall, in sight but out of reach; Nigel would call for it with arms raised and face turning from the bird to the person being addressed: [bò, bò]. This was presumably an imitation of the adult syllable [bɜːd] *bird*, and probably Nigel's only imitative expression. (If it was an imitation, it was an imitation of the syllable, not the word; Nigel is still far from being capable of abstracting words at this stage. Although this and the 'commotion' sign sometimes overlapped – and the syllable *bird* may have been one of the sources of that also – the two were quite distinct signs, with different meaning and context and different accompanying bodily postures.) The special significance of the bird, its value as a symbol of objectivity and continuity, was reflected in the fact of its being called for by a special sign, never by the sign [nà] which had the generalized meaning of 'I want'.

Finally there was the repeated [g̊ʷɣig̊ʷɣig̊ʷɣi ...], Nigel's version of the 'alternating prosody' that appears almost universally in infant babbling: essentially it is an alternation of the fundamental prosodic values of y and w, vocal postures that form the articulatory basis of contrasting phonological systems in adult languages the world over. The vowel qualities are simply the transitions between these two postures; the w is often accompanied by some contact in the velar or uvular region, and sometimes glottalic closure. With Nigel the origin of the sound was quite clear: he had heard himself make it while falling asleep, a by-product of the sucking movement with joint of thumb held against the lips. But instead of merely babbling with this sound, Nigel – who did very little babbling – put it to use in his protolanguage. It still sometimes came out while he was going to sleep; but he usually said it when he was not in his cot but wanted to indicate that he was feeling sleepy. He would curl up on the floor, look at his mother, close his eyes and say [ɡʷʶɪɡʷʶɪɡʷʶɪ...]; then open his eyes and look at her again. The message was 'I'm sleepy: shut the world out – and maybe someone will put me to bed?'

By this time Nigel could understand various sets of utterances addressed to him by the three adults with whom he exchanged meanings, his "meaning group" of significant others:

Utterance type	**Example**	**Nigel's response**
where's ...?	Where's the window?	looked at it
	Where's teddy's eye?	pointed to it
go and get your ...	Go and get your bib	fetched it
game routines	Round and round the garden	held out hand, palm upwards
do you want ...?	D'you want your bird?	smiled, sighed

Meanwhile at ten months Nigel had taken his first steps forward, holding on to someone or something, and had tried, unsuccessfully, to stand without support; the following week he managed to sit down voluntarily from a standing position. He now for the first time 'waved' goodbye – actually opening and closing his fist, with elbow bent and forearm pointing up. His only other gesture was a demand for music ('sing a song' or 'put a record on'), which he expressed by beating time with one arm, sometimes accompanied by the regulatory sign [ʒ̃].

3 Ten and a half to twelve months

At eleven months Nigel was able to get to his feet by steadying himself against a flat surface, such as a door or a wall, and to roll over and over continuously. He now fed himself for the first time, holding the spoon in his fist; one day he helped himself to an apple from the fruitbowl and tried unsuccessfully to gnaw it (he was just getting his second tooth).

Meaning	Expression	Function	Orientation
'give me that'	nà ... mid to low	instrumental	object
'give me my bird'	bò mid to low	instrumental	favourite object
'make music'	gesture: beating time	instrumental	service
'do that'	ɜ̀, n̄ŋ mid to low	regulatory	other person
'do that – I insist'	m̄n̄ŋ ƒ high to low	regulatory	other person (intensified)
'yes? here I am'	ɛ̀ low	interactional	other and self (response)
'nice to see you; and let's look at this'	ʔò, ʔɔ̀, dɔ̀ mid to low	interactional	other and self (mediated by object)
'nice to see you – at last!'	ən̄n̄ŋ ƒ high to low	interactional	other and self (intensified)
'goodbye'	gesture: opening and closing fist	interactional	other and self
'that's interesting'	ò̃, œ̀ mid-low to low	personal	self: cognitive
'look, a commotion'	bò̃, dɔ̀, ò̃ mid-low to low	personal	self: cognitive (prominence)
'that's nice'	à mid-low to low	personal	self: affective
'that tastes nice'	n̄ŋ mid-low to low	personal	self: affective (taste)
'I'm tired'	gʷɤi ... low	personal	self: withdrawal

Figure 2 Summary of Nigel's protolanguage at ten and a half months

Next day was his first 'disobedience', the rejection of an act of meaning addressed to him: being told not to scratch the table, he went on doing so, looking expectantly at his mother for her response.

He still asked for his toy bird [bò], [vò], and now added another specific demand 'I want some powder (on my hands, so that I can hit the drums)'; this was a string of syllables [ǧəbʷǧəbʷ...] ("gabugabu..." or "bugabuga...") in imitation of my ritual *a little bit of powder!* The general demand 'I want – ' was still [nà ...]; and both [ɜ̀] and its intensified form [m̄n̄ŋ] were very frequent as the means of getting people to do things, usually forms of entertainment such as bouncing him on one's knee, making his rabbit jump in the air or tapping different objects to see what noise they made. Such expansion in his protolanguage as there was at this stage was mainly in the interactional and personal areas, and in responses.

Nigel now frequently expressed his personal involvement with his surroundings. As a sign of general interest, [ò̃], was now being replaced by [ʔdɔ̀] or [dɛ̀ə], 'look!', the former being his own 'invitation to share attention' and the latter possibly an imitation of *there*. He now added signs for specific interest in various kinds of commotion: [ʔdɔ̀] 'a dog commotion' (barking), [œ̀ œ̀] 'an aeroplane commotion' (noise of aircraft overhead), and – being excited at the sight of a football game, with people running in all directions – [bə̀], [və̀] 'a ball commotion'. As a sign of pleasure, [ɛʸiː] replaced [à] in the general sense of 'I like –', [nŋ̀] still being reserved for taste (and gradually disappearing). When he had had enough of the outside world, he shut it out with [g̊ʷɣi ...].

The form [dɔ̀] was still used as greeting: 'nice to see you; let's look at this picture together'. It was now used when the other person was already present, simply as a means of interaction. Nigel had a little board book of coloured pictures; he pointed to a picture, looked at the other person and said [d̂ɔ̀] 'let's look at this'. This was the first step in the separation of the two components of interaction and attention; in this same context, Nigel introduced a new expression [ɛʸa] which was oriented less towards the other person and more towards the picture – the other person being invited to say its name, "Yes, it's a rattle". Here was the first intimation of the connection of a sign with (the demand for) a name; and Nigel sometimes used this same expression when something was named as it was being given to him: "Here's a rusk for you" – [ɛʸa] 'that's what it is (and that's what I wanted)'. It is interesting to note that in the same week Nigel used a personal name for the first time: [ānnā]. It was a greeting to Anna, and it was unique in being on a high level tone instead of the falling tone that was characteristic of all his other signs.

Nigel was now beginning to respond to acts of meaning with acts of meaning of his own. He had done this from the start in a context of simple interaction, responding to his mother's call; he still used [ɛ] in this sense, and now added an intensified variant [àː]^{ff}, a raucous yell which he used only to respond when called from somewhere out of sight. But he now started responding in other contexts too – provided the response came within his functional competence, such that the meaning was one that he could himself initiate. He could not respond to a question seeking information, because he could not himself offer information, and it would be the best part of a year yet before he could use language in an informative function. But he could initiate acts of meaning with a sense of 'I want'; and just before 11 months he learnt to respond verbally to offers, acts of meaning by others where the response called for from him was '(yes) I want', such as "Do you want a drink?" and "Shall I sing you a song?". Previously his response to these had been a smile, together with a general bodily expression of satisfaction; now he began to accompany these with a long breathy [ɛ̀ː] on a low falling tone. This was, in origin, a sigh, part of the total bodily response; Nigel frequently sighed as a relaxing of concentrated attention when the attention had been rewarded. He now turned this into a linguistic sign, meaning 'yes, that's just what I wanted!'.

This step of turning a natural response into a symbolic one seemed to open up for Nigel the potential of responding as a mode of meaning, and he now began to use expressions that had hitherto served to initiate, in a responding sense also. [nã ...] is beginning to disappear, and is never used in this way; but the regulatory [ɜ̰] comes to function – without accompanying smile – in a response context, especially where some joint activity is suggested: 'Shall we go out for a walk?' – [ɜ̰] 'yes let's'.

The long-drawn-out [ɛ::] still persists, and shortly afterwards it occurs in a new setting. At just under 12 months, on the day Nigel first stood up on his own, and first managed to put a holed disc on to a stick, he was turning over the pages in his board book, looking carefully at each picture and saying [ɛʸa] as he did so. He looked at me expectantly and, to make the meaning perfectly clear, took hold of my finger and pressed it gently on to the picture: [ɛʸa]. "It's a ball", I said. "E-e-eh!" – 'yes, *that's* what I wanted you to do'.

Nigel's responses now give some indication of the extent of his understanding of the speech that is addressed to him. He can respond to a range of offers, such as those mentioned earlier, with a 'yes please do that'; and to various instructions, such as 'sing a song', by carrying them out. He shows understanding of particular words: hearing "aeroplane", he said [œʷœ]; hearing "big noise", he made one. He now 'waves' (right hand raised, fingers opening and closing on palm) not only on leaving, seeing someone getting ready to leave, or seeing them return, but also in response to the word "byebye". Asked "Where's Nigel's nose?", he touches it. Such situations were not entirely without ambiguity. On one occasion Nigel gave his 'big noise' yell, apparently out of context; his mother looked startled, then realized something she had just said, and laughed. "I said *nose*, not *noise*," she said. Nigel gave a very convincing impression of being embarrassed by his mistake.

Appendix 2

Table 1 NL 1: Nigel at 10½ months

Function	Content systems	Expression Articulation	Tone	Gloss
Instrumental	demand, general	nã - - -	mid	"give me that"
	demand, specific (toy bird)	bø	mid	"give me my bird"
Regulatory	command, normal	ɛ̃	mid	"do that (again)"
	command, intensified	m̃m̃	wide; ff	"do that right now!"
Interactional	initiation → normal (friendly)	= ø; 'dø; 'dɔ	narrow mid	"nice to see you (and shall we look at this together?)"
	→ intensified (impatient)	ɛ̃nnɛ̃	mid	"nice to see you—at last!"
	response	e; ɛ	low	"yes it's me"
	interest → general	= ø	low	"that's interesting"
	→ specific (movement)	'dɔ; bø; ø	low	"look, it's moving (? a dog, birds)"
	pleasure → general	a	low	"that's nice"
Personal	→ specific (taste)	m̃m̃	low	"that tastes nice"
	withdrawal	gʷɤγ- - -	narrow low	"I'm sleepy"

Note: All above on falling tone; mid = mid fall, narrow low = low fall over narrow interval, etc. At 9 months, Nigel had two such meanings, both expressed as [ø] on narrow mid-low falling tone; one interactional, "let's be together", the other (possibly slightly wider interval) personal "look, it's moving." He also had, however, three meanings expressed gesturally: two instrumental, "I want that," grasping object firmly, and "I don't want that," touching object lightly; and one regulatory, "do that again," touching person or relevant object firmly (e.g. "make that jump in the air again"). The gestures disappeared during NL-1 to NL-2.

In this and subsequent tables, favorite items are indicated by *, and rare or doubtful items by ? Where two or three items are related in both meaning and sound these are shown by =, accompanied by an index number where necessary.

Table 2 NL 2: Nigel at 12 months

Function	Content systems			Expression		Gloss
				Articulation	Tone	
Instrumental	demand, general → toy bird			nä - - -	mid	"give me that"
	demand, specific → powder			bø; b'ø; vø	mid	"I want my bird"
				gáb^w - - -; bug^w - - -	mid	"I want some powder"
Regulatory	command, normal			ɔ; ɜ; m̃ŋ	mid	"do that (again)"
	command, intensified			m̃ŋ	wide; ff	"do that right now!"
Interactional	initiation → greeting, personalized			na; an : a	high level	"Anna!"
	greeting, general → normal (friendly) → object-oriented			ʔ dɛə	mid	"look (a picture)!"
		→ intensified (impatient) → person-oriented		*=dɔ; dœ; ɔ; œ	mid	"nice to see you (and shall we look at this?)"
				ʔ ɔm̃ŋ; ŋm̃ŋ	mid	"nice to see you–at last!"
	engagement (and response to gift)			*ɛk̯a;œ^wa	mid	"what's that?; there it is (that's what I wanted)"
	response → to interaction			ɛ: ; ɔ:	low long	"yes it's me; yes, I see"
	→ to regulation			a	mid ff	"yes?!"
		interest → general		* = dɔ; dœ; ɔ; œ	mid	"look, that's interesting"
		→ specific → dog		dɔ	mid low	"a dog!"
		→ ball		b'ɔ; b'œ; vɔ; vœ	mid low	"a bus!"
		→ airplane		œ^wœ	mid low (both)	"an airplane!"
		→ nose		dou	mid low	"a nose!"
Personal	participation → pleasure → general			e^ʔi:	mid low	"that's nice"
	→ taste			ʔm̃ŋ	low	"that tastes nice"
	→ [?]			ʔgegege	narrow low	"[?]"
	withdrawal			g^wɤɣ - - -	narrow low	"I'm sleepy"

Table 3 NL 3: Nigel at 13½ months

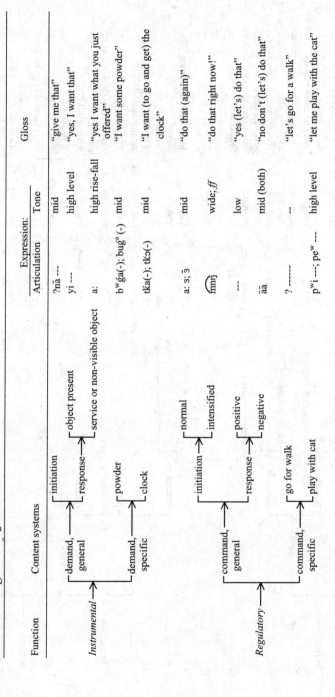

Table 3 continued.

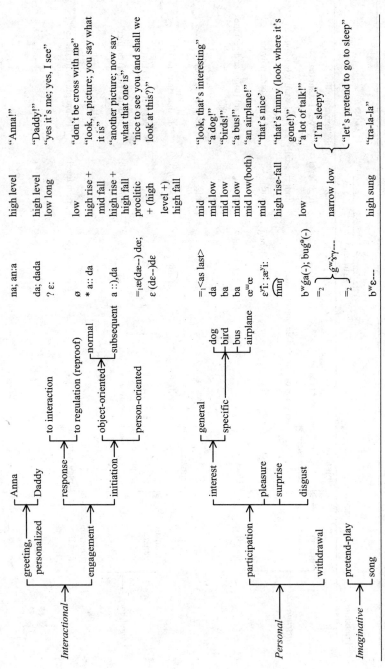

APPENDIX 2

Table 4 NL 4: Nigel at 15 months

Function	Content systems				Expression		Gloss
					Articulation	Tone	
Instrumental →	demand, general	initiation → object present			ṅṅṅ	high fall, *ff*	"give me that!"
		response → service or non-visible object			*= n; a; yi	high squeak	"yes I want that"
	demand, specific	powder			? a:	high rise-fall	"yes I want what you just offered"
		clock			bʷga(-); bugᵊ(-)	mid fall	"I want some powder"
Regulatory →	command, general	initiation → normal			tka (-)	mid fall	"I want (to go and get) the clock"
		intensified			=a	mid fall or level	"do that (again)"
		response → positive			a	high fall, *ff*	"do that right now!"
		negative			ɜ̃—	low fall	"yes, (let's) do that"
	command, specific	go for walk			ʔãã	mid fall (both syllables)	"no, don't (let's) do that"
		draw curtains			ʔ-------	—	"let's go for a walk"
Interactional →	greeting, personalized	Anna			da	mid fall	"it's dark; let's draw the curtains"
		Daddy			na; an:a	high level	"Anna!"
	engagement	response to reproof			da; dada	high level	"Daddy!"
		initiation → object-oriented	normal		ʔ ø	low fall	"don't be cross with me"
			subsequent		*a ::da; adᵊda; adʸdeʸa	high rise + mid fall (downjump)	"look, a picture; now say what it is"
					a ::da	high rise + high fall (upjump)	"another picture; now say what that one is"
		person-oriented			=₂ ɛdɛ	mid high level + fall (no jump)	"nice to see you (and shall we look at this?)"

395

Table 4 continued.

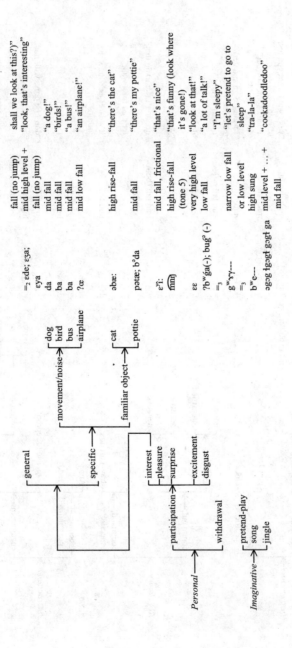

APPENDIX 2

Table 5 NL 5: Nigel at 16½ months

Function	Content systems				Expression		Gloss
					Articulation	Tone	
Instrumental	demand, general	initiation	normal		=m	short high fall, *ff*	"give me that!"
			exploratory		aa	mid level + high level	"that's new; let me see it"
		response	plaintive		=₂ ɛːhe	mid level + mid-low level	"somebody DO some thing!"
					*nː ə; yi	high squeak	"yes I want that"
	demand, specific	food	general		=₂ afia	mid level + mid fall	"where's my food?"
			specific	rusk	ᵃɹoʊ	proclitic + mid fall	"I want a rusk"
				toast	dooba	mid fall spread over both syllables	"I want some toast"
		ritual object	powder		bʷɔga	proclitic + mid fall	"I want the powder"
			clock		tikᵊɔkᵊ	mid fall spread throughout	"I want the clock"
		pottie			pᵊta	proclitic + mid fall	"I want my pottie"
Regulatory	command, general	initiation	normal		a; e	mid fall or level	"do that (again)"
			intensified		= a	high fall, *ff*	"do that right now!"
		response			ɛ; ɛ̃; m	low fall	"yes (let's) do that"
	command, specific	suggestion (joint)	go for walk		?‑‑‑‑‑‑‑	—	"let's go for a walk"
			draw picture		doᵊ	mid fall	"let's draw a picture"
		request	draw curtains		da; ɛːda	(mid rise +) mid fall	"it's dark; draw the curtains"
			come for lunch		la	mid fall	"come and have your lunch"

Table 5 continued.

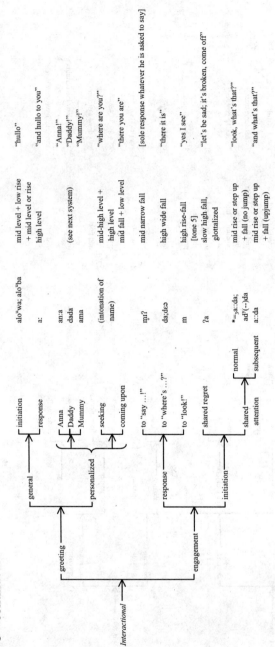

APPENDIX 2

Table 5 continued.

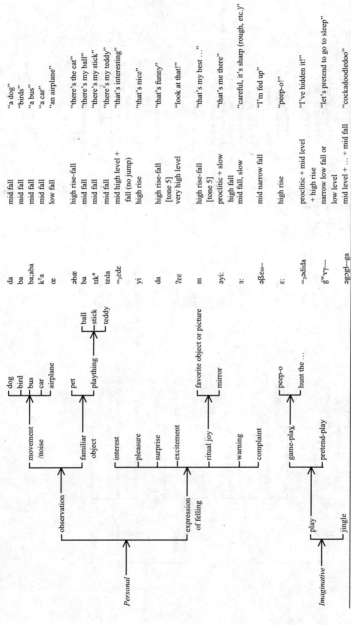

Personal	observation	movement/noise	dog	da	mid fall	"a dog"
			bird	ba	mid fall	"birds"
			bus	ba:aba	mid fall	"a bus"
			car	kʼa	mid fall	"a car"
			airplane	œ	low fall	"an airplane"
		familiar object	pet	abæ	high rise-fall	"there's the cat"
			plaything — ball	ba	mid fall	"there's my ball"
			— stick	tɪkª	mid fall	"there's my stick"
			— teddy	tɛda	mid high level + fall (no jump)	"there's my teddy"
	expression of feeling	interest		=ˌɛdɛ	high rise	"that's interesting"
		pleasure		yi	high rise-fall [tone 5]	"that's nice"
		surprise		da	high rise-fall [tone 5]	"that's funny"
		excitement		ɜːˁ	very high level	"look at that!"
		ritual joy — favorite object or picture		m	high rise-fall [tone 5]	"that's my best …"
		— mirror		əyi:	proclitic + slow high fall	"that's me there"
		warning		ɜː	mid fall, slow	"careful, it's sharp (rough, etc.)"
		complaint		əʃɛœ—	mid narrow fall	"I'm fed up"
Imaginative	play	game-play — peep-o		ɜː	high rise	"peep-o!"
		— hunt the …		=ˌɜdida	proclitic + mid level + high rise	"I've hidden it!"
		pretend-play		gʷʌy—	narrow low fall or low level	"let's pretend to go to sleep"
	jingle			əgɔgɪ—ga	mid level + … + mid fall	"cockadoodledoo"

Note: Here for the first time is a set of options which do not form a simple taxonomy. The personal names Anna, Daddy, Mummy may be combined either with high level tone meaning "I'm looking for you," or with mid falling tone, meaning something like "hullo, there you are!"

399

Table 6 NL 6: Nigel at 18 months

Function	Content systems				Expression: Articulation	Tone	Gloss
Instrumental	demand, general	initiation → normal			ɑː; ɛː; m	short high fall, *ff*	"give me that"
			→ exploratory		aʔa	mid level + high level	"that's new; let me see it"
		response			ɑː; ɛ; yi; m	high squeak	"yes I want that"
					=afia; ɛhɛ	mid level + mid fall	"where's my food?"
	demand, specific	food → general → basic			*more*	mid fall	"I want some more"
			→ supplementary		*cake*, etc.		"I want some cake (etc.)"
				→ specific [8]	*powder*, etc.		"I want the powder (etc.)"
		ritual object [4; + coord.] → pottie			*pottie*		"I want my pottie"
		music [5]			*Dvořák*, etc.		"I want the "Dvořák" (etc.) record on"
		plaything [7]			*ball*, etc.		"I want my ball (etc.)"
		lift			*fish*		"I want to be lifted up to where the fish picture is"
Regulatory	command, general	initiation → normal			ɛ; ɛ	mid fall or level	"do that (again)"
			→ intensified		=₁ a	high fall, *ff*	"do that right now!"
		response → inclusive			œ; ɛ; ɜ	mid fall	"yes, let's do that"
		→ exclusive			dʉ; dʌo	mid fall	"yes, I want you to do that"
	command, specific	suggestion [5; incl. 1 struct.]			*book*, etc.		"let's look at a book (etc.)"
		request [5]			*lunch*, etc.		"come for lunch"
		request for permission [5; incl. 1 struct.]			*stick-hole*, etc.		"can I put my stick in that hole? (etc.)"
		request for excursion [8; + coord.]			*train*, etc.		"let's go out and look at trains (etc.)"
		assistance → come with			=₂ aːha; ɛːhɛ	mid level + mid fall	"come with me and …"
		→ pick up			ɛ	mid fall + gesture	"pick me up"

400

APPENDIX 2

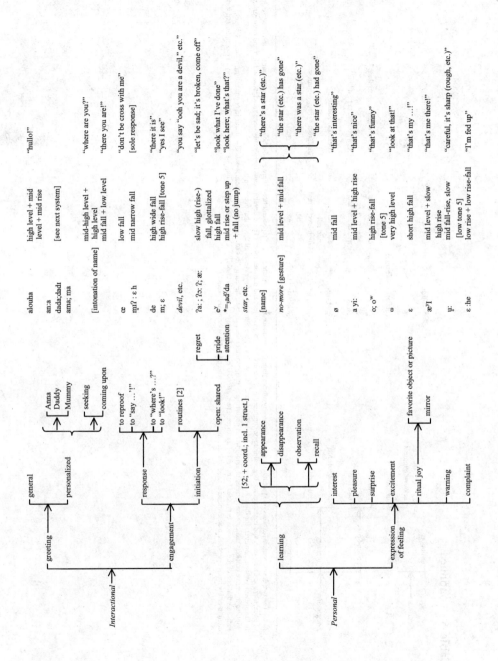

Table 6 continued.

Heuristic	initiation		*=ˌadʲda	mid rise + high level + high fall	"what's that (called)?"
	response →	acknowledgment	m		"I see"
		imitation	[imitation of name]		"it's a …"
Imaginative	pretend-play	go to sleep	gʷyy—	narrow low fall or low level	"let's pretend to go to sleep"
		be a lion	ɪaːo	mid or low fall, ff	"let's pretend to be a lion"
	jingle	cockadoodledoo	gɔgɬ—gɔ	mid level + … + mid fall	"cockadoodledoo!"
		dadikeda	oːdadʲkᵃda	high level + mid level + low fall	"dadikeda" (finger-drum sound)
	rhyme		[supplying final word of rhyme]		

Note: The two-level, content–expression system with simple taxonomy of meanings is now no longer an adequate form of representation. There are the beginnings of a grammar – an intermediate level of vocabulary and structure; and meanings are beginning to be combined (e.g. observation of an object and demand for it). These developments had already been anticipated in NL 5 and even earlier. In the present version, however, for the sake of continuity, NL 6 is shown as if it were still the same kind of system as all those that preceded it. Figures in square brackets indicate the number of single words occurring as options under the particular heading; "coord." indicates that these words also occur in coordination. + "incl. 1 struct." indicates that one of the options is expressed by means of a structure (e.g. *stick-hole* "can I put my stick in that hole?") Under each such heading just one word is given, by way of example, and it is cited in orthography; phonetic transcription is used only for those expressions which are not vocabulary items.

Appendix 3

SPECIMEN OF NIGEL'S CONVERSATION ON THE DAY HE REACHED EIGHTEEN MONTHS

Nigel is sitting on the kitchen shelf having his syrup. He finds an old piece of rusk. [əɹòu] ('rusk') he says happily, starting to nibble it.

"You don't want more rusk after all that tea!" says his mother.

Nigel looks hopefully at the bottle of syrup. [nōumə̀] ('no more'), he says, slowly and deliberately.

This is a routine, and his mother responds appropriately. "No more because Dr Thompson said no more than one teaspoonful for a little boy!" She points to a bowl of fruit. "Now this is apricots and you'll have some tomorrow for tea."

[ɛbkɔ]. This is a reasonable imitation of "apricots".

His mother lifts him down, and he runs to the front door. [dɔ̀] ('door'), he says five times, meaning 'I want to go outside'. She opens the door of the apartment, and Nigel runs out to the front door, just opposite. It is getting dark. Through the window at the side Nigel can see a clear sky, with the moon and stars.

[dà] ('star'), he says. He points to the moon. [ad^{y}dà] ('what's that?').

"That's the moon," his mother says.

[mũː] ('moo!'). This is Nigel's imitation of an adult imitation of a cow.

"No it's not what the cow says," says his mother. "It's 'moon', not 'moo'!"

The cat appears. [bæ̀ː] says Nigel ('pussy!'). [bæ̀ː]

"Yes that's the pussycat."

Nigel looks hopefully at the main door. [nōumə̀], he says.

"No, we're not going out of the house any more today."

[nōumə̀] (nine times).

The end of the day; Nigel's mother is putting him to bed. "And when you get up in the morning, you'll go for a walk," she says.

[tìk^{a}wa]

"And you'll see some sticks, yes."
[lòu]
"And some holes, yes."
[dà] (three times)
"Yes, now it's getting dark" (but he may have meant 'and I'll see the star' – a large poster he passes by in the street).
[ò̤] (thirteen times) ('I want')
"What?" says his mother.
[ò̤] (seven times); then plaintively [ò̤ò̤] ('please!')
"What do you want in bed?"
[ωː]
"Jamie?" (his doll)
[ȝ̃, ȝ̃] ('no!')
"You want your eiderdown!"
Nigel grins. [ɛ̀ːː] ('yes that's it!')
"Why didn't you say so? Your eiderdown!"
[àilə] (three times) ('eiderdown')
"There you are!"
Nigel clutches it contentedly, thumb in front of mouth.
[g̊ʷʁig̊ʷʁig̊ʷʁi...] ('now I'm going to sleep')
He says a few last words to himself. [bà] (three times) ('buses'). [bɨ] (?) [ÌGˣɔGˣɔ] ('and the weathercock') [dʉ̀] ('and stones') [tìkwa] ('and sticks') [dà] ('and the star').

With this inventory of the sights of the day, or perhaps of the morrow, he falls asleep.

INDEX

acquisition 26, 30, 34, 56, 66, 89, 137, 198, 210–11, 250, 277–8, 293, 309, 350
act
  of meaning 6, 12, 14, 18–9, 23, 113–25, 131–47, 187, 206, 214–7, 238, 244, 248–52, 282, 301, 303, 329–32, 336, 341, 354
    communicative 113, 214
    semiotic 11, 19, 68, 185, 296
    social 115, 141, 301
    speech 23, 138, 247
    symbolic 114, 145, 198, 214
action and reflection 123, 125, 203–4, 336
adolescence 11, 327, 366, 368
adult
  English 23, 50, 77, 119, 148, 151, 224, 263, 349
  grammar 22, 205–6, 224, 256
  grammatical system 39, 78
  language 8, 12–3, 28–33, 37, 40, 45, 48–51, 54–7, 60–2, 65–70, 75–94, 101–2, 107–11, 118–20, 133, 135, 140, 143–6, 150, 157–62, 173, 178–86, 190, 195–6, 203–7, 213, 222–4, 235, 239, 244, 257, 262, 286–8, 297–8, 304, 318, 354, 368
  linguistic system 30, 48–51, 61, 78, 82–4, 87, 92, 96, 98, 103, 108, 110, 117, 222

semantic (system) 29, 66, 89, 117–8, 125, 135–6, 158, 163, 182, 186, 289, 292
semiotic 120, 161, 219, 283
speech 12–3, 29, 61, 121, 189, 198, 205, 232, 343, 348
system 28, 30, 33, 35, 40, 44, 48–9, 54, 81, 92, 107, 122, 161, 163, 184, 195, 197, 244, 247
anaphoric 186–9
aphasia 269
articulation (see also intonation) 13, 21–3, 65, 85, 102, 113, 135, 202, 213, 220, 241
articulatory 12–3, 21–3, 26, 62, 66, 102, 333

Bernstein, B. 34, 48, 56, 70–1, 250, 272, 275, 278–9, 289, 305
bi-stratal 92, 97, 199, 204
brain 7, 9–10, 14–15, 18–20, 26–7, 60, 354
Braine, M.D.S. 29–30, 33, 56
Brown, R. 30–1, 211
Bullowa, M. 198, 209, 262

chants, chanting 51, 271, 277, 324
child
  development 196–7, 208, 212
  language 13, 35, 43, 56–7, 182, 207–10, 251, 259, 274, 300, 309, 323, 328–9

tongue   11, 15, 111, 209, 217–9, 222–3, 255, 317
Chinese   251, 256, 262, 331, 354, 369–71
Chomsky, N.   210, 250
Christie, F.   351
clause(s)   19, 21, 31, 54, 57, 66, 87, 120, 186, 190–1, 203–4, 222, 232–5, 243, 262–3, 272, 284, 293–4, 298, 335, 341–2, 344, 357–8, 361, 364, 367
Cloran, C.   338, 340–1, 351, 361
code   80, 227, 232, 249, 278–9, 301, 311
coding   30, 58, 82, 85, 102, 109, 116–20, 123, 133–4, 161, 199, 218, 228, 232, 301, 303, 310, 332, 341
cognitive   29, 49, 53, 63, 89, 118, 182, 208, 240, 250, 295, 300–1, 310, 330
cohesion   121, 186–8, 294
communication   35, 87, 101, 210–2, 252, 257, 275, 277, 289–90, 308, 312, 325
  process   51, 77, 83–4, 136, 163, 187
  role(s)   46–7, 82
  system(s)   91–2, 200, 218, 262, 354
communicative competence   110, 138, 249, 328
competence-performance   232, 249
complementarity   345, 349–50, 352, 369
component
  experiential   344, 355
  ideational   23, 51, 58, 81, 87, 110, 117, 136, 179–82, 207, 293–4
  interpersonal   23, 48, 54, 69, 81, 87, 108, 117, 179–82, 208, 248, 293–4, 343
  pragmatic   136, 178, 184–5, 222
  textual   163, 189, 191, 293–4

congruence, congruent   229–35, 238, 350, 364, 367
construe   10, 11, 14–5, 18–20, 23, 112, 121–2, 140, 197–207, 211–7, 223–4, 251–9, 262, 311, 328–30, 335, 344–5, 352–69
content-expression   11, 35, 52, 65, 67, 85, 92, 118, 133, 199
context of situation   12, 19, 67, 81, 87, 101, 115, 121, 134, 203, 206, 286–7, 290, 295, 302–4, 344
context-bound   121
context-free   121, 134, 137
continuity   15, 67, 87, 92, 108–9, 112, 116–7, 121, 123, 142–3, 162, 183, 200, 204, 207, 218, 294, 350–1
conversation(al)   47, 57, 83, 100, 111, 115–22, 125, 131–42, 191, 200–2, 210, 223–4, 247, 257–9, 262–9, 284, 329, 361
culture(s), cultural   9, 15, 29, 32, 35–6, 48, 55–6, 70–1, 84–5, 88, 91, 95–6, 101, 105, 111, 149, 196, 202, 209, 212, 217, 251, 281–91, 301, 303, 305, 311, 313, 317, 322, 325–7, 349, 363–4
Darwin, Charles   210, 215
declarative   20, 23, 48, 54, 58, 83, 101, 150–1, 180, 183, 206, 234–5, 243–4, 255–7, 297, 343
deictic centre   358, 363–4
Derewianka, B.   353, 368
development   6, 9–11, 14–5, 20, 26–35, 43–58, 63–7, 71–4, 78–80, 83, 86–92, 97, 101, 105–17, 121–25, 135–46, 151, 159, 162–3, 166, 181–3, 190–2, 196–200, 208–13, 217–25, 244–5, 250–1, 254,

258–62, 274–6, 281–2, 285, 298–303, 308–14, 317, 323–9, 332, 335–7, 341–2, 346, 349–50, 353–8, 366–71
cognitive 53, 300
language 6, 26–35, 52, 55, 63–7, 71, 73–4, 78, 89–91, 101, 105, 109–14, 137–8, 142–5, 162, 183, 190, 196–8, 210–3, 219, 223–5, 250–1, 281, 298–303, 308–9, 312–4, 317, 323–9, 332, 335, 346, 350, 353, 366, 369–71
semantic 64, 86, 89
semiotic 9, 14, 218, 251, 349

developmental
functions 32, 34, 41, 49, 67, 70, 85–6, 104, 108, 179, 217
linguistics 196–7, 208–10, 312
process 32, 49–51, 68, 108, 121, 179, 182, 196, 200, 282, 297, 300
device(s) 43, 82, 109–10, 187, 198, 250, 296, 368
dialect 64, 140, 269, 278, 371
dialectic 116, 122, 158, 253–4, 341, 352
dialogic 252–8, 338, 358, 364
dialogue 14, 28, 38–40, 46–9, 53–4, 59, 77–9, 82–6, 97–103, 110, 116–9, 134–40, 144–52, 163, 171, 174, 180, 185–6, 190–1, 206, 212, 219, 222, 226–32, 236–8, 247–50, 253, 256–9, 284, 287, 294, 314–5, 342, 361
discourse 57, 59, 121, 140, 185, 188–92, 203, 212, 220, 224, 229, 258, 299, 303, 314, 323, 331, 342–4, 349, 352, 365–6, 370
Dixon, J. 250, 262

education(al) 34, 49, 110, 223, 250, 270–1, 275, 278–9, 282, 308–9, 313–4, 323–8, 346–55, 358, 361–5, 368–9
empirical 68, 126
English 23, 34–6, 40, 43, 50, 66, 75, 77–8, 107, 119, 148, 150–1, 188, 195, 224, 235, 262–3, 269–71, 277, 293, 297, 302, 312, 322, 324, 334, 342, 349, 354, 369, 371
epigenetic(ally) 10, 26
ergative 181, 222, 345
ethnographic 49, 247
evolution(ary) 15, 26, 35, 85, 96, 110, 118, 121, 123, 152, 162, 180, 183, 197, 204–7, 235, 249, 255, 299, 303, 322, 331, 338
exchange
of attention 7, 138, 213, 216, 252
of goods-and-services 233–5, 255
of information 134, 146, 200, 234–5
of meaning(s) 7, 115, 121, 138–9, 142–6, 158, 212–4, 230, 232, 240, 244, 284, 289, 299, 301, 325, 346
of symbols 150, 179, 226
exophoric 188–9, 294
experiential(ly) 23, 42, 45, 54, 252, 258–9, 262, 302, 335–6, 339, 343–4, 352, 355, 358–9, 363–4, 368–9
expressive-conative 29, 49
extralinguistic 38, 47, 71, 87, 94, 100, 118, 301

Fillmore, C.J. 31, 57, 301
Firth, J.R. 34–5, 48, 90, 95, 286, 290, 341
formal 8, 18, 118, 163, 253, 262, 269, 275, 289, 323, 343, 349

function 14, 23, 32–58, 60, 67–87, 93–7, 100–9, 118–22, 133–7, 147, 150–1, 157–63, 174, 177–85, 190–2, 200, 206–7, 214, 219–22, 228, 235, 238–43, 272–80, 288–9, 292, 296–9, 304, 314, 318, 324–5, 330–1, 335–6, 338, 350, 352, 359
functional-semantic 93, 123, 207

genesis of language 38, 207
genre(s) 185, 289–90, 370
gestural(ly), gesture(s) 7, 12, 43, 50, 91, 112–5, 118, 125, 131, 145–6, 165–7, 170, 181, 199, 210, 212–7, 222, 239, 310–1, 330, 354
glossematics 31, 251
glossogenic 76, 97, 110
goods-and-services 18, 23, 144–7, 150, 152, 200, 203, 206, 226–7, 232–5, 239, 243–4, 247, 255–6
grammar 8, 14–5, 18–23, 26, 29–30, 35, 39–54, 62, 65, 67, 69–70, 82–5, 97–8, 101–3, 118–9, 123, 135–6, 140, 144, 161, 198–217, 211, 218–224, 228, 234, 254–7, 262, 270, 278, 280, 284, 292, 310–11, 318, 323, 331–52, 354–7, 364–70
grammatical
  metaphor 339–40, 347–9, 352, 365–9
  structure(s) 29–30, 53, 82, 98–9, 120, 134, 185, 199, 220, 280, 295, 317, 344
  system(s) 39–40, 46, 51, 54, 57, 69, 78, 101, 228, 235, 297, 342–3
grammaticalized 181, 199, 255, 335

Hasan, R. 233, 259, 279, 317, 328, 338–40, 351, 353, 361–2, 372
heuristic 34, 38, 41–3, 50, 52, 71–2, 80, 85, 93–4, 97, 104–5, 110, 161, 169, 274–80
higher-order 10, 11, 14–5, 18–20, 23, 355
holophrase(s) 40, 109, 172
Hymes, D. 102, 290–2

iconic 114, 145, 198, 215–6, 329–3, 351
ideational 21, 23, 29, 49, 51, 54–5, 58, 69–70, 81, 87, 102–3, 108, 110–11, 117, 120–1, 135–6, 163, 179–85, 192, 199, 203–7, 220, 239, 248–9, 286, 288–9, 293–5, 301, 339–45
imaginative 34, 38, 51–2, 55, 58, 68, 71–3, 76, 85, 93–4, 116, 133, 161–2, 191–2, 221, 275–7, 330, 360
imitation(s), imitative 9, 12, 36, 48, 61, 64–6, 75–9, 92–3, 97, 109, 113, 144, 173, 214–8, 293, 309, 330, 332
imperative(s) 20, 23, 26, 31, 177–9, 183, 205–7, 223, 229, 234–5, 255–6, 262, 272, 294, 297, 335, 338
infancy, infant(s) 7–11, 15, 19, 27, 63–4, 112, 121, 137, 161, 196–9, 205, 208–210, 212, 252, 310, 327, 329, 353–5, 369
information-seeking
  question(s) 148–9
informative 34, 38, 41, 55, 58, 73, 83, 135, 150, 179, 206, 312, 344
Ingram, D 57, 89
innate 26, 29, 61, 144, 198

innatism 250
instrumental 11, 34, 37, 40–52, 58, 67, 71–4, 77–80, 84–5, 93–7, 100, 104–5, 117–8, 133, 145–6, 158–61, 168, 177, 240, 271–2, 277, 288, 299, 330
interaction
 linguistic 43, 85, 111, 178, 276–7, 281, 283, 289–90
 semiotic 158, 299
 social 46, 180, 273, 284, 301
 symbolic 118, 158, 292
 verbal 48, 64, 161, 188
interactional 11, 34, 37–8, 40, 42, 46, 50, 52, 71–5, 80, 84, 93–9, 104, 110, 115–8, 133, 145–9, 158–62, 168–9, 177, 183, 223, 240, 244, 273–80, 290, 304, 330
interactive 122, 141, 178–80, 198, 206, 224, 300–1, 312, 321, 329
interface, interfacing 8, 19–20, 26, 102, 199–200, 229, 254–5, 331
interpersonal 8, 19, 21, 23, 29, 48–51, 54–5, 69, 71, 81, 87, 102–3, 108, 111, 117, 120–1, 136, 163, 179–80, 182–5, 203–8, 215, 220, 230, 239, 248–9, 258–9, 286, 288, 293–5, 328, 330, 335–40, 343, 346, 352, 355, 358–9, 363–4
interrogative 23, 48, 54, 58, 83, 101, 120, 150–1, 180, 183, 206, 234–5, 243–4, 256, 297, 335, 338, 343
intersubjective 137–9, 141–2, 145, 149, 203, 212, 217, 310
intersubjectivity 139, 212, 215, 251, 253
intonation(al) 10, 12, 20, 50–1, 53, 65, 77, 85, 98, 102, 106–7, 109, 113, 135–6, 143, 148, 162, 177, 184, 186–92, 199, 202–5, 220, 223, 232, 241, 256, 262, 293–4, 297, 318, 344
intruder 56, 69, 102

Jakobson, R. 90, 210

Karmiloff-Smith, A. 211, 223
kinetics 8

language
 adult 8, 12–3, 28–33, 37, 40, 45, 48–51, 54–7, 60–2, 65–70, 75–88, 91–4, 101–2, 107–11, 118–20, 133, 135, 140, 143, 144, 146, 150, 157–62, 173, 178–86, 190, 195–6, 203–7, 213, 222–4, 235, 239, 244, 257, 262, 286, 288, 297–8, 304, 318, 354, 368
 child 13, 35, 43, 56–7, 182, 207–8, 210, 251, 259, 274, 300, 309, 323, 328–9
 early development 32–3, 71, 74, 212, 223, 251, 332, 371
 function(s) of 31–5, 38, 42, 44, 47, 49–51, 55–6, 66–73, 83–7, 100, 102, 150, 182, 269, 272–9, 288–9, 317, 322
 human 8, 23, 110, 185, 205, 218, 355
 natural 211, 219, 256, 312, 335, 345
 Phase 1 96, 104, 109
language-based theory of
 learning 327–8, 351
language-creating process 101, 111, 198, 310, 312
learning
 how to mean 26, 28, 60, 87, 90, 95, 295, 298, 353, 368

language 41, 60, 96, 111–2,
    308–11, 325, 332, 338–9,
    346, 349–50, 353
process 29, 71, 277, 295, 300,
    309, 327, 332, 347, 369
strategy 302, 332, 366
through language 111–2, 308,
    317, 319, 325, 349–50, 353
Lemke, J.L. 262, 338, 350–1
Lewis, M.M. 20, 57–8, 89, 105
lexicogrammar 8, 11, 18, 65, 67,
    82, 92, 98, 102, 109, 118,
    134, 136–7, 140, 183, 199,
    204, 211, 218–9, 254,
    289–90, 301, 322, 331, 333,
    336, 348
lexicogrammatical 14, 28, 45, 82,
    84, 87, 90, 93, 98, 102–3,
    109, 118, 120, 192, 200, 202,
    211, 222, 230, 241, 248, 284,
    289, 293, 295, 300–1, 303,
    310, 344, 351, 358
lexicosemantic 89, 135
linguistic
  interaction 43, 85, 111, 178,
    276–7, 281, 283, 289
  resource(s) 112, 144, 273, 313,
    368, 371
  structure(s) 29, 40, 41, 44, 48,
    56, 114
  system 30–3, 40, 45, 48–56,
    59–65, 69, 73–8, 81–8, 91–3,
    96, 98, 103, 108, 110, 117,
    123, 144–5, 162, 196, 197,
    199, 203–4, 207–8, 213,
    222–4, 228, 247–8, 281–3,
    287–8, 290–1, 298, 300–2, 322
linguistics 18, 31, 57, 64, 196–7,
    208, 210–2, 218, 224, 247–8,
    250, 291, 309–12, 322, 338,
    342
listener(s) 23, 46, 136, 198, 210,
    217, 219, 257, 308, 317, 331,
    335, 339

literacy, literate 328, 340, 346, 349,
    352, 363–4,
  Breakthrough to literacy 309
logical-semantic relations 337,
    339–40, 344

macrofunction(s) 104, 108,
    119–20, 136, 140, 147, 262,
    335
Malinowski, B. 49, 56, 90, 95, 208,
    285–6, 290
Martin, J. 250, 262, 328, 348–51,
    368, 372
material 7–14, 18–9, 37, 48, 67, 71,
    93, 105, 118, 135, 190, 224,
    247, 252–9, 270, 272, 277,
    283, 294, 298, 304, 345
mathetic 23, 42–5, 48–54, 58,
    80–1, 87, 103–8, 119–20,
    122, 125, 135–6, 140, 161–3,
    168–9, 172, 174, 178, 180–5,
    192, 199, 203, 205–6, 221–2,
    242–3, 255–6, 286, 296–9,
    304, 318, 352
Matthiessen, C. 224, 344
meaning(s)
  ideational 103, 120–1, 136, 163,
    183, 199, 204–5, 239, 295,
    301
  interpersonal 21, 103, 120–1,
    136, 163, 183, 204–5, 239,
    248–9, 295, 339, 352
  act(s) of 6, 12, 14, 18–9, 23,
    113–25, 131–47, 187, 206,
    211, 214–7, 238,
    244, 248–52, 282, 301, 303,
    329–30, 332, 336, 341, 354
  potential 6, 11–5, 28, 32–5, 41,
    51, 55, 68–9, 78, 84–7, 90,
    94–6, 108–9, 111, 114–21,
    133, 137, 141–4, 162, 192,
    199, 207, 217, 219, 247, 253,
    285–91, 295, 297–8, 301–4,
    312, 314, 321, 336–43, 350–6

meaning-making 9, 251, 257
mental 142, 197, 212, 217, 272, 309–10, 319, 321, 345, 358
meronymy 358
metafunction(s), metafunctional 54, 108, 117, 120, 136, 185, 220, 224, 262, 335–6, 339–40, 343–6, 352
metalanguage(s), metalinguistic 275, 323, 345
metaphor(s), metaphorical 14, 70, 137, 213, 299, 309–10, 334, 336, 339–41, 344, 347–50, 352, 364–9
microfunctions, microfunctional 11, 253, 330, 333
microlinguistic act(s) 285
microsemantic 285
microsemiotic 96, 111, 305
modal 45, 223, 237
modalities 8, 23, 121, 343, 359
modality 54, 108, 136, 163, 183, 208, 235–8, 294, 296, 337
monologic 257–8, 360, 364
monologue 28, 98, 280, 284
mood 19, 22–3, 48, 54, 58, 78, 103, 108, 120, 136, 163, 178–80, 183–4, 203–8, 222–4, 228–30, 235, 255, 258, 293–9, 333, 335, 338, 343, 358
morphology 28, 35, 254
mother-tongue 224–5

narrative(s) 58–9, 98, 104, 114, 117, 119, 126, 134–5, 140, 150, 163, 169, 180, 185–6, 192, 202, 206, 258, 284, 287, 315, 324
network 8, 13, 15, 48–9, 78, 86, 115, 144, 227–8, 230, 232–3, 237, 247, 249, 282, 299, 335
Nigel 21–3, 26, 28, 35–8, 40–7, 50–4, 57–9, 64–5, 67, 73–89, 91–113, 114–37, 140–51, 157–63, 175, 175–92, 200, 203–6, 214–8, 220–24, 232–45, 247, 252, 257–62, 282–85, 288, 293–305, 318, 320, 324, 333, 337–8, 340–8, 356
noun(s) 20, 181, 188, 223, 323–4, 333, 348, 357, 365–8

observer 56, 69, 102
Oldenburg-Torr, J. 13, 20, 218, 251, 259, 328, 330–1, 335, 339
ontogenesis 112, 144, 151, 204, 212, 226, 249, 259, 327
ontogenetic(ally) 81, 117, 140, 205, 207, 256
ontogeny 85, 182, 197, 207

Painter, C. 13, 20, 218, 222, 224, 251, 259, 328, 331, 335, 337, 339, 353, 356, 358, 363
performative 26, 179
personal
    and (the) heuristic 40–1, 44, 50, 52, 80, 278–9
    function(s) 38, 72, 75–6, 93, 161, 278
Philips, J. 15, 259, 337, 340, 356–7, 365
phonemes, phonemic 12–3
phonetic 8, 12–3, 20–1, 36, 61, 64, 66, 94, 162, 202, 254
phonetics 8, 18, 331
phonological(ly) 8, 13, 28, 31, 33, 57, 61, 66, 89–90, 102, 118, 144, 162, 191–2, 202, 221, 241, 284, 297–8, 300
phonology 8, 18, 35, 61, 67, 82, 85, 92, 98, 183, 191, 199, 204–5, 210–11, 218, 310, 322, 331, 341

phylogenetic(ally) 84, 197, 205, 256
Piaget, J. 223, 295, 358
play 51, 330
plurifunctional 41, 45, 53, 102
polarity 58, 337, 342
potential
   meaning 6, 11–15, 28, 32–5, 41, 51, 55, 68–9, 78, 84–7, 90, 94–6, 108–9, 111, 114–21, 133, 137, 141–4, 162, 192, 199, 207, 217, 219, 247, 253, 285–91, 295, 297–8, 301–4, 312, 314, 321, 336–43, 350–6
   semantic 60, 75, 177, 184, 199
   semiotic 8, 24, 75, 80, 138, 249, 295, 342
   semogenic 252
   systemic 8, 12
pragmatic 23, 41, 44–5, 50–4, 57–8, 79–81, 86, 93, 95, 101–8, 119–22, 125, 135–6, 147–8, 151, 161, 163, 168, 170–1, 174, 177–85, 184, 192, 199, 203, 205–6, 221–2, 232, 242–3, 255–6, 262, 286, 294, 296, 298, 304, 318, 352
pragmatic/mathetic 44, 58, 81, 109, 125, 178, 182, 184, 207
pre-linguistic 35, 65, 112, 145
pre-speech 139–40
pre-symbolic 213, 251–2
pretend 34, 73, 93, 133, 176, 192, 208, 275, 277, 330
prosody, prosodic(ally) 12–3, 21–3, 26, 36, 66, 92, 94, 135, 203, 239, 248, 333
proto conversation 7, 138–42, 252
protolanguage 92–6, 102–3, 107–9, 157, 188, 210, 311
protolanguage(s) 9, 11–15, 18–21, 26, 64, 77–8, 82, 84, 88, 113–9, 123, 125, 133–6, 139–43, 146–9, 190, 199–200, 203–5, 207, 212, 215–20, 224–5, 238–40, 242, 244, 251, 253–7, 259, 262, 311–2, 317, 324, 330–7, 344, 346, 349, 351, 354
protolinguistic 12, 15, 20–1, 116, 147, 199, 205, 208, 216, 218–20, 223, 241, 251, 253–4
psycholinguistic 28–9, 33

reality-constructing 125, 242
reconstruction 301, 347–8, 352
reconstrue 19, 257, 347–8, 352, 364, 367
referential 12, 20–1, 29, 49, 332–3
reflective 114–5, 117, 146, 179, 204, 239–40
register(s) 87, 140, 287–8, 291–2, 299, 305, 323, 349–50, 368–70
regression 347, 352
regulatory 11, 34, 37, 40–1, 43–4, 46, 49–50, 52, 58, 71–2, 75, 77–8, 80, 84, 93–4, 96–7, 100, 104–5, 117–8, 133, 145–6, 158, 160–1, 168, 177, 181, 240, 272–3, 277, 288, 298, 330
reinforce, reinforcement 61, 76, 109, 143, 273–5
relational 102, 294, 358, 365
representational 29, 49, 202, 276–8, 280, 336
request(s) 31, 43, 45, 53, 72, 75, 77–8, 117, 144, 147, 158, 160, 170, 174, 177–9, 199, 220, 223, 256, 298, 311, 318, 360
rhetoric 142, 208, 247, 365
rhetorical 121, 140, 203, 292, 323, 341, 358
rhymes 55, 93, 271, 275, 324
rhythm(ic) 10, 21, 192, 271, 275, 308

role-playing 48, 103

science(s) 27, 88, 224, 270, 347, 349, 367–371
secondary (education) 309, 323, 328, 349–50, 353, 365–371
semantic analysis 31, 56
  categories 56, 302, 366
  choice 239, 285, 287
  configurations 87, 177–8, 199, 291, 299
  potential 60, 75, 177, 184, 199
  space 331, 336, 344, 350
  structure(s) 98–99, 185, 199, 285, 287
  system(s) 29, 33, 36, 42, 57, 64, 66, 69–71, 75–6, 87, 89–91, 94, 96–7, 101, 109, 111–2, 116–7, 120, 123, 125, 136, 143, 59, 163, 178, 180–3, 186, 192, 207, 211, 219, 228–9, 235, 249, 282, 285–6, 288–9, 292–4, 300, 302–3
semantics 8, 18, 28, 67, 82, 85–6, 92, 98, 110, 113, 117, 163, 178, 183, 199, 204–5, 211, 218, 228, 248, 275, 282, 288, 295, 301–2, 309, 322, 324, 331, 349, 368
semiotic act(s) 7, 11, 19, 68, 185, 213–4, 296
  construct(s) 121, 287, 344
  development 9, 14, 218, 251, 349
  potential 26, 75, 80, 138, 249, 295, 342
  process 227–8, 235, 327–8, 344, 351
  strategies 119, 135, 221, 294, 297–9
  structure(s) 94, 96, 108–9, 115, 283, 287, 290–1, 293, 295, 303–4
  system 11, 15, 18, 60, 67–8, 88, 90, 96, 179, 195, 211, 214–5, 217–8, 226–9, 234, 262, 283, 292, 332, 336–7, 342, 351
semiotics 162, 180, 292, 299, 368
semogenic 88, 252, 312, 336, 352
social
  act(s) 115, 134, 141, 301–2
  construct(s) 116, 122, 141, 302, 304
  context(s) 29, 48, 56, 68, 94–6, 108–10, 118, 136–7, 162, 185, 211, 226–8, 248, 281, 286–8, 290–2, 295, 299, 301–2, 305, 312
  interaction 46, 180, 273, 284, 301
  meaning 94, 137, 251, 227, 282
  process(es) 10, 20, 26, 32, 112, 116, 121, 141–2, 212, 228, 251, 255, 295, 300, 302, 355
  reality 138, 141, 299, 301–2
  roles 46, 77, 82–3, 86, 99, 134
  semiotic 90–1, 96, 101, 109, 140, 228, 282, 284, 286, 290, 301, 303
  structure(s) 32, 70, 281–2, 289, 304
  system 90, 94–6, 101, 108–11, 121, 123, 137–8, 154, 281–2, 287, 289–90, 292, 301–2, 304, 343
social-contextual 144, 151, 228–9
socialization 48, 56, 71, 137–8, 208, 272
society 262, 279, 289, 305, 323
sociolinguistic 28, 32–4, 60, 89, 110, 137, 287, 289
sociosemiotic 90, 107, 109, 142, 299
speech 11–3, 15, 22–3, 28–9, 31, 36, 44, 48, 54, 57–8, 61–3, 68–70, 72, 74, 83, 95–6, 99–100, 103, 113, 121, 125, 138, 140, 143–4, 148, 161,

169, 183, 189–90, 198, 202–3, 205, 211, 219–20, 223, 226, 228–30, 232, 235, 238–9, 244, 247, 274, 278, 281, 284, 292, 294, 296, 303, 308, 311, 312, 314–5, 317–8, 335–6, 343, 348, 350, 361–2

strata, stratum   8, 14, 40, 43, 45, 65, 88, 92–3, 102, 200, 211, 228, 230, 333, 336, 351

stratification(al)   31, 34–5, 89, 337

structure
grammatical   29–30, 53, 82, 134, 185, 199, 220, 280, 295, 317, 344
linguistic   29, 40–1, 44, 48, 56
semiotic   96, 115, 283, 287, 290–1, 293, 295, 303–4

subjective reality   116, 123, 125, 134, 142

syntax, syntactic   28, 35, 48, 210–11, 254, 278–9, 300, 309–10, 323

systemic   7–8, 11–4, 20–1, 44, 49, 78, 94, 162, 220, 224, 233, 248, 262, 339, 366

systemic-functional   108, 226

system-structure theory   31, 34

taxonomy, taxonomies   86, 97, 103, 135–6, 161, 183, 258–9, 334–5, 346, 356, 358, 361, 364

temporal   6, 31, 190, 205, 286, 296, 359, 361

tenor   121, 291–4, 303

text-forming   163, 188, 191

textual   50, 55, 70, 120–1, 163, 186, 189, 191, 205, 220, 288–9, 293–5, 343–4

texture   70, 185–8, 190, 203–4, 289

thematic   31, 358

Thibault, P.   8, 19, 251

tone   21–3, 44–5, 50–1, 53, 58, 77, 81, 98, 102, 106–7, 119–20, 122, 125, 132, 135–6, 147–8, 150–1, 159, 162–3, 168–73, 183–4, 189, 205, 214, 221–3, 232–3, 242–3, 248, 255, 262–3, 272, 294, 296–7, 307, 318, 324, 330, 343

tonic   150, 172–4, 186, 189–91, 204, 307

transitivity   19, 22–3, 31, 54, 57, 103, 108, 120–1, 136, 158, 180–1, 183, 203, 222, 255, 262, 293–4, 301, 335, 345, 358

Trevarthon, C.   7, 112, 138–9, 212–3, 215, 252, 262, 329–30

tri-stratal   31, 48, 51, 67, 92, 97, 199–200, 204, 218

universal(s)   35–6, 43, 85, 88, 255

variation   7, 9, 20–1, 88, 140, 217, 317, 323, 362, 370

verb(s)   89, 187, 235, 237, 323, 333, 348, 357, 365, 367

verbal   35, 41, 48, 52, 59, 64, 81, 88, 103–4, 119, 136, 147–8, 161–3, 179, 188, 191–2, 235, 243, 256, 282, 351, 357, 364, 369

vocabulary   28, 33, 35, 40–1, 43–6, 48, 52–3, 60, 62, 65–7, 79–80, 82, 85–6, 89, 97–8, 109, 140, 161, 222, 254, 278, 292, 294, 310–1, 314, 324, 331, 335, 337, 348

vocal   9–10, 12, 19, 23, 33, 38, 62, 65, 67, 74–5, 77, 85, 112–3, 115, 125, 146, 199, 213, 215–6, 330

vocalization(s)   10, 12, 35, 66–7, 76, 146, 160, 166–7, 218

voice   21, 62, 129, 239, 294

quality   21, 23, 102, 203, 256, 324
vowel   13, 23, 145, 215, 221
Vygotsky, L.   250, 342

WH-interrogative(s)/WH-question(s)   23, 26, 100, 148, 150–1, 180, 244, 258
Whorf, B.L.   301, 317, 319
word(s)   6, 8, 9, 11, 15, 20, 22, 28, 30, 33, 40–5, 51, 53, 55–6, 58, 62, 64–70, 74–80, 86–9, 91–3, 97–8, 102, 105, 109–10, 125, 127, 130, 138, 140, 147, 149–50, 161–2, 172, 179, 181, 183, 186, 188–91, 199, 206, 210–11, 215–6, 218–22, 228, 241, 243, 248, 252, 269, 275, 277–8, 280–1, 284, 286, 288, 290–1, 296, 299–301, 303–4, 312, 319, 321–5, 328, 330–1, 334–5, 342, 344, 346, 354–6, 359, 363–5, 367–8, 371
wording(s)   82, 84, 94, 102, 118, 120, 133, 145, 199, 202, 204, 218, 222–3, 230, 284, 310–2, 323, 337, 348–9, 367

西方语言学原版影印系列丛书

编号	书名	作者
06884/H·0963	语义学与语用学:语言与话语中的意义	K.Jaszczolt
06878/H·0957	字面意义的疆域:隐喻、一词多义以及概念概论	M.Rakova
06883/H·0962	英语语篇:系统和结构	J.R.Martin
06877/H·0956	作为语篇的语言:对语言教学的启示	M.McCarthy 等
06887/H·0966	布拉格学派,1945-1990	Luelsdorf 等
06881/H·0960	认知语法基础 1	R.W.Langacker
07694/H·1090	认知语法基础 2	R.W.Langacker
06686/H·0965	论自然和语言	N.Chomsky
06880/H·0959	语料库语言学的多因素分析	S.T.Gries
06882/H·0961	美国社会语言学:理论学家与理论团队	S.O.Murray
06879/H·0958	英语教学中的教材和方法——教师手册	J.Mcdonough 等
07592/H·1055	英语语言文化史	G.Knowles
06885/H·0964	分析散文	R.A.Lanham
07596/H·1059	语法化	P.J.Hopper
08727/H·1451	古英语入门	B.Mitchell 等
07594/H·1057	美国英语入门	G.Tottie
07593/H·1056	英语语言史:社会语言学研究	B.A.Fennell
07595/H·1058	语言学入门纲要	G.Hudson
08673/H·1422	语言的结构与运用	E.Finegan
08738/H·1454	语言艺术的学与教	D.Strickland
10244/H·1590	认知语言学	William Croft, D. Alan Cruse
11598/H·1734	语篇研究:跨越小句的意义	J. R. Martin, David Rose
11597/H·1733	语用学:多学科视角	Louise Cummings
	语言引论(第 8 版)	V. Fromkin 等

北京大学出版社

邮 购 部 电话:010-62534449　　联系人:孙万娟
市场营销部电话:010-62750672
外语编辑部电话:010-62767315　　62767347